E. F. (Edward Frederick) Knight

A narrative of travel in Kashmir, Western Tibet and Gilgit

E. F. (Edward Frederick) Knight

A narrative of travel in Kashmir, Western Tibet and Gilgit

ISBN/EAN: 9783742835444

Manufactured in Europe, USA, Canada, Australia, Japa

Cover: Foto ©Andreas Hilbeck / pixelio.de

Manufactured and distributed by brebook publishing software (www.brebook.com)

E. F. (Edward Frederick) Knight

A narrative of travel in Kashmir, Western Tibet and Gilgit

IN HIMIS LAMASERY.

A NARRATIVE OF RECENT TRAVEL
IN KASHMIR, WESTERN TIBET, GILGIT, AND
THE ADJOINING COUNTRIES

BY

E. F. KNIGHT

AUTHOR OF 'THE CRUISE OF THE FALCON'
'THE CRUISE OF THE ALERTE' 'THE FALCON ON THE BALTIC'
'SAVE ME FROM MY FRIENDS' ETC.

WITH A MAP AND 54 ILLUSTRATIONS

SECOND EDITION

LONDON
LONGMANS, GREEN, AND CO.
AND NEW YORK: 15 EAST 16th STREET
1893

PREFACE

VARIOUS circumstances took me to Kashmir in the spring of 1891. I did not see much of the Happy Valley itself; but for the greater part of a year I was travelling among those desolate mountain-tracts that lie to the north of it, where the ranges of the Hindoo Koosh and Karakoram form the boundary between the dominions of the Maharajah and that somewhat vaguely defined region which we call Central Asia.

Great changes are now being effected in Kashmir: we are actively interfering in the administration of the country, and introducing much-needed reforms, which will produce important results in the immediate future. The affairs of this State are likely soon to attract a good deal of attention, and therefore a description of the country as it is to-day, and some account of the relations which exist between the Indian Empire and her tributary, and of the steps that are being taken to safeguard Imperial interests on that portion of our frontier may not be inopportune.

I have, so far as is possible, confined myself to a narrative of my own experiences, to a plain statement of what I myself saw, without attempting to theorise as to what ought to be done or left undone on the frontier. The Indian Government can be trusted to do everything for the best, as heretofore; and while it is foolish for people at home to airily criticise the policy of those highly-trained Anglo-Indian experts who have made the complicated problems of our Asiatic rule the study of a lifetime, it is still more foolish for one to do so who has spent but a year in the East, and who, therefore, has just had time to realise what a vast amount he has yet to learn.

In the course of my journey I was luckily enabled to accompany my friend, Mr. Walter Lawrence, the Settlement Officer who has been appointed to the Kashmir State, on one of his official tours, and saw something of his interesting and successful work; I visited the mystic land of Ladak with Captain Bower, the explorer of Tibet; reached Gilgit in time to take part in Colonel Durand's expedition against the raiding Hunza-Nagars; and fell in with other exceptional opportunities for observing how things are managed on the frontier, both in peace and war.

My thanks are due to the editors of the 'Times,' the 'Graphic,' and 'Black and White' for the permission they have kindly given me to reproduce in this book portions of articles which I wrote for those papers.

The illustration of the Devil Dance at Himis is a reproduction of a drawing (by Mr. J. Finnemore, from my photographs) which appeared in 'Black and White.'

PREFACE

The whole region included in the sketch-map which accompanies this volume is an intricate mass of mighty mountains cloven by innumerable ravines. In order to avoid confusion superfluous detail has been avoided; the principal valleys alone have been indicated, while the two great parallel watersheds of the Hindoo Koosh and the Western Himalayas have been purposely emphasised, at the expense of the no less lofty subordinate branches of either chain.

Kashmir has been called the northern bastion of India. Gilgit can be described as her farther outpost. And hard by Gilgit it is that, in an undefined way, on the high Roof of the World—what more fitting a place!—the three greatest Empires of the Earth meet—Great Britain, Russia, and China. Hence the title I have given to this book.

E. F. K.

CONTENTS

CHAPTER I

SNOW—THE ROAD INTO KASHMIR—A KASHMIR CUSTOM-HOUSE—THE JHELAM—DOMEL—URI—THE RESIDENT'S RECEPTION . . . 1

CHAPTER II

BARAMOULA—KASHMIRI BOATMEN—ACROSS THE WOOLAR LAKE—THE VALE OF KASHMIR—SALE OF THE STATE TO GOLAB SINGH—REFORMS IN ADMINISTRATION—A STORM ON THE LAKE . . 19

CHAPTER III

CLIMATE—SRINAGUR—THE EUROPEAN QUARTER—SRINAGUR MERCHANTS—PROGRESS AND DEVELOPMENT OF THE STATE—RESOURCES OF KASHMIR—PROPOSED RAILWAY—THE TAKHT-I-SULIEMAN . 33

CHAPTER IV

NATIVE SERVANTS—'DASTUR'—PREPARATIONS FOR JOURNEY—BY RIVER TO ISLAMABAD—THE SETTLEMENT OFFICER'S COURT—SUPPLIANTS—SYSTEM OF LAND-TENURE—REVENUE—OFFICIAL EXTORTION—FORCED LABOUR 48

CHAPTER V

A TOUR WITH THE 'BANDOBAST WALLAH'—TEMPLE OF MARTUND—BRAHMIN AND MUSSULMAN CULTIVATORS—RETURN OF FUGITIVE PEASANTS—THE DISHONEST PATWARI—TEMPLE OF PAYECH—A DESERTED VILLAGE—SUCCESS OF THE SETTLEMENT—A VILLAGE OF LIARS—FRAUDULENT OFFICIALS 70

CHAPTER VI

A PICNIC ON THE DAL LAKE—THE FLOATING GARDENS—WE SET OUT FOR LEH—ON THE GREAT TRADE-ROUTE—THE SIND VALLEY—CAPTAIN BOWER'S TIBETAN EXPEDITION—GOOND—SONAMERG—'CHITS' 84

CHAPTER VII

THE WESTERN HIMALAYAN RANGE—THE ZOJI LA—CLIMATE OF LADAK—MATAYUN—DRAS—TIBETAN SCENERY—TASHGAM 102

CHAPTER VIII

KARGIL—OASIS CULTIVATION—TIBETAN TABLE-LANDS—SHERGOL—A BUDDHIST COUNTRY—THE LAMASERY—RED LAMAS—SKOOSHOKS—THEORY OF INCARNATION 117

CHAPTER IX

CHARACTER OF THE LADAKIS—THEIR DRESS—THE PEYRAK—POLYANDRY—LAW OF ENTAIL—MAGPA WEDLOCK—PRAYER BY MACHINERY—MANIS AND CHORTENS—MULBEK—THE NAMIKA LA—KHARBU—PRAYING-WHEELS 136

CHAPTER X

THE FOTU LA—LAMAYURU—ITS LAMASERY—LAMAS' MUSIC—MERCHANTS FROM LASSA—TRADE WITH TURKESTAN—NEED FOR A CONSULATE AT YARKAND—THE INDUS—NURLA—SASPUL—NIMU—BAZGO—PRAYING-WATERWHEELS 151

CHAPTER XI

THE HUNTING OF DAD MAHOMED—LEH FEVER—CITY OF LEH—THE BAZAARS—CARAVAN TRADE—POPULATION OF LEH—MORAVIAN AND ROMAN CATHOLIC MISSIONS—DR. REDSLOB—BOWER'S PREPARATIONS—POLO 165

CHAPTER XII

IBEX-STALKING—TIBETAN BEER—HIMIS FESTIVAL—THE GIALPO'S ESTATE—THE PILGRIMAGE—A LADAKI NACH—MONASTERY LANDS—THE LAMASERY OF HIMIS 183

CHAPTER XIII

THE MYSTERY-PLAY AT HIMIS—FIRST DAY'S CEREMONIAL—THE LAMA MASK—THE DEVIL DANCE—THE TREASURES OF THE LAMASERY—THE IDOL CHAMBER—SECOND DAY'S CEREMONIAL—THE CONSECRATION OF ANIMALS—A HARLEQUINADE—RETURN TO LEH—THE LAMASERY OF TIKZAY—THE SKOOSHOK 200

CHAPTER XIV

A REVOLUTION—NATIVE CHRISTIANS IN LEH—BAZAAR RUMOURS—COMMENCE MARCH THROUGH BALTISTAN TO GILGIT—LINGUA FRANCA—THE TRUCULENT AFGHAN—DEFILES OF THE INDUS—SKIRBICHAN—GOMA-HANU 215

CHAPTER XV

THE CHORBAT LA—THE KARAKORAM RANGE—THE PROVINCE OF BALTISTAN—BALTIS—A MUSSULMAN COUNTRY—A DEPOSED RAJAH—KAPALU—ITS RAJAHS—A JOURNEY ON A SKIN RAFT—BRAGAR . . 229

CHAPTER XVI

SKARDU—KATSURAH—WEATHER-BOUND AT SHIKARTHANG—THE BANNOK LA—NANGA PARBAT—ON THE GILGIT ROAD—THE DARDS—ASTOR FORT—APPLEFORD'S CAMP 246

CHAPTER XVII

RAIDS ON THE GILGIT AND ASTOR DISTRICTS—THE GILGIT GARRISON—NATIVE MISMANAGEMENT—THE GILGIT AGENCY—SPEDDING AND CO.'S NEW MILITARY ROAD—DESERT CONDITION OF THE COUNTRY AND DIFFICULTIES OF TRANSPORT—STRATEGICAL IMPORTANCE OF GILGIT AND CHITRAL—SPEDDING AND CO.'S STAFF AND COOLIES . 261

CHAPTER XVIII

ON THE SLOPES OF NANGA PARBAT—MARCH TO GILGIT—ASTOR COOLIES—THE HATTU PIR—RAMGHAT—THE INDUS VALLEY—THE SHINAKA REPUBLICS—HOME RULE—BOONJI—THE FLOOD OF 1840—THE INDUS FERRY—CHAKERKOT—A DESERTED VILLAGE . . . 276

CHAPTER XIX

THE GILGIT VALLEY—GILGIT—THE KASHMIR ARMY—REGULARS—IRREGULAR LEVIES—THE IMPERIAL SERVICE TROOPS—WORK OF THE GILGIT AGENCY—COSSACKS ON THE PAMIRS—HUNZA ENVOYS—MARCH TO SRINAGUR—A PATHAN DASTUR—IDGARH—SIRDARKOTE—THE BORZIL PASS—MINEMERG—THE VALLEY OF GURAIS . . 295

CHAPTER XX

THE RAJDIANGAN PASS—VIEW OF THE VALE OF KASHMIR—SRINAGUR AGAIN—WAR RUMOURS—REINFORCEMENTS FOR GILGIT—RETURN TO ASTOR—AN EARLY WINTER—CLOSING OF THE PASSES—DIFFICULTIES OF A MOUNTAIN CAMPAIGN—COMMUNICATION INTERRUPTED—LOSS OF LIFE ON THE PASSES—CAPTAIN YOUNGHUSBAND—ARRIVAL OF THE GUNS AND FIFTH GURKHAS—A BLIZZARD ON THE PASS 312

CHAPTER XXI

DESCRIPTION OF HUNZA-NAGAR—DEFENCES OF THE VALLEY—KANJUT RAIDS ON CARAVANS—SLAVE-DEALING—THE THUMS—THE MAULAI SECT—RELATIONS BETWEEN HUNZA AND CHINA—RUSSIAN EXPEDITION TO THE VALLEY—CAUSES OF COLONEL DURAND'S EXPEDITION—OUR ULTIMATUM—FORMER KANJUT VICTORIES—SPEDDING'S SAPPER AND MINER CORPS 326

CHAPTER XXII

GOLF—PILGRIMS FROM MECCA—CAMP AT CHAKERKOT—ATTITUDE OF THE NATIVES—COMMISSARIAT DIFFICULTIES—A HUNZA SPY CAUGHT—THE ENEMY'S PLANS—COLONEL DURAND'S FORCE—THE PUNIALI LEVY—A COUNTRY OF MAGICIANS—THE FAIRY DRUM . . . 338

CHAPTER XXIII

SPEDDING CONSTRUCTS A TEMPORARY ROAD TO CHALT—SCENERY OF THE KANJUT VALLEY—NOMAL—GUETCH—THE CHAICHAR PARI—CHALT FORT—CHAPROT—MOUNT RAKAPOSHI—OUR TROOPS REACH CHALT—THE REPLY TO COLONEL DURAND'S ULTIMATUM—THE THUM'S CORRESPONDENCE—THE HUNZA-NAGAR FIELD FORCE—OCCUPATION OF THE KOTAL—OUR FORCE CROSSES THE FRONTIER 350

CHAPTER XXIV

THE FIGHT OF DECEMBER 2—ADVANCE ON NILT—STRENGTH OF NILT FORT—THE GURKHAS AND GUNS COME INTO ACTION—THE RIDGE CROWNED BY THE PUNIALIS—COLONEL DURAND WOUNDED—A FORLORN HOPE—THE MAIN GATE BLOWN UP AND THE FORT TAKEN BY ASSAULT—LOSSES ON BOTH SIDES—TWO V.C.'S—CAPTURE OF ENEMY'S SUPPLIES 366

CHAPTER XXV

THE FIGHT OF DECEMBER 3—WE ARE REPULSED WITH LOSS—ROAD-MAKING UNDER DIFFICULTIES—DETERMINED STAND OF THE KANJUTS—AN EIGHTEEN DAYS' CHECK—DESCRIPTION OF THE ENEMY'S LINE OF DEFENCE—LIST OF OFFICERS WITH FIELD FORCE—HUMOURS OF THE CAMPAIGN—VIGILANCE OF THE ENEMY—WORK OF SPEDDING'S ENGINEERS 385

CHAPTER XXVI

RECONNAISSANCES—THE ABORTIVE ATTACK OF DECEMBER 8—A NOISY NIGHT—A LETTER FROM THE THUM—FOOTBALL UNDER FIRE—ANOTHER FRUSTRATED ATTACK ON DECEMBER 12—A HALF-HOUR'S TRUCE—NAGDU'S DISCOVERY—DEPARTURE OF SPEDDING'S PATHANS 399

CHAPTER XXVII

THE FIGHT OF DECEMBER 20—THE STORMING-PARTY—THE CLIFF SCALED—CAPTURE OF THE FOUR SANGAS—THE ENEMY'S POSITION TURNED—FLIGHT OF THE GARRISONS—BEHAVIOUR OF THE IMPERIAL SERVICE TROOPS—ANOTHER V.C. 416

CHAPTER XXVIII

ADVANCE OF OUR FORCE—PRISONERS TAKEN TO CHALT—SUBMISSION OF NAGAR—FLIGHT OF THE THUM OF HUNZA—SUBMISSION OF HUNZA—OCCUPATION OF NAGAR 428

CHAPTER XXIX

OCCUPATION OF HUNZA—HUNZA CASTLE—THE ZENANA—HUNZA WINE—LOOT IN THE THUM'S PALACE—THE ROYAL LIBRARY—THE THUM'S CORRESPONDENCE—A TREASURE-HUNT—THE SECRET CHAMBER . 443

CHAPTER XXX

A FLYING COLUMN IS SENT UP THE VALLEY—A CHRISTMAS NIGHT'S BIVOUAC—GULMIT FORT—FRIENDLINESS OF THE KANJUTS—PASSU—RETURN OF FUGITIVES—THE WAZIR HUMAYUN—KHAIBAR—KHUSRU KHAN—GIRCHA—DIFFICULTIES OF THE UPPER KANJUT VALLEY 457

CHAPTER XXXI

MISGAR—LITTLE GUHJAL—AN INDIAN ULTIMA THULE—A HUNZA MERRYMAKING—THE KANJUT SWORD-DANCE—A HUNZA PANTOMIME—DISARMAMENT OF THE TRIBESMEN 473

CHAPTER XXXII

FROM GILGIT TO RAWAL PINDI—A TROOP OF KINGS—THE INDUS VALLEY ABOVE BOONJI—SEVEN MARCHES IN SNOW—THE ZOJI LA IN WINTER—RAWAL PINDI, AND HOME 485

WHERE THREE EMPIRES MEET

CHAPTER I

SNOW—THE ROAD INTO KASHMIR—A KASHMIR CUSTOM-HOUSE—THE JHELAM—DOMEL—URI—THE RESIDENT'S RECEPTION

On February 26, 1891, leaving the then very dense fogs of London, I embarked on the good ship 'Rome,' of the Peninsular and Oriental Company, bound for Bombay. The winter had been a notoriously severe one, and a great portion of the northern half of our globe was still under snow. Whenever we sighted high land between England and Port Said we had proofs of this. On doubling Gibraltar we saw the Sierra Nevada, on the Spanish coast, gleaming white from the jagged summits almost down to the base, while on the African shore Mount Atlas supported the misty heaven on cold, pale shoulders. Farther on we beheld the hills of Candia and Cephalonia, the mountains of Albania and the Morea all robed in snow; and, a sight of wonderful beauty visible far away one dawn as we steamed towards the Straits of Messina, the dome of Etna, pale pink and unsubstantial looking, floating in mid-air; for all the lower portion being uncovered with snow could not be seen for the distance, and blue sky seemed to intervene between the sea-horizon and the splendid summit hanging above like some fairy island carved out of delicate pearl.

Mr. Charles Spedding, C.E., who was my fellow-traveller to Kashmir, in which country he is constructing the strategical roads concerning which I shall have a good deal to say, feared that we might find it impossible to penetrate the Himalayan region to our destination for some time after our arrival in India, as the passes would probably be closed until a much later season than usual after a winter of such unexampled severity. The announcement by the Indian meteorologists, which we read in the papers, to the effect that the snowfall on the Himalayas had averaged forty feet during the winter, did not tend to reassure us.

I was destined to have a considerable experience of snow for the next twelve months. With the exception of the few days occupied in travelling from Bombay to Rawal Pindi and back, I believe that I was never out of sight of snow the whole while I was in India, hot season and cold, and I was very often wading through it for days. This visit to the burning East was, therefore, rather a unique one, frostbite and not sunstroke being the danger to be apprehended most.

On March 23 we arrived at Bombay. From here to our immediate destination, Rawal Pindi, is little more than a three days' journey by express train; but we traversed India in leisurely fashion, remaining a day or two at Bombay to see the Caves of Elephanta and the Towers of Silence, enjoying the while the hospitality of the luxurious Yacht Club; halting another day at Agra to visit that surely fairest building ever raised by man, the magical Taj; and two or three days more at Lahore, so that it was not until the morning of April 5 that we alighted from our train at Rawal Pindi station, and saw before us to the north the snow-covered ranges of the Outer Himalayas.

We had come to the barrier of those seemingly interminable dusty plains of India which we had been traversing for days, and already found ourselves in a different climate. The fresh hill-breeze was deliciously cool and invigorating, and the clear blue sky was of a different tint and pleasanter to look at than the heaven of the sultry South. Rawal Pindi is one of the most important cantonments of troops we have in the world, and military works on a vast scale are now in progress there; but I can say nothing about these from personal observation, for Spedding, into whose hands I had implicitly confided myself, would allow of no halt; he issued his marching-orders before we left the train, and we were to start on the road to Kashmir at once.

We therefore drove straight from the station to the house of Mr. Dhanjibhoy, a courteous Parsee gentleman who contracts to carry mails, passengers, and baggage between Rawal Pindi and Srinagur, the capital of Kashmir. He informed us that there were still eight feet of snow on parts of the road, and that landslips and avalanches had destroyed it in places and carried away bridges, but that it was now more or less passable, and that he was running the mail to Srinagur, a distance of 225 miles, in forty-eight hours. Passengers with baggage, however, could not travel nearly so fast as this.

By the time we had breakfasted Mr. Dhanjibhoy had all ready for us, and our caravan started. Four or five of those clumsy, slow, and altogether unscientifically constructed little vehicles known as *ekkas*, and which, I suppose, have been in use in India ever since wheels were invented, carried our native servants and our baggage, while we ourselves got into a *tonga*, a handy little two-horse trap for bad roads, in whose favour a good deal could be said. A Punjabi coachman drove us with true Mussulman fatalist recklessness at a good twelve miles an hour towards the hills, a lad hanging on behind anyhow he could, blowing a horn to give warning of our wild approach whenever we were about to turn a corner. We changed horses every five miles or so, and in less than an hour and a half we reached the outposts of the mountains, and had to somewhat moderate our pace. The road now wound along the sides of pleasant valleys with wooded slopes and cultivated bottoms vivid with the green of young rice. We gradually ascended, the air getting perceptibly cooler, till we reached the dak bungalow or post-house—it is scarcely necessary to translate the word in these days of Rudyard Kipling—of Tret, which is twenty-five miles from Rawal Pindi. The ekkas came in long after us; our progress along the road had, of course, to be regulated by that of our baggage, and as the ekka horses are not changed at the stages, but have to go right through, our rate of travelling was not rapid.

The next day, having allowed the tardy ekkas to get a good start, we were off again. We only accomplished fourteen miles this day, to Murree; but the road zigzagged up the hills by a steady incline all the way, and was trying for horses.

At first the country we passed through reminded one of the fair valleys on the Italian slope of the Alps in spring. We drove through woods of fragrant deodars and firs; the fruit-trees, the violets and other flowers were all in blossom, while clear cool water ran merrily down every hollow. But when we got higher the air was cold and the scenery had a wintry aspect. The road was in very bad condition, and in places was being repaired by large gangs of coolies. When we were a little distance from Murree we came into deep snow, and it was impossible to take tongas or ekkas farther. But some twenty coolies were at hand to help us here; they carried our baggage on their heads, and we tramped up to Rowbury's Hotel. Murree, once the seat of the Punjab Government, is a favourite hill-station and sanatorium in the hot season, and streets of charming little bungalows wind along the well-wooded hillsides, commanding fine views over the Himalayan ranges far away to the north; while from the high points one looks over the great plain of India stretching like a vast blue sea to the south. But Murree is 7,600 feet above the sea, and all the bungalows were deserted at this season; many of them, indeed, were quite snowed up to their roofs still, and the snow was lying eight feet deep in the streets.

Ekkas were not to be procured beyond Murree, and all our heavy baggage had to be carried on the backs of coolies for the rest of the way. But it was arranged that tongas should be sent from Srinagur to meet us at the point where the road again became practicable for horses, to carry ourselves and our light baggage. So as to give the coolies a good start, Spedding halted us for three days at this cheerless but bracing spot.

On April 9 we were off again. We had to walk a few miles to the point where the road was open; here we found the tongas awaiting us, and we rattled away down the hills. The journey for the next few days was one calculated to try the nerves a bit. The road was in very bad condition: landslips had been frequent; rickety temporary bridges took the place of those that had been swept away; where the road had fallen bodily into the abyss, a track only just sufficiently broad to allow the tonga to pass had been cleared by the navvies. Once one of our horses and a wheel of the tonga did slip over the side, on which we promptly jumped out. Luckily, there were some navvies by who rescued carriage and animals, pulling them back before they rolled over the precipice. Our reckless coachman, too, had an unpleasant fashion of driving at full gallop along these dangerous places and round the sharp turns where no parapet existed at the edge of the cliff.

The relays were frequent, and, without exception, when the fresh horses were put in at a stage they jibbed and plunged madly for a few minutes, the sore backs which had been inflicted on the poor animals by native negligence being obviously the cause. It is lucky that the post-houses where the changes are made are always at an easy part of the road with no precipice very near, else serious accidents would be the rule and not the rare exception on this road.

We passed gangs of navvies working on the wrecked road at frequent intervals. They were of various hill races, Kashmiris, Baltis, and Pathans, good-natured fellows, ready to laugh and interchange a joke, and also to help us by pushing on the tonga over a bad bit, or clearing fallen boulders from our path.

After driving some way we entered the valley of the river Jhelam, the classical Hydaspes, which formed the Eastern limit of the conquests of Alexander the Great. It is said that he embarked on it to descend to the Indus. He must have had a rough and anxious voyage if it was then the foaming, rushing, rock-encumbered torrent it is now. This portion of the river is not navigable for a craft of any description, but quantities of small logs—to be used as railway-sleepers in

India—are cut in the forests of Kashmir and thrown into it. These are washed down to the Punjab, where the agents of the Maharajah collect as many as are not dashed into matchwood. When we first caught sight of the Jhelam it was running far beneath us, but we quickly descended to its bank, which we followed for the remainder of this day's journey, once more in an agreeable spring climate, having left winter behind at Murree.

The Jhelam here forms the frontier between British India and the territories of the Maharajah of Kashmir, and when we reached the village of Kohala we crossed the river by a suspension bridge and were in the native State, a fact which was unpleasantly, though somewhat amusingly, brought to our notice by the presence of a very curious and thoroughly Oriental Customhouse.

This was quite a new institution, ordinary travellers between India and Kashmir not having been worried by this civilised nuisance hitherto. It seems that the Durbar had suddenly bethought itself to make an attempt at taxing the sahibs who now throng into Kashmir every hot season, so the *hukm* was issued that a Custom-house should be established at this place; but how it was to be organised and managed was, of course, left to chance, and not considered in the least.

On crossing the river we found ourselves in a dirty little bazaar, where we were confronted by the ominous inscription, 'Custom House,' in English and Persian, painted on a board which hung outside one of the huts. Then came out to us the Kashmir Customs official, in a long gown, with nothing official in his appearance—a polite man who spoke no English and only a few words of Hindustani, with whom, therefore, it was difficult to carry on the abstruse financial argument that ensued. After some search he found and brought to us the Customs regulations, written in Persian, which we could make nothing of, and which evidently puzzled him too; so he tried to simplify matters by quietly suggesting that we should pay 6 per cent. duty on the value of all our property. We asked him how he proposed to assess us, but he easily got over that difficulty; he assured us with a charming smile that he had full confidence in the honour of the sahibs, and would accept our own valuation without question. We then explained to him that we had not the slightest idea as to what our belongings were worth, but wished to clearly understand from him what articles were liable to duty. To this he replied that his instructions were not very definite, but he was under the impression that there was a tax of 10 per cent. on guns and of six rupees a gallon on wine and spirits.

Then the argument took another direction. He said he thought that sportsmen and other *bonâ fide* travellers were exempt from duty, but that merchants were not so; that he considered contractors were merchants, and that, consequently, Spedding was liable to full dues, whereas I possibly was not. This led to a discussion on the definition of terms, and to subtle questions of philology, till this pundit, finding that he was like to lose himself in dim metaphysical labyrinths, shifted his ground to a very practical standpoint, and discovered that there was one thing at least of which he was quite certain—his orders were that nothing should be allowed to pass his hut until the duty had been paid, and he proudly pointed to a pile of bales and boxes which he had impounded from the carriers, and among which, to our consternation, we recognised the heavy baggage which had been sent on with the coolies, and which we imagined to be far ahead.

After this interesting argument had continued for some time in the centre of a crowd of amiable-looking natives, we wearied of the amusement, and then the Kashmiri had to yield before the stubbornness of the sahib. It ended in his allowing us to go by with all our property, the heavy articles being again sent on with coolies, in consideration of a written agreement on our part, to the effect that we would pay the dues at some future time when the claim against us had been definitely made out, subject to our right of appeal to the higher authorities. I never heard any more of this business. I believe that the impossibility of carrying on a Custom-house on these principles, at any rate at the expense of the sahib, was so obvious that it was decided to allow English travellers to go through free as of old, and to only raise duty, as heretofore, on merchandise entering the country.

So, having won the day, we proceeded to drive on into Kashmir territory. The road from Kohala onwards, which completes the connection between Rawal Pindi and Srinagur, was constructed by the Kashmir State in accordance with an arrangement we have with our tributary, whereby the Maharajah is bound to make strategical roads within his frontier for the purposes of Imperial defence. This is the only road practicable for wheels in the whole of this country. It was commenced in the reign of the late Maharajah. The progress of the work, however, was very slow for a time, only thirty miles of it having been finished, after several years' labour, when Mr. Spedding contracted to complete the remaining portion without delay. He brought his work to a satisfactory conclusion in 1890, having overcome all the extraordinary natural difficulties which this mountainous district opposes to the engineer. It is spoken of by competent judges as being one of the finest mountain roads in the world. It is needless to speak in this place of its strategical importance, and I shall have plenty to say later on concerning its prolongation, on which Mr. Spedding is still working—a military road connecting Srinagur with Gilgit, the extreme northern outpost of Kashmir, and, therefore, of the regions under British influence.

The scenery through which we now drove was very pleasing. The steep slopes of the mountains were well cultivated to a considerable height. The laboriously built-up terraces of soil were irrigated by little artificial canals carrying the water from tributary nullahs for miles along the hillsides; the groves of peach, walnut, apricot, almond, and other fruit-trees, mostly now in full blossom, the vines trained up the poplars as in Italy, and the scattered patches of various grain, showing the existence of a considerable and industrious peasantry. The whole of the Kashmir State is practically independent of rain. A fairly hard winter, storing a sufficiency of snow on the mountain tops, so that the gradual thaw through the summer keeps the irrigation canals constantly brimming, is all that is wanted to ensure an abundant harvest. Every great famine that has occurred in Kashmir has been caused, not by summer drought, but by a too mild winter, or by heavy rains in the hot season, which have flooded the plains and destroyed the crops.

Above this terraced cultivation were the pine-forests and the pastures on which numbers of sheep and goats were feeding; while, far above, seen through gaps of the lower ranges, rose the great snowy peaks.

The road now followed the precipitous left bank of the Jhelam, passing sometimes over galleries that had been carried along the face of perpendicular cliffs, sometimes under tunnels that had been driven through rocky buttresses. Here, too, the avalanches and landslips that had followed the enormous snowfall of the winter had damaged the road in many places, destroying parapets and bridges.

This night's halting-place was the dak bungalow of Dulai, forty miles from Murree. This is a comfortable post-house, as are all those on the Kashmir section of the road, dak bungalows being, I believe, a hobby of the present ruler. Among the official notices posted on the walls in the name of the Maharajah of Kashmir and Jummoo, I read an abstract of the new game laws for the State, forbidding the employment of dogs for driving, the killing of the females of ibex and other animals, and the selling of heads by natives. It is to be hoped that these much-needed regulations will be observed, for in recent years an indiscriminate slaughter has threatened to exterminate the wild creatures of these hills.

On the following day we only travelled one stage to Domel, and put up in what is the prettiest dak bungalow in Kashmir, situated at a beautifully verdant spot at a bend of the foaming river, and commanding a delightful view both up and down the valley.

A walk through the little bazaar after breakfast brought me to the fine iron bridge, built for the State by Mr. A. Atkinson, which here spans the river. It is constructed on the cantilever principle, and the stone piers that support it are Oriental in their shape and elaborate decoration. This is a good example of the admirable manner in which our Anglo-Indian architects adapt Eastern form and art to our utilitarian public works. This bridge also serves the purpose of a sacred building, for Hindoo idols have been placed in the niches of the stonework, the offerings of maize that lie in their open palms showing that they do not want for devotees. Close by, the Kishenganga River joins the Jhelam, and is spanned by a light suspension bridge which surmounts an old native wooden cantilever bridge, now broken-backed and falling in. Wherever

KASHMIR CANTILEVER BRIDGE

anything more permanent and solid than a rope bridge is required in Kashmir it has been customary, from time immemorial, to build it on the cantilever principle, generally of one arch, the supporting timbers projecting one over another from the bank, their shore ends being weighted down with masonry. These Kashmir bridges are strongly constructed, and some still in use are of great antiquity. It is said that one of them first suggested the idea of the Forth Bridge.

At Domel, Spedding met General de Bourbel, the Engineer-in-Chief to the State, and certain of his own staff. As he had business to discuss with them, we halted here for a few days, and a pleasanter spot could not have been chosen for the purpose.

On crossing the bridge on the morning after our arrival, I found a picturesque encampment which served to remind me that I was now well on my way to Central Asia. This was a large caravan from Yarkund that was bringing a considerable freight of carpets and tea across the mountains to India. The men, warmly clad in clumsy robes and sheepskins, were natives of Chinese Turkestan, big, jovial-looking, rosy-cheeked fellows of Tartar type.

There is a considerable Sikh colony in the neighbourhood of Domel, and as one of the most important Sikh religious festivals commences on April 12, all the people of that faith—men, women, and children—were gathered here from far and wide, clad in their festal raiment. They bathed in the sacred Jhelam, feasted or fasted according to the law, and made merry. It was interesting to see these cheery, simple, fine people enjoying their holiday, a people for whom the Englishman cannot but have much sympathy, remembering how bravely they fought against us first of all, how well they fought for us later on in the Mutiny days, and are fighting for us still when occasion demands.

But everything at this festival was not beautiful to see. Two or three opium-sodden, fantastically skipping, howling, naked fakirs had found their way here, covered with filth, hideous, evil-featured, with insane fanatical malice glittering in their eyes—our greatest enemies in all India these.

It was while we were here that the news of the Manipur disaster reached us. I noticed that there appeared to be an impression abroad that there were troubles ahead on the frontier; vague rumours were in the air of coming disturbances in the North-West. The Black Mountain fanatics were again preparing for war just beyond the mountains to the west of us, and within sight of the Murree hills. We heard that the Chins had risen, that a general outbreak of the Miranzais had taken place, and that our troops would be attacked by a force of nearly 10,000 Afridis, Akhils, and Mishtis. Spedding remarked, 'I should not be surprised if we see some fighting before we leave this country'—a surmise which proved correct.

Another guest arrived at the bungalow during our stay. This was Captain Bower, of the 17th Bengal Cavalry, well known as a traveller and explorer in Central Asia, but who has since this made his name still more famous by his extraordinary journey across Tibet from Ladak to Shanghai. He was now on his way to Srinagur to organise his caravan, and intended to set out for Ladak as soon as the passes between Kashmir and the Tibetan frontier were open. I had some interesting conversations with him concerning those desolate regions, and he pointed out to me on the map a long blank space stretching across the north of India. 'I hope to do away with a good deal of that blank,' he said, ' when I return.' He suggested that I should accompany him as far as the Chinese frontier, and see the curious Buddhist country of Ladak. I was very glad to seize the opportunity of visiting that region in the company of one who knew it so well, and agreed to join him. As will be seen, I had no cause to regret my decision.

On April 13, leaving Spedding and the other engineers to complete their business, I drove off with Mr. Millais, one of Spedding's staff, to Uri, where Spedding has built himself a bungalow, there to await him.

It was a forty-eight miles' drive through a lovely country, the reckless tonga-drivers, as usual, to all appearance, trying how nearly they could break our necks. Turning round a sharp corner at full gallop we collided with another tonga coming in our direction, neither driver having heard or heeded the other's horn. Having nearly been precipitated over the cliff on this occasion, our next adventure was to drive through a cascade and knock down a pundit. At this particular spot, a water-course on the hillside having broken away from its proper channel, was pouring from a height above on to the road, forming a powerful shower-bath for whosoever should pass beneath. The pundit in question was availing himself of so splendid an opportunity for performing his ablutions. He had stripped all his clothes off, and was standing in the middle of this cascade as we turned the corner and drove into him. He had his eyes shut, and the falling water drowned the noise of our approach. The collision did not injure the pundit, but our startled horses once more nearly sent us over the cliff. We had only two more narrow escapes on this day. First, we met a marriage procession of such exceedingly gaudy colouring that our horses were, not unnaturally, dazzled and alarmed at this rainbow apparition, and with their usual stupidity attempted to escape from it over the road edge to the certain perdition of the rocks below.

Our last escape was the most serious of all; for this time it was not the mere risk of breaking one's neck that was incurred, but of committing sacrilege in the worst degree and making oneself liable to imprisonment for life in the gloomy dungeons of Hari Parbat, the Bastille of Srinagur. We ran over a sleeping cow, most luckily without doing it serious harm. I suppose every schoolboy is aware that the population of Kashmir is for the most part Mahomedan, while the royal family and ruling caste are Hindoos. It is a long time since I was a schoolboy, and they did not teach us these things then, so I must confess that I myself was ignorant of the above fact until within a few months of my departure for Kashmir. The majority here have to submit to the religious prejudices of the small minority. Until recently the killing of that sacred animal, the cow, was punishable with death. Imprisonment for life is now the penalty, and many an unfortunate Mahomedan, I believe, is lying immured in Hari Parbat because that in time of famine he has ventured to kill his own ox to save himself and family from starvation. English travellers are naturally bound to observe the laws of this State while travelling in it, and though in their case imprisonment cannot, of course, be enforced, an immediate banishment from the realms of the Maharajah would follow the crime of wilful sacrilege. The Englishman must forswear his national diet while he is a dweller in Kashmir; so for the next nine months—that is, until I crossed the frontier into the Kanjut valleys—I never tasted beef.

Millais and myself passed a few days in Spedding's bungalow at Uri. We had plenty of society, for the summer visitors were beginning to throng into Kashmir, and as many of these were Spedding's friends, he had invited them to put up at his bungalow on their way through. Mothers, accompanied by their daughters, were among our guests, travelling up to Srinagar without male escort. Every summer English ladies wander about Kashmir alone, taking their caravans of native servants, baggage animals, and coolies, pitching their tents at night, and riding the stages in the same independent fashion as their brothers and husbands would.

Kashmir is one of the few countries in which it is possible for a lady to travel about in this unconventional manner. This is, indeed, the safest land I have ever seen or heard of. The firm rule of the Mussulman and Hindoo conquerors, who have successively oppressed this peaceable, not to say cowardly, race, the terrible penalties that used to be inflicted for any offence against the person or property of travellers, the excellent Oriental custom by which a whole district is made liable for crimes committed within its boundaries, have produced this result. The natives dare not be dishonest, at any rate on a big scale or in an open manner, and a traveller of the dominant British race, man, woman, or child, is treated with a servile civility which no doubt proceeds rather from fear than from any natural tendency to be kind to strangers.

After a few days Spedding arrived at Uri, and on April 21 we saw a rather interesting function. Our newly-appointed Resident in Kashmir, Colonel Prideaux, of Abyssinian fame, accompanied by Mrs. Prideaux, came through Uri on his way to Srinagur, and halted for tiffin at our bungalow. The natives prepared to receive the representative of the Empress with due honour. A large crowd of men gathered in front of the bungalow, and in the Oriental fashion brought their *dalis* or presents, which they solemnly placed on the ground—baskets of dried fruit, potatoes, offerings of odorous onions, fish, too, from the river, a goodly show of comestibles.

There is a little fort here, and the garrison, about a dozen in number, turned out to present arms when the great Sahib should arrive. The uniform of these sepoys

C

of the Maharajah was very gay—bright red stockings, blue tunic faced with red, yellow pyjamas and red and blue turban.

All the native gentlemen of the neighbourhood were, of course, present, both Hindoos and Mussulmans. The most noticeable among these was the Nawab of Uri, an old Mahomedan, who is the titular ruler of this district, but who, of course, does not enjoy the power his ancestors possessed before the Dogras took the land. He was a fine-looking old man; his bent form was robed in snowy white, and from under his voluminous white turban peered a lean, handsome, eagle face. He was accompanied, as befitted his position, by some twenty followers. I observed that though he spoke freely to the Englishmen and Mahomedans present, he had not a word to say to the Kashmiri pundits, whom he appeared to look upon with great contempt. The Hindoo Dogra rulers of this country belong to a manly, warlike race, which one can respect and admire; but the native Hindoo is a despicable being. These Kashmiri Hindoos are always known as pundits—why I am unable to say, for it is an utter misuse of that term, which is supposed to imply learning, a quality very scarce among these people.

At last we heard the tonga horns sounding far up the gorge, and soon after the Resident and his retinue drove up. He received the salaams of the gathered people, and his servants collected their vegetable offerings.

The Colonel was entering on the Residentship of Kashmir at a most critical time, when a clever and tactful man was needed to undertake the responsibility of safeguarding our interests at Srinagur without causing unnecessary friction. That we have got such a Resident in the person of Colonel Prideaux appears to be the general opinion.

CHAPTER II

BARAMOULA — KASHMIRI BOATMEN — ACROSS THE WOOLAR LAKE — THE VALE OF KASHMIR — SALE OF THE STATE TO GOLAB SINGH — REFORMS IN ADMINISTRATION — A STORM ON THE LAKE.

On April 24 we started for Baramoula, where we were to leave the cart road and take to boats. This, our last day's journey on the road, carried us through the fairest country we had yet seen. We drove through pleasant groves of chestnuts, walnuts, peaches, pears, cherries, mulberries, and apples, all of which are indigenous to this favoured land, while the wild vines hung in festoons from the branches. The fresh grass beneath the trees was spangled with various flowers—great terra-cotta coloured lilies, iris of several shades, and others—while hawthorn bushes in full blossom emulated the whiteness of the snows above. The mountains, too, were craggy and grander in outline than any we had yet seen. Highest of all were the dreary, snow-streaked wastes, lower down forests of deodar crowned the cliffs, which in their turn often fell sheer a thousand feet to the green, lawn-like expanses below. Sparkling cascades dashed over many a high precipice. It was a land of running water, of fruit, and flowers, and birds, and sweet odours, that made one think that the beauties of far-famed Kashmir had not been exaggerated by the Oriental poets.

But though in the territory of the Maharajah, we

were not really yet in Kashmir proper; the term now, as of old, before new conquests had so far extended the State, being restricted to the Vale, or rather great alluvial plain, of Kashmir, together with the valleys running into it. It was not till we reached the town of Baramoula that we emerged from the defile that forms the gateway of Kashmir, and saw before us the commencement of that fair oasis which is so curiously embedded in the midst of the rugged Himalayan system. By Baramoula the hills recede on either side of the Jhelam Valley, cultivated plains border the river, and the raving Jhelam itself broadens into a slowly-flowing stream. Just beyond Baramoula the last spurs of the hills slope gently into the vast plain which stretches to the far-away, dim, snowy ranges. After having been shut in for days within the narrow horizons of the Jhelam gorges, with the loud tumult of foaming torrents ever in one's ears, it seemed pleasant and strangely soothing to thus suddenly open out this extensive landscape, and come to the banks of this calm, broad water, which did not raise a murmur to break the stillness of a glorious evening.

The distance from Baramoula to Srinagur by land is thirty-two miles; but the usual method of proceeding to the capital is by boat, up the sinuous Jhelam and across the Woolar Lake, a twenty hours' journey. By the banks of the river we found our servants awaiting us amidst the piles of baggage. A number of *doongahs*, as the Kashmiri travelling boats are called, were drawn up along the shore hard by, and the rival crews clamoured round in their usual persistent way for our custom. We engaged as many boats as were necessary for our party, which had now been increased by several of Spedding's staff, and embarked.

A doongah is a sort of large punt, fifty feet long or more, partly roofed over with matting, supported by a wooden framework. The two ends of the boat are left open, and here the men, women, and children forming the crew steer, work their short paddles, or quant. Most of the roofed-in portion is placed at the service of the traveller who engages the doongah, and here he puts up his bed and impedimenta; but a small space in the

DOONGAHS

stern is cut off by a mat and reserved for the crew, generally consisting of one man, his wives and progeny, who live and do their cooking there.

The Hanjis, or boatmen, form a separate class in Kashmir. They are fine-looking men, athletic, hard-working, and extremely courteous, if they are not allowed to go too far and become a nuisance, which they readily do. Their women when young are often beautiful, and the children, of whom they appear to be very fond, are the prettiest little creatures imaginable; but the Hanji is often a great scoundrel, though if kept well in hand he is too great a coward to display his bad qualities. The Hanjis are Mahomedans of a very lax sect; they assert that they are the descendants of Hindoos who were forcibly converted under the old Raj, so cannot be expected to be very orthodox. As they still entertain a regard for the religion of their ancestors, they compromise matters by neglecting the observances of either creed. They are naturally considered a degraded class, and other Mussulmans will not marry into their families.

Our servants occupied one doongah, in which they could prepare our meals, while we Englishmen had a doongah each to live in. There is not much privacy in one of these craft, and while travelling at night light sleepers must not expect repose, unless they kick the captain at intervals to explain their wishes; for while towing along the bank, or paddling, the men sing wild choruses and the women chatter unceasingly; but even kicking the captain cannot suppress the squalls of the numerous babies.

Before we got under weigh I had time to look round Baramoula. The town is on the right bank of the Jhelam, which is here traversed by a long cantilever log bridge of several arches. Close to the bridge stand the ruins of a fort which was destroyed by the earthquake of 1885, one of the most violent ever recorded in this often-convulsed region, and which here caused great loss of life.

Baramoula is a typical little Kashmiri town, with narrow dirty streets, thronged by a dirtier and not particularly picturesque population. The houses are built of sun-dried brick, with the woodwork of eaves, doors, and lattices more or less artistically carved. The gabled mud roofs are densely overgrown with long grass, interspersed with bright flowers. I had often read of the roof-gardens of Kashmir, and now knew what was meant. On looking down from above on a Kashmir town this almost universal custom produces a pleasing effect, even the tops of the mosques and Hindoo temples being thus converted into gardens and tiny fields, over which, in the summer days, the birds and butterflies hover in numbers.

We were towed and paddled through the greater part of the night, but when I awoke at dawn I found all quiet—even the babies were still, and our crews were sleeping. Our little fleet was brought up alongside the bank where the Woolar Lake flows into the Jhelam, close to the village of Sopor. I now saw around me the Vale of Kashmir in its entirety; a vast green plain with lakes and many winding streams, surrounded by a distant circle of great mountains, shutting it in on all sides with a seemingly impassable barrier of rock and snow, rising in peaks of immense height, some of the highest in the world indeed, gleaming dimly in the morning light. It is not strange that the invaders who came upon this sweet oasis after months of travelling among the fearful and arid mountain regions that lie beyond waxed enthusiastic over its fertile beauty and hailed it as the first paradise.

The Vale of Kashmir is about 5,200 feet above the sea; it is oval in shape, being, roughly, one hundred miles long and twenty miles broad; while the Woolar Lake is ten miles in length and six in breadth, but its waters, flooding the extensive swamps and low pastures, often extend over a far greater area. At some remote period the whole plain was submerged, forming a great inland sea, of which many native traditions speak. Then the waters broke through the mountain dam at Baramoula, deepening and broadening the channel of the Jhelam, the only outlet, with the result that the Woolar has shrunk to its present dimensions; while the greater portion of the old lake bed is now a rich alluvial plain, cloven by numerous streams and some rivers of considerable size, such as the Jhelam and the Sind, which, rushing down the mountain gorges from the glaciers and perpetual snows, pour themselves into the lake, and so ultimately into the Jhelam, near Sopor. Before the breaking away of the barrier at Baramoula, the level of the lake was some 600 feet higher than it is now. The liberated waters washed away vast quantities of the softer soil, so that the plain of Kashmir is much lower than the bed of the old lake. But there still remain isolated portions of this ancient bed that were left by the subsiding waters; these are the Karewahs, as they are called, flat-topped hills, with steep cliff sides rising some hundreds of feet above the plain, which form a striking feature in the scenery of the Vale.

Soon everyone in our fleet was up and about, but we did not get under weigh, as we had to await Spedding's house-boat, which was to join us here. A house-boat is no uncommon sight now on the Jhelam and the canals of Srinagur, the rich natives having followed this fashion so well adapted to Oriental tastes, and on some of the reaches of the classical Hydaspes one could almost imagine oneself to be at Henley.

While we waited, our boatmen lay about lazily, and the dirty, pretty children commenced to play at that most ancient of games, tipcat, with their also dirty, pretty child-mothers. There was a dak bungalow on the shore close to us, a favourite resort of English fishermen, and we found the walls of the house worth inspecting; for here were recorded, with more or less artistic skill in charcoal and pencil, the stories of the sahibs' sport. I saw pictures of fifty-pound mahseers, with descriptions of how and when the monsters were caught. The artists had allowed their imaginations to run riot in some cases, and each successive sportsman attempted to describe a bigger record than his predecessor. One wag had parodied these fishermen's tales, by drawing on the wall a gigantic creature which he represented himself to have caught while in bed in the bungalow, accompanied by a graphic description of the spirited play it had given. The picture was easily to be recognised as of a creature we also have in England, but on a much smaller scale, remarkable for its agility and troublesome bite.

Inflamed possibly by these drawings of the veracious sahibs, all our servants settled themselves down to a serious morning's fishing, but with no result. The boatmen slept for some time and they awoke in a depressed frame of mind, for, though hungry, they dared not eat, as the great religious fast of the Mahomedans was now in progress. Not being able to satisfy the appetite of hunger, they bethought themselves to attempt instead the gratification of what appears to be as strong an appetite with the Kashmiri—the greed of money, and in a mild way they struck for *rassad*, or extra pay for rations, in consequence of the delay here. They demanded two annas a day each, on which it was pointed out to them that half that sum was the daily rassad according to the State tariff. 'But,' urged the chief spokesman of the strikers, argumentative and fond of hearing himself talk like all his race, 'this, sahib, is the Ramazan, and for us good Mussulmans no food must pass the lips to-day ; but at night we may eat, and we feel already that our hunger will be very keen. We will then eat twice as much as usual, so should have double rassad.' When we refused to yield to this plausible argument the men commenced to groan and weep bitterly, as they will on the smallest provocation, especially when they have failed to extract an extra pice, for of such stuff is the native of the Happy Valley.

As a rule, an Englishman coming for the first time to this country takes a great fancy to these plausible, handsome Kashmiris, finding them clever, cheery, and civil, and it is not until he has been some time in the country that he discovers that these are among the most despicable creatures on earth, incorrigible cheats and liars, and cowardly to an inconceivable degree. The Kashmiri is clad in a long woollen gown like a woman's, called the *pheran*, which it is said the conqueror Akbar by edict compelled the men of this race to wear, with the avowed intention of destroying what manliness they may have had and turning them into women. It appears that his method has proved eminently successful. It is true that the Kashmiri has several useful qualities. He is a clever artisan and an industrious farmer, he has great physical strength and endurance, he can be very courteous when in hope of gain or inspired by fear ; he is distinctly a man of peace and easy to rule, but he is not admirable save to that school which affects to despise courage as a relic of barbarism.

He is in many respects a difficult, paradoxical creature to describe. To dislike him one must know him, one must have seen, for instance, a great, strong, bearded man submitting to having his ears boxed a dozen times in succession by a Punjabi half his size, and whom he could crush with one hand, weeping and raising piercing shrieks like a naughty child that is being whipped, and finally rolling on the ground and howling at the feet of this lad of a more plucky race. On the other hand, one must have observed his covert insolence to some griffin globe-trotter, who does not understand the rascal yet and treats him too leniently. He will presume on any kindness that is shown him until, at last, going too far, he is brought to reason by the thrashing he has long been asking for. I believe a Kashmiri likes a beating and the consequent luxury of a good howl; for he certainly neglects all warning, and persists in some offensiveness until what he knows will be the inevitable chastisement comes.

A Kashmiri will unresistingly take a blow from anyone, even from a Kashmiri, I should imagine, should one be found to strike—a very rare occurrence, for though these people wrangle among each other like the proverbial washerwoman, they never come to blows by any chance, having attained such a depth of cowardice that they actually fear one another. I had been a good deal among Mahomedans in other countries, and had always associated dignity and courage with the profession of that creed, so was disagreeably surprised to discover this cowardly, cringing, cackling race among the followers of the Prophet.

Tartars, Tibetans, Moguls, Afghans and Sikhs have all in turn overrun the Happy Valley, whose inhabitants have always quietly submitted to each new tyranny. Their very abjectness has been their salvation; for their conquerors, not having to fear them, did not attempt to exterminate them or to dispossess them of their lands, but left them to cultivate the rich soil and carry on their industries—like the bees, to work for the advantage of others, their enslavers appropriating the results of their labour. They still cultivate the best lands, and are likely to prosper under the beneficent *régime* which the Indian Government is introducing. It is to be hoped that the greater liberties they will now enjoy will tend to make something like men of them; but it will take long to raise them from the degradation into which they have been sunk by so many ages of oppression.

In order to obtain a clear understanding of what is now taking place in Kashmir, and of the object of our present interference in the management of that country, a few facts connected with its more recent history should be borne in mind, and these I may as well briefly set out here.

Kashmir, having been wrested from the Pathans by the Sikhs in 1819, was attached to the Punjab until the termination of the Sutlej campaign and our occupation of Lahore, when it fell into the hands of the British.

Instead of retaining this country, whose immense value to us was not realised at the time, we at once assigned it by treaty, dated March 16, 1846, to Golab Singh, the Maharajah of Jummoo, in consideration of the valuable services he had rendered us. In exchange for the independent sovereignty over this extensive region, he was to pay us the very inadequate sum of 75 lacs of rupees, and engaged to come to our assistance with the whole of his army whenever we were at war with any people near his frontier. He also acknowledged our supremacy, and agreed to pay a nominal annual tribute—consisting chiefly of Kashmir shawls—to our Government. Not only the Vale of Kashmir, but all the hill countries beyond which had been recently subjugated by the Sikhs, including Ladak, Baltistan, and the Astor and Gilgit districts, by this treaty became the appanage of the Maharajahs of Jummoo.

During the reign of the present ruler, Pertab Singh, the Indian Government has lent to the Kashmir State several selected officers, both civil and military, to superintend the much-needed reforms in the administration of the country. Without this interference on our part Kashmir would have been quite unable to carry out her treaty obligations. She was threatened by bankruptcy and general disorganisation, while her unpaid and discontented army was in no condition to protect the frontier.

I shall describe in the proper place what I saw of the work of these British officials; but I may state here that our present active policy in Kashmir, while having for its object the safeguarding of our Imperial interests, will bring about a great amelioration in the condition of the population. This is not a benefit, moreover, that is being forced upon a people against its will. The natives would much like to see yet more interference on our part. The only class that does object—and with good reason—to our supervision of the affairs of the State during the present critical time is that small body of Hindoos from which the officials are selected—corrupt even for Oriental officials—who grind down the unfortunate Mussulman peasantry with their outrageous rapacity and with the forced labour which they exact. These do not at all relish our newly-introduced revenue reforms, which, while they enrich the treasury and bring a secure prosperity to the people, deprive these ruffianly pundits of their loot. The members of the ruling family, including the president of the State Council, Rajah Amar Singh, are quite alive to the necessity of these reforms, and have loyally backed up the efforts of our officers to set things right.

The Mahomedan cultivators, who form the vast majority of the population, being a peaceful, clever, unfanatical, money-loving people, appreciate the enormous advantages they gain under the new order of things, and for purely selfish reasons heartily welcome the reforming sahib.

It was late in the afternoon before the house-boat arrived and our fleet got under weigh again. The crews, famished as they were, paddled along lustily to a not unmusical though monotonous chorus.

We were soon well away from the land on the broad inland sea. The air was still and sultry, and there came a stormy sunset with magnificent colouring. The uninterrupted wall of mountains which surrounded us, many of whose peaks out-topped Mont Blanc by thousands of feet, presented a very fine appearance in the distance, the vast snowy wastes being lit here with a pale yellow light, here glowing like molten gold, and here gleaming purest white; while the deep, shadowed defiles that clove the hills were purple black. But on the lake itself night was already falling, and by the dim light all that we could distinguish round us was the dark water and the high summits of those Himalayan deserts of rock, ice and snow, which the sun's rays had not yet left. There was something unearthly in the colouring and in the desolation of the scene as well as in the immensity of the distances. It might have been some landscape of the ruined moon, so lifeless and strange it seemed.

The storm signs were not deceptive. One of the violent squalls that are frequent here swept down on the lake, and loud thunder rolled over the mountains, while quite a rough sea at once got up on the broad waters. The matting was blown off the roofs of the doongahs quicker than it could be taken in by the crews to prevent capsizing. The water tumbled on board each craft, and forthwith a tremendous commotion arose among the boatmen. Such a noise I never heard before—men, women, and children were lamenting, weeping, and howling to their prophets in one terrified chorus. It was vain to attempt to paddle the heavy boats against so strong a wind, so the whole fleet had to scud back before the storm towards the mainland on our lee, where stood a small village. In their terror the men tumbled over each other in hopeless confusion, each one giving orders and cursing his fellows instead of lending a hand. We had almost reached the shore when, with a heavy downpour of rain, the wind suddenly shifted and threatened to drive us out into the broadest part of the lake; whereupon the panic became worse than ever among these great, bearded cowards. Luckily the wind soon shifted again to a quarter that was fair for us, and the scared mariners struggled hard with their paddles to attain the safety of the dry land as quickly as possible.

During the storm the surrounding mountains appeared more fantastic than ever; rainbows spanned the peaks; and for some time after the sun was set one far-off, snowy plateau shone out with an uncanny yellow light when all else was dark.

The howlings of our gallant fleet had awakened the village; so all the inhabitants were gathered together on the shore to shout instructions to us as we approached, while all the village dogs were standing there too, with energetic barking contributing their share to the fearful din.

All the boats were at last successfully beached, the howlings and barkings gradually subsided, and our boatmen proceeded to break their long fast and gorge themselves with food.

The season of the Ramazan is not a good time for travelling in a Mahomedan country: the people get quite stupid with their alternate starving and guzzling. The orders were that after a four hours' rest we should start again and prosecute our journey by moonlight; but at the appointed time the admiral of our fleet came to us to complain that several of his men were sleeping so soundly after their heavy supper that he was quite unable to wake them. He was afraid, I suppose, to kick them up himself, and wished us to perform the operation for him. He was informed that it was not our business to rule and kick his men; that was his province, while it was ours to rule and stir him should he fail in enforcing obedience to his orders.

On this he succeeded somehow in bustling up his replete followers and we paddled off again, the wind having dropped and all being quiet save for the snoring of those of the men off duty, the night-long jabbering of the women—what on earth can these Hanji ladies find to talk so much about?—and the crying of babies.

CHAPTER III

CLIMATE—SRINAGUR—THE EUROPEAN QUARTER—SRINAGUR MERCHANTS—PROGRESS AND DEVELOPMENT OF THE STATE—RESOURCES OF KASHMIR—PROPOSED RAILWAY—THE TAKHT-I-SULIEMAN.

On waking on the morning of April 26 we found that we had left the lake and were ascending the Jhelam once more—not, as after it has passed Baramoula, a torrent raging down deep gorges, but a placid stream as broad as the Thames at Kew winding sluggishly across the fat alluvial plains. Our men had now put aside the paddles and were tramping along the bank with the towlines, acquiring another splendid appetite for a night of gormandising to follow a day of religious fasting.

The sky was clear, the air cool and pure, after the storm; it was veritable Kashmir spring weather, than which it would not be easy to find any more healthy or agreeable. The climate of this Paradise of Asia appears to be well-adapted to the European constitution. The few English children who have been born and brought up here are as strong and rosy-cheeked as if they had been bred at home; while there is no necessity for their leaving the country when they have attained a certain age, the separation between parents and children, which forms for our people the great drawback to an Indian career, being quite avoidable in Kashmir. Had we not sold this magnificent country, a great military cantonment would no doubt have been

D

long since established here. This would not only have been most advantageous from a strategical point of view, but would have avoided much of the sickness and mortality which thins the ranks of our white army in India.

The heavy boats were towed but slowly, so we often disembarked and walked along the banks which have here been artificially raised to prevent the water overflowing the adjacent land, much of the plain at this season being considerably below the level of the river.

All round us was to be seen the great circle of dazzling snowy ranges that encompasses the plain. We traversed fine pastures, now blue with a species of iris very common in Kashmir. We passed villages pleasantly embowered amongst walnut, mulberry, and other trees, while frequently the great chenars or plane-trees, which form one of the features of the Happy Valley, stood like giants above the others. It was a land of birds too. Numbers of those little Parsees, the larks, were singing a joyful morning hymn to the rising sun, there was a cooing of doves and a calling of cuckoos, while brightly-coloured and quaint little hoopoes, our old friend the epops of Aristophanes, were darting among the foliage, elevating their impertinent crests as they stared at us with an expression that plainly said, 'What right have you people in our country?'

At last we saw ahead of us the two landmarks of Srinagur, which are visible far across the plain—the prison and fortress of Hari Parbat topping a dome-shaped hill, and the higher peak of Takht-i-Sulieman, which rises precipitously 1,000 feet above the city, and on whose rocky summit stands a temple upwards of two thousand years old.

After several hours of slow progress up the winding reaches of the river, we traversed the scattered suburbs and entered the Asiatic Venice. Srinagur, 'The City of the Sun,' contains a population of something under 100,000. When approached by one of its numerous waterways it appears a pleasing place at first sight and worthy to be the capital of a great State, but the traveller is somewhat disillusioned when he leaves the waterside to penetrate the narrow streets.

Leaving our slow doongahs to follow us, we hailed some of the gondolas of Srinagur; long, swift canoes known as *shikarahs*, in which we reclined luxuriously on soft cushions as we smoked and surveyed the busy and interesting scene. Many picturesque craft of all sorts were travelling on the river: clumsy cargo barges laden with timber, grain, or oil; mat-roofed doongahs full of passengers and their baggage; darting shikarahs, in which sat smiling merchants in fine silk robes, carrying samples of their wares with which to tempt the newly-arrived sahib; boats, too, containing what our Indian novelist modestly terms dainty iniquities, clad in gauzy raiment; while now and then the gorgeous galley of some noble hung with rich awnings would be paddled swiftly past us by a crew of twenty boatmen or so in gay uniform.

The steps of the ghauts, which afforded access to the river from the streets, were crowded with people— women who had come down with their pitchers for water, Hindoos gravely performing their ablutions, and naked children. On those ghauts that led down from the lower quarters of the city the thronging Mussulmans were as noisy as a Saturday-night crowd of Irish in a low part of one of our big towns; laughing shrilly and chattering as a rule, but in many cases volubly quarrelling, women as well as men, in true Irish style, cursing each other, shrieking, the neighbours taking part in the slum row; but with all their furious excitement never daring to come to blows, in which last respect Paddy's behaviour would no doubt have been very different.

The houses on the banks are of many storeys, most of them richly ornamented with carved wood, and with something of medieval Europe in their appearance, while the sloping roofs of nearly all are overgrown with verdure. The dome of one Hindoo temple was very characteristic: it was covered with long grass thickly studded with scarlet poppies and yellow mustard. Mulberry-trees, with vines winding about them, find room to grow between the houses, producing a pretty effect. The temples of the Hindoos and the mosques of the Mussulmans, some very handsome, are scattered among the other buildings. On all sides, too, are to be seen the remains of the ancient temples and palaces, testifying to what a magnificent city Srinagur must have been before the iconoclastic Mahomedan invaders destroyed, so far as they could, all the monuments of the idolaters. The embankments of the river present these relics of the remote past at almost every step. Many of the ghauts were obviously once the stairs of ancient temples. Carved friezes, columns, and great blocks of stone form the foundations of the modern rickety houses of mud and wood. The Hindoos once more rule the land, but they can no more build like the men of their faith in those old days, who raised such massive and beautiful edifices to their gods.

Our boatmen paddled us on, past the mansions of the merchants and the somewhat ugly palace of the Maharajah, under numerous bridges built on stacks of logs on the cantilever principle; and my first impressions of the capital on this fine afternoon were distinctly favourable, for there is a quaint beauty in these city waterways, and the charm is enhanced by the ranges of snowy mountains and the flashing glaciers which as a rule form a background to the view.

No European is permitted to take up his quarters in any portion of the native town, and he is forbidden even to enter it by night. There is a certain district set aside for his use, and to this we now repaired. This is outside the city, on the banks of the river, and extends for some distance, forming a pleasant little colony. Here are the Residency, the British church, the English library, the hospital, and of course the inevitable polo and cricket ground, golf links, race-course, and rowing club.

A European is not allowed to own property on Kashmir soil. If he builds himself a house—which until quite recently would have been forbidden, and is now only winked at in a few instances—he does so at his own risk; he can be evicted at a moment's notice, the house as well as the land it is built on being the property of the Maharajah. Of old, before such free access as now was granted to Europeans, the few who entered Kashmir were received in princely style as guests of the Maharajah, and even now the British traveller stands in somewhat the same position, being treated with exceeding courtesy and liberality; the present ruler, for instance, has built several bungalows in the Munshi Bagh and other orchards on the river bank, which he places at the disposal of visitors at a very nominal rent. But as some 300 of our fellow-countrymen now visit Kashmir in the hot season, this accommodation is quite insufficient, and the great majority either live in boats on the river or in tents on the bank. The Jhelam, where it flows through the European quarter, presents quite a lively appearance. Gay house-boats and capacious family doongahs line the shore, and when the heat of the day has passed the water is covered with rowing-boats, whose occupants are men in flannels and girls in Thames-side summer dress.

Along one of the prettiest reaches of the river

THE CHENAR BAGH

stretches the Chenar Bagh, or Garden of Plane Trees, so called from the magnificent chenars which here shade the grassy lawns that descend to the water. This Bagh is sacred to the bachelors. Here the subalterns on leave and other young men pitch their tents beneath the trees or occupy doongahs moored to the bank. It is indeed a lovely spot, the groups of grand trees, the fresh sward and broad water, presenting the appearance of some fine old park at home, and as one looks up the reach, the rocky pinnacle of the Takht-i-Sulieman, with its crowning temple, forms a noble background to the scene.

In this place, too, one can well study the ways of the Hanji class, for the women and children of the doongah boatmen are always at work under the trees, where they pound the maize in great wooden mortars, are busy over their cooking-pots, or arrange each others back hair—a complicated process, I should imagine, for the Mahomedan women wear their hair after the old Kashmir style, plaited behind into a long pigtail, which forms a broad mat at the top and is interwoven with threads; not an ugly fashion, but if one may judge from the mutual shikaring which one generally sees in progress in one of these feminine groups, apt to afford cover to wild creatures. A Hanji woman is clad in a long loose robe like a nightgown, which, it is to be supposed, was once of some bright hue, but which is of about the same colour as her own dirty if often handsome face. Living is cheap here, and the young subalterns have an enjoyable time in their free Chenar Bagh; merry smoking-concerts frequently occur in camp, and the tinkling of the banjo is almost unceasing. The Chenar Bagh has rather a wicked reputation, but it is the recognised Bohemia of Srinagur, from which married couples are rigidly excluded—for have they not their own respectable Munshi Bagh allotted to them.

The Chenar Bagh was somewhat empty when I first saw it, in consequence of the Miranzai, the Black Mountain, and other little expeditions, and some officers who had obtained leave and had travelled all the way to Srinagur were immediately recalled. But when I returned here in the autumn, some of these expeditions having come to an end, I found the bachelor quarter crowded with young warriors taking their rest after the wars.

We moored our fleet along the bank and dined this night with Mr. Lawrence, the Settlement Officer appointed to this State, who kindly asked me to join him on one of his official tours in the Valley, an invitation of which I was very glad to avail myself.

On turning out of bed on the morning after our arrival, I was pestered, as a new comer—not that one is exempt after a summer's sojourn here—by the persistent merchants of Srinagur, who are very troublesome until one learns how to deal with them. They thronged around me in multitudes, hungry for my rupees. There were men bearing hot-water pots eager to shave me and cut my hair, whether I would or no; tradesmen who wished to sell me Kashmir shawls, carpets, silver or copper work, *papier maché* articles and carved wood; there were tailors, too, with specimens of cloth, shoemakers, makers of cooking pots, of chairs, of portmanteaus, of saddlery, of plum-cakes, of guns, of beds, of every conceivable necessary and luxury; and there were plenty of kindly capitalists anxious to lend me as much money as I chose to ask for. These, with the exception of some of the tailors —who were pundits—were Mussulmans, fine-looking, bearded men in white robes, some having quite the features of Hibernian Celts, some of Jewish cast of countenance, while many were something between the two types, and might have passed as samples of that rather anomalous creature, the Irish Jew.

They were all adepts at blarney, and with a jovial persuasive volubility extolled their own wares and cried down those of their neighbours in more or less broken English. Their pertinacity was extraordinary. The sweetly-smiling, long-robed ruffians would not take no for an answer. 'I do not want you to buy, sir,' would say one in a gentle, deprecating way, after some emphatic refusal on my part to have any dealings with him. 'Please to quite understand, sir, that I do not wish to sell. I only ask you to do me the honour of looking at some of this excellent workmanship. It will not fail to interest you.' Then, if I should order him to be gone, and explain that I was busy, 'In that case I would not on any account interrupt you,' he would urge, 'but I have nothing myself to do, sir, so I will sit down here and wait until you are quite unoccupied; then I will show you some beautiful things.' And thereupon he would squat down on the grass in front of the boat, surrounded by his merchandise, to remain there silent and motionless, contemplating me with a smile of patient amiability.

But some of these merchants will go to great lengths. They will step from the shore on to the overhanging prow of one's doongah, intrude into one's cabin, press their wares on one, and absolutely decline to move until they are forcibly ejected.

All this may be amusing at first, but one soon wearies of it. One discovers that to enjoy any peace one must be a trifle brutal. Some sahibs obtain comparative privacy with a stick. A hawker of the lower class here will understand nothing less than this as a hint that he must take himself off. Then he departs smiling; it is all in the day's work; to cheat a sahib out of one anna will recompense him for many blows.

The wares thus spread out before the traveller by these irrepressible touts are often of great beauty, so that it is difficult to look at them and resist the temptation to buy. The artistic metal-work of Kashmir is too well known in England to need description here, but I may, however, mention that an English firm, Messrs. Mitchell & Hadow, is now competing with the native merchants. This firm employs a quantity of the most skilful workmen, and produces carpets, silver, and copper-work of the best quality, together with other specialties of Kashmir art. Those who find no pleasure in bargaining with a keen Oriental, who is certain to outwit and cheat them to a greater or less extent, and wish to obtain undoubtedly good articles at a fair price, can be recommended to this firm.

I had not been long in Srinagur before I realised that I was in no sleepy Oriental State that had been allowed to go on in the same way from time immemorial, and would continue doing so. Kashmir is in a transitional state, and reforms of the most radical description are taking place. It will be deeply interesting to watch the progress of affairs.

Until quite recently permission to enter Kashmir was only granted to a very limited number of Europeans each year, and even now a passport from the Resident is necessary for every civilian visitor; but, practically, this once exclusive State has been completely thrown open to travellers. That Englishmen should be allowed to own property and engage in manufacturing industries, or establish agricultural colonies, is often spoken of as the probable outcome of the opening out of this country. But such a step will not be taken without serious consideration. At present the British Resident tries all cases that may arise between Englishmen and natives in his own Court, and can arbitrarily expel from the State an offending fellow-countryman. This system, of course, amply satisfies the small need that now exists for such jurisdiction; but should Kashmir be opened, as is suggested, to British enterprise, litigation between our countrymen and natives would obviously become more frequent, and some properly-constituted British or mixed tribunal would have to be introduced, entailing further heavy responsibilities on the Imperial Government.

Another more serious objection might have been hitherto raised to the proposed schemes for the development of Kashmir. It would have been imprudent to have permitted the formation of a considerable colony here unless proper precautions were taken for its protection. The disorganisation of the State had spread to the large army of mercenaries which the Maharajah maintains. Arrears of pay for months, in some cases for years, became due to the sepoys; they did not even receive their proper rations; an intense dissatisfaction naturally grew up, and insubordination was general. Evilly-disposed officials would not have been slow to argue that this state of things was due to the interference of the Indian Government in Kashmir affairs and to the consequent depletion of the Treasury. Such a feeling might have easily led to a military mutiny, an attack on the white residents, and a frightful disaster. There have been times, too, when the price of grain has risen to famine rate in the city, and bread riots have been imminent. Indeed, the handful of British men and women who encamp on the banks of the Jhelam outside that teeming city, enjoying their summer holiday, are not altogether unlike the thoughtless population that lived under Vesuvius of old. Here, too, the treacherous fires slumber below. Few of these laughing sahibs who despise this cowardly, cringing people, suspect the secrets of those crowded bazaars so near, the scheming, the raging discontent, the hatred of that Hindoo official class whose privileges to rob and oppress the people are now being curtailed.

But these sources of danger will soon cease to exist. The revenue reforms, as I shall presently show, will increase the prosperity of the State and enable it to pay its way. British officers have been appointed to organise the Kashmir army. Colonel Neville Chamberlain, the Military Secretary to the State, has set himself energetically at work to convert these levies into disciplined and serviceable troops, and insists that they shall be fed, paid, and clothed as they should be; while the Imperial Service Regiments that are now employed for the frontier defence, and which I saw fight gallantly a few months later, have been brought to a state of high efficiency by the officers of the Gilgit Agency. The causes of discontent have been removed, and military mutiny is now probably as remote a contingency in Kashmir as it is in India.

Should British enterprise be admitted into this country there will undoubtedly be ample scope for it. The resources of Kashmir have never been exploited. According to some authorities, only one-third of the available land is under cultivation, and even that does not produce nearly what it might. It is probable, therefore, that should the long-talked-of, more-than-once surveyed railway be made, Kashmir will become an exporter of grain, ghee, and other agricultural produce; she is so, indeed, on a small scale, at the present moment, despite the heavy expenses of transport by road. The railway will also bring prices to more or less of a level with those in the Punjab, and put a stop to those violent fluctuations that now occur, superfluous plenty and famine alternating. In the great famine of

1878, for instance, when enormous numbers of the cultivators perished, the seed corn was eaten by the famishing people, and the fields could not be sown; while, on the other hand, the absence of facilities for transport has led to enormous waste after an exceptionally plenteous harvest. Short-sighted dealers and others have then hoarded the grain in expectation of better prices, until it has rotted away in their ill-constructed godowns.

This proposed railway, connecting Srinagur with the lines of India, should prove an unmixed benefit to the Kashmir State and people. Negotiations on the subject have long been in progress between the Indian Government and the Kashmir Durbar. Some time since it was understood that its construction had been definitely settled, and that as soon as the rate of the guaranteed interest on the capital, and some other details had been arranged, this important work would be put in hand.

I believe that valuable minerals exist in some parts of this country, but they will never be utilised until European capital is introduced. There should be a large export, too, of the delicious fruits of Kashmir. At present all the industrial enterprise of the country is practically centred in the Maharajah. His, for instance, are the sawmills; his the monopoly of manufacturing wine and brandy. French specialists conduct this last business for him, and the wine, both red and white, which they produce, is of excellent quality. I do not think it is too much to say that the vineyards of Kashmir should some day make India independent of France, for claret of the ordinary description at least. While on the subject of wine, I may mention that I have never tasted better cider than that which Mr.

Lawrence makes for his own use from the apples of the country. This gentleman, as befits his post as Settlement Officer, takes the greatest interest in all the agricultural possibilities of Kashmir, has tried many interesting experiments in his own garden at Srinagur with foreign fruits and vegetables—most of which thrive very well when imported here—and supplies valuable cuttings free to such farmers as have sufficient intelligence to appreciate and ask for them.

Of the various sights of Srinagur itself, its mosques, its ruined temples, I shall say nothing; for these have been often written about, and there are at least two guide-books fully describing the city. One is written by Dr. Neve, of the English Mission Hospital in Srinagur—an excellent institution, by the way, and though the attempt to convert Mahomedans and Hindoos may not have been very successful, and may possibly not be even advisable, the noble charity that cures these people of their bodily ills deserves every encouragement. The other guide-book is by Dr. Duke, the Residency physician. Both these are well written and full of information as to Srinagur and the State generally.

But I must speak of the view which I enjoyed one morning from the Takht-i-Sulieman, or Throne of Solomon, the isolated peak which, rising precipitously from the edge of the river opposite the European quarter, towers a thousand feet above the plain. It is a view that no traveller should miss. I looked down on the many windings of the river and the numerous canals traversing the Asiatic Venice, with its temples, and glittering mosques, and garden-roofed houses, all lying extended beneath me like a plan. Beyond spread the irrigated plain with its flooded rice fields. In the distance was the great gleaming sheet of the Woolar, and still nearer, at the foot of the hill on which I stood, the smaller, but most beautiful Dal Lake. The Maharajah's vineyards are on the sloping shores of the Dal; so, too, are the exquisite *baghs* or pleasure-gardens of the kings of old—beautiful lawns descending to the pellucid water, well planted with magnificent trees, and having shady groves, among which are winding walks and retired pavilions. Here was the Versailles of the Mogul Emperors, where, in the summer evenings, the luxurious feasts were given, when the branches of the chenars were hung with thousands of coloured lamps, while nautches and musicians entertained the gathered guests. I have made a promise that this should be in one respect a unique book on Kashmir—I would refrain from quoting ' Lalla Rookh '—else this would have been my opportunity. And last, looking beyond the lakes, I saw around me, far off, the grand and mysterious wall of mighty mountains, encompassing the plain with wastes of perpetual snow, on this particular morning looking even more imposing than usual ; for the purple crags and the snows merged into similarly coloured clouds with which the sky was overcast, so that one could not distinguish where mountain ended and cloud commenced. A wonderful effect, as if the encircling Himalayas were the limit of this lower world, and that over yonder were the gigantic steps into the heavens.

CHAPTER IV

NATIVE SERVANTS—'DASTUR'—PREPARATIONS FOR JOURNEY—BY RIVER TO ISLAMABAD—THE SETTLEMENT OFFICER'S COURT—SUPPLIANTS—SYSTEM OF LAND-TENURE—REVENUE—OFFICIAL EXTORTION—FORCED LABOUR.

AFTER a short and very pleasant stay in Srinagur, in the course of which I made the acquaintance of the different British officials who have been selected to assist the Native Government in the administration of this disordered State, I set out on my travels, not at all sorry to have some hundreds of miles of rough marching, after the luxurious laziness of steamers, trains, tongas, and doongahs.

I had already provided myself with an old Mahomedan servant at Bombay, one Babu Khan, of whom I have not yet spoken, a knowing old rascal, who spoke a little English and hung about the seaport when out of work so as to secure the fresh-landed, innocent griffin as a master. How respectful he was! How attentive! What unbounded devotion he professed for the 'noble Sir,' who was to him 'both as father and mother!' How skilled in subtle and unanswerable excuse for every fault! How sleeplessly watchful for an opportunity of cheating me out of a few annas—but never allowing anyone else to do so! Yet, on the other hand, as so many of these men are, what an excellent servant on the road he really was! A cook who could produce a dinner for a gourmet out of the simplest materials at the end of a hard day's march; willing, and clever at making a *bandobast*. What a useful and expressive word, by the way, that word bandobast is! The dictionary gives 'management, arrangement,' as the English equivalents for it, but what a lot more it really signifies!

On being asked whether he would go to Leh with me—a chilly and disagreeable journey for a native of India—Babu Khan replied, with a profound bow: 'I will go wheresoever my sahib goes; to the wars, if he wishes it,' and forthwith took the keenest interest in the preparations for the journey; for every purchase I made, whether effected through his instrumentality or not, brought to him the usual present from the vendor, according to *dastur*—another comprehensive word, the dictionary translation of which is 'commission,' or 'custom.'

It not only covers customary commission, but customary anything else. It is a word that one soon comes to hate. Vain is it to try to have things done after your own ideas. You point out how some piece of work can be accomplished in a more expeditious or satisfactory way, and the Oriental to whom you address your remarks listens patiently, quite agrees with all you have said, and then politely but doggedly replies, 'Sir, that is not the dastur'; that ends the argument. Whoever succeeded in persuading an Asiatic to break through the old traditional method, the sacred dastur? It is a fetich to him. Some sahibs, I believe, commence their Indian career by making a rule of beating a servant who dares utter the objectionable word. But this has not the slightest effect; one might as well try to knock the Himalayas down. The passive resistance that the immemorial custom offers to the sacrilegious innovating spirit of the foreigner wins the day at last; and the fretful sahib, for his liver's and sanity's sake, struggles no more, and prudently submits to the inevitable.

Thus my servant, after explaining to me what it was the dastur to carry on the road, passed several days in the bazaar making the necessary purchases. It was the dastur, I discovered, to travel with what, after my experience of other countries, appeared to be an extraordinary quantity of pots and pans. But I should never have got a dinner out of the old ruffian with less; it would have been against dastur, an unholy meal.

It was also dastur, as I afterwards found out, to poison me regularly once a month. I had to put up with it. For all the pots and pans had then to be taken to a bazaar, if one was near, to be re-tinned. Now the tin employed for this purpose in Kashmir, and often in India, is an amalgam containing little tin and a good deal of lead, as may be demonstrated by rubbing a freshly tinned article with a handkerchief, which is at once blackened. I had a solid tin canteen among my cooking things, and Babu Khan on one occasion stretched dastur to the absurdity of having even this covered with the above impure compound. This monthly poisoning of his 'father and mother' brought Babu Khan a profit of about twopence as commission from the tinker on each occasion. I should define dastur as an Asiatic custom, rendered sacred and inviolable by age, and always favourable to the Asiatic as against the European. I never heard of an unpatriotic dastur that worked the other way. Dastur is, indeed, the Guardian Angel of the East.

For an English reader purposing a journey into these regions, the following particulars may be of use.

I will commence by pointing out that it is quite unnecessary to provide oneself with any special outfit before leaving England, as everything needful for the march can be procured at a much less cost in Srinagur than at home. Ten coolie-loads of baggage and stores should suffice for the single traveller. The regulation coolie-load is fifty pounds, so one's impedimenta must be distributed accordingly. As mules, ponies, and yaks are employed for carriage where possible instead of coolies, the baggage should be so stowed as to adapt itself to all these modes of transport. Small *yakdans*, or mule-trunks, are excellent for containing one's clothes and valuables; these leather-covered trunks are sold in pairs, and whereas one trunk makes an average coolie-load, the two, connected by a couple of strong straps, can be swung on to the back of any sort of baggage animal. When in camp, the two yakdans form one's bed, two poles, with a canvas bed laced between them, being extended from one yakdan to the other, iron sockets being attached to the yakdans to receive the pole ends. *Kiltas*, or leather-covered baskets, which, as Duke says in his guide, are shaped like Ali Baba's jars, are useful to hold one's cooking things and stores, of which last a considerable quantity will be required for a long journey. For though one can generally obtain sheep, fowls, and eggs in all parts of the State, it is only in the bazaars of a few towns and villages, which can be counted on the fingers of one hand, that stores of any description can be procured. Hence a sufficiency of tea, candles, sugar, flour, ghee, rice and tobacco must be carried, while each traveller must please himself as to what he will take in the way of luxuries, such as tinned soups, jams, spirits, and the like.

A folding chair and table, a portable leathern bath,

a rifle, and a photographic camera also formed portion of my collection of necessaries, which, when gathered together, appeared an appalling mass to me, accustomed as I was to the simplicity of travel in wild parts of North and South America and the Colonies. But if one must do in Rome as Rome does, still more must one do in the East as the East does; one is not permitted to be simple: one must have servants, and luxuries, and dignity. In short, one must do as dastur enjoins.

Rough clothing for the road can be procured at Srinagur at an extraordinarily cheap rate. For instance, my pundit tailor turned me out a suit (a Norfolk jacket and knickerbockers) of *puttoo*, or native cloth, for about seven shillings. In anticipation of the extreme cold which I knew I was to encounter later on, I also got him to make me an overcoat lined with sheepskin and high Yarkand boots of cloth and felt.

I had supplied myself with ammunition-boots, which I used to consider the best foot-covering for rough walking; but, like many Englishmen who visit Kashmir, I soon became converted to the native grass shoes and *chaplies*. The former are roughly-made sandals of rice grass, a loop passing inside the big toe to keep the shoe in its place. On dangerous hillsides, where it would be impossible to walk in boots, one steps with firm confidence when shod with this supple sandal, which allows the foot to grasp all the irregularities of the rock.

The summer heat is intense in the gorges of Kashmir, and then the leather chaplies are much to be preferred to boots; while to cross a pass late in the season in the latter is to court almost certain frost-bite. In that extreme cold the circulation in the feet must in no way be impeded; they must move freely in grass

SRINAGUR.

shoes and thick leather socks, or, better still, in several loose socks or mocassins of sheepskin. It was by taking these precautions that later on a large party of us crossed the Himalayas in mid-winter without mishap. I have now abandoned my old opinion that heavy boots are the best to march in. The natives in the East are, I think, right in this matter. They certainly know more about marching than we do. Let he who doubts this compete with a Kashmiri.

I engaged a second servant before starting, a Kashmiri of the bheestie or water-carrying class, one Subhana, a sturdy individual, whose duty it was to keep near me on the march with the camera, and also to assist Babu Khan generally in camp.

Before setting out with Bower to Ladak I carried out my promised tour with Mr. W. R. Lawrence, the Settlement Officer to the State. He was assessing the land revenue in the neighbourhood of Islamabad, a two days' journey up the Jhelam; so on May 4 I started in a doongah for that place with my servants and necessary impedimenta.

I fondly imagined that I had left luxury behind me at Srinagur, and would live simply for a time; but I was quite mistaken, the faithful Babu Khan would not have it so. He proved himself to be a cook of infinite resource, and turned out for me in some mysterious manner a lunch and dinner of I know not how many rich courses daily. I foresaw that a long sojourn in Kashmir, with him as my attendant, would make an incurable dyspeptic of me. Later on I took this deadly *chef* with me into desert mountain regions, where it was difficult to obtain supplies; but even there he contrived to put before me the same perniciously sumptuous repasts. Then I led him still higher into the mountains, until the rarefied cold air became intolerable to his Indian lungs, so that pleading pneumonia he left me. This alone saved me; for it was in vain to impress upon him that I preferred a simple diet on the march; he had travelled with some sahib who had been in the custom of doing himself too well; thus Babu Khan, to his list of unalterable dasturs, had added that of ruining the liver of every master he served.

This was a very pleasant lazy two days' journey up the winding river, by ancient temples, crowded villages, groves, and leagues of rich pasturage supporting numerous kine. One could rest on the slowly-moving boat or walk on the bank alongside it as the spirit moved one. The scenery was always lovely, especially in the evening, when indescribable effects of water, foliage, sunset clouds and far, faint, moonlit snows would be produced. Indeed, a land of singular beauty, not without good reason called the Earthly Paradise, and reputed throughout all Asia as Holy Ground.

Babu Khan, now that he was travelling alone with me, began to wax communicative. He explained to me that the extraordinary English which he spoke had been picked up in England. He narrated to me some of his English experiences, and spoke to me of the sultry English climate, the coolie labour on English plantations, the number of Chinamen in the country, and other matters which had escaped my own observation when travelling at home. I asked him in what part of England he had seen these strange things. He replied that he had been in Melbourne, and in a province a long way inland from it, where they grew sugar. He was evidently under the impression that Australia is the sea-girt isle from which the roving Britons come.

On the morning of May 5 we appeared to have

made little if any progress since the previous evening. There, still close by us, loomed the Takht-i-Sulieman. We had indeed travelled many leagues by water ; but the Jhelam, as if loth to leave the pleasant plains for the mountain gorges, pursues its slow course by as sinuous a way as possible, constantly doubling back upon itself in long loops, like the well-known pattern on the Kashmir shawls, which, by the way, say the natives, was first suggested by these very windings of the river as seen from the summit of the Takht.

This was a morning not easily to be forgotten, cloudless, fresh as it might have been in Paradise in the youth of the world ; and this is the sort of figure that naturally suggests itself to one travelling in this wonderful valley. Shortly after dawn, when the dew was still on the pastures and a thin haze was in the air, a very curious and fairy-like scene lay before us. The whole plain was here overgrown with the small blue iris in full flower, presenting the appearance in the distance of a great still blue sea. Of exactly the same tint was the sky above us and the lower portion of the mountain range on the far horizon, where the snow was not lying. Thus plain and sky and hills were not distinguishable one from another. One seemed to be looking into an infinite pale blue space, cloven in the centre by a jagged band of pearly white—the distant snowy uplands trembling in mirage. But one must have seen it to realise the unreal beauty of the picture.

There was a good deal of interesting human life to observe on the river as we progressed up it : huge cargo boats towed laboriously by strings of men ; naked fishermen in canoes drawing their nets, of whom my servant would purchase, after much bargaining and ample dasturi, fish for my dinner ; wealthy pundits in travelling doongahs with their white-robed wives, and piles of mysterious-looking luggage. On nearing one village I heard a great tumult, and perceived on coming up that all the inhabitants, including the dogs, were quarrelling over a mound of grain on the river-bank. It was, I believe, a discussion as to the amount due to the Maharajah as revenue.

The crew of my doongah consisted of one man, some women, and several small children. It was interesting to watch the way the Hanji parents bring up their progeny. The education is simple. The three R's are neglected as useless accomplishments, while a thorough instruction is given in the three arts of towing, punting, and paddling.

The boatmen are kind to their children, but will not permit them to shirk their tasks. Thus, to-day the smallest child, a pretty little girl of three or four, had to take her little lesson. She was too small to tow, but she was put on the bank to trot alongside her brothers and get accustomed to stepping out barefooted on the rough track. She came to a place where the path, cut in the face of the steep mud cliff, was only a few inches broad for a short distance, and where a false step would mean a ducking. The little maiden got frightened, and refused to attempt the dangerous passage; but the boat did not stop for her; her parents laughed, and left her there weeping. Seeing that no one would return to pick her up she philosophically wiped her eyes and tripped across the place quite merrily. Her nervousness had been mostly simulated; Kashmiris, even at four years old, have good heads on precipices, and the little humbug advanced without fear when she realised that malingering was useless. She was then brought on board, was much applauded and caressed, and was rewarded with apples for having done her lessons like a good child. One nice trait of these people is their keen affection for their children. These half-naked boat urchins live happy lives, and I think many English children would like to exchange places with them and enjoy this free outdoor existence for a time on the rivers of the Happy Valley.

This was a night of disturbance. We were brought up along the bank, and hardly had the side mats been let down on either side of the cabin, and all been made snug for the night, than we were besieged by an army of wild cats. They scampered all over the boat and carried off meat, fish, bread, and all the eatables they could get at. I lit a candle and chased them out several times, but no sooner was I in bed again than back they came, running across my face in their search for further loot.

On the next morning, May 6, we met two mounted natives on the bank. They brought me a letter from Mr. Lawrence, who had sent me a horse so that I might ride out to his camp in time for breakfast, leaving the doongah to follow up the winding river.

I found my friend encamped just outside Islamabad in a pleasant orchard by the river, a resting-place of the ancient kings, known as the Wazir Bagh. He was sitting at his tent door, surrounded by a crowd, dispensing justice like some Caliph of the Arabian Nights.

I was in time to witness a strange sight. Two suppliants came up who, after the manner of Kashmiris, had carefully got themselves up in pitiable plight with a view of attracting sympathy for their cause. These two big men had stripped themselves naked, save for the loin rag, and had smeared their bodies all over with foul wet, blue mud from the river bed. Even their hair and faces were thickly covered with the filth, through which their eyes glittered comically. It was an absurd spectacle, calculated to move one rather to laughter than to tears. They came up and stood before the Settlement Officer, quietly salaamed, and then suddenly and of one accord commenced to weep, groan, and shriek most dismally, while they wrung their hands or clasped them imploringly, writhing their bodies as in agony. Then they picked up dust in their hands and poured it over their heads and bodies, which, streaking the layer of wet mud, rendered their appearance still more fantastic. After a few minutes of this buffoonery, which, I think, Mr. Lawrence allowed to have a little play in order that I might observe this strange feature of the Kashmir character, he gave a peremptory word, and they ceased their noise as simultaneously and suddenly as they had commenced it—for a Kashmiri can summon tears and heartbroken sobs and stop them at will—and then both together they poured out their grievance in an eloquent oration.

Their story was, that while they were working in their fields an official had taken from them by force some grass straw of the value of twopence. The said official had moreover plucked their beards; in evidence of which they each produced two or three hairs, which they affirmed had been pulled out. Mr. Lawrence told them that he could not listen to men who presented themselves to him in so filthy a condition. If they appeared in the evening clothed and clean he would attend to their case. The Court was therefore adjourned until the plaintiffs should be washed, and we went in to breakfast.

These queer people employ all manner of tricks

in order to attract the attention of great men. Once, in Srinagur itself, Mr. Lawrence, on coming out of his bungalow, found a strange object in front of his door, surrounded by a contemplative crowd. On walking up to it he discovered that this was an ancient naked pundit standing on his head. This acrobatic sage had thrown aside his garments, and was thus patiently balancing himself while he awaited the Settlement Sahib's coming out. The Settlement Officer ordered him to be turned right side up, and the case was forthwith dealt with.

Sometimes the method adopted to excite pity is unpleasant, as when, on one occasion, a weeping man appeared carrying a small bundle which emitted a dreadful odour. On being asked what he desired, he cried out: 'Oh, Sahib! I have come back from the Punjab to my native village; but they will not give me back my land. Lo! here in this bundle is my dead child, and I have not even so much as a bit of ground in which to bury the body.'

Our Bandobast Wallah, as the natives call the Settlement Officer—an instance of the comprehensiveness of that word bandobast to which I have already alluded—had a great task before him when he was set to put the complicated revenue system of this State into order. During my short tour with him, and in the course of conversation, I gathered some information on this subject, and was enabled to partly realise what had to be done, and what a great deal this efficient officer has already succeeded in carrying through. Many men, I imagine, would have despaired before the herculean task; for what Augean stables of corruption there were to clear out, what hydra-like abuses that, having apparently been destroyed, would come to a head again as soon as the officer's back was turned! But Mr. Lawrence takes the keenest interest in his work, is not easily discouraged, and pursues his end with untiring energy and patience.

How very few people at home really understand of what sort of men our Indian Civil Service is composed; how arduous is their work; what vast responsibilities are theirs; how, above all suspicion themselves, they inspire the corrupt natives with an absolute confidence in their integrity as well as in their wisdom. India is surely a school for administrators such as the world has never seen; and when troublous times do come, England will need the services of these highly trained men, and learn to appreciate their merits.

The following facts will explain the present condition of this primitively governed State, and will show the difficulties the Settlement Officer has to contend with and the direction his labours take.

In the first place it must be understood that all the soil is the property of the Maharajah. The *assami*, or hereditary farmers, cultivate the land on a very wasteful sort of metayer system, under which they have to pay, as revenue to the Maharajah, two-thirds of their crops, he supplying seed-corn and cattle when necessary. What this revenue amounts to is unknown, for no Budget is issued, and the emptiness of the Treasury is often pleaded as an excuse for the neglect to pay the troops and carry out treaty obligations. In the autumn of 1891 an English official was sent by the Indian Government to inquire into the finances of the country. His report, I believe, was confidential.

But whatever the value of the revenue, there can be little doubt that it is not what it should be. Of the total produce of the country a far smaller fraction than the supposed two-thirds reaches the coffers of the State, and a very meagre proportion remains with the cultivator, while the bulk is swallowed up by the grasping official middlemen who stand between State and cultivator. Moreover, under the present system of robbery and oppression much less is produced than would be the case under a better order of things. It is no advantage to the assami to get the most he can out of the fertile soil, for any surplus over what is sufficient to allow him a bare subsistence is wrung from him by the tax-farmers, who, at the same time that they plunder the peasant, embezzle the revenue due to the State.

It is the work of our Settlement Officer to put a stop to this official extortion, to hold forth inducements to the assami to extend the cultivation of the land by giving him the fruits of his labour, to assess the revenue that shall be paid by each district, and to see that the State be not defrauded of its dues—in short, to largely better the condition of the cultivators while augmenting the receipts of the Maharajah's treasury and enabling the country to pay its way.

The revenue of Kashmir is for the most part collected in kind; it is only in the neighbourhood of the towns that the State receives its due in specie. Mr. Lawrence has abolished some of the more absurd forms of payment, and maize and rice are the only substitutes for cash now received in the districts near the capital. It had been the custom to exact quantities of bulky and perishable commodities, such as apricots, the difficult transport of which across hundreds of miles of mountain tracks resulted in enormous waste. Sometimes new and arbitrary requisitions are suddenly made, apparently for the sole object of giving trouble to the peasantry. Such poetic taxes as love-philters and violets seem rather appropriate to the Vale of Kashmir, and these are still levied ; for one district has to supply a certain weight of *chob-i-kot*, the root of a mountain herb which is in repute as an excellent aphrodisiac, while from another district so many maunds of violets are required annually.

The State officials are supposed to ascertain the yearly value of the cultivated land of each village community, and to raise a revenue proportionate to it. This assessment is, almost without exception, irregular and unjust. If it have any principle underlying it, it may be said that this is the competition of thieves, for this alone regulates the amount that is extorted from the cultivators. Some villages are grossly over-assessed, while others are equally under-assessed; and therefore one of Mr. Lawrence's chief duties is to have a proper survey and valuation of the lands of each village made, and to then fix a definite annual revenue in place of the present uncertain and often ruinous demand.

The State is divided for purposes of revenue into districts called *tahsils*, each containing a number of villages, and being under an official known as a *tahsildar*. The tahsildar is an Oriental edition of a French préfet, but is more powerful and far more irresponsible. He has the civil and criminal jurisdiction over his district, and enjoys unequalled opportunities for enriching himself at the expense of State and people.

Each village has its *lambadar*, a personage with whom every traveller in Kashmir has plenty of dealings; for it is he that is sent for when one enters a village, and he has to provide one with coolies, sheep, fowls, and other necessaries. It is he, too, who often receives the pay for these; and how much he retains as his dastur, and how much he hands over to the unfortunate coolies and farmers, it is difficult to say. The lumbadar is the hereditary tax-collector of the village. He is responsible to the tahsildar of his district for the revenue which he collects, and is supposed to receive about 2 per cent. of it as the reward of his labours. This should be an important and respectable office, but is very far from being so if one may judge from the appearance of the average lumbadar. He is generally as dirty and ragged a wretch as any assami of his village, and often represents it rather as the recipient of kicks than halfpence. A lumbadar is, indeed, in some parts of the country not much better than the village scapegoat, and I have known one run away from his home in despair as his village was unable to meet the requisitions made upon it, and his responsible back had to bear the whole burden.

Still, as the Settlement Officer explained to me, the condition of a village, in the Vale of Kashmir at any rate, much depends on the character of its lumbadar, and the post is sought after. In what way he can be a useful man to his village is a striking instance of the extraordinary corruptness of Kashmir administration. It appears that if the lumbadar be an influential person, and can hold his own with his superiors, the village will be prosperous, and the sign of this prosperity will be a gigantic indebtedness. The more flourishing the village, the more hopelessly bankrupt will it be, the greater the arrears of revenue due to the State. There are several causes for this paradoxical state of things, but the following will suffice as an illustration.

A powerful lumbadar never renders the State its due. He bribes the officials above him to leave his village in peace. He and the assamis will enter into collusion with the tahsildar of the district. Instead of paying the full revenue to the State, they will allow heavy arrears of revenue to be entered against the village, while half of this amount is secretly handed over to the tahsildar as an honorarium for his leniency. A weak lumbadar cannot contrive this. It seems that under him payments will be heavier, arrears fewer, and the assamis will groan beneath extortionate demands. To arrive at the true arrears of a village behind all the complicated embezzlement and falsification of accounts would, of course, be a hopeless task, and Mr. Lawrence has recommended to the Durbar that all arrears, with the exception of the Musada—State advances in seed-grain and cattle—shall be wiped off, and that the revenue shall be paid regularly in such a way as will preclude the continuance of these rascalities. In the districts he has already settled. Mr. Lawrence has still to work through these hereditary officials, but has made it difficult for them to earn many fraudulent perquisites. The lumbadar in these districts is now in a better position, receiving 5 per cent. of the revenue; and as there is now an appeal to the Settlement Officer, any proof of peculation would bring instant dismissal from a lucrative post. The lumbadars, so far as one can see, are improving in their morals. Besides, when the exact revenue to be paid by a village has been fixed, and all irregular requisitions have been abolished, there will be little scope for the old blackmailing and other official tricks.

The assessment in Kashmir is for ten years, not for thirty, as in India, for it is anticipated that the new cart road to the Punjab and the coming railway will greatly increase the value of land, so that an early re-assessment has been deemed necessary in justice to the State.

It must be understood that the bankruptcy of a village in no way incommodes the inhabitants, save that it prevents them from working for any surplus produce which the State can call upon. The Kashmir cultivator is quite reckless about the accumulation of these arrears. He knows that the State cannot recover them, while ejectment from his miserable home is no great punishment. The State, indeed, rarely resorts to ejectment, as it can gain nothing by it. When the revenue collector arrives at a village it is curious to observe sometimes how the farmer's cattle, goods, even his crops, vanish as by magic, having been taken up into the mountains for concealment, his earthen pots and his blanket being all that is left to him. The assami has but two objects in life—to earn his bare living from his fields, and to escape that curse of Kashmir, the *begar*, or forced labour. He dare not accumulate wealth, and exists from hand to mouth. The new reforms are now giving him his chance for the first time, and being a shrewd fellow, he is not slow to avail himself of it, as I well perceived during my stay in the country.

And it is, indeed, quite time that something should be done before the State is hopelessly ruined. Any traveller visiting Kashmir can see for himself how the officials of the Maharajah in all parts of the country kill for him the goose that lays the golden eggs. The people do not seek to make money, for if the officials heard of it, it would at once be wrung from them. For instance, the contractors on the Murree road offered high pay for the use of the farmers' bullock-carts in the winter season, when these were not required for agricultural work; but the farmers, knowing that the profit would not be theirs, refused to supply them. A shikaree will often beg a sahib who has employed him to write a paper for him, stating that his pay has been but one-half of that really given, so that he may deceive his rapacious tyrants and retain some portion of his earnings. For the same reason Pathans and other foreigners are employed as navvies on the road, it not being possible to procure a sufficiency of free labour among the native population. Numbers of the peasantry have deserted their lands and fled to other countries—to the free Punjab, or even to half-savage Yaghistan—leaving their share of the village revenue to be paid by their neighbours. In remote districts things are still worse, and entire villages have been abandoned because life under the local tyrant had become a burden too heavy to be borne.

But a native of this State suffers from a form of oppression far more severe than the extortion of the tax-collectors; the latter at least leaves him a bare subsistence, but that of which I am now speaking signifies separation from family, and in too many cases torture and death. I have already alluded to the begar, or forced labour. Now this in itself is a just and useful institution, not by any means unknown in Europe. What, for example, is an English juryman but a begar? It is quite right that the villages should supply men when necessary to keep in repair the roads that traverse their districts, or to carry letters, or even for purposes of coolie transport. There is no hardship in a properly conducted and legitimate forced labour, and the people themselves have no objection to it. In such a country as Kashmir it is indispensable for the conduct of public affairs. The short-sighted natives would never combine for the common good unless compelled to do so by the ruling powers.

But there is a just begar and a begar that becomes the most harmful instrument that can be placed in the hands of an unscrupulous official. Many thousands of villagers have been driven off every year to toil as carriers of burdens on the Gilgit road. Gilgit is a name of terror throughout the State. An enormous transport service is needed, as I shall show further on, to supply the garrisons on the northern frontier with grain; and the Kashmir authorities have been utterly careless of the comfort, and even of the lives, of the unfortunate wretches who are dragged from their homes and families to trudge for months over the wearisome marches of that arid country. They fall on the road to perish of hunger and thirst, and, thinly clad as they are, are destroyed in hundreds at a time by the cold on the snowy passes. When a man is seized for this form of begar, his wives and children hang upon him, weeping, taking it almost for granted that they will never see him more. A gang of these poor creatures, heavily laden with grain, toiling along the desert crags between Astor and Gilgit, on a burning summer's day, urged on by a sepoy guard, is perhaps as pitiable a spectacle as any to be seen on the roads of Siberia. But these are not convicts and criminals, they are Mussulman farmers, harmless subjects of the Maharajah.

One important result of our intervention in Kashmir, and especially of the position we have taken up at Gilgit, will be the removal of this barbarous system. The Gilgit road begar, already much mitigated, will soon be a thing of the past. A properly organised coolie corps is taking its place; and the military road, which Spedding is now constructing, will allow of the use of mules instead of men.

Such being the horrors of the transport begar—and the Gilgit road, though the worst, is not the only one in the State on which the system is conducted with cruelty—men are naturally willing to pay a good deal to be exempt from it, and this, of course, gives our typical official an opportunity he is not likely to miss. Most of the begar has to be carried on in the summer months, when the passes are open, at the very season that the villagers are needed in their fields, the crops suffering from their absence. It is then that the grasping official swoops down on a district, and while raising the complement of men required by the State, levies blackmail from all the others. It has been calculated that for one man who is taken on this forced labour, ten purchase their immunity from the officials, as much as one hundred rupees being paid in some instances. The village is thus impoverished and rendered incapable of paying its share of revenue to the State.

The begar and its accompanying blackmail assumes many forms. Thus recently, when a dozen carpenters were required for Government work in a distant region, every carpenter in Srinagur was impressed by the police, and had to pay for his liberty. Sometimes all the men of a trade—the bricklayers, for instance—getting wind that it is intended to make one of these raids upon them, fly from the capital to the mountains for a time, public and private building work coming to a standstill until they return.

It is obvious that this widely-extended system of forced labour cannot be abolished by a stroke of the pen. It is recognised that begar must be carried on in a modified form for some time, at any rate, if only to avoid the famines that would necessarily result from the absence of transport and the interruption of communication.

Still, our Settlement Officer has been able to entirely do away with the system in some cases. Where this is not possible, he is removing the grosser abuses, making the official blackmailing a difficult matter, and equalising begar throughout the land.

All Hindoos are exempt from forced labour, the burden falling on Mahomedan villages only. Some of these also escape it, for it occasionally happens that a whole village is sold by its cultivators for a nominal sum to some influential Hindoo, on condition that he obtains for them exemption from begar, while they remain on the land as his tenants. So many other more or less fraudulent methods for attaining the same end are practised that the incidence of the begar falls very oppressively on certain poor and unprotected villages which cannot afford to purchase immunity.

Mr. Lawrence has now persuaded the Durbar to abolish these exemptions, and make every cultivator— Brahmins only excepted—do his fair share of work. When begar has been thus modified and equalised, it will fall but lightly on the population, and will be nothing like so oppressive a burden as is the military conscription in European countries.

CHAPTER V

A TOUR WITH THE 'BANDOBAST WALLAH'—TEMPLE OF MARTUND—BRAHMIN AND MUSSULMAN CULTIVATORS—RETURN OF FUGITIVE PEASANTS—THE DISHONEST PATWARI—TEMPLE OF PAYECH—A DESERTED VILLAGE—SUCCESS OF THE SETTLEMENT—A VILLAGE OF LIARS—FRAUDULENT OFFICIALS.

AFTER breakfast on the morning of my arrival in camp I rode out with Mr. Lawrence, who had some work to complete in the neighbouring villages before holding his Court in the evening.

First we entered the town of Islamabad, a picturesque place of one thousand houses or so. Passing the tanks of clear water, which are crowded with sacred fish, fed regularly by the Hindoos, we passed into a large building, in which Mr. Lawrence holds a land-measurement class. Here were assembled a number of Brahmins of all ages, children and very old men, eager to learn the use of the chain and the elements of surveying, so that they might be employed on the assessment work.

As we went in, a very stout old gentleman, the headman of the district, rose and made an eloquent speech, in which he pointed out the great advantages which would ensue from the proposed reforms in the tenure of land. He exhorted the students to acquire the art of land measurement as speedily as possible. He told them that his sole desire was to see them get on in the world, that he had always been deeply interested in their welfare, for was he not to them both as father and mother. Many of his listeners, I observed, smiled feebly on hearing all this. I suppose the old humbug, when he possessed the power, had tyrannised over and ill-used them as much as any other official.

After the Settlement Officer had inquired into the progress of the students, examined their plans and calculations, and awarded prizes, we rode to the top of the *kareewah* above the town, to see the famous ruins of Martund, the Temple of the Sun. After ascending a steep cliff about 500 feet in height, we found ourselves on an extensive plateau stretching to the foot of a low range of mountains near us. This plateau was no doubt the original bed of the great prehistoric lake, before the breaking away of the barrier at Baramoula had liberated the waters, and the softer alluvial soil had been washed away.

After crossing the kareewah for a few miles we reached the temple. The site is a sublime one. These gigantic ruins stand in the middle of a solitary waste, commanding a magnificent view over the Vale of Kashmir and the Himalayan ranges—an impressive relic of the bygone days of Kashmir greatness. This temple is supposed to have been built in the fifth century. The stones composing it are so massive that it has to a great extent resisted the shock of earthquakes and Mussulman iconoclasm. The architecture is of the Aryan order. The ruins form a great quadrangle surrounded by a beautiful colonnade. The stately entrance, the fluted columns, indeed the whole character of the structure, at once call to mind the monuments of ancient Greece. For the relations between Greek and Asiatic art I must refer the reader to the authorities. There is an interesting description of this temple by

Captain Cunningham in the 'Asiatic Society's Journal' of September 1848. We met two Brahmins close by; they told us that the temple was only considered holy, and visited for devotional purposes, every third year, the year which, according to their calendar, has an extra month—the Brahmin leap-year.

After visiting some villages and inspecting a class of industrious young Brahmins, who were engaged in taking measurements of some land that was to be brought under cultivation, we rode back to camp through a particularly fertile district. Here were orchards of mulberry, apricot, walnut, pear, almond, apple, and other fruit-trees, fields of rice, maize, and the various grains from which the alimentary and burning oils are extracted. The Kashmir Hindoos, by the way, are more thorough-going vegetarians than their co-religionists in India, for they do not cook their food with ghee or clarified butter—which they export to the Punjab—but with vegetable oils, such as the oils of mustard, of peach-stones, and walnuts, generally employing several together in the same dish.

Whenever we came across waste land it was covered with the blue iris which spreads all over this country, and is so deep-rooted that it renders the reclamation of the soil difficult. However, it is a favourite food with the sheep, and is dried and stacked for winter fodder. I noticed that the willows by the wayside had been closely pollarded, and that the upper twigs of some had been woven together into what appeared to be large nests. On inquiry I was told that the willow branches, like the iris, are cut for fodder, and that the nests are for the convenience of the small boys who are perched up there when the crops are on the ground, to scare away the crows and stray bears by slinging stones and shouting. A larger variety of purple and white iris is often seen growing in isolated clumps in the Vale, not spreading for great distances like the commoner small, blue species. Each of these clumps represents a Mussulman burial-place, it being the custom of the Kashmir followers of the Prophet to plant this beautiful flower above their dead.

When we returned to camp Mr. Lawrence sat in the cool of the evening under the fruit-trees of the Bagh, which was noisy with the song of birds, and listened to the petitions of the people.

They squatted in a patient, respectful semicircle at a distance from him, while the baboo clerks called them up one by one to come forward and tell their tales. There were several complaints of over-assessment in the district, and the cultivators threatened that they would desert their farms unless a reduction was made. This is a threat which is frequently carried out, for the assamis lose nothing by going away from their homes, as they can readily obtain employment on some Hindoo's land, or migrate to the village of a wife's relatives. But their own village suffers by their desertion, for the annual revenue to the State has to be made up, and the remaining villagers, who possibly already have more land on their hands than they can cultivate, have to pay the share due from the abandoned farm.

On the following morning, after *chota haziri*, camp was struck, and we rode off to a village ten miles from Islamabad, where Mr. Lawrence was to hold an important settlement meeting. This place, called Wachi— I don't vouch for the spelling—is prettily situated among some fine chenar trees. It is inhabited by Mussulmans; but just beyond the little river which flows by it is another village of Brahmin cultivators. There are not many of these last in the country; the Kashmiri Brahmin is a city man, and is not so good a farmer as the Mahomedan. We were told that there were only three Mussulmans in this Brahmin village, a carpenter, a barber, and another; but the pious three had a primitive little mosque among the houses of the idolaters, at which the barber was wont to officiate as priest.

After the settlement meeting we crossed the river to this village, and, accompanied by a crowd of Brahmins and Mussulmans, ascended what from below appeared to be a peaked hill, but which proved to be a flat tableland—another kareewah—surrounded by steep cliffs, standing out of the plain like an island. From here we looked far over the plain, with its winding rivers, fields, groves, and numerous villages, from which rose many other kareewahs like the one we stood on. Mr. Lawrence now obtained a bird's-eye view over the scene of his immediate labours, and proceeded to question the assembled people as to the different village lands. They made many complaints of the water-supply, asserting that the farmers on the neighbouring highlands were increasing their cultivation to the detriment of the plain, absorbing an undue quantity of water, and leaving an insufficient amount to find its way by the irrigation-canals to the lower cultivation. This is, of course, a common grievance in this country, and is not easy to settle.

While we stood on this hill an ancient pundit, finding that I was a stranger in the land, endeavoured to explain to me the outward signs by which a Mahomedan can be distinguished from a Hindoo peasant in the Vale of Kashmir. It appears that, whenever possible, the followers of the two religions do things in exactly opposite ways. They wind their turbans in different directions; one buttons his robe from right to left, the other from left to right. The Mahomedan mounts his horse from the left side, as we do; the Brahmin from the right side. The distinction between the two in this country is, indeed, generally more outward than inward. The observers of neither faith have cause to boast of the religion of their forefathers. The ancestors of most of these people were converted backwards and forwards—Vicar-of-Bray-like—according to successive dynasties. They are now neither good Hindoos nor good Mussulmans. One result of this is that fanaticism is seldom displayed, except, of course, when Shiahs and Sunis meet—those Nonconformists and High Churchmen of Mahomedanism.

I walked through both these little villages with the Settlement Officer, entered the houses, and began to understand how these people live. Their houses look picturesque from a distance, and are generally surrounded with chenars, walnuts, and mulberries, but they are not pleasant places within. They are built of unbaked bricks, held together by a wooden framework, have thatched gabled roofs, and are generally of two storeys, the ground-floor being occupied by the cattle in the winter, the upper floor by the family. The rooms are dark, and no attempt is made to keep them clean or comfortable, the cooking pots in many cases constituting all the household goods. There is little indeed for the tax-collector to seize on.

The peasant himself, though generally handsome and well-proportioned, is a dirty-looking object. His garments are of the same muddy colour as his house and fields, and consist of a skull cap—the turban not being worn in the fields—pyjamas, and a long gown of puttoo cloth or linen, according to the season. There is little picturesqueness of costume to be observed among the peasantry throughout all the territories of the Maharajah. There is a disagreeable monotony of squalid and usually ragged dress; it is dangerous for a cultivator to parade what wealth he may possess, so he makes an ostentation of extreme poverty.

Mr. Lawrence told me that the total wardrobe of an assami is worth about five rupees, and that a suit lasts two years. The moderate sum of four shillings a year will therefore cover a farmer's, tailor's, and haberdasher's bills. A small income goes a long way here. A man possessing five rupees a month can marry and maintain a family, if not given to extravagance—a rare vice in Kashmir—and can even support two wives on that sum. I discovered, however, that there are some farmers even in Kashmir whose spendthrift ways bring their families to ruin. I inquired what form of gambling or other dissipation is to blame for this, and was informed that there are three expensive vices on which a foolish peasant can waste his substance—salt, snuff, and sugar. Luxurious dog! The explanation of this is that all necessaries in the way of food, as well as clothing, are produced on a man's farm; but he has to go to the bazaar for the above three articles, and money is needed to obtain them.

The cultivator of the plain appears to live a cheerless sort of life, having no distractions or amusements, unless the game of outwitting the revenue collectors reckoned as such. In winter the family spin and weave puttoo after supper. There are few merrymakings, and the different families in a village do not associate much with each other.

On May 8 we continued our progress and visited

several villages, two soldiers with lances riding ahead of us to keep off the people, who crowded up anxiously with their petitions. Each village had its eloquent spokesman, who, when the grievance was a general and not an individual one, pleaded the cause of all the assamis. In one village this orator complained that the villagers were being 'choked by their misfortunes.' Three years before, when the famine and cholera raged in Kashmir, and killed or drove away one-half of the population of the valley, nearly all the assamis had fled from this village, in which the pestilence had been working exceptional havoc. Only five families had since returned to their homesteads. 'Therefore we are not enough,' said their spokesman, 'to cultivate the lands of the absentees; yet the whole revenue, as before, is demanded of the village. How are we to pay it?' 'Would you like other cultivators to come here, take up your abandoned lands, and help you to pay the revenue?' asked Lawrence. 'That is what we desire,' was the ready reply. The Settlement Officer made a note of the matter, and he told me that he would have no difficulty in finding men willing to take up well-irrigated lands such as these were.

In another village a refugee, who had returned from the Punjab, prostrated himself on the ground and petitioned Mr. Lawrence to restore his land to him, which had been seized in his absence by the Patwari, or hereditary village revenue accountant. It appeared that this man had been appropriating all the abandoned lands in order to sublet them. This was the very sort of abuse of his position on the part of an official that the Settlement Officer was most anxious to put down. He promptly gave his decision as we walked along. The Patwari had to surrender the land at once. This quick Arabian Night-like justice is what is wanted here, and impresses the Oriental mind.

On May 9 we passed by another of the famous old temples of Kashmir, that of Payech, a small but beautiful building, dedicated to the Sun God, which, concealed as it is in a grove away from the road, has escaped the destructive zeal of the Mahomedan, and is in almost perfect condition.

Then we rode off to our next camp near the village of Koil; the laden coolies gradually trooped in, and our servants, accustomed, like all Asiatics, to camp-life, soon had our tents pitched by the apricot trees on the windy plain, and were preparing our dinner.

The villagers, who had been patiently squatting afar off until Mr. Lawrence was ready to receive them, now came up. One old pundit presented himself in tears with a wisp of straw round his neck and a lump of hard clay in his hand. He explained that these symbolised the treatment he had met with. He had been choked to death by his tyrants as by the wisp of straw, and he had been beaten to the earth and crushed as by that bit of clay—in plain words, he wanted his rent reduced a trifle. Mr. Lawrence happened to smile at the metaphors of this absurd old gentleman, and then all the natives round, who up to that moment had stood with solemn faces seeing nothing funny in the incident, became of one accord convulsed with merriment. They perceived that the sahib had smiled, so they, too, would assume a sense of the humorous if they had it not. They probably laughed in the hope of conciliating the Bandobast Wallah, even as junior members of the Bar ostentatiously show their appreciation in court whenever a judge makes what he obviously imagines to be a joke.

A neighbouring village was interesting as an example of the good Mr. Lawrence has already effected. This was once a considerable place, but the houses are now in ruins, and on the waste lands the squares of grass-grown ridges show the borders of former paddy fields. The whole of the inhabitants fled to India in the fatal year of 1879. These people are now flocking back. A year before our visit there were but seven families in the village, we now found thirty; for during the previous twelve months twenty-three families had returned from the Punjab, where they were doing well, the report of Mr. Lawrence's settlement work in their native land, and of the security from oppression that was already enjoyed in the settled districts, having reached these exiles.

The Kashmiri assamis have entire confidence in the justice and wisdom of the British officials. These fugitives, who had been residing in the Punjab since 1879—before that year Kashmir peasants were not permitted to leave their country—had been able to observe the condition of the cultivators in that province under our rule, and realised that the same happy state of things would ultimately prevail in all Kashmir. The lumbadar told us that several more families were expected to return this year. These people certainly love their country; as the Kashmir proverb puts it, 'Every bird is fond of its own twig'; and now that our interference has made life supportable for them in their old homes, the fugitives will quickly re-occupy the land where their presence is so much needed. It is not from over-population, but from the reverse, that the Vale of Kashmir suffers.

The next day, May 10, was the last of this tour, and we rode to the place where we had appointed our doongah to meet us. It was a day full of work for Mr. Lawrence. Ahead of us rode the spear-bearing chaukidars in gay uniforms. Several officials accompanied us, and behind toiled on the long train of dingy coolies carrying our tents and baggage. We always had a crowd about us; the cultivators of one district walking with us to the frontier of their land, where they would leave us to the cultivators of the next district, who, in their turn, would escort us through their territory, and so on.

We passed through a village of liars; but by thus particularising one place I do not wish to give a false impression as to the credibility of the Kashmiris. I mean that in this village the liars were even yet more barefaced in their mendacity than any I had yet come across. As usual, the village spokesman came up to disparage the condition of the land and obtain a reduction of the assessed revenue. He brought with him a lump of stone and some sand in one hand, a few mouldy straws, some grains of diseased rice, and two rotten walnuts in the other, which he represented as fair samples of the soil and produce of their poor property. We were walking between admirable crops and over a rich loam even while this orator was addressing us.

As a matter of fact this village, in consequence of a collusion between cultivators and officials, was very much under-assessed, as Mr. Lawrence soon discovered. He informed the spokesman that the State should no longer be defrauded in this manner, and that while all arrears would be wiped off, a larger revenue would be imposed, which the village would be compelled to pay regularly.

The Kashmiris are unblushing humbugs. While their spokesman had been graphically describing the misery of their condition, the assamis had ranged themselves before us as a melancholy chorus, and whenever he had paused for breath they had broken in with pitiable lamentations and weeping. But now, finding that Mr. Lawrence could not be outwitted, and that the game was up, they at once good-humouredly resigned themselves to the higher assessment, and laughed merrily at the defeat of their representative and the sorry figure he cut as the Settlement Officer exposed his falsehoods. A Kashmiri, as a rule, is not at all abashed, but merely rather amused, when he is detected in some barefaced attempt at fraud, and smilingly compliments the person who finds him out on his superior cleverness.

In this particular case, as in others, the Settlement Officer had found it necessary to demand an increase of revenue from a district. He is opposed to any over-leniency in this respect. The cultivators, degraded as they are, and working for mere subsistence, require a stimulus to labour, which a just assessment, combined with a fixity of tenure, ought to give them.

We rode on, and as we approached the limits of each village saw before us the stolid, silent men rolled in their blankets, squatting down in a long row, looking in the distance like so many gorged vultures—the assamis waiting to escort us across their land and assert its worthlessness in specious falsehood.

They all said they could not procure a sufficiency of water, as the farmers on the hills above had stolen their share. This was a universal complaint, even on the mountain farms. A man who cultivates the highest land of all, at the edge of the eternal snows, would not have the slightest hesitation in making the same impudent excuse for avoiding a just revenue. Between

G

corrupt officials on the one hand, and lying peasants on the other, it must be somewhat difficult to arrive at the truth. The Settlement Officer's work is no sinecure.

We came to a village which had fallen a victim to one of the worst abuses of the Kashmir system. Hindoo officials had here tyrannised over the Mussulman cultivators, and had driven them in despair to sell their lands to their oppressors for very nominal sums. These fraudulent sales are, I believe, to be cancelled, a measure which, of course, will be bitterly opposed by the Hindoo official class. Mr. Lawrence has suggested to the Durbar that these ignorant and shortsighted cultivators should not be permitted, at least for the present, to sell or mortgage their hereditary rights in the soil. The cart-road into India, and the coming railway, are likely to greatly increase the value of the land in the Valley; speculators in land will consequently be abroad, from whom the cultivators should be preserved. A free power to alienate would ruin the peasantry.

And now, the tour being over, we rode down to the river and embarked on our doongahs, having first bid farewell to the crowds of peasants who had come down to see off their benefactor, the Bandobast Wallah. Their expressions of gratitude to him were orientally effusive. The assamis wept because he was leaving them, and applied to him every term of reverent adulation. I imagine that even Kashmiris have some sense of gratitude, and that a portion of this demonstration, at any rate, represented genuine feeling. These people undoubtedly have good reason to be thankful that the Indian Government has taken their cause up, and has sent so capable an officer to conduct the Settlement. Nearly all the suggestions he has made have been accepted by the Durbar, and these extensive reforms are being steadily carried out.

It now remains to be seen whether the hoped-for end will be attained, which is, I will repeat, to benefit the State revenue and extricate Kashmir from her present insolvent condition, and at the same time to convert the cultivators from degraded and oppressed paupers into well-to-do farmers, as in the Punjab.

The Sind Valley, which I twice traversed later on, has been settled throughout by Lawrence, and the good results are already manifest. The assamis of that Tahsil are obviously far more prosperous and happy than those in the unsettled districts. The farmers there expressed themselves as perfectly contented with what had been done; they said that Lawrence Sahib had been their saviour; they had hitherto been as beasts of the field, but now they felt that they were men.

CHAPTER VI

A PICNIC ON THE DAL LAKE—THE FLOATING GARDENS—WE SET OUT FOR LEH—ON THE GREAT TRADE ROUTE—THE SIND VALLEY—CAPTAIN BOWER'S TIBETAN EXPEDITION—GOOND—SONAMERG—CHITS.

As soon as we were settled down in our doongahs, the boatmen paddled, towed, and punted us back to Srinagur with extraordinary energy, so that we reached the city before night. They were highly delighted when Mr. Lawrence gave the order for the homeward journey; for the morrow was the Eed, the great Mahomedan holiday, when feasting and merrymaking suddenly succeed to the month-long fasting and penance of the Ramazan. During this holiday it is next to impossible to get any work out of one's servants. They attire themselves in their best garments, and betake themselves to the bazaar to enjoy a bout of gluttony and dissipation, and stagger home stupefied with excess in food, opium, and preparations of Indian hemp.

My next expedition was to be to wilder regions, in the company of Captain Bower. I found that he had sent a number of coolies on to Leh with the bulk of the necessaries for his long journey across the Tibetan wilderness; but as he had purchased horses at Srinagur, which he purposed to employ for the transport of his stores beyond Leh, and as the road, still deep in snow, was impracticable for animals in places, he was compelled to postpone his own departure a little longer.

Doctor Thorold, the only European who was to accompany him on his dangerous adventure, had gone on to Leh with the coolies, and had written back a very unfavourable account of the condition of the road. He reported that there were several marches through soft snow, and that the nullah that led up to the Zoji La Pass was blocked by a gigantic curtain of precipitous snow and ice, up which it would be necessary to cut a zigzag path with ice-axes before it would be possible for horses to effect the ascent.

So I had to pass a few days at Srinagur, where the British summer colony had already collected, and appeared to be enjoying itself thoroughly with dinner-parties, balls, picnics, horse-racing, cricket, polo, and other amusements.

A picnic in the Nasim Bagh, on the shore of the Dal Lake, is an event to be remembered. I was present at one given by the Resident. The Anglo-Indians, I think, understand picnics better than do our people at home, having taken some hints from those luxurious inventors of picnics, the Asiatics. No more delicious spots can be found for open-air revelry than the fair gardens that surround the capital of Kashmir, where sloping lawns, beautiful groves, flashing cascades and fountains, marble terraces and pavilions, combine to form ideal places for the purpose. Indeed, the genius of picnic seems to rule the whole shores of the Dal; the desire for careless pleasure, feasting and flirting is inspired by the cool breeze that blows over the broad lake through these pleasant groves and gardens; and this is not to be wondered at, for were not these planted by those grand old picnicers, the Emperors Akbar, Jehangir, and Aurungzebe? Often did the fair Noormehal and other ancient queens of beauty picnic in these sweet retreats.

I should not be surprised, by the way, if the very word picnic, whose origin, I believe, is unknown, were some old Kashmir name for the pleasant pastime of which this Happy Valley was the birthplace. I am sure that some of our ingenious etymologists could readily prove this.

We repaired to the Resident's picnic by water, in shikarah boats, a journey well worth taking for its own sake. After passing from the Jhelam into the Dal, we traversed a portion of the lake which is so densely overgrown with aquatic plants that it is difficult to realise one is on a lake at all. Tall rushes and reeds, and in places groves of willows, rise from the water; and this vegetation is intersected by a labyrinth of small channels, through which the boat progresses. These water-alleys are exceedingly pretty; on either side is the fresh, green water-jungle, while in the more open spaces are floating fields of lilies and singharas. The singhara is the Kashmir water-nut, which overgrows many of the lakes and rivers, and furnishes the chief article of food to the fishing-population. This seemed to be a favourite haunt of the golden orioles, which I saw flashing all round me in the sunlight. In places one might have imagined oneself to be on some quiet nook of the Norfolk Broads; but on looking up, the far snowy ranges and the nearer craggy heights of Solomon's Throne and Hari Parbat soon dispelled that illusion.

Here, too, I saw some of those floating gardens of Kashmir, of which I had often read. One would not observe these unless one's attention were attracted to them; for they merely look like well-cultivated banks of earth. But the term floating garden is no misnomer. They are not of natural growth, but are constructed by the peasants, who produce upon them cucumbers and other vegetables for the Srinagur market. The following passage from Moorcroft's travels clearly explains how these gardens are formed:—'The roots of aquatic plants growing in shallow places are divided about two feet under the water, so that they completely lose all connection with the bottom of the lake, but retain their former situation in respect to each other. When thus detached from the soil, they are pressed into somewhat

HARI PARBAT.

closer contact, and formed into beds of about two yards in breadth and of an indefinite length. The heads of the sedges, reeds, and other plants of the float are now cut off and laid upon its surface, and covered with a thin coat of mud, which, at first intercepted in its descent, gradually sinks into the mass of matted roots. The bed floats, but is kept in its place by a stake of willow driven through it at each end, which admits of its rising or falling in accommodation to the rise or fall of the water.'

The Nasim Bagh, or Garden of Bliss, is on the sloping bank of the Dal, where the lake is not overgrown with vegetation, but forms a fine open expanse of clear water. Here, under the shade of magnificent plane-trees, the servants of the Resident had pitched the great tents for the picnic; the gay pavilions, the bright costumes of the natives and of the English ladies in their summer frocks, the numerous pleasure-boats darting on the lake, combining to form a pretty picture.

But I had now to put aside for some time the luxury of picnics in the pleasant Happy Valley, for Bower was impatient to be off into the desert lands beyond the Himalayas; and though the reports from the Zoji La were still very unfavourable, he decided to start from Srinagur on May 17, and push on across the mountains, if possible.

From Srinagur to Leh is a distance of 260 miles, divided into nineteen marches, all of which are usually practicable for baggage-animals. But the road was in so bad a condition after the hard winter, that we knew we should have to employ coolie labour for our baggage, and would be lucky if we got all Bower's horses across the pass unladen.

This is the great trade-route between India and Yarkand *viâ* the Karakoram Pass, and also between Kashmir and Lassa, and other commercial centres of Tibet and Turkestan; consequently, the road, for a Kashmir road, is a good one; but this is not saying much for it. At its best it is but a rough bridle-track, dangerous for ponies at certain points, so that, as on every other route in these regions, the traveller must not be surprised to lose a baggage-animal over the cliff. It is safer to entrust one's valuable property to the surer-footed coolie.

The first stage from Srinagur—to Gunderbal—is generally accomplished by water; so the horses and baggage were sent ahead early on the morning of May 17, while we followed later in the day in a rapid shikarah boat. Having traversed some of the pretty channels of the Dal Lake, we entered a narrow canal which winds through the slums of the city. It was a dirty, odorous, but picturesque waterway, spanned by stone bridges built of the great carved blocks, pilasters, and friezes of the old Hindoo temples. The embankments and ghauts on either side were also full of these relics of Kashmir's palmy days: images of deities, defaced by the fanatical Mussulmans, were to be seen all round, and in the open spaces were extensive foundations and massive ruins of the ancient City of the Sun.

People were bathing at all the ghauts. The water of these canals appears too filthy even to bathe in, and yet the population of this great capital entirely relies on it for drinking purposes. That cholera plays fearful havoc here occasionally is not to be wondered at. The prudent sahibs, who encamp in the European quarter, send to the Dal Lake for their water; but a Kashmiri would, of course, never think of taking such a precaution, and is satisfied with the abominable fluid that stagnates under the city slums. The late Resident, Colonel Parry Nisbet, R.E., worked out and urged the adoption of an easy and not expensive plan for the supply of pure water to Srinagur; but the Kashmir Public Works Department—which requires some looking into—put obstructions in the way of the proposed water-supply, so that cholera still reigns supreme.

Having traversed the suburbs, we were paddled across the weed-grown Anchar Lake, which brought us to a flowery pasture-land, where the Sind River, having issued from its mountain gorges, divides into many channels and hurries to the Woolar Lake. We now found the water discoloured by the glaciers and melting snows, and icy cold.

We gradually approached the hill-country, and at last reached the village of Gunderbal, at the very mouth of the Sind Valley; and here, by the river bank, we found our tents pitched and our followers awaiting us. As soon as we had disembarked, a deputation of very obsequious people came down to us, headed by the lumbadar of Gunderbal, who was anxious to supply us with firewood, sheep, and all else that we might require. We never had any trouble in obtaining coolies and supplies on the Leh road, for Captain Bower had been furnished with a *parwana* by the Kashmir Durbar, and injunctions had been sent on to every official on the route to render him assistance. So our journey was like a royal progress; and it is not unpleasant to travel like a king for a change.

But this Leh road is not altogether an easy one for an ordinary sahib travelling in a private capacity. The village authorities will often boycot him, refusing carriage and supplies, except at exorbitant rates. This is stated to be a temporary result of the Settlement Officer's reforms. It is understood by the people on this road that he has abolished begar, that all labour is free, and that consequently the old official tariffs are no longer in force. The lumbadars and other officials are profiting by this popular theory, and, urging that they have no power to compel the villagers to work or sell supplies, make these extravagant demands. If this continues, travelling in this country will become impossible for the British subaltern, in these hard days of the depreciated rupee. I met two young officers who had started to spend their leave shooting in Ladak nullahs, but who had turned back in disgust at the impositions they met with at every step. The sporting sahibs brought plenty of money into the country, and gave employment to shikaris and others, but now the officials who pretend to be the spokesmen of the people kill the goose that lays the golden egg. Free-trade will not do here. The Kashmiri, for his own good, must be made to work and to sell at reasonable rates. Only last autumn the peasants tried to boycot the city of Srinagur itself, in the hopes of enhancing the price of their hoarded grain, and nearly brought on serious bread riots and bloodshed.

It will be a great pity if the Kashmir nullahs become too expensive for our subalterns on leave from the plains of India. This is the most extensive, and in many ways the best, of the Himalayan holiday-grounds. To shoot among these solitudes is a splendid training in itself for a young subaltern, and far better for him than to loll at Simla or other hill-stations, where, if reports are true, too much of the soldier's time is occupied in gambling and flirting—excellent amusements both, but which are wrongful indulgences for the boys, and should be reserved for officers of a certain age, whose joints are too stiff for mountaineering. Some middle-aged officers, indeed, hold that no leave to the hill-stations should be granted to youngsters. Let them go to the mountains and get hard in the chase of the ibex and the Ovis poli, while the oldsters enjoy the monopoly of the sedater joys of Simla.

At Gunderbal, all our followers and baggage being collected together, we were able to apportion the loads and ascertain how many coolies or baggage-animals we should require on the road. I found that the belongings of myself and my two servants, including two tents and an abundance of stores, would load fourteen coolies. Dr. Thorold had preceded Captain Bower to Leh with the bulk of the stores for their expedition, but there was a goodly pile left to be carried on by us. Bower was taking seventeen ponies with him, and intended to purchase others on the road. They looked in good enough condition now, and were to be well fed and exempted from carrying loads until the frontier was crossed; but many were destined to perish later on among the Tibetan wastes.

The men who were to accompany Bower on his expedition were awaiting him here—an outlandish-looking lot: Mussulmans from Turkestan, pig-tailed Buddhists from Ladak, of ugly but amiable Mongolian features, and half-breed Argoons. I do not know how many of these accomplished the long journey or how many deserted, but there were, at any rate, two thoroughly reliable natives with him, whose tall figures, handsome Aryan faces, and fair complexions distinguished them from the stunted, swarthy Tartars, and who carried the undertaking through to the end. One of these was a young Rajpoot of good family, a Government surveyor keen to distinguish himself as an explorer for the Intelligence Department; the other was Bower's orderly, who had obtained leave to accompany him, a fine young Pathan, with all the pluck, devilry, and love of fun of his race. Ours was a very Babel of a camp, no less than six languages being regularly spoken in it.

The Sind Valley, which we had now to ascend for our first five marches, is considered to contain some of the loveliest scenery in Kashmir, and though I did not visit it at a favourable season, I could see that it de-

serves its reputation. At dawn on May 18 our camp
was struck, the pack animals which had been hired
in the village, and which were to carry our baggage
until we got into the snow, were laden, and we com
menced our long march, which, for Bower, was to lead
to one of the most extraordinary journeys of exploration that has ever been accomplished, for it will undoubtedly be recognised as such when his tale is told.
He was to disappear into absolutely unknown regions,
the most inhospitable in the world, and be not heard
of until he arrived, a year afterwards, on the shores of
the Pacific Ocean at Shanghai, having succeeded in
considerably altering the aspect of that great blank
space in the map which had been such an eyesore to
him.

Asiatic servants are certainly wonderfully skilled in
striking camp, getting the caravan off, and making all
comfortable again at the end of a day's march. On
the first day of a journey there is a little delay and
confusion, but all settles down by the second. Indian
servants, with all their faults, are in many respects
the best in the world. It is difficult to imagine an
English butler tramping along over difficult mountain tracks, now baked by the fierce suns of the Indus
gorges, now risking frostbite on icy passes, and then,
after each hard day's march, setting to work to construct a fireplace of a few stones, and, with the aid of
some primitive pots and pans, to turn out a capital
dinner of many courses, as my khansamah had to do
for many months at a time.

Our two khansamahs made the following bandobast
as to how they should feed us on the road. On one
day Bower's khansamah was to prepare our chota
haziri before starting, and our dinner when we got into

camp at night; while my servant was to go ahead at dawn with a coolie-load of cooking-utensils and food, and have our breakfast ready for us at some suitable half-way spot on the march. The following day they would exchange duties, and so on. Each servant, of course, used only his own master's sheep, fowls, stores, &c. There was no combining of Bower's and mine for a meal. One day's dinner was entirely supplied by him, the next day's by me. A different system might have been more convenient, but could not have been permitted by our masters, the servants; it would have been quite against dastur. The Oriental is in some ways an extreme individualist. He cannot conceive it possible that the sahibs themselves are otherwise. That two men travelling together should consider their stores common property is to him opposed to the universal laws of selfish human nature. Thus, the servants of different masters do not work together well: they so profoundly mistrust each other's honesty, they are ever on the watch to outwit each other. They are sure to quarrel if they attempt partnership. Each identifies himself with his particular sahib; and though exacting a sufficient dastur from him, he will allow no one else to do so. Any other sahib's servant is to him a dangerous foe, against whom he has to protect his own employer. Bower's servant would have robbed me, and my servant would have robbed Bower, for the benefit of their respective masters. They observed each other closely; they would squabble over a pinch of salt, if one should help himself to it from the other's *kilta*. One day, when it was my turn to supply the dinner, Babu Khan got cleverly to windward of Bower's man: he pretended not to be able, at the moment, to find any of my jam, so that, in order not to waste time, Bower ordered his very reluctant servant to place on the table a half-empty jam-pot of his own. This untimely consumption of Bower's stores was never forgotten or forgiven by his man; from that hour he nourished a vindictive hatred against Babu Khan, and at every dispute threw this pot of jam in his teeth.

Perhaps it is as well thus, for if two Indian servants combined against their masters, what ruinous proportions would dastur assume! Another advantage of this bitter rivalry was that each of our khansamahs would try to turn out a better dinner than the other. We consequently fared well, and Bower left me to plunge into the desert beyond Leh in excellent condition.

So Bower and myself set out on the morning of May 18, alternately riding and leading two of his horses; for though, like himself, they were to be kept fit for the Tibetan hardships, it would do them no harm to carry a man occasionally. Our friend the lumbadar did not encourage us. He said that the pass was impracticable, and that on this side of Sonamerg the road had completely fallen away. On being asked when it would be repaired, he replied that he could not say, but that nothing would be done for some time, as the villagers had no tools to work with. And yet this is the chief road into Central Asia!

Our road lay up the valley, winding along the slopes at some height above the rushing torrent. Here was particularly noticeable a phenomenon which prevails all over Kashmir and in most portions of the Himalayas. Whereas the mountains on our right hand, which faced the north, were clothed with dense forests, those on our left hand, facing the south, were everywhere arid and treeless; so sharp is the demarcation between the growth on one side and the barrenness on the other side of a mountain, that we could see the tops of the pines forming a dark fringe along the summits of all the bare ridges to our left, showing the limit of the forests rising on the farther side.

This, our first day's march, was an easy one to the village of Kangan, near which we encamped in a grove of chenars. On the next day, May 18, we accomplished another stage to Goond. This village is situated amidst the finest scenery of the Sind Valley. The bottom of the valley is here broad and undulating, well-cultivated in places, with groves of fruit-trees surrounding the comfortable-looking farmhouses. The river often divides, enclosing pretty islands of emerald grass or of tangled bushes. A little later in the season, when the roses, jasmine, and honeysuckle, which grow in wild profusion, are in flower, this must be one of the fairest spots on earth. The mountains, which here enclose the valley, rise in forest-clad domes, between which are deep, shady dells, reminding one somewhat of the Jura country.

The loveliness of the land even made Bower's Pathan orderly wax enthusiastic. He gazed at the fertile vale with a keen admiration, which took a very practical form. 'What pasture for goats and sheep!' he exclaimed. 'What corn-fields! Why has not somebody taken this country from the people? These miserable Kashmiris do not deserve to have it. They could not fight for it. Why don't the Black Mountain men come down on this? I wish I was raiding here with a lot of good Pathans! Why don't the English take it?' And so he went on, with wondering warmth. No doubt the British have fallen greatly in his estimation for not having annexed this valley. It would have been vain to explain politics to him—to speak of treaties and breaches of faith. His political ethics were of the good old simple sort, which he summed up thus:— Those who are weak and cannot fight should not be allowed to possess.

We had already ascended to some elevation, as was shown by the chilliness of the night-air, and we noticed that the snow-line on the hills was much nearer to us than it had been lower down the valley. It was not possible to take laden horses beyond Goond, so coolies were collected for us by the lumbadar.

The next stage to Goond is Gagangir, but on May 20 we made a double march to Sonamerg. The path still wound up the valley, now by the torrent, now high above it. We soon reached our first snow, lying in patches across the road. The vale lost its softer beauties, and narrowed to a grand gorge with towering crags. The difficulties of the road, such as they were, commenced. Down every side-nullah, which clove the precipices on either side, huge avalanches had fallen to the river-bed, and along the very steep slopes of these avalanches our way lay. In places great accumulations of snow filled the bottom of the gorge, through which the torrent had forced a narrow channel, rushing between two walls of snow thirty feet in depth. That the winter had been an exceptional one was testified to by the number of fine trees that had been swept away by the avalanches. It was a wild scene, and the signs of devastation were apparent everywhere. Bower's horses had to be led with great care across these snow-inclines, where a false step would have meant a fall over the cliffs into the foaming, rock-encumbered Sind.

H

Sonamerg is a miserable little village situated in a very beautiful spot. Here one is no longer in a narrow gorge, for the hills recede and the valley opens out, the river flowing between broad, rolling pastures. The enclosing mountains are of grand outline, and in the lower portions of their deep nullahs are fine pastures: higher up are dark forests of pine, while higher still, above the tree-zone, glittering glaciers are wedged between barren crags.

Sonamerg signifies the Golden Meadow, the yellow crocus, which thickly studs the pastures, no doubt having suggested the name. Here, as on the *cirques* of the Alps, the little streams that pour down from the surrounding snows keep these broad pastures green and fresh through the summer heats, and one walks knee-deep in grass and flowers. We had been gradually ascending since we left Gunderbal, and were now 8,650 feet above the sea, at about which elevation the pleasantest summer climate is found in Kashmir. A great portion of the English colony at Srinagur was wont to migrate here in the hot season; but for ladies the journey is a somewhat long and rough one, and Sonamerg has therefore been supplanted as a sanatorium by Gulmerg, where the Resident has his headquarters every summer.

It was difficult, when I saw these famous rolling meadows of Sonamerg, to realise what a lovely luxuriance would be theirs later on. The aspect of the country was indescribably dreary. The pastures were under snow, and where it had melted away in patches there was dark mud alone visible, the young grass not having yet pushed through; though here and there, in the warmer nooks, the hardy crocus, outstripping other vegetation, was thrusting out already its golden petals.

The little group of log huts, inhabited by herdsmen, which composes the hamlet of Sonamerg—the highest in the Sind Valley—looked even more filthy and wretched than it really is, in contrast to the pure snow surrounding it; and to intensify the prevailing melancholy of this wintry scenery, dark snow-clouds were hanging on all the mountain peaks, and a steady sleet was falling from the overcast heavens when we arrived in camp.

We noticed that from here to the summit of the pass, and beyond, the snow was covered with the corpses of locusts, which, fortunately for the Vale of Kashmir, had attempted a raiding expedition across the Himalayas at too early a season. Later on I came to a dead horde of these rash robbers at a higher altitude than that of the summit of Mont Blanc.

We encamped on a patch of muddy ground where the snow had melted. The wind howled down the valley all night, driving cold rain and sleet before it. It was certain that heavy snow was falling on the pass, and it appeared probable that we should be delayed on this side by bad weather—a rather serious matter, for our following was a large one, and no supplies to speak of are procurable here.

The lumbadar told us that Dr. Thorold had arrived safely at Leh six days since. He said that the Thanadar of Dras was sending thirty coolies across the pass to assist us, and that we should meet them at the next stage, Baltal. He also gave us all the news concerning the few sahibs who were travelling on this road, in Baltistan, and in the neighbouring countries. He knew exactly where each was, and what sport he had had. The marvellous manner in which news, important or trivial, is conveyed about Asia from mouth to mouth has often been observed. An item of information will reach a bazaar—no one knows how—from a spot a thousand miles away with incredible speed. In Kashmir territory this is very noticeable, but there is a good reason for it here. There are but few practicable roads through this mighty mountain system, and each of these becomes, as it were, a telephone of communication.

We had to change our coolies at Sonamerg. The official in charge of them, who had accompanied us from Goond, of course demanded bakshish before he left us, and also—still more of course—required of us a *chit*, or written testimonial. Here everyone with whom one has dealings, from one's barber and coolies up to the rajahs of the districts one traverses, expects one of these chits. Even a native whom one casually meets on the road, and with whom one enters into conversation for five minutes, often requests his chit. All the importunate merchants of Srinagur, all the boatmen when they solicit custom, produce their piles of chits, given to them by different sahibs. The Kashmiri, simple in this matter only, sets an enormous and quite fictitious value on the chit. He has faith in it as a sort of talisman. If one discharges a servant for theft, he will suffer unmurmuringly the mulcting of his pay, but to refuse him a chit, even if it state at full all his shortcomings, is almost to break his heart.

A Kashmiri undoubtedly prefers to have an abusive chit than no chit at all, but a chit of some sort he must have. So indifferent is he, indeed, as to whether his chits praise him or completely take away his character, that he does not take the trouble to get them translated for him by some city *munshi*, but presents them all, good and bad, for your consideration. One official on this road is the proud possessor of many chits. He handed one to me, and gazed at me with a solemn expression of conscious merit as I read it. This chit was from a captain sahib, and ran thus :—'This man is the greatest thief and scoundrel generally I have ever come across.'

CHAPTER VII

THE WESTERN HIMALAYAN RANGE—THE ZOJI LA—CLIMATE OF LADAK—
MATAYUN—DRAS—TIBETAN SCENERY—TASHGAM.

THERE was a keen bite in the air when we set out on the next morning, May 21, from our encampment on the wind-swept plateau. The guide-book describes this, the march to the foot of the Zoji La, as a beautiful one over 'rolling meadows'; but for us it was rather over rolling snow. We floundered through undulating fields of deep, soft snow; we crossed avalanche slopes of snow and débris, and had occasionally to wade in the icy river under a snow cliff thirty feet high, which formed the base of some great avalanche too steep to travel over.

This was a short but fatiguing march of ten miles to the halting-place of Baltal. There are no inhabitants at Baltal, but three or four rough stone huts are clustered together, which serve as refuges for the *dak wallahs* and coolies crossing the pass. Here we found the thirty coolies that had been sent from the other side by the Thanadar of Dras to assist our men in getting the baggage over. These fresh coolies were natives of the Dras district, stunted, ugly, and of the Mongolian type—very different-looking people from the handsome Kashmiris, the limit of whose country we had now reached. They were warmly wrapped in shapeless filthy garments, and wore warm mocassins of skins on their feet to preserve them against frost-bite.

Their head-man, a weather-wise person, said the pass was now difficult, but not dangerous, provided the weather was favourable. It was snowing hard when we reached the huts, but he was of opinion that it would clear up later on, and, if it did so, he recommended that we should start at three in the morning, so as to get across the worst part of the pass before the sun should soften the snow. He explained that it would be quite impossible to proceed so long as the snow fell. He informed us that an Afghan horse-dealer, on his way from Turkestan to Kashmir, was now weather-bound at Dras. He had attempted the pass two days before, but had to give it up and return, though not before he had lost several of his horses. No horses had yet crossed the pass this year. We heard that a shikaring sahib had got over with coolies one moonlight night, when the snow was frozen hard, some weeks earlier; but that a wind had overtaken them, so that they had to leave all the baggage on the summit of the pass and hurry to Matayun for their lives, he and several of the coolies being badly frostbitten.

One has to pick one's weather carefully to cross a Himalayan pass in winter and spring, and when one does get a slant—as they say at sea—one must hurry over quickly; for the sudden, fierce winds that often spring up are then very formidable, and sometimes destroy whole caravans of travellers with their deadly cold. A few months before this 300 mules and their drivers were thus overtaken and lost on the Gilgit road. The Zoji La has a bad reputation for the icy gales that sweep across its exposed snow-downs.

The Western Himalayas traverse the territories of

the Maharajah from north-west to south-east, from the Indus Valley on the Chilas frontier to the Chinese frontier near Spiti; and the Zoji La (La is Tibetan for pass) is the lowest depression in the range, being only 11,500 feet above the sea; consequently, the wind concentrates itself in this deep gap of the great mountain wall, and rushes through it with high velocity.

This range, whose average height must be over 17,000 feet, and which contains, among other peaks, the mighty Nanga Parbat (26,620 feet), divides the Kashmir State into two nearly equal portions, and thus forms a stupendous natural barrier, not only between regions widely differing in climate and in other physical respects, but between peoples as far as possible apart in race and religion.

To the south of the range is the land of the Aryans; to the north the people—save in the Dard districts near Gilgit—are of Mongolian stock. In Ladak, the country we were now to enter, the inhabitants are Buddhists, and though subject to Kashmir, they still look upon the Grand Lama as their real lord. When one is in Ladak one is practically in Tibet; the same strange scenery and climate, the same language, dress, and customs of the queer pigtailed inhabitants are found in both countries.

The Sikh and Dogra rulers of Kashmir crossed this range, which formed the old natural frontier, and in turn subdued all the countries to the north of it as far as the great watershed of the Karakoram and Hindoo Koosh mountains. They effected the conquest of Ladak between 1834 and 1842. It was then ruled by a native rajah who acknowledged China as his paramount Power, and the Grand Lama at Lassa as his spiritual chief. There is no natural division between Ladak and Chinese

Tibet; the highlands of one are continued into the other, and the same rivers flow through both countries. The frontier between Western Tibet (as Ladak is sometimes called) and Chinese Tibet was settled definitely some years back.

In Kashmir there is a regular rainfall, even if it be inconsiderable, and the heavy winter snowfall stores the water necessary to refresh the country in the summer months. It is consequently a green land of woods and pastures. But the contrast between Kashmir and the region beyond the mountains is very remarkable. The rainclouds from the south, which have come over India from the distant seas, are intercepted by this lofty range. So on crossing the Zoji La one suddenly enters the great bleak wastes of Central Asia, where there is practically no rainfall, and where even the winter snowfall on the mountain-tops is but light, so that at 16,000 feet above the sea one often finds no snow left lying in summer.

Ladak, like Chinese Tibet, is for the most part a desert of bare crags and granite dust, with vast arid table-lands of high elevation—a land where are no forests or pastures, where in places one can march through a long summer's day and never see so much as a blade of grass; but in which, by means of artificial canals bringing down a little water from high snows, small patches of the granite dust are irrigated and carefully cultivated here and there—tiny green oases, so sharply defined from the surrounding desolation that, as Shaw in his book says, they look like bits of some other country cut out with a pair of scissors and dropped into a desert: a cloudless region, always burning or freezing under the clear blue sky; for so thin and devoid of moisture is the atmosphere that the variations of temperature are extreme, and rocks exposed to the sun's rays may be too hot to lay the hand upon at the same time that it is freezing in the shade. To be suffering from heat on one side of one's body while painfully cold on the other is no uncommon sensation here.

Ladak can boast of being the highest inhabited country in the world : the average elevation must be very great. Grain is cultivated in places at 15,000 feet. Leh itself, the capital, is 11,500 feet above the sea, but is considered by the highlanders of the Rupshu district so low as to be unhealthy in summer, and they only visit it in winter. These strange creatures complain of suffocation when they descend to the Vale of Kashmir, and would die if they stayed long in its dense air.

One never hears of any other pass than the Zoji La on the Leh road—and it is, indeed, the only difficulty one encounters, for it is here that the southerly wind deposits its heavy burden of snow ; but, as a matter of fact, a great portion of the road beyond, though left bare of snow in early spring, is at a considerably higher elevation than the summit of the Zoji La, at one point attaining 13,400 feet.

From the above description one would imagine this barren region to be depressing and uninteresting in the extreme, but it is, on the contrary, fascinating to an extraordinary degree. There are few countries I would so gladly revisit as Western Tibet.

Near Baltal the road leaves the Sind Valley and ascends a tributary nullah. The bottom of this nullah was now entirely filled with snow, under which a rushing torrent had tunnelled a way. There is a summer and a winter route across the Zoji La, the former and longer one zigzagging up the nullah to the ridge, the latter and shorter one, which we were to take, being up a precipitous gully which leads directly to the summit of the pass, upwards of 2,000 feet above. In this gully an enormous mass of snow accumulates every winter, whose very steep incline it is possible to scale without danger when the snow is firm; but in summer this route is impracticable, for then the swollen torrent has worn away great tunnels and cavities, above which the gradually decreasing snow-roof becomes exceedingly treacherous, and anyone venturing upon it runs considerable risk of falling through and losing his life. This was the steep curtain of snow which Doctor Thorold had described as extremely difficult for horses to scale, and it certainly looked so from below.

As the head-man, to whose local knowledge we of course submitted, had given the word that we should start at 3 A.M. if the weather should clear, we did not consider it worth while to pitch our tents, but took up our quarters in one of the rest-houses, which were crowded with our men. We selected the biggest hut, where we found a group of coolies squatting round a large fire in the middle of the mud floor. The only firewood procurable was that of the dwarf birch, which here covers the hillsides; the smoke of this is peculiarly suffocating and irritating to the eyes, and as there were few orifices in the roofs and walls to allow its escape, we were kept weeping and coughing till bedtime.

The wind howled and the snow fell outside for several hours; but at four our guide, who had been keeping watch on the weather, woke us, and said that we could now start. We turned out, to find the aspect very cheerless: the moon had risen, and was feebly gleaming on the snowy waste through a frozen haze.

The wind had dropped, but the snow was still falling lightly. The guide explained that there had been but little fresh snow, and that the surface of the old snow would be now frozen hard and easy to walk on. So horses and coolies were sent ahead, while Bower and myself smoked a pipe over the embers of the fire, knowing that we could travel faster than the others, and soon overtake them.

It is a sixteen-miles march from Baltal across the pass to the next stage, Matayun. The mass of snow which during the preceding hard winter had filled up the gully, choking the torrent and piling high above it, was indeed prodigious. The snow, as the guide had foretold, was firm at first, and even the horses did not sink into it much. He was also right in his weather forecast: the day proved windless, hot, and fine. We luckily reached the top of the gully before the sun had risen high and softened the snow. The scaling of that steep rampart would have been almost impossible a few hours later for the horses, and we should in all probability have lost some in the deep drifts.

Whereas the ascent had been almost perpendicular, the descent on the other side of the pass was so gradual as to be imperceptible. Indeed, Matayun is only 500 feet lower than the Zoji La, which is like no ordinary pass, and may rather be described as a gigantic step, upwards of 2,000 feet in height, by which one rises from Kashmir on to the elevated table-land of Tibet.

From the summit of the pass we proceeded along the level bottom of a snow-covered valley, which gradually broadened, and was bordered by rugged hills, on which the dwarf birch-trees alone grew. The gaunt, leafless branches of these trees, the vast undulating wastes of snow, and the dark crags combined to form an intensely dreary and melancholy picture.

It was a long and tedious march. As the sun gained power the snow became very soft, so that the ponies sank deep at every step, often fell, and reached camp very tired. It was hard work for the laden coolies, and even for our two unladen selves. When we came to some rocky space bare of snow, the contrast

IN CAMP: LADAKI COOLIES.

after the stumbling, floundering, and dragging of legs out of deep holes in the drifts was so great that to walk on the solid ground felt as restful as if one had been sitting down.

The glare of the snow of course necessitated the use of goggles. Some of the coolies wore snow-spectacles of their own manufacture. Meshes of horsehair were employed instead of coloured glass to fill the rough wooden frames—a plan which seems to answer very well.

At last we came to where a clear stream babbled along the valley over a pebbly bottom, which we frequently crossed by snow bridges. It flowed in the direction we were going, and showed us—what we could not otherwise have detected—that we had crossed the great watershed and had commenced the descent. This was the Dras River, whose valley the Leh road now follows for nearly five marches.

As we toiled across the weary fields of snow the only living things we saw were certain queer little beasts that are very familiar to travellers on these highlands. Every now and again we would hear an uncanny shrill whistling, and on looking in the direction whence it came would observe a little marmot sitting up on its hind legs on the top of some rock and gazing impertinently at us. These marmots drive dogs frantic with their exceedingly irritating ways. A dog seldom succeeds in catching a marmot. The marmot stands still, lures him on with jeering whistles, and then, but not until the infuriated dog is just on him, drops into his hole between the rocks; when the disappointed dog has retired to a safe distance, he pops out again like a jack-in-the-box and resumes his tantalising jibes.

There is something quite fiendish in the behaviour of this little imp. The Ladak Buddhists say that it is possessed of a man's soul, a malicious person being on death re-incarnated as a marmot; and they would not kill one on any account. Bower's two spaniel pups, Benjamin and Joseph, had never seen marmots before, and seemed to be rather afraid of them, not venturing very near, but barking weakly in response to the marmots' whistling, and then beating a rapid retreat. But though not daring to tackle marmots, the two puppies had splendid sport with some Kashmiri coolies they met near Matayun, and of whom, of course, they were not in the least afraid. On the other hand, the average Kashmiri, who is afraid of everything, exhibits abject terror if a sahib's dog, be it only a toothless little puppy, approaches him. Benjamin and Joseph had discovered this, and used to have great fun. Whenever they saw a Kashmiri they would run up to him barking, whereupon, in almost every instance, that fine-looking, athletic, bearded disgrace to the human race would behave as a five-year-old English child would be ashamed to do, howling, weeping, and throwing himself down in the snow in deadly fear.

This day the puppies had also the luck to 'stick-up' the Maharajah's mail. Encountering the dak wallah, they of course badgered him with their playful barkings. The poor wretch threw down his mail-bag, rolled himself in his blanket, and cast himself, screaming for protection, at Bower's feet. We called the dogs off, and left the postman lying on the snow weeping bitterly, his nerves completely upset by this unprovoked attack. The puppies were highly amused, and decided that Kashmiri-baiting altogether beat marmot-hunting as a sport, and was, besides, so very much safer.

All our men at last straggled into Matayun, most of the coolies having occupied ten hours on the road. Here amidst desolate scenery we found a house of refuge rising from the snow. This was one of the usual *serais* of this country, consisting of a square of low, flat-roofed buildings enclosing a central courtyard. There was room for all of us in the dark little chambers, on the floors of which we soon had our fires burning and the welcome tea was got ready by our servants.

Here we found the Afghan merchant who had failed to cross the pass, with some members of his caravan.

He told us that he had left Kashgar in the preceding autumn, and had wintered at Leh; so he did not appear to be in any hurry. These people do not believe that 'time is money.' They like to get a high profit on their venture, and care little how long they may have to wait for it. To turn over money quickly and enrich oneself by frequent small profits is not the Oriental's way of conducting a business; it is, among other things, too lacking in dignity for an Asiatic. This Afghan was wearing over his clothes a *choga*, or robe of Russian chintz. Bower asked him why he did not purchase English chintz. 'It is not of nearly such good material,' he replied, 'as the Russian; besides, the English do not make striped chintz such as we like, but of strange and displeasing designs.' It seems that our manufacturers do not study the tastes of their Asiatic customers so much as they might. Some of the chintzes sent out here are indeed remarkable. A short time since all the notables in Chitral were arrayed in gay robes covered with representations of a pirouetting ballet-girl, a large consignment of cotton stuff with this elegant design having arrived from England.

The next day, May 23, we had another fifteen-miles tramp through snow to Dras, a scattered little village containing a capacious serai, in which the Thanadar had ordered a chamber to be swept and garnished for us. The inhabitants of Dras are of various races, and, limited as is the population, no less than four languages are in constant use here—Kashmiri, Tibetan, Balti, and Brokpa, the last being the tongue of a shepherd-race inhabiting the high valleys.

The Dras people are Mussulmans; for we had not quite got into the Buddhist country yet, though we saw here large stones on which idols were carved, showing that the Buddhist creed had once prevailed in this district, as it also did formerly in all the countries between the mountains we had crossed and the Hindoo Koosh range, Baltistan having only adopted Mahomedanism in comparatively modern times.

Dras is situated amidst just the sort of desert scenery the Buddhists seem to love: treeless, craggy mountains, with great *couloirs* of ruddy gravel sloping from them to an unfertile plain. But, according to the Tibetan standard, this would be considered a rather rich land, for short grass was growing here and there among the rocks, while round the village stood some disconsolate-looking poplars, struggling for existence. By means of irrigation, a little barley is cultivated here.

Beyond Dras there was but little snow lying, though occasionally, on the next two marches, we came to avalanche-slopes, and had to pick our way across loose moraines of mixed snow and débris; but there were no real difficulties, and we were able to discharge our coolies at Dras and engage horses for our baggage.

On May 24 we descended the valley to the next stage, Tashgam. The scenery was becoming more Tibetan as we advanced. The mountains were flatter at the top than in Kashmir. The high desert-plateaus, so characteristic of Tibet, were already extending above us, instead of the serrated and pinnacled ranges we had seen on the other side of the Zoji La. The mountain-sides, too, were of Tibetan ugliness, not clothed with forests or pastures, but formed of piled-up rocks and loose gravel. The only plant-life visible on the barren heights were a few scattered and stunted pencil cedars (*Juniperus excelsa*). There was no grass in the stony valley-bottom; but rose and gooseberry bushes grew on the river brink in places.

I

Here and there, even on the most arid spots, clumps of a small slate-coloured plant, something like fennel in appearance, were growing. Bower at once recognised this as an old, familiar friend, and explained to me its great merits. This was Boortsa, or Eurotia, a most invaluable plant to travellers on the high desert-valleys and plateaus of Tibet, and without which vast regions would be quite impassable for man and beast. It is full of an aromatic oil that smells something like camphor. It burns the better the greener it is, as Bower demonstrated by applying a match to a growing clump, which blazed up readily. On those wind-swept, bitterly cold wastes, where there is no wood or grass, the boortsa is the only fuel save cattle-dung, and is often the only fodder procurable for one's animals. It was not growing very luxuriantly in this comparatively low-lying and fertile valley. It flourishes best, it seems, in extremely arid regions, and at a much higher elevation—for we were now at little more than twice the height of Ben Nevis above the sea.

We saw a fair amount of animal-life this day—larks, choughs, and snow-pigeons flying round us, marmots whistling on the rocks, and lizards darting among the sun-heated stones. The villages we passed were dirty but snug little rabbit-warrens of places, all the huts standing on a common foundation—a rocky height or an artificial stone embankment—and huddled close up to each other, as if for warmth.

We were certainly marching through a very changeable climate, for summer and winter alternated several times this day. At one moment the heat would be tropical, the next moment a bitter blast would rush down the mountain-side from the snowy wastes and glaciers ten thousand feet above, bringing with it snow and icy rain; for we had not yet quite reached the rainless regions. Some of the moisture-laden clouds from the south are driven across the mountain-range to reach as far as this.

When sitting down this day to tiffin, with the sun blazing on one cheek and the other cheek in the freezing shade, one almost felt, as was remarked at the time, that it was a question by which one would be attacked first—sunstroke on one side of one's head, or frostbite on the other.

We put up for the night in the serai of the little village of Tashgam. One need not pitch the tents at any stage between Matayun and Leh, as there are State rest-houses for the accommodation of travellers, for the use of which no charge is made.

On arriving, Bower announced that he wished to purchase some horses, and a good part of the evening was passed in chaffering with the natives. Like men all the world round who deal in horseflesh, these were pretty sharp customers and plausibly mendacious, but Bower, after much bargaining, bought some animals at a reasonable rate. One of these men was a striking example of the miserly spirit with which the Asiatic will regard the most insignificant article of property, when compared with the small value he sets on time and labour. The price of a horse having been agreed upon, this man refused to throw into the bargain a bit of old home-made rope which served as a halter, the value of which was infinitesimal. He did not yield the point until the next morning, some time after our caravan had started, when, our own men being far ahead, he expressed his readiness to lead the horses for Bower all the way to the next stage, eighteen miles away, and return home on foot, without remuneration.

There are no such things as unconsidered trifles for the ordinary Asiatic; he eagerly clings to his every possession. I caught my servant, for instance, hoarding on the march all sorts of odds and ends—empty bottles, meat-tins and jam-pots, sheepskins and feathers—the whole lot worth, say, one shilling, but for the carriage of which all over the Maharajah's dominions by some seventy marches Babu Khan would have quietly left me to pay some thirty times as much. I had a great emptying-out of kiltas at Leh, and threw away a coolie-load of rubbish, to the unutterable grief of the poor old man, bereft thus of his hoarded treasures.

At Tashgam we were still among Mahomedans, but these were converted, or perverted, Ladaki Buddhists, and spoke the Tibetan tongue. Instead of the greeting of 'salaam,' the word with which we were welcomed here, and on all the road beyond, was the Tibetan equivalent, *jooly*.

CHAPTER VIII

KARGIL—OASIS CULTIVATION—TIBETAN TABLE-LANDS—SHERGOL—A BUDDHIST COUNTRY—THE LAMASERY—RED LAMAS—SKOOSHOKS—THEORY OF REINCARNATION.

On May 25 we travelled two stages to the village of Kargil, a distance of twenty-four miles. This is the capital of the extensive district of the same name. The Thanadar of Dras, who had met us at Matayun, was still with us; but at Kargil he handed us over to the thanadar of that district, who in his turn escorted us to the next district; and so on. For such are the marks of honour with which one travelling like Bower, on Imperial service, is received in Kashmir; his march is like a royal progress.

This day the place selected for our midday halt and meal was near the hamlet of Chanegund. There was a characteristic bit of Ladaki scenery on the other side of the river, of which I decided to take a photograph. I was perched on a rock, and was about to withdraw the cap from the lens, when a most unexpected gust of wind—for it was a calm day—struck the apparatus, and sent it rolling down the rocks. When I picked it up I found the camera seemingly beyond any possibility of repair in this wild country, where skilled mechanics there were none. My dismay at this catastrophe can be imagined. I was deprived of the means of taking pictures now that I was at the very threshold of one of the most interesting countries in the world to delineate. I gathered the fragments together and marched on, in no good temper with things in general. My foolish Babu Khan tried to sympathise with me. 'It must have cost so many rupees,' he lamented. The waste of hard cash, and not the irreparable loss of my pictures, was all he could realise.

The scene I was about to photograph would have made a good illustration of the method of irrigation by which small patches of this desert are reclaimed. The mountains that sloped to the torrent-bed on the other side of the valley were perfectly bare and very steep; but nearly half-way up this dreary wall of rock, some thousands of feet above the river, one long, thin, green, horizontal line extended both up and down the valley as far as one could see, following for leagues every inequality of the mountain-side, round projecting bluffs and retreating hollows. This was an irrigation-canal, that brought water from the glacier-fed stream of some distant nullah—a stream which had probably to be tapped high up, before it was swallowed and lost in the great slopes of débris that form the bases of the mountains.

Some of the cliffs, along whose face this little canal had been carried, appeared from where we were to be quite inaccessible, and a great deal of patient labour must be needed to construct and keep in repair such a work as this. The line of these canals is always easily distinguished by the narrow belt of wild vegetation which the water nourishes on its course, the green band standing out brightly against the everywhere else naked hillside.

Nearly opposite Chanegund was a small hamlet with a curious little bit of cultivation round it, which was to have been the central object of my photograph. A fan-shaped slope of débris here issued from the mouth of a dry nullah, and to this some of the water from the canal high above had been carried down, converting it into a triangle of vivid green.

From Chanegund our way led through a desert ravine with mighty cliffs towering on either side. The narrow bridle-path was generally high above the torrent, carried along the face of precipices, or winding over great landslips of brown rocks. The road had been broken away a good deal in places, but our surefooted little hill-ponies bore us across with perfect safety.

Not far from Chanegund the Dras stream flows into the Suru River, the united waters joining the Indus some twelve miles farther on. To follow these valleys would seem to be the natural route to Leh; but the Indus, for some twenty-five miles below its junction with the Suru, is hemmed in by such lofty and perpendicular precipices, rising for many thousands of feet on either side above the raging torrent, that the natives, adepts as they are at opening out hill-tracks, throwing frail wooden scaffoldings and ladders from ledge to ledge across the face of cliffs, have here not found it possible to make a coolie-road of the roughest description—and what is called a rough road in this country is calculated to make one's hair stand on end. The road to Leh, therefore, at this point diverges up a tributary nullah of the Suru, as a reference to the map will show, and after crossing two passes descends to the Indus Valley near Khalsi, five marches from Chanegund, and above the impracticable gorges.

In order to avoid the same difficulties, the road from Leh to Skardu, by which I travelled later on, instead of following the Indus all the way, leaves it at Hanu, and pushes into the highlands, to cross a pass nearly 17,000 feet above the sea.

In the course of my journey I marched through the whole Indus Valley—this one bad bit, which defies the native roadmaker, excepted—from Leh, to where the river flows across the frontier into the unexplored region of Chilas. Such a long series of stupendous gorges exists, I should imagine, in no other portion of the globe. On the so-called roads which penetrate these ravines one has to scale cliff-sides by means of small wooden pegs let into the rock, or swarm up a tree-trunk leading from one narrow ledge to another twenty feet above it. In places one creeps along the face of a perpendicular wall of rock, holding on to the slight crevices with fingers and toes, a fall of hundreds of feet being the consequence of a false step. These tracks are very fatiguing as well as difficult, for there is a terrible lot of going up and down stairs on nearly every day's march. Every now and again, in order to circumvent some impassable precipice overhanging the river, the road abruptly ascends some six thousand feet or so, to descend again as steeply on the farther side of the obstacle. In comparison to such ways as these the Leh road is an exceedingly easy one.

Near the junction of the Dras and Suru we rode through a typical Tibetan oasis. It was as a bit of Devonshire in springtime dropped down in the midst of sands and crags arid as those round Aden. This little plot of cultivation was about two hundred yards square, and was intersected like a chessboard with tiny irrigation-ditches, through which the cold, clear, mountain water babbled merrily. It was the greenest and freshest garden imaginable, and all the birds and butterflies for miles around appeared to have found this out, and were collected in this pleasant place. Here were patches of young corn and deep grass full of flowers, among which the currant, gooseberry, and rose bushes grew luxuriantly, while willows and fruit-trees afforded a grateful shade. The narrow fringe of uncultivated, partly-watered land which divided the oasis from the surrounding wilderness was blue with iris blossoms. It amazes one to discover that by judiciously scattering a little water over granite dust such exuberant fertility can be brought about.

For the greater part of the way to Leh the traveller finds himself winding along deep and narrow gorges, where the scenery is often extremely grand, but also gloomy and somewhat depressing, in consequence of the absence of vegetation. At intervals these gorges suddenly open out, the mountains on either side retreating, and leaving a broad, flat valley-bottom between them; it is in these openings only that cultivation is practicable, and here what, if left to Nature, would be a stony and sandy desert, is converted by the industry of man into a fertile oasis. After marching for hours down some barren and sunless defile, it is pleasant to suddenly emerge on one of these open, sunlit spaces, green with waving corn and groves of fruit-trees.

Kargil, our this day's destination, is the most extensive oasis in this part of the country. It fills a broad and beautiful vale, which the Suru River enters, and out of which it flows, by narrow gorges. Though surrounded by bare mountains, this green valley has a very pleasing appearance after the desolate country that is traversed to approach it. The natives of Ladak think a great deal of the Vale of Kargil, and consider it to be one of the most fertile districts in the universe.

It is, indeed, a sort of paradise for Tibet, which after all is not very high praise.

As we neared the serai, the Thanadar of Kargil, accompanied by several gaily-attired notables, rode out to meet us. They brought us the usual *dalis*, or presents, as tokens of their respect: large metal dishes of dried currants and apricots, and a basket of sugar candy. They also held out rupees to us in their open hands, a generosity which, like the courteous Spaniard's gifts, must, of course, not be understood too literally. The proper thing is to touch the proffered coins with one's finger, in polite signification of acceptance, but not to take up the rupees. These offerings of money are always made to the honoured visitor, and the sum varies in proportion to the wealth and position of the two parties. Thus, a rajah will send one a large bowl of rupees, which have to be gratefully acknowledged, and then returned. As one marches along these roads, one is continually met by natives who step forward to present their little offerings: two lumps of sugar, or three dried apricots, or what not. One can often tell a man's trade by his dali. Each brings of what he has or produces. Thus, the miller comes out of his mill with a little saucer of flour; the farmer with a handful of corn; the very poor man with a bunch of wild roses, to show that he has no possessions save those things that Nature gives to all men freely; and the tax-collector, or other official, quite as appropriately, makes his sham gift of the rupees he has extorted from his neighbours. I need scarcely say that in many cases these kind attentions are intended as gentle hints that bakshish would not be unacceptable.

As soon as we were settled in the rest-house, on an open whitewashed verandah, where we put up our beds and table, and made ourselves generally at home in full view of the admiring population, which crowded round to gaze at us, I bethought myself of my wrecked camera, and after an examination was inclined to think that I could patch it up sufficiently for use if I had the necessary tools. I consulted the lumbadar, who told me that there was a very clever carpenter in the village, for whom he would at once send.

This skilful artificer soon arrived: a good-natured Ladaki, with a stolid face like that of a Chinese idol, puckered up into an inscrutable and perpetual smile. He spoke little, considered the ruins of the camera, nodded his head as if perfectly satisfied with his capacity for dealing with the job, went off, and came back with all his tools, consisting of a hatchet, a sledgehammer, a large coarse saw, and a drill three-quarters of an inch in diameter. What he proposed to do with the camera I know not; but I rescued it from his hands just as he was about to attack it with the saw, and peremptorily bade him begone.

The wooden framework of the camera had been broken in several places, and the bellows were torn away. It was not an easy business to tackle without tools, but I set to work, so anxious was I not to be deprived of my means of taking pictures. I procured some native glue, and employed this where possible; then I extracted a few superfluous screws from the apparatus, and with them screwed together the broken portions. The only tool at my disposal for boring the preliminary holes for these screws was a large needle, which I made red-hot with a candle-flame and an improvised paper blowpipe, a tedious but successful process, which surprised and delighted the crowd of spectators. Then I replaced the broken focus-glass with a half-plate, from which I had washed off the chemicals, and on which I had pasted a bit of tissue-paper; and at last, to my own astonishment and great satisfaction, the camera was mended and apparently solid enough. For all practical purposes it indeed proved as good as ever. The good-natured people round seemed as pleased as myself at my success, and a chorus of some Tibetan equivalent for bravo greeted the result of my labours. While I was thus employed Bower was horse-dealing again, and succeeded in adding a few more animals to his troop of baggage-ponies.

Our next march—May 26—took us through scenery of true Tibetan aspect. Close to Kargil the road leaves the valleys for a time, and after ascending the bare mountain-side, we found ourselves on a stony table-land of considerable elevation. From here we perceived many similar plateaus all round us. The prospect was grand and interesting, and the immensity of the landscape gave a pleasant sense of freedom after the contracted views in the narrow gorges we had been traversing. Between these high table-lands we could see the profound defiles of the different rivers winding in and out, and here and there the green patch of an oasis, far beneath, relieving the prevailing barrenness. We also saw the summits of the surrounding mountains, which had been invisible from the valleys below—dreary masses of rock, bare of forest or pasture, and streaked with snow. The sky was cloudless, and of the beautiful transparent pale blue characteristic of the Tibetan regions. The wind, too, up here was of Tibetan keenness, absolutely dry, and deliciously bracing. As Euripides said of the Athenians, so, too, the Ladakis are 'ever delicately treading through most pellucid air.' One feels as if one could never get tired in such a climate.

In this thin, dry air, far-off objects appear quite near; mountains sixty miles away might be heaps of stones forty yards off, and *vice versâ*. There is no atmospheric effect to give any idea of distance. All the details of a landscape seem equally distant, and one looks out upon the world almost as did the boy cured of blindness, quoted by Bishop Berkeley, to whom all at first was like a picture painted on the eye. It is impossible here to judge the distance of even familiar objects whose size one knows, for the air has a curious magnifying effect, due to a form of mirage. Black yaks or sheep on far hillsides appear monstrously big; a solitary tree, plainly visible, may be two days' journey off. We saw a woman walking in the valley below us; she looked like a giantess. There was a lack of proportion and perspective that produced a strangely unreal effect. It was like a land in a dream.

After crossing this table-land we descended to the valley of the Wakka, a small tributary of the Suru. We passed the village and fair oasis of Paskil, and rode into a strange gorge, with rock pinnacles on either side, shaped like castle towers and cathedral spires. The scenery was becoming more uncanny as we advanced, which was as it should be; for we were now entering the country of those uncanny people, the Tibetan Buddhists. We followed this wild defile for many miles, the road crossing the torrent several times, and often zigzagging high up the cliff-side in order to avoid projecting spurs. At last, after a rather long day's march, and being utterly weary of these imprisoning crags, we suddenly opened out another of those pleasant cultivated vales that are so grateful to the traveller, and perceived our welcome destination, the village of Shergol, ahead of us.

This is the first Buddhist village on the road. It is a labyrinth of rather well-built mud houses, with narrow alleys between. The curious, calm people were sitting on the flat roofs as we approached, and appeared to be silently meditating on Nirvana, or other far-off, solemn

SHERGOL GOMPA.

things, but their minds were most probably vacant of any idea. Towering above the houses were gigantic *chortens*, or sarcophagi, of dried mud, gaily painted, containing the ashes of pious lamas.

On the mountain-side, near the village, is a *gompa*, or monastery of lamas, to which I hastened with my camera as soon as we had established ourselves in the serai. The illustration will show what this extraordinary place is like. The Buddhist of Tibet, while he despises the beautiful, has a love for the horrible and grotesque in Nature. He builds his monastery on what to ordinary men would appear to be the most undesirable spot possible: he perches it on the summit of some almost inaccessible pinnacle, or burrows into the face of some frightful precipice. Like the solitaries of the 'Thebaid,' he seeks scenes of desolation, and in this desert country he has no difficulty in finding what he requires. The Lamasery, or Gompa, of Shergol, is carved out of a honeycombed cliff, forming with some other cliffs of the same description a giant flight of stairs on the slope of a bleak mountain of loose stones. The gompa itself is painted white, with bands of bright colour on the projecting wooden gallery, so that it stands out distinctly against the darker rocks. There is not a sign of vegetation near; all round is a dreary waste of stones alone.

From this lamas' retreat the view of the mountains on the other side of the broad valley is in itself particularly fantastic. I shall often have to employ this last adjective when writing of Ladak. It expresses the genius of the land. The country itself is fantastic, and the fantastic race who dwell in it do all they can to assist Nature, and make their surroundings still more fantastic than they are. These mountains which face the monastery are of considerable height, and their slopes, though possibly formed of rugged débris, from this distance appear perfectly smooth, falling to the bed of the river in regular furrows and in waves overlapping each other, like those one often sees on a stream of lava that has cooled. These undulations are of various vivid colours—great streaks, a mile long, of pink, ochre, white, green, blue, brick-red, and here and there of coal-black. The effect is very curious.

It looks as if some Brobdingnagian child had been making experiments with its first box of paints, and had daubed the mountain-side with one colour after the other. This must form a delightful scene to the meditating lamas of the Gompa. They would have painted all the mountains just like this had they been able. I daresay they would tell one that some pious incarnation with miraculous powers had come from Lassa and executed this work of art. I wonder, by the way, what these people would do in the way of improving, to their ideas, the appearance of the clear blue heaven that hangs above their country, were they able to get at it.

We were at last well in the land of the pigtails. All the men in Shergol wore these appendages in the Chinese fashion, and had features of the pure Tibetan type, there being little, if any, admixture of Aryan blood here. I soon realised that I had reached a very strange land, a country of topsy-turveydom, where polyandry prevails instead of polygamy, where praying is all conducted by machinery, and where, in short, the traveller fresh from beyond the mountains is bewildered by the quaint sights, the strange beliefs, superstitions, and customs he comes across every day.

For some time I was greatly puzzled while wandering through this region. It all, in a way, seemed so familiar to me. Surely I had somewhere, long ago, lived amid this curious people and in such a weird land as this—but when and where? Was I myself a Ladaki re-incarnated in England by mistake? was I a degraded Mahatma, now recognising feebly once more the long-lost country of my origin? The idea was not a pleasant one, and I felt quite relieved, at last, when the explanation of this mysterious feeling flashed across me. Yes; I had lived before among these people. I remembered that when a small boy I had read 'Gulliver's Travels,' and that the voyage to the flying island of Laputa had made a great impression on my imagination. I had conjured up that kingdom to my mind just such a perspectiveless, artificial, unreal-looking land as this; and just such a people as these queer Ladakis had those no more queer people, the Laputans and the sages of Balnibarri, appeared to my fancy. They are fantastic in the same way. Both are as ingenious in grotesque and objectless invention as they are stupid and clumsy in the ordinary avocations of life. The Ladakis, like the Luggnaggians, have their immortals, the ancient and dreamy skooshoks, whose acquaintance I was to make later on. How pleased, too, would these lamas, who love to have their homes as near the sky as possible, be if they could separate them from the mountain and dwell in gompas floating in mid-air like Laputa, far above the world of ordinary men, which to them is so vain and uninteresting.

I did not visit the interior of Shergol Monastery, but walked across the stony desert to the foot of it, and saw for the first time the lamas I had so often heard of, who passed by me as if not observing me, evincing no curiosity, not even saluting me with a jooly, but apparently wrapped in their own thoughts.

These were Red lamas, who alone are found in Ladak; whereas the Yellow lamas, who are in many respects more ascetic and strict than the Red, are the prevalent sect in Chinese Tibet. The Red lamas are, for the most part, as dirty and ragged as the itinerant beggar-monks of Southern Europe, whom they much resemble in appearance. One could not fail at once to recognise these men as monks. There is a remarkable

K

likeness, so far only, of course, as form and outward appearance is concerned, between the Buddhist Church in Tibet and the Church of Rome; and anyone who has seen the religious ceremonies at Himis, for example, cannot but conclude that this likeness is too complete to be due to mere coincidence.

The Red lama wears a red petticoat, and throws over his shoulders a large red shawl, which leaves his left arm bare. His head is close-shaven, and when out of doors he dons a little red cap with ear-flaps, of the same shape as that worn by the laity. He always carries about with him a praying-wheel, a rosary, and a bottle of holy water.

Ladak is still almost as theocratic a country as Chinese Tibet, despite its conquest by the Kashmir State half a century ago. The lamas, who, as I have already said, recognise as their spiritual, and in some respects temporal, ruler, the Delai Lama, or Grand Lama of Tibet, at Lassa, are too powerful to have suffered much from the interference of the Dogra Government. No less than one-sixth of the population of Ladak are in the Church, either as monks or nuns; and as almost each family, wealthy or poor, contributes one or more of its members to the priesthood, the Church is a popular institution, and any interference with its privileges is bitterly resented. Unwarlike and timid as the Ladakis are, they are ready to fight in defence of their lamas, and a few years since, when it was proposed to increase the revenue paid by the monasteries, the country was on the brink of revolution, and artillery had to be brought out to overawe the rioters in the bazaar at Leh. The lamas of Lassa are always intriguing and fostering sedition in Ladak. The Kashmir Government now forbids any communication by letter on secular business between the lamas of Ladak and those of Chinese Tibet; but a good deal of correspondence is smuggled across the frontier. Some letters that have been intercepted have been found to contain very compromising matter.

The Church of Ladak is very well endowed. Its extensive estates comprise much of the most fertile land in the country, and on this the State exacts as revenue only one-sixth of the amount per acre that has to be paid in the case of private land. It is also said that the monasteries own pastures and cultivated land in remote valleys, the existence of which is unknown to, or ignored by, the authorities, so that no revenue at all is levied on them. A rich monastery, too, has no difficulty in obtaining leniency of assessment by the bribery of the tax-collectors. When Lawrence extends his Land Settlement to Ladak he will certainly have some difficult problems to deal with.

These lamaseries appear to be organised in a very business-like way. There are two classes of monks in each. There are, in the first place, the working monks, who attend to the temporal interests of the community. These cultivate the land, collect the rents of the monastery tenants, travel through the villages to beg alms for the brotherhood, and advance coin and grain to farmers at a usurious rate of interest. Among this class is the steward, who keeps the monastery accounts. The second class is composed of the spiritual monks, who have nothing to do with worldly matters, but devote their time to dreaming and religious exercises, and to whom, to judge from their abstracted expression and general appearance, the bladder-flappers of the Laputan sages would be useful attendants, to wake them up when it was time to wash. Their sole duties are to mumble and intone words they do not understand, and to dance the complicated figures of the sacred dances. From this class the abbot is chosen, and in a few cases a monastery has as its spiritual head a very holy person indeed, no less than a skooshok, or incarnation. When Lord Roberts visited Srinagur, the Skooshok of Spitak Gompa was presented to him. This personage is supposed to have been re-incarnated seventeen times, and in his first stage to have been a contemporary of Buddha.

Mr. Ramsey, late Assistant-Commissioner (as our Resident in Ladak is called), has put his researches into the form of an excellent dictionary of Western Tibet, in which he gives a complete account of these skooshoks. It seems that after a man has attained a high pitch of virtue, and has thus escaped liability to re-birth in any of the six ordinary spheres, he can, when he dies, either enter the Nirvana he has earned, or return to the earth as an incarnation, or skooshok. Only four monasteries in all Ladak now have resident skooshoks as their spiritual heads—saints who have rejected the desirable Nirvana in order that they may live again to do good to their fellow-men.

When one of these is about to die, he calls around him his disciples, and tells them where he will be re-born and all the circumstances of the re-birth. As soon as he is dead the disciples repair to the place he has indicated and search for a newly-born child which bears the sacred marks, and is for other reasons the most probable incarnation of the departed saint. Having found the child, they leave him with his mother till he is four years old, when they return, bringing with them a quantity of praying-books, rosaries, praying-wheels, bells, and other priestly articles, among which are those that belonged to the late incarnation. Then the child has to prove that he is the new incarnation by recognising the property that was his in his previous existence, and by relating reminiscences of his past. If he is successful in this, as is nearly always the case, he is acknowledged as the skooshok, and is carried off for ever from his home and family, to be educated in the sacred mysteries, first in the gompa of which he is to be the head, and afterwards, for some years, in the sacred city of Lassa. He then returns to his own gompa, therein to take up his residence in a separate building, not busying himself with the worldly affairs of the brotherhood, but dreaming away the long, quiet years until the time comes for him again to die, and be re-born in another earthly body. All those who know this country best affirm that skooshoks and lamas, as well as the people, have an absolute belief in this strange theory of metempsychosis, and that even the selection of the property of the late skooshok by the child is not due to collusion or trickery—at any rate, of a conscious sort. But the Ladakis have a magnificent capacity for belief. One of their articles of faith is an exceedingly convenient one in a country where morals are so lax as in Tibet. It appears that in some districts, when an unmarried girl gives birth to a child the father is presumed to have been a god, and the child is devoted, as a sacred creature, to the priesthood.

It is strange, by the way, that one never hears of Mahatmas in Ladak or in Tibet proper. The lamas know nothing of the mysterious beings who are supposed to dwell in their midst, and who, while disdaining to manifest themselves to their own people, apparently delight in carrying on a telepathic communication of a trivial, if miraculous, kind with their alien disciples in England and America. The nearest approach to a Mahatma that one comes across in these regions is the skooshok; but I much doubt whether a European esoteric Buddhist would accept one of these incarnations as his spiritual master. Bower traversed Chinese Tibet from end to end, but found no signs of a Mahatma.

No one can treat with ridicule the beautiful teachings of Prince Siddhartha, and it is not altogether strange that among the enlightened peoples of Europe he now has followers as well as admirers; but these inhabitants of the Himalayan highlands have corrupted almost beyond recognition his pure and wise doctrines, and have buried with absurdities all that was eternally true in them. A visit to Tibet is apt to destroy many illusions. It is better to read of Buddhism in the glowing pages of 'The Light of Asia' than to contemplate it from too near. As it exists in these regions, Buddhism is fantastic, and most interesting to study; but it is as degraded a system of idolatry as has ever been practised by a people outside savagery. The priests themselves have long-since forgotten the signification of the many complicated ceremonies, forms, and symbols of their religion, and all that remains is an unmeaning superstition.

The laity take a conveniently lax view of their religious duties. 'I know nothing about my religion' the Ladaki peasant will tell one. 'It is not my affair. It is the business of the lamas. We pay them to pray for us and see that all is right with our souls.' The bulk of the praying is, as everyone knows, carried on by machinery in Ladak. For instance, wheels containing rolls of prayers are turned by water-power; and every time a wheel revolves it is working out the salvation of the man who put it up: every turn exempts him from some infinitesimal portion of time which would otherwise be passed in one of the six inferior spheres. If he have a big enough wheel and sufficient water-power, he may hope to close one after another the gates of these spheres, and attain the 'perfect peace' on death. Ramsey, in his book, describes these six spheres, which come thus in order of merit:—*Illa*, or gods; demigods; man; animals; *eedak*, a fabulous animal always suffering hunger or thirst, having a large belly and a long, thin neck, through which enough food can never pass; temporary hell. In order to escape these existences it is only necessary, according to Tibetan belief, to twist round a wheel so many millions of times. Piety here appears to have nothing to do with moral conduct; it is but a question of the multitudinous turning of wheels, waving of flags, and mumbling of syllables that have no sense.

But, after all, this Tibetan belief is not so far more foolish and corrupt than some forms of so-called Christianity we come across in Europe. The tenets of some of our own sects gone a little madder than they already are would not be unlike those of Ladak, a land, indeed, which, even as Laputa, is a living satire on the civilisation of the world.

CHAPTER IX

CHARACTER OF THE LADAKIS—THEIR DRESS—THE PEYRAK—POLYANDRY—LAW OF ENTAIL—MAGPA WEDLOCK—PRAYER BY MACHINERY—MANIS AND CHORTENS—MULBEK—THE NAMIKA LA—KHARBU—PRAYING-WHEELS.

HAVING photographed the gompa, I returned to the serai, in front of which I found a crowd of natives assembled, Bower in the midst of them, bargaining over some horses that had been brought for his inspection. These men did not jabber and lie, fawn and smile falsely, after the manner of a Kashmiri who is trying to sell something, but argued the point out in a quiet, frank, good-humoured way that impressed one favourably. One comes to like these amiable Ladaki Buddhists; they are highly spoken of by all who have travelled in their country, as being truthful, honest, hospitable, and straightforward. They are a harmless, simple race, with none of the narrow bigotry and caste prejudices which draw so impassable a chasm between the peoples of India holding other creeds and ourselves. A Ladaki Buddhist has no objection to eating food with a Christian, or to drinking out of a cup that has been used by him. He does not look upon us as unclean beasts. He does not hide his women from our gaze, and these uncomely creatures wander about openly and unveiled, stare the Englishman boldly in the face, and greet him with a cheerful smile. All this makes Ladak a far pleasanter land to travel in than either a Hindoo or a

Mahomedan country, with their barriers of reserve and seclusion, which make it so extremely difficult for the stranger to acquire any but the most superficial knowledge of the natives. The Ladaki, on the other hand, will welcome one to his house, admit one into his most sacred buildings, and allow one to be present at any of his religious ceremonies, concealing nothing, and ready to give any explanation that is required of him.

Following a religion that never persecutes, he is very tolerant to other creeds, though he adheres firmly to his own. He seeks to make no converts, but treats the unbeliever with a good-natured pity. He knows in his heart that his European friend is doomed, on death, not to enjoy Nirvana and be absorbed into Deity like himself, but to be re-born in lower and vile forms, or to be hunted through space by demons into the abyss of dark nothingness; but he is too polite to allude to this. He is sorry in his mild fashion for the unfortunate man, but sees no reason to treat him uncharitably in this world on account of his coming misfortunes in the next.

In Ladak both men and women are warmly clothed, even in summer. The male costume consists of a thick woollen frock reaching to the ankles, girded in the middle with a cloth band; on the head is a little cloth cap with two ear-flaps, which are generally turned up, so that from a distance a man appears to be provided with a pair of long ears like a satyr. The women, too, are so well rolled up in clothes that they display figures of about the elegance of a beer barrel; they wear shapeless frocks reaching to their ankles, thick cloaks of sheepskin, and boots as clumsy as those of the men. The very limited charms with which they have been favoured by Nature are not heightened by any artifice. Their coiffure is peculiarly unbecoming to their coarse Tartar features. On either cheek hangs a great bunch of coarse black hair, while the ornament known as the *peyrak*, which is peculiar to ladies of Tibet, covers the top of the head and falls some way down the back. The peyrak is a piece of leather studded with flat turquoises; it is about two feet in length and about eight inches broad. The turquoises vary in size from that of a two-shilling piece downwards; they are found in Chinese Tibet, are of a greenish colour, and of infe-

LADAKI WOMEN, WEARING THE PEYRAK.

rior quality. However, a good peyrak may be worth as much as twenty-five pounds. All the personal property of a Ladaki woman is invested in the turquoises of her peyrak, so that while walking behind her it is easy for a fortune-hunting swain to estimate at a glance the value of an heiress.

The men wear a long pigtail like the Chinese, and their Mongolian physiognomies, with small Tartar eyes and flattish nose, give them a decidedly Chinese appearance. But a jolly Ladaki is a man one can understand and get on with, and his character is entirely different to that of the inscrutable, and, to the European idea, scarcely human, inhabitant of the Celestial Empire.

One of the first things that strikes the traveller in Ladak, especially if he comes from the poverty-stricken adjoining country of Baltistan, is the extremely well-to-do appearance of all the people. The houses are well-built, and there is often an attempt at comfort and ornament that seems quite luxurious after the miserable huts and the squalor of the other mountain races. It must be allowed that the Ladakis are a very dirty people indeed; but this is from choice, and not from poverty, for it is rare to see a man or woman who is not well clad and well nourished. Beggars and very poor people are but rarely met with here; and it is easy to see that the cultivators are fairly prosperous, and exempt from the hard hand-to-mouth struggle for bare subsistence which is the lot of their Mahomedan neighbours.

This happy condition of the Ladakis is due to the curious, and, to our ideas, unpleasant custom of polyandry, to which the merit must be allowed of keeping the population within reasonable limits in an unfertile region. Polyandry appears to be singularly well suited to the country and to the character of this people. Europeans who have resided here say that, so far as they can observe, the system is attended with no peculiar evil results of its own.

The improvident Mussulman Baltis, with their plurality of wives and large families, are miserably poor, and drag along a pitiable existence on the verge of starvation. But it is far more necessary to keep down the population in Ladak than in Baltistan. A great portion of the Baltis inhabit valleys at a comparatively low elevation above the sea, where the summer heats are often as intense as in the Punjab. Inured to extremes of climate, they are consequently fitted to emigrate, which they do in great numbers, engaging themselves as coolies and navvies.

But the Ladakis, accustomed to high elevations only, succumb to bilious fever when they reach the plains, and soon die when taken from their highlands. Again, their religion, language, and strange ways generally, differing so vastly from those of all neighbouring countries, necessarily isolate them; they are naturally unwilling to leave their mountains to live among aliens prejudiced against them, and not likely to receive them in too friendly a manner. For this race emigration is not a feasible relief to over-population, so polyandry has been devised as a substitute.

The custom of polyandry is intimately connected with the law of entail which prevails in Ladak. This ancient Tibetan civilisation has developed a system of land-tenure almost as complicated as our own, and which is admirably adapted to maintain the prosperity of the cultivator, despite the natural poverty of the country.

The first curious point to notice in this system is that the eldest married son of a family is placed in a better position than his own father, and is practically the head of the family. For as soon as the eldest son marries he enters into possession of the family estate, a small portion only being retained by his parents for the support of themselves and their unmarried daughters; and that portion also becomes the property of the eldest son on the death of the parents and marriage of the daughters. But the eldest son, when thus marrying and taking possession of the family estate, is obliged to support the two sons next to himself in age; and these two are not allowed to contract independent marriages, but share the wife of their eldest brother, becoming the minor husbands of that lady. The children of this strange union recognise all three husbands as father, but pay more respect to the eldest, as the head of the family. If there are more brothers than two, the others do not share the family wife, but have to leave the estate and seek their fortunes outside, becoming lamas, or earning their living by working as coolies, or, if they be fortunate, as *magpas*: and what the profession of magpa is I shall presently explain.

The two younger brothers, though minor husbands to the wife, are always in an inferior position, and are often little better than servants to the eldest brother, who is looked upon as the sole owner of the property by the Kashmir State, and as such is alone made responsible for the revenue and contribution of forced labour.

If the eldest brother dies, the wife, provided she has no children, can rid herself of his brothers, who are her minor husbands, by a simple ceremony. One of her fingers is attached with a thread to a finger of her dead husband. The thread is then broken, and by this action she is divorced from the corpse, and consequently from the two surviving brothers at the same time.

This is a country where women's rights are thoroughly understood and respected. The ladies of Ladak labour under no legal disabilities, and, far from being treated as inferiors, after the usual Oriental fashion, in many respects are in a better position than the men. If there be no son, the eldest daughter inherits the land, and in this case the Ladak heiress enjoys a delightfully independent condition, which, I imagine, would satisfy the most exacting of those ladies at home who are shrieking against the restrictions and obligations of our old-fashioned matrimonial law. The happy heiress of Ladak does not, unless she wish it, marry an eldest son and his two younger brothers with him according to the system I have just described, but if she prefers it—and she generally does prefer it—she enters into another kind of marriage contract, with one man at a time, a contract which, so far as she is concerned, binds with no strong ties, but which is recognised as being quite respectable, and for which the lamas have arranged a special religious ceremony. The lady selects some—according to Tibetan standard—well-favoured younger brother of a large family, who, therefore, has no interest in the lands of his family or share in his eldest brother's wife, and she makes this person her magpa, as this sort of husband is called. The magpa husband of an heiress has to behave himself if he wishes to retain his position. He is the property of his wife, and cannot leave her, except in the case of gross misconduct on her part. But if she is displeased with him, she can turn him out of doors, and be rid of him, without any excuse or form of divorce. Ramsey says she generally gives him a sheep or a few rupees when thus discharging him. She is then quite free to take unto herself another magpa.

A Ladaki rarely divorces his wife. He is a very practical-minded and complaisant husband; his jealousy takes no violent form; he is, as a rule, willing to dispassionately discuss his dishonour with a detected lover, assess the damages his wife's indiscretion has inflicted on him, and compound the matter for a sheep or a few rupees.

Polyandry has a tendency, as is well known, to keep down the population in more than one way, and a noticeable feature of this country is the paucity of children: though one sees women everywhere, the children are few and far between, and those one does meet appear to be rather silent and sedate little creatures, mildly happy, as Buddhists should be, but not much given to childish games. In Mahomedan Baltistan, on the other hand, the women scurry away into the houses as the unbelieving sahib approaches—one scarcely ever sees them. But a Balti village rings with the merry noise of playing children, and one comes across shoals of the dirty, ragged, or naked little creatures, full of fun, though half-starved, tumbling about in every lane and field.

Shergol is the farthest outpost of Western Buddhism; and beyond this we were constantly encountering by the wayside some signs of the creed of the lamas—altars, images, and monuments of various sorts. If one judged from the multitude of these, one would conclude this to be the most religious country in the world. This is what one would expect in a land where religion takes outward and visible forms only, which the traveller can see for himself as he goes along; where all the praying of the inhabitants is performed for them by the idols of their own making, devotion and doctrine taking material form in stocks and stones. Each day's journey now brought us into a more religious region, until, in the vicinity of Lamayuru and Leh praying flags, altars, *mani*, and *chortens* were to be seen scattered over the whole face of the country, every prominent pinnacle of rock being fashioned into a prayer or idol.

On May 27 we had an interesting march of eighteen miles to Kharbu. Outside Shergol we saw the first mani, or wall of praying-stones. The illustration represents a typical mani. This is a massive stone wall or embankment about eight feet in height, its top sloping from the centre to either side, like the roof of a house. Every one of the large flat stones that form this roof is elaborately carved in the pictorial characters of Tibet with prayers, generally with the inscription, '*Om mani patmi Om*,' a prayer that is repeated in a variety of ways many millions of times each day in this country, and which is, perhaps, the most largely employed prayer in the universe. The translation of these mystic

MANI AND CHORTENS.

syllables is merely, '*O! thou jewel in the Lotus, O!*' If a native be asked what this phrase signifies, he will reply that he does not know, but that the words are very holy, and that the repetition of them is a sacred duty. Ramsey says one explanation is that each of the six syllables of the prayer represents one of the six spheres in which a soul can be re-born, and that by constant repetition of them the doors of each of these spheres may be closed, and hence Nirvana be obtained on death. Thus, *Om*, repeated often enough, will close the gate of the Fairy sphere, *ma* that of the Demigod sphere, and so on.

These walls of stone, some a mile in length, are found everywhere in Ladak, generally at the entrance of villages, but sometimes far away from any habitation. The thousands of stones composing a mani will all pray for one of the faithful, or, rather, by their magic power lessen the periods of purgatory for him and bring him by some space of time nearer Nirvana, whenever he walks by them, provided he take care to leave the mani on his right hand. Thus it is that a road always divides on approaching a mani, a path running on each side, so as to accommodate a traveller coming from either direction.

The stones forming a mani vary in size from a few inches to four or five feet in diameter. The carvings are often artistic and beautiful. Images of Buddha and designs of mystic figures are represented upon them, as well as prayers. The carving is done by pious lamas, generally from Lassa, who travel through Buddhist countries in order to perform this holy duty, and hasten thereby for miserable mankind the release from the evils of existence. To wander over the face of the earth through all one's life and chisel holy symbols on every crag one passes on the wayside is, according to this people, the noblest pursuit to which an earthly saint can devote himself.

At either end of the mani in the illustration is a large chorten, of the shape most frequently met with in Ladak. After the corpse of a Buddhist has been burnt by the lamas, some of the ashes of the dead man are mixed with clay and moulded into a little idol, which, if the deceased was a man of wealth, is placed by itself in the middle of a chorten built expressly for it; if he was a poor man, his idol is placed in some old chorten, with other idols of the poor. I have found the cavities of ancient chortens filled with these little images.

About three miles from Shergol we passed the village of Mulbek, a curious place, with many manis and chortens, and a monastery perched on the rocks above. By the roadside near the village is a colossal idol of the god Chamba, carved on the face of an isolated rock. At the foot of this I found Subhana, who had gone ahead with the camera, awaiting me with a broad smile on his face. He had come to the conclusion that this idol was just the sort of thing I should like to photograph, and he was evidently highly pleased with himself when I proceeded to take a picture of it. Subhana prided himself on knowing what was worth photographing and what was not; and this intelligent Kashmiri, after a little experience of my ways, hit the mark as a rule. Sometimes, it is true, I found him patiently waiting for me, with camera ready, before some object so entirely devoid of any sort of interest that it was puzzling to conjecture by what strange workings of his mind he had come to consider it pictorially valuable.

The idols of Ladak were, of course, regarded by Subhana and our other Mussulman followers with a contemptuous amusement. Those who had not visited the land before seemed to think that we had brought them into the midst of the most wicked idolaters on earth.

When we entered the village of Mulbek the male population was sitting in groups, silent and motionless, on the flat house-tops. As we passed each house, the dingy-faced, pigtailed men on the roof would rise to

ROCK IMAGE NEAR MULBEK.

their feet of one accord, make an obeisance, utter the word of greeting—jooly—in solemn chorus, squat down again simultaneously, and then in a moment become apparently quite oblivious of us, and lapse into silent meditation. There was something very weird in this performance; but it was quite in accord with the spirit of this enchanted land. There were many little black cattle in the alleys of the village, and the tiniest and tamest goats I have ever seen came out of the houses to make friends with us. The Ladaki goats are the prettiest creatures of their kind, with long, soft hair; but they are very perky and conceited. They look more like nice little clean toy goats out of the Lowther Arcade than anything else. All domestic animals are remarkably tame in Ladak; for good Buddhists treat with kindness those lower forms of life into which it may be their bad lot to be re-incarnated some day. Not only man, but also all creatures under his domination—horses, sheep, goats, fowls—are diminutive here; whereas the wild animals on the high mountains are of gigantic size—the Ovis poli for example, that Brobdingnagian among sheep.

Near Mulbek the road passes through one of those weird ravines so frequent in this country, where the crags of concrete and sandstone are worn away into fantastic shapes simulating cathedral spires, great terraces and turrets of castles, vast organs, and other forms. Here the Buddhist has his sacred place on many a pinnacle and in hollows of the cliffs. There are numbers of curious little buildings carved out of the soft rock and decorated outside with paint, not now inhabited, the homes of Lamas long-since dead. On some of the peaks, too, are cairns of stones—altars whereon the natives place the horns of beasts and other offerings for the gods. The traveller, too, who penetrates this defile is protected by sacred writings on the face of the cliff, which frighten away the evil spirits of the air. An enchanted land indeed, where signs of magic rites meet one at every step; a strange world, such as one has seen before in dreams alone, and which on this day looked more unearthly even than usual. The sky above was of the blue of the Tibetan turquoise. There was an absence of perspective, and one could form no idea of distance. As one marched on, far mountains appeared to advance to meet one, and all the stony waste was trembling with mirage.

In the course of this march we ascended a side-nullah to the summit of a ridge forming the watershed between the Wakka and another small tributary of the Indus. On this pass—the Namika La—we were 13,000 feet above the sea, that is, 1,500 feet above the Zoji La. But there was no snow, and here we found the easiest bit of road we had experienced since leaving Srinagur. The ridge is a plateau of earth, white with a deposit of nitre or other salt. We then descended into a broad valley hemmed in between bare mountains. We passed two or three villages, and in every case the Buddhists, as usual, avoiding the easy plain, had gone out of their way to build their monastery and dwelling-houses on isolated and precipitous rocks. One of these villages presents a very strange appearance. At the entrance of an extremely desolate side-valley stands a steep hill, topped by a dome of soft rock. This dome is capped by a monastery, and its sides all round are honeycombed with the dwellings and tombs of the village, the whole looking like a gigantic wedding-cake that had been nibbled by mice. A very holy lama dwells here.

After passing long rows of chortens and manis, we reached our destination, Kharbu. Above this village towers a great precipice, on whose serrated summit are the ruins of what must once have been an extensive town and a strong castle—just the sort of grotesque mountain-stronghold Doré would have loved to draw when illustrating some mediæval legend.

As we neared the village strange music greeted us, and we saw four men with pipes and metal drums squatting on a house-top, who had been sent to do us honour with their wild and barbaric, but not unimpressive, strains. Often, as we rode into one of these silent villages of Ladak, we would be startled by the sudden braying of a trumpet above us, and on looking up would see on the walls of a lamasery hanging over some dizzy height, a red-draped lama blowing a long brass shawm to welcome us.

From the serai at Kharbu we looked over the mud-houses of the village, on whose flat roofs the people were sitting under the numerous praying-flags which fluttered in the evening breeze. The sacred syllables are painted on these flags, and, as the wind shakes them, they produce the same result as the manis and the praying-wheels. Nearly everyone we saw here was carrying a hand praying-wheel. This is a little cylinder containing rolls of the usual prayers. It is held in the hand, and turned by the action of the wrist, after the manner of a child's rattle. One sees the Ladaki men unceasingly twisting these little instruments while walking on the road, or chatting and bargaining in the bazaar; for to concentrate the attention on the revolution, or even to be conscious of it, is quite unnecessary—one can attain the Perfect Peace by automatic muscular action.

Bower and myself strolled outside the village until we found ourselves in a field of chortens, where an intelligent native met us, whose hut was built amidst the crowded tombs of departed saints. He spoke a little Hindostani, and was pleased to reply to our questions. We asked him what he knew of the ruined town extending along the crags above us. 'That,' he said, 'is Old Kharbu. It was a well-fortified castle before the Dogras came. That white building was one of the palaces of the Rajah of Ladak. In my father's time all the villagers lived in the castle up there; but when the Maharajah's troops came here and deposed our Rajah, they burnt the old town, and no one has dwelt there since.'

A very unhandsome lady, who also lived among the tombs, but who, to judge from the number of turquoises on her peyrak, must have been a person of some consequence, now came up, and was ready to take part in the conversation, our first friend acting as interpreter. She told us she had three husbands, but that all were now away getting wool. She explained to us that when her eldest, or principal husband, was at home the other two had to keep out of the way. Thus, if he happened to return first from his wool-gathering, he would place his stick or winter boots outside the house-door, to intimate to his juniors that he had taken up his residence in the family mansion, and that their presence there was undesirable until he should go away again.

CHAPTER X

THE FOTU LA—LAMAYURU—ITS LAMASERY—LAMAS' MUSIC—MERCHANTS FROM LASSA—TRADE WITH TURKESTAN—NEED FOR A CONSULATE AT YARKAND—THE INDUS—NURLA—SASPUL—NIMU—BAZGO—PRAYING-WATERWHEELS.

On May 28 we marched to the next stage, Lamayuru. It was one of the usual cloudless Ladaki days: the sun's rays, passing through the thin air, which lessened little of their power, fell upon us with scorching fierceness, while the wind at this elevation was keen. All this part of the country is higher than the Zoji La, the valley of Kharbu being nearly 12,000 feet above the sea, and Lamayuru 11,520.

When we reached the village of Hinniscoot, which is built on the steep slope of a hill, with a ruined castle above it, we found some sepoys of the Maharajah's army awaiting us, who had been sent from Leh to escort Bower for the last six marches into that city.

Shortly beyond this village we crossed a ridge, the Fotu La, the highest point of the Leh road, being 13,400 feet above the sea. Here, though we were 2,000 feet higher than the top of the Zoji La, we found no snow lying; but the higher mountains on either side were deeply covered. On the summit of this ridge stands a great chorten, under the lee of which we took shelter until a sudden and violent mountain-storm had passed by us. The wind blew with great force, howling like a gale at sea as it swept down upon us from the snow-filled gullies high above, driving snow and hail before it.

The scene from here was very wild. On either side of us towered rocky peaks wrapt in clouds, and we looked through this gap in the mountains over an immense sea of high, upheaved plateaus, snowy domes, and profound ravines, the whole appearing to be completely waste, as if this had been some landscape on the dead moon—crags, accumulations of stones, stretches of bare yellow earth and snow, but not a tree, nor a blade of grass, nor any sign of life, the scattered oases nestling in the valley depths not being visible from here.

We descended from the ridge and passed into a dreary defile, which was a good preparation for the extraordinary spectacle that was to meet our eyes as we emerged from it. The defile was narrow, with a flat bottom, where was a dry watercourse; on either side the sandstone crags rose perpendicularly, cloven into the usual fantastic shapes of towers and organs. It was an uncanny place, and opened out suddenly at its farther end on a broad, barren valley with wastes of pebbles, dry earth, and boulders, through which a little river ran. At the farther end of the valley, just before it narrowed again into a gorge, we saw the village of Lamayuru on a steep, bare hillside, with its gompa crowning the crags above.

But what made this view so very striking, and elicited exclamations of astonishment even from our followers, was the enormous number of monuments of Buddhist worship that were crowded up on either side of the road for the two or three miles that lay between us and the village. Thousands of chortens, standing in rows and in groups, long manis of carved prayers, and cairns, covered the desert ground, and the effect was indescribably weird.

We walked to the village through this silent city of tombs and altars, all of which appeared to be of great age. The outskirts of Lamayuru itself were still more densely crowded with lofty chortens, some bril-

LADAKI GROUP.

liantly painted and elaborately carved. We wound in and out through a labyrinth of these, and the road occasionally passed under a chorten by a gateway lofty enough to allow of a man on horseback riding beneath. The quaint houses of the little town, many of which were in ruins, were perched on pinnacles of rock and on other as uncomfortable positions as could be selected. A very dirty but polite group of the principal citizens, with long gowns and pigtails, most of whom were twirling their prayer-wheels, came out to welcome us, and with soft footsteps walked before us to the serai through narrow alleys, the mild-eyed Buddhists gazing at us from the roof-tops as we passed. In the 'Arabian Nights' there is a description of a Mussulman prince who comes to a strange city of idolaters, terrifying to the imagination, where dwell magicians. Were I illustrating the old tale I should draw just such a place as is this weird Lamayuru.

This is far the most picturesque spot on the Leh road, and I was very disappointed in not being able to take some photographs here, for the camera-bearer loitered this day, and never came in until after sunset.

Bower and myself paid a visit to the lamasery, which is a large and interesting one. To reach it we had to walk through the heart of the town, or, to speak more accurately, climb up it; for one ascends the narrow streets by flights of rough and steep steps hewn out of the rock, crossing deep chasms by log bridges; and so precipitous in places is the face of the cliff, that to get from one house to another on a ledge above it a ladder is necessary. It is the most perpendicular, rambling, and generally most eccentric human settlement that it is possible to imagine. The irregular little windows of the houses are, as a rule, in the upper storeys only, so that one walks up a street between two bare, leaning mud walls. Dirty people and clean goats seemed to be all living together within these buildings; for the heads of both appeared at the windows and on the house-tops, peering down upon us. Sometimes the houses met above our heads, or the street was roofed over with beams and mud, so that only a dim light penetrated below to show us the way as we crept up these tunnel-like thoroughfares. It was as some subterranean city in a nightmare.

When we had nearly scaled the town, some of the lamas—those ugliest, dirtiest, and gentlest of human beings—came down to meet us, attired in flowing robes that had once been red, but which had been toned down by years of dirt to a darker and more artistic shade.

The monastery is perched on the very summit of the rugged crags, and is about two hundred feet above the lower portion of the town. The buildings composing it fit themselves into the crevices and irregularities of the precipices, being in places supported on wooden scaffoldings and overhanging the abyss—an insecure-looking habitation, but strongly and skilfully constructed. On the sides of the gate by which we entered some large praying-wheels were fixed. These were cylinders some two feet in diameter, containing rolls of prayers, and turning on pivots projecting from the wall. Each of the monks, as he entered, gave one of these wheels a push with his hand and so made it whirl round for a few seconds, vainly imagining that by a constant repetition of revolutions he could at last effect his escape from the trammels of earthly existence; like some silly captive squirrel that perpetually runs up the treadmill of its turning cage in the fond belief that it is hurrying to liberty.

A French traveller in these regions describes an amusing scene of which he was a witness. A lama on passing one of these prayer-wheels piously turned it. Before it had ceased revolving another lama, coming the other way, put his hand on it and set it travelling in a reverse direction, to his own credit account, and thus deprived the first lama of the full advantage of his own spin. A fierce argument forthwith ensued between the two, which at last led to blows. The peaceful

Buddhist never resorts to violence unless it be over some very serious question, such as the above, when his unkind brother was postponing Nirvana for him.

Passing through the gompa gates we were taken into a dimly-lighted hall, in which the air was odorous with incense. The walls and roof were draped with richly-coloured hangings of Chinese silk and paper, on which were dreadful designs of fiends and dragons. Strange ornaments of paper and feathers, and several glass bowls of incantation water, were arranged on the platforms under the walls. There were some rather well-executed images of Buddha, and of many hideous deities of good and evil.

The abbot, who had been muttering *Om mani padmi Oms* in a low voice all the time he was with us, now inquired whether we would like to hear the musicians of the lamasery play. We replied in the affirmative, and five lamas, provided with long shawms, gongs, and cymbals, sat on the floor in the middle of the chamber and executed for us the sacred music of the Tibetan Buddhists, fantastic as everything else Tibetan, with abrupt changes and strange discords; while now and again the music would suddenly cease, and with subdued voices the monks would engage in a wild and melancholy chant in the minor key. It was music such as I had never heard before in the East—barbaric, but in a way singularly impressive, well fitted to the mystic Buddhist faith—music that was older than the creeds of Europe, and seemed to awaken vague reminiscences of a far barbaric ancestry, or of the former existences through which, according to the Buddhist doctrine, the soul has passed. As competent judges have assured me, this Tibetan music is composed with more real science, and is of far higher merit, than the average

European listener would be aware of. But there are delicate distinctions in it almost inappreciable, modulations of quarter notes which, to our ears, produce an effect of flatness and sameness.

The music over, the lamas took us to the idol-chamber. They showed us an image of Buddha, and many other idols of brightly-coloured demons and fearful, fabulous monsters, which they said had been made for the monastery by a great lama from Lassa. At one end of the room was a large disk, or shield, on which was carved, with some artistic skill, the image of a God with a number of hands radiating to the circumference of the shield. Any European conversant with Buddhism would have been able to name without hesitation the deity thus represented; but on questioning the lamas, they replied that they did not know what God this was, but that it was a very holy and potent idol, which the learned lama from Lassa had brought to them to worship.

On May 29 we marched about eighteen miles to Nurla. Below Lamayuru the valley again contracts, and we travelled several miles down a narrow gorge, the road zigzagging among the crags, in places being carried along the cliffs, and often crossing the torrent by wooden bridges.

In this ravine we met a caravan of Tibetans who were on their way from Lassa to Kashmir with a number of horses laden with brick tea. We entered into conversation with the chief, who spoke Hindostani. He said they had left Lassa in the preceding autumn, and had wintered at Leh to await the opening of the Zoji La. This brick tea is not very palatable to Europeans, but is held in high estimation by the Kashmiris, for it fetches two rupees or so a pound in the bazaar at Srinagur; whereas Indian tea of inferior quality can be purchased there for a few annas a pound. The Chinese levy a duty on Indian tea. It is, however, often smuggled across the frontier, fifty horse-loads at a time.

Our commercial arrangements with China in this part of the world are, by the way, in a somewhat unsatisfactory condition, and the presence of a British Consul at Yarkand is much needed. I believe that a bit of red-tapeism at home stands in the way of our having a representative in Chinese Turkestan. It is asserted that, as Consul in Chinese territory, he would necessarily be under the control of our Minister at Pekin, to whom he would have to forward all his reports. This would entail such delay and confusion as to render the Consulate practically useless. The remote province of Turkestan is almost a *terra incognita* at Pekin, and is in some respects outside the jurisdiction of the Celestial Government. To be of any avail the Yarkand Consulate should be placed directly under the Indian Government, which understands the conditions and requirements of our relations with Chinese Turkestan as our Embassy at Pekin and our departments in England cannot do. But to have it thus would not be according to Cocker, and we have therefore no Consul at all. The result is that the Russians, who maintain a Consulate at Yarkand, have things their own way there, and the trade between India and Turkestan is crippled, as far as possible, to the advantage of the Russian traders. For instance, merchants who are Indian subjects of ours pay dues on entering and on leaving any city in Chinese Turkestan; while, on the other hand, the Russian merchants pass free of toll. This partiality is a direct violation of Lord Elgin's

Tientsin Treaty, by which it was stipulated that England should not be debarred from any commercial favour that was granted by China to any other nation. It is high time that there should be someone at Yarkand to guard the interests of our subjects who trade there. Every English traveller in Turkestan is met by the resident Indian merchants with bitter complaints of the treatment they receive. It is a clever bit of Russian policy to make the fact of being a British subject an obstruction to one's business and a serious pecuniary loss in Central Asia.

Since the commercial treaty that was entered into between the Governments of India and Kashmir in 1870 we have a representative, known as the British Joint-Commissioner, at Leh, which town is the centre of the trade with Eastern Turkestan, as well as with Tibet. His duty it is to settle all disputes between our subjects and natives of Kashmir on the one hand, and the Central Asian merchants who are subjects of Russia and China on the other hand. The presence of this officer at so important a centre has already produced excellent results: most of the abuses that hampered the trade on this route have been swept away, and the merchants are no longer so outrageously blackmailed as before on their way through Kashmir territory. The duties that were once levied on caravans passing through Leh were abolished some years ago by the Maharajah's Council; but it is said that the officials of that city quietly ignored the order, charged the tolls, and pocketed them all for a year or so afterwards, before they were detected.

This day we passed another small Tibetan caravan of donkeys laden with wool. The men told us they had come from the Chung Tung, or Northern Plateau, by way of Rupshu. The wool trade between Tibet and India is now considerable, and Englishmen who have taken up this enterprise at Darjeeling are making large profits. The Chinese Tibetans who travel with these caravans on this road swagger along with a somewhat arrogant air, and, as natives of holy and free Tibet, look down with contempt on their conquered brethren of Ladak, are given to bullying them, and often impress the Ladaki coolies to carry their goods through the country for nothing.

After descending the gorge for several miles, we at last opened out the broad valley of the Indus, up which our road was to lie for the rest of the journey to Leh, and I saw for the first time that mighty river, even here of considerable volume, swollen and discoloured with the melting snows of unexplored regions of Tibet, and roaring in a series of furious rapids between its desert shores.

We crossed the river by a long cantilever bridge, rode through a Dogra fort which defended the passage, whose garrison turned out to salute us, and commenced our ascent of the valley. Soon rows of manis and chortens indicated the approach to a village, and we entered the extensive oasis of Khalsi, where we had our tiffin by an artificial pond of clear water under the shade of walnut-trees. We looked round on rich crops of peas, barley, and lucerne; multitudes of apricots; wild lavender and iris growing among the rocks; and murmuring streams of coldest, clearest water flashing by, that had converted the desert of granite-grit and gravel into this pleasant garden. The line of demarcation between cultivation and complete barrenness was very remarkable here. When we set out again after our midday halt, we stepped over the outer irrigation-ditch, about eighteen inches broad, from deep lucerne on one side, to a desert of sand and pebbles on the other, where not a plant grew.

We journeyed on through a dreary land quivering in mirage until sunset, when we came to the long row of tombs again—a cheering sight, as signifying the approach of our destination and dinner—and then entered another sweet oasis, that of Nurla, where, as usual, we partook of our meals and slept *coram populo* —all the village coming out to stare at us—on the verandah of the serai.

The next day's journey (May 30) was of seventeen miles, in the course of which, as the guide-book justly remarks, there is but one small patch of vegetation. At this patch, accordingly, we halted for breakfast. An heiress—for such she must have been, to judge from the way she bullied her husband when he came up, a mere magpa he, no doubt—was working in the fields, and on turning one of her numerous little irrigation canals on to a plot of barley, released a quantity of water, which poured down in our direction as we were enjoying our fowls and tea, and threatened to irrigate us out. Our servants and sepoys on this set up cries of consternation and indignation, and the woman, terrified at the danger into which she had inadvertently placed the two great sahibs, hurried up with her spade, and promptly dammed the canal up again and saved us.

It was then that her miserable slave and magpa slouched up, and she proceeded to heap abuse on him in a shrill voice all the while we were at breakfast, as if the accident had been his fault, poor wretch. He wisely replied nothing to the scold who ruled him He looked like a man whose spirit had been completely broken by much ill-usage. If I were he, I should try

M

and summon up sufficient courage to beg her—since she evidently no longer loved her poor magpa—to give me the customary parting rupee or sheep, and discharge me. It was a sad sight, and set one thinking to what depths women's rights, as advanced by some extreme ladies at home, would drag down the hapless male. Unless we look to it we shall all be as magpas some day.

After breakfast we were off again over heated crags and sands and slopes of gravel, while dust-devils rose up mysteriously all round us, soaring like great columns of white smoke into the blue sky, in a few moments to burst and scatter into clouds. Then once more we came to the outlying manis and tombs, and saw before us the orchards of the oasis of Saspul, behind which, in striking contrast, were wastes of yellow sand and reddish gravel glowing in the sunshine, and still farther off was a great range of dark mountains with snow-covered peaks—Devonshire, the Sahara, and the Alps seeming to combine to form this incongruous landscape.

We traversed one of the usual dishevelled suburbs of old tombs, broken walls, and ruined, deserted huts which surround a Ladak village, and passed through the irrigated land, grateful to the eyes after the glare of rocks and sands, with a noise of babbling water and singing birds in our ears, and the smell of lavender and many flowers in our nostrils, to the serai.

The description of one day's march on this road is very like another, tomb-surrounded oases alternating with desert ravines and plateaus; the scenery, however, is not really monotonous, but is always varying and interesting.

On May 31 we travelled to Nimu. As the Indus

for some miles rushes down a precipitous gorge, our road left the valley and ascended to the stony plateaus above. It was a windless and oppressively hot day. The sky above was no longer of the Tibetan blue, but of a yellowish tint, and instead of the marvellous Tibetan clearness of atmosphere, a haze hung over the country, rendering distant objects indistinct. This was the typical climate of the steppes of Turkestan, as distinguished from that of Tibet. The copper sky and the haze were due, not to the presence of any moisture in the air, but to the finest dust held in suspension, which, having been carried up into the higher strata of the atmosphere by storms on far distant deserts, was floating over Ladak.

The extreme dryness of the air was becoming more noticeable as we left the Himalayan range farther behind us. Here mouth, throat, and nostrils feel uncomfortably parched, and the skin is chapped and cracked. I remember that three of us once tried to whistle to one of Bower's dogs, but found it impossible to do so with our dried-up lips.

We met this day a band of poor Mussulman Baltis on their way to seek work in Kashmir or India—simple, ugly, good-natured people, with long elf-locks curling down their cheeks, clothed in filthy and scanty rags, and of a half-starved appearance. Several of them had suffered from frostbite while crossing a pass leading from their country, and had lost fingers and toes. The Ladakis look very comfortable and well-fed by the side of these poor creatures. The Baltis are an unfortunate and oppressed race; but, as the result of our interference, things will be better with them for the future. In consequence of the proximity of their country to the Gilgit road, it is these men chiefly who are impressed to carry loads on that deadly track, while thousands of them have been captured and sold as slaves in Turkestan by their neighbours, the Kanjut robbers.

Our midday halting-place was in a bagh of blossoming apricot-trees outside Bazgo. This village covers the side of a rocky hill. High above it, on the crags, are the ruins of an ancient fortress, which once resisted a very long siege, and two large lamaseries. I ascended the cliffs and explored the strange wilderness of great rocks, riven as by earthquakes, on which these buildings stand. The gompas, surrounded by precipices and pinnacles, command extensive views, but over stony desolation only, not so much as a blade of grass being within sight to remind the lamas of the despised life of earth.

At Bazgo I saw a praying-waterwheel for the first time, a cylinder full of rolls of prayers fixed across a stream upon an axle, and turned by the running water. It is indeed strange, if these people really believe in the efficacy of their praying-machinery, as they are said to do, that they put up so few of these waterwheels. The traveller in Ladak seldom comes across them, and yet, revolving day and night as they do unceasingly, it stands to reason that they must perform more work than the praying-flags and hand-wheels. An enormous amount of praying power is wasted in the rushing Indus, which, properly utilised, might be made to insure Nirvana on death to every soul in the country. Good missionaries from Lassa should see to this.

LAMASERY AT NAZUM.

CHAPTER XI

THE HUNTING OF DAD MAHOMED — LEH FEVER — CITY OF LEH — THE BAZAARS — CARAVAN TRADE — POPULATION OF LEH — MORAVIAN AND ROMAN CATHOLIC MISSIONS — DR. REDSLOP — BOWER'S PREPARATIONS — POLO.

ON June 1, our sixteenth day out from Srinagur, we marched two stages and completed our journey to Leh. Our route lay across a hot and glaring desert; but though there were no habitations or cultivation, the whole road was lined with chortens, manis, and cairns, and all the big boulders of rock that were scattered over the waste had little heaps of stones or horns of cattle on their tops, piled up as propitiations to the gods by pious travellers.

At a small oasis where we halted for tiffin we were met by two mounted Dogra officers of the Maharajah's army who were old friends of Bower and had travelled with him in Central Asia, so that there was a cordial greeting between them. One of these officers had distinguished himself by tracking down the murderer, Dad Mahomed, for which feat he had received the large reward that had been offered by the Government, and had been publicly thanked in open Durbar at Srinagur. The story of this capture is interesting. This Dad Mahomed, a Pathan from Quetta, a notorious ruffian and assassin, who had established himself as a merchant at Leh, murdered the English traveller, Dalgleish, on the

Karakoram Pass, where the caravans of both happened to be encamped on the same night. Dalgleish's followers were cowardly Lakadis and Russian Turkis, who made no attempt to defend him. After the murder Dad Mahomed cut the Ladakis' pigtails off, and amused himself by firing at the wretches as they fled down the pass. He made the Mussulman Turkis take an oath on the Koran not to reveal what he had done. He then escaped into Turkestan with his Pathan followers.

The Indian Government was soon apprised of this murder, and Captain Bower, who was then setting out to travel in these regions, was instructed to discover and arrest the assassin if possible. All Bower was told as to the whereabouts of the fugitive was to the effect that he was somewhere in Central Asia, which, I need scarcely say, is a geographical term comprising a very large slice of the earth's surface, so that the mission must have appeared a somewhat vague and hopeless one.

Bower crossed the mountains into Chinese Turkestan, where our fellow-subjects, the Hindoo merchants settled there, as is their custom, welcomed the English traveller and gave him every assistance in their power. The Chinese authorities refused to take any steps in the matter, but the Hindoos soon obtained for Bower all the information he required, and he was put upon the track of Dad Mahomed. That gentleman got wind of Bower's intentions, and evidently did not consider himself to be safe in any part of Central Asia, for he commenced to travel backwards and forwards over enormous distances, often under an assumed name and in disguise, so that all trace of him should be lost, and he was heard of in Bokhara and Balkh, as well as in the cities of China. The trade-routes, the only practicable roads over the thinly-populated regions of Central Asia, are limited in number, and form, as I have before remarked, telephones, as it were, of news. It is difficult to keep one's goings and comings secret in such a country, so that while this exciting chase was being carried on Bower was never for long off Dad Mahomed's tracks, and Dad Mahomed was always still better informed as to the movements of so conspicuous a personage as a European traveller.

The fugitive never ventured within Bower's reach, and invariably kept a few hundred miles between himself and his pursuer; so Bower soon realised that this was a difficult game to stalk, and that he might pass the rest of his life rushing up and down the wastes of Asia, and fail to catch this wily and rapidly-moving Pathan. Bower thereupon changed his tactics; driving, and not stalking, was obviously the proper way of conducting this sort of chase, and he made his plans to drive Dad Mahomed into a previously-laid trap. First he sent the Dogra officer I have mentioned and another reliable man of his party, both well disguised, to Samarcand with definite instructions, which they carried out with great intelligence. Then Bower, with the rest of his men, proceeded to energetically follow up the Pathan, allowing him no rest, and at last, by turning his line of flight, compelled him to escape in the direction of Samarcand. Dad Mahomed unconsciously fell into the trap: he entered Samarcand, and was promptly recognised by Bower's two men. While one of these shadowed him, the other went off to the Russian general, produced Bower's letter, and told the story. The general at once sent some Cossacks with the man, the murderer was seized and carried to the prison. Bower was anxious to march the prisoner into India through Kashgaria and

Kashmir, as a good example to any other ruffians there might be in those parts; but Dad Mahomed could not, of course, be delivered over to him until an extradition warrant had been obtained from the Russian Government. There was a considerable delay in receiving a reply to Bower's request, and difficulties might have been raised had not the prisoner, before any decision on the subject was come to, been good enough to solve the knotty problem by hanging himself in his cell.

Some Pathans of Dad Mahomed's tribe were in Samarcand at the time, who threatened Bower's followers, and told them that neither they nor their master would ever reach Kashmir alive. No one, however, ventured to interfere with Bower on his return journey, and the story of this successful drive spread through all the bazaars of Central Asia and caused a great impression. 'How far-reaching,' men would say to each other, 'is the arm of the Indian Sarkar? It can even stretch across Kashmir to seize and destroy in the depths of Asia the man who has had the temerity to slay a sahib.'

The Dogra officers informed us that there was an epidemic of Russian influenza in Ladak, to which Dr. Marx, the Moravian missionary, had fallen a victim. This disease had been raging for some time in Central Asia, and Bower told me that eighty Chinese soldiers had died of it while he was in Kashgar. The epidemic in Leh, however, turned out to be, not influenza, but a fever peculiar to this province, somewhat resembling typhus, but of a milder nature; its symptoms are fever and very high temperature lasting for twelve days, intense headache, a slight rash, and disordered mental faculties, followed by extreme prostration for several weeks. It breaks out regularly in Ladak every spring,

LEH.

and is probably due to the filthy habits of the people when confined within their dark, unwholesome huts, during the intense cold of the winter, through which they practically hybernate; so that in early spring, when they come forth debilitated by the poisonous air they have been breathing for months, the fierce sun has plenty of material out of which to engender a pestilence. The Buddhists attribute its origin to the Mahomedans in Leh, for they argue that it always follows the exhausting fast of the Ramazan. This fever is rarely fatal; but the Moravian missionaries, who had devoted themselves to the care of the sick natives, were attacked without one exception, and two died of the *sequelæ*.

We rode on after our tiffin, with our escort, across the burning sands and pebbly wastes of the Indus Valley till we came to the isolated rock of Pitak, rising from the river-bank, with an ancient gonpa and fort at its summit. Here two spurs of the mountain-range to the north of the Indus open out, leaving a great sand plain between them. At the head of this plain, about five miles from the Indus, and at the point where the hills approach again to form a narrow valley, stands the city of Leh, surrounded by cultivated fields, groves of lofty poplars and other trees. The streams that flow down from the nullahs behind it and water this oasis are afterwards sucked up by the arid sands, and never reach the Indus. The Indus at Pitak is 10,500 feet above the sea, Leh is 11,500 feet, so that one gradually ascends 1,000 feet in the course of the five miles' journey across the sands.

As one approaches this important city, the capital of Western Tibet and of Western Buddhism, it presents a really imposing appearance. Towering above all the groves and houses stands the massive palace of the deposed *Gialpos*, or Rajahs of Ladak, with many irregular storeys and lofty, inleaning walls, and with giant chortens containing the ashes of kings surrounding it. Higher up, on the crags behind, is the gompa, and behind all rises a mighty snow-covered mountain-range, across which lead the roads into Turkestan and Tibet.

Our late Joint-Commissioner, Mr. Ramsey, has greatly improved the road between Leh and Dras, and for the last five miles has carried it in a perfectly straight line from Pitak to the gates of the city. But the Ladakis, fantastic as usual, loving zigzagging and tortuous ways and abhorring regularity, often avoid this easy route to take a longer and rougher one. There is, however, some reason for this eccentric conduct: there are no manis by the side of the new road, so that to walk these five miles, though saving in time, is an unprofitable and absolutely wasted effort so far as preparation for the next world is concerned; it is, therefore, more advantageous to follow the rugged old winding native road, well-provided as it is with rows of praying-stones, and far superior to the new one from a theological point of view.

Mr. Ramsey, by the way, was anxious to improve the road from Leh across the Karakoram Pass, the principal trade-route into Central Asia. He called together the merchants of Leh, pointed out the advantages of his scheme, and asked if they would contribute a trifling sum each towards the cost of the work. Their spokesman, who happened to be the same Dad Mahomed whom Bower subsequently hunted to the death, was a political economist of the true Oriental school. 'No,' said he, 'we are better without a road. It would, as you say, save much time in the journey

LEH BAZAAR.

and lives of baggage-animals, and men; but a good road would bring more merchants here, goods would become cheaper, and our profits would consequently be less.'

We rode up to the city, passed through the walls by a small wicket-gate, and found ourselves at the head of the bazaar, which has been built since the Dogra conquest—a long, broad street, such as Srinagur cannot boast, bordered by the shops of the merchants, and with the great white palace rising conspicuously at the farther end. The passing through this wicket into the bazaar is a sudden burst from the wilds into civilisation. The merchants, many of whom are white-robed Hindoos from Kashmir, were sitting cross-kneed among their wares at the entrance of their shops. Several of the leading men met us, to salaam and proffer their dalis of dried fruits, sugar, and vegetables. But the bazaar was comparatively deserted at this early season. I was informed that later on, when the passes into Central Asia are open, this place would be full of life, and be exceedingly picturesque and interesting for a stranger to behold.

Leh, conveniently situated as it is about half-way between the markets of India and those of Central Asia, has become the terminus for the caravans from both regions. In the summer, traders arrive at Leh from every part of India, and from Turkestan, Tibet, Siberia, and the remotest districts of Central Asia. Here the goods and produce of the south are exchanged for those of the north. It is seldom that a caravan from India goes north of Leh, or that one from Central Asia proceeds south of it. The merchants, who have been travelling for months along the difficult roads from either direction, meet here and dispose of their loads, to a great extent by barter; but before they commence the long, weary homeward journey, they rest here for a month or two, so that the bazaar and the environs of the city are thronged with the camels, yaks, and other beasts of burden, as well as with men from all corners of Asia. At this time there is such a motley collection of types and various costumes, and such a babel of different languages, as it would not be easy to find elsewhere. Savage Tartars in sheepskins, and other outlandish men, jostle with the elegant Hindoo merchant from the cities of Central India, and the turbulent Mussulman Pathan scowls at the imperturbable idolaters from the Celestial Empire. Leh in September is, indeed, one of the busiest and most crowded of cities, and the storekeepers and farmers who have to supply this multitude must make a very good profit for the time.

Leh is therefore a very cosmopolitan city, even in the dead season; for there are resident merchants and others of various races and creeds. Small as is the permanent population, at least four languages are in common use here—Hindostani, Tibetan, Turki, and Kashmiri—while several others are spoken. Six religions have their followers in Leh: there are Buddhists, Mahomedans of three sects (Sunis, Shiahs, and Maulais), Hindoos, and Sikhs. The people are fairly tolerant to each other's beliefs, and intermarriages in families of rival creeds are not infrequent. There is a mongrel race here of Arghons, as they are called—the half-caste offspring of Mussulman Turki caravan-drivers, who enter into temporary (Nikah) marriages with Ladak Buddhist women. These Arghons adopt the religion of their wandering, and often unknown, fathers, and are Mahomedans of a lax sort. The result of all this intermarriage is that the Buddhists and Mahomedans have mutually modified each other's peculiar customs, and have yielded to each other's prejudices. The Mussulman women at Leh, as a rule, go about freely and unveiled, like their Buddhist sisters, and are only to be distinguished from the latter by the fillets and coin ornaments they wear on their heads. The idea of polyandry is loathsome to a Mahomedan, while a Ladak lady is averse to sharing her husband with other wives; so one finds here that a Mussulman has seldom more than one wife, and that a Buddhist woman has generally but one husband, the contact of the two extremes, polygamy and polyandry, having developed the intermediate custom of monogamy.

We were put-up in the British Joint-Commissioner's residence, a bungalow outside the town surrounded by a grove and garden. This is the centre of the European quarter, such as it is, consisting only of the Moravian mission-house, the European cemetery, and a dak bungalow containing a library of books left behind by travelling sahibs, and under the charge of the native postman.

There are only four graves in the European cemetery. One is that of the murdered Dalgleish, and two of the others are of English travellers who died of the effects of thin air and the difficulty of breathing at high altitudes.

The present Joint-Commissioner in Ladak is Captain Evans Gordon, an energetic and able officer, as are most of those appointed by the Indian Government to this unsettled and peculiarly-situated State. He had not yet arrived at Leh, as his presence had been required at Srinagur; so we were unfortunate in not meeting him here.

We found at the Residency Dr. Thorold, who was to accompany Bower on his adventurous journey, and who had preceded him with the stores. It was lucky he had done so, for there was not even so much as a native doctor in Leh, and Dr. Thorold had been of great service in attending on the Moravian missionaries, all of whom had been attacked by the fever. After talking the matter over with him, Bower decided not to proceed on his journey until they were out of all danger, and stood in no further need of medical assistance.

The only European residents in Leh were the members of the two missions, the Moravian and the Roman Catholic. The latter mission had but recently been established, and consisted of only two Fathers, an Englishman and a Dutchman, who had just arrived in the country, and had not yet acquired the vernacular or commenced their labours. The Moravian mission is an old institution. Shortly before our arrival there were three missionaries attached to it, two of whom had their wives with them. All European travellers to Leh have carried away pleasant and grateful recollections of this happy, simple, harmonious little community, which was now being so sorely tried. Dr. Marx had already succumbed to the fever, while the two others, Dr. Redslop and Mr. Shaw, were both laid up with it. Dr. Redslop died while I was in Leh. The ladies were also attacked by the fever, and one of the little children died at this time from other causes.

The Moravians have not, I believe, made any active attempts at converting the natives to Christianity, in which they have acted rightly and wisely. An ill-judged and tactless precipitancy in dealing with these strange people would have ruined all their chances of success. I do not think they entertain any hopes of proselytising for a long time to come. Those who send out the Moravians do not expect of them sensational reports of so-called conversions. But these missionaries have tended the people in their sickness, have fed the poor, and have, in short, by the example of their own devoted lives—ever doing their duty towards their neighbours—given an excellent demonstration of what the religion of the true Christian is. The Ladak Buddhists are a somewhat uncharitable people, callous to the sufferings of others, while the religion they profess is degraded, selfish, and in nowise resembling the doctrine that Siddartha taught; but from what I saw, I think many of them entertain an honest and grateful appreciation of the work of the Moravians and an admiration of their virtues. It is possible that from admiration some may be led to imitation, and to the adoption of a higher standard of ethics than is their present one.

The Moravians maintain a little hospital at Leh. The perpetual dustiness of the air, and the manner of their life in winter, makes the natives of Ladak particularly subject to ophthalmia and other diseases of the eye, for the treatment of which they flock to the hospital in great numbers. In one year Dr. Marx performed thirty operations for cataract alone.

Dr. Redslop was a man who had acquired a complete mastery of the Tibetan dialects, and no European knew so much as he of the Tibetan people. He was wont to meet and discourse with the lamas and others who came from Chinese Tibet, and acquired a mass of information, most of which, I fear, will be lost with his death. He had many friends at Lassa, and his intention was to visit that great centre of Buddhism when all his arrangements were complete; it is certain that, if any man could have overcome the prejudices of the lamas and have obtained permission to visit that mysterious closed city, it was he.

The province of Ladak is governed by a Wazir; but this official remains in Jummoo, while his lieutenant, the Naib Wazir, has his residence in Leh. This gentleman treated Bower and myself with the greatest kindness, and did all that was in his power to assist us.

Bower's destination had necessarily to be kept secret at this time, for, had the native Buddhists suspected it, they would have communicated with the lamas of Tibet, who would have thrown every obstacle in his way, and most probably, by intimidating his followers, have compelled them to desert at an early stage of the journey, or would have resorted to force to drive the expedition back into Kashmir territory. It was therefore Bower's intention, when nearing the Chinese frontier by Changchemno, to turn suddenly off from the more frequented routes, and plunge into a part of the country so desert and uninhabited that the lamas would be unaware of his whereabouts until he was far in the heart of Tibet. Then the desertion of his followers would be improbable, as being a more perilous course than to follow him faithfully onwards; while it would be too late for the lamas, should they discover him, to attempt to send him back by the way he had come.

The Naib Wazir was alone taken into Bower's confidence at Leh, and the natives, though they must have marvelled at the scale of his caravan, probably supposed that he was merely bound on a sporting-expedition to the high valleys of Ladak.

Bower soon had his caravan ready. He purchased a quantity of grain at Leh, some more horses, and a number of sheep, which were to serve as beasts of burden as well as for meat, for each was to carry two little sacks of grain on its back. He had an order on the Treasury of Ladak for a considerable sum he was to take with him for the purposes of his journey. It occupied some time to count this out, for it was paid in antique gold and silver coins of various countries, and also in the impure gold-dust which the Ladakis obtain from the sands of the Indus, and with which they pay their revenue to the State.

The Naib Wazir carefully selected the explorer's Ladak followers for him, and cautiously made inquiries as to the character and resources of the country into which Bower was first to penetrate on crossing the frontier. Little information could be obtained concerning it, save that it was unpopulated, desert, and considered impassable. It was a *terra incognita* even to the nomads.

The previous winter had been so severe that the difficulties attending such a journey would doubtless be greater than in ordinary years, and natives reported that even the comparatively easy passes on the earlier and well-known stages were still quite impracticable for laden animals.

Here I began to realise better what an adventuresome expedition this was of Bower and Thorold. They were now about to plunge into an absolutely unexplored region, a region of the most elevated table-lands in the world, where even the very valley-bottoms are higher above the sea than the summit of Mont Blanc; to discover their own passes across huge mountain-ranges; probably for weeks, if not for months, at a

N

time to depend entirely on the supplies they were carrying with them, finding neither fuel nor grass by the way; possibly, after long, arduous journeys across the mountain solitudes, to arrive at insuperable natural barriers, compelling them to retrace their steps and commence again in some other direction; to be boycotted by the natives, or to meet with still more active hostility; to encounter the deadly cold of the Tibetan tempests; to lose most of their animals on the road; and to run no inconsiderable risk of perishing, with all their following, on the inhospitable deserts. But Bower was resolved to clear up the geographical problems of this mysterious and unknown land. With his discoveries he would fill up that great blank space on the map of Asia. As the world now knows, he accomplished his task; after a year's wanderings, unheard of, their fate altogether unknown, the two Englishmen at last re-appeared at Shanghai, to the relief of all their friends.

For one reason and another Bower remained at Leh for two weeks before he commenced his onward march.

My own programme was, after seeing the interesting Buddhist festival at Himis, to march across-country to Gilgit, at the farther extremity of the Kashmir State, where I had arranged to meet Spedding. I had also to await at Leh a reply from our Resident at Srinagur, to whom I had applied for permission to travel on the Gilgit road.

I have already explained that no Europeans, save officers of Her Majesty's Service, are allowed to travel in Kashmir territory without a passport from the Residency. But this passport does not extend to the road between Gilgit and Kashmir, which is closed to private travellers. So great is the difficulty of sending up a sufficiency of necessaries to the Gilgit garrison during the four months that the passes are open, so limited are the supplies procurable on that barren route, and so great is the drain on the scanty population for coolie labour, that this prohibition is a very necessary one. For the last two years Europeans, whether officers or civilians, who have applied for permission to travel to Gilgit or to shoot in the nullahs of that district—a favourite one for Himalayan sportsmen— have done so in vain. With two or three exceptions only, the officers of the Gilgit Agency, and Spedding, with his staff, who are constructing the new military road, are the only Englishmen who have been admitted into the country. However, as I did not require large trains of coolies to carry my loads, was not bound for sporting purposes, and had shown good reasons for my wish to visit Gilgit, I was in hopes that my application would not be refused.

I passed my time very pleasantly at Leh for a few days, wandering about the environs and taking photographs. The Naib Wazir also got up some amusements for us, notably polo, the indigenous game of all the highland country between Tibet and Chitral, as well as of Manipur. At Leh it is the custom to play in the bazaar, all business being suspended for the purpose. The Naib Wazir issued the order, all the shops were closed, and the strains of a native band, in which kettle-drums, trumpets, and *surnais*—the sound of which last is like that of bagpipes without the drone—were the principal instruments, gave notice to the citizens that the play was about to commence. The players were all Ladakis, mounted on capital little ponies. There can be no doubt that, though this game is native to the country, we have much improved upon it, and polo as played by British officers in India is a far superior sport. We sat on the flat roof of the Court House, with the Naib Wazir and other notables, to view the curious spectacle, while the populace

RAJAH'S PALACE, LEH

crowded all the other roofs on either side of the ground. The band played without pause, the air always becoming more rapid and noisy when either side was approaching a goal, and subsiding to low and querulous notes if the chance were lost. When a goal was won there would be a triumphant and discordant outburst of music. In some parts of Baltistan it is the custom for the beaten side to dance for the amusement of the spectators.

I was surprised one day, while walking down the bazaar, to see some small Ladaki boys playing at a game that was undoubtedly cricket, with two wickets, polo-sticks for bats, and wooden polo-balls. They made runs, caught each other out, and, so far as I could see, observed the orthodox rules. I shall not attempt to prove that cricket, which we flatter ourselves to be a pre-eminently British pastime, is in reality an ancient Tibetan game introduced into Europe by the Jesuit Xavier, or some other traveller of old, who had visited these parts. I think it more probable that the Moravians have played the game here among themselves, or with any sahibs who might have been passing through Leh, and that the Ladaki urchins, having been employed as fielding fags, have taken it up in their usual imitative manner. Later on I was instrumental in introducing golf into Hunza and other regions, where it had certainly never been seen before. We used to impress little boys as caddies, and I afterwards frequently saw them practising the great game of North Britain on their own account, with their fathers' polo sticks and balls.

On June 5 a sahib arrived at Leh, the first we had seen for some time; this was Mr. Hunter, the well-known sportsman, who has shot big game in all parts of the world, and had just arrived from Changchenmo with a collection of fine heads as trophies of his success. So we were four sahibs at dinner this night, and Hunter produced from his stores a much-travelled bottle of port, which had been carried by him across Africa to Kilimanjaro and back. I was once taken to task by some critics, and accused of gloating too much, in a book of travels, over the good things I came across at rare intervals in the way of eating and drinking. It is all very well for a possibly dyspeptic or sedentary person in London to find fault thus; but when one has been on the march for months, and living constantly in the open air, one comes to consider eating and drinking anything but unimportant matters, and the way we enjoyed that unwonted luxury—the bottle of port—this night is a thing I cannot forget, and feel myself bound to gratefully record.

CHAPTER XII

IBEX-STALKING — TIBETAN BEER — HIMIS FESTIVAL — THE GIALPO'S ESTATE — THE PILGRIMAGE — A LADAKI NACH — MONASTERY LANDS — THE LAMASERY OF HIMIS.

On June 6, having some ambition to slay an ibex, I set forth with a native shikari whose home was in the Snemu Drokpo, the particular nullah in which I intended to try my luck, and which runs into the Indus Valley near Nimu. Iamps, a hamlet at the head of this nullah, is two days' march from Leh.

The first day we marched to Tharu, and encamped in a willow-plantation by the side of the Leh road. The country round this spot is particularly dreary—a howling wilderness of granite boulders, where the dust devils are nearly always to be seen, springing up from the plain silently and mysteriously, even on a windless day.

My tent was pitched on a patch of grass by the brink of the stream, recommended as a camping-ground by our careless shikari, who should have known better; for shortly after dinner a distant murmur, ever-increasing in volume, was heard, which was soon recognised as the sound of rushing water, and of a sudden down came a foaming wave, and the tiny stream had swollen to an impetuous torrent. There was a tremendous scurrying in the camp: the servants and coolies attempted to perform wonderful engineering feats by damming a channel here and digging a trench there; but all in vain, so the tent and scattered cooking-pots and other impedimenta had to be carried hurriedly to higher ground. As this phenomenon happens every night in summer, it might have been foreseen. All day long the hot sun melts the snows on the high mountains above, and the nullahs carry off the liberated water; but as the distance to the snow-fields is considerable, it is night before the water has descended to this level. In the night it freezes hard on the mountains, and no water finds its way into the nullahs, so that the streams in the daytime are shrunken for the lower portion of their course.

On June 7 we ascended the Suemu nullah, a cheerless ravine with only a little boortsa growing on its slopes, and halted for breakfast at a hamlet called Rapsta. Here came out of a house to greet us the two brothers of my shikari, together with the wife common to the three, a young woman with rather pleasing features, carrying a baby in her arms. They brought me yellow and red roses; for these people, like most Asiatics, are fond of flowers, and in summer generally go about with wild blossoms in their caps. Here, for the first time, I tasted the Lakadi beer, or *chung*, which is made from *grim*, a species of barley that ripens at high altitudes. This beer has the muddy appearance of Thames water below bridge, and tastes rather like inferior cider; it is not unpalatable, however, and is refreshing on a hot day. The wife brought me a bowl of this beverage, having first thrown a handful of flour into it and stirred it up well with a stick, a mixture which is certainly sustaining.

The three husbands and their lady chattered away in a friendly manner over another large bowl of beer and flour. I discovered that my shikari was the eldest brother, consequently the owner of the family estate, and lord over his two younger brothers. He took both away with him when we resumed our march, and employed them as coolies to carry our baggage, the lady being left at home alone.

As eldest brother, my shikari was the best dressed and cleanest of the family. The minor husbands, the wife and child, were astonishingly dirty, and looked as if they had never been washed in their lives. The natives of Chinese Tibet are reputed to be the dirtiest people in the whole world, even more dirty than the Ladakis. I do not see how this can be, unless there are indeed Mahatmas in that country, and it is these who are spoken of; for Mahatmas, of course, could have accumulated an immortality of dirt, and would have an advantage in this respect over the mere mortal Ladakis.

We reached Iamps, a place high up the nullah, where two or three families occupy some miserable huts. There is a little grazing here for the cattle, but it is difficult to understand how even these few people can extract their subsistence out of so barren a spot. Here my tent was pitched for the next four days, during which I clambered about the mountains after the shy ibex; but I was not in luck, and after some of the hardest and most fatiguing work I have ever experienced, I abandoned this monotonously unsuccessful pursuit.

June 8 was my first day on the hillside. We had a terrific climb up and down the parallel spurs above the nullah, over high gaps, often in deep snow, sometimes 16,000 feet or more above the sea, and nearly always on difficult ground, for fourteen hours—and all in vain. We only saw female ibex, and these, according to the Maharajah's game laws, must not be shot. The view from these heights was splendid, and enabled one to form a good idea of the character of the country. One realised, as one could not from the valleys along which the road is taken, what an elevated and extremely desolate region Ladak is, and what a large proportion of its surface is above the line of perpetual snow and the zone of vegetable life.

Each day we toiled along the high ridges, sometimes overlooking the Bazgo nullah and seeing the oases of the Indus Valley spread out like maps far beneath us; and always with the same immense panorama of snowy uplands, cloven by labyrinths of profound ravines, stretching before us, reaching to the mountains of ice and snow that bar the way to China. We clambered over the crags and slopes of loose débris, to see plenty of female ibex, it is true, for these appeared to be perfectly aware of the law which protected them; but the few males we stalked down were small. I only shot one, whose horns proved to be of inconsiderable size, not the sort of trophy to exhibit to Himalayan sportsmen. My shikari was very disappointed; he said there was scarcely enough grass for the males yet, but that in ten days it would have grown up, and that then there would be good sport in this nullah. He knew that he was to receive extra pay in the event of my securing a good head, so he was uncomfortably energetic and keen, and would allow me no rest, even after tiffin, but would insist on my toiling on over crumbling landslips and hazardous cliff-faces until I began to entertain an intense loathing for him and ibex-stalking generally. So on June 11 I rose against my tyrant, and insisted on striking camp and returning to Leh.

I sent the baggage on by road, while the shikari and myself travelled across the mountain-tops to Nimu, on the chance of being rewarded for all this toil at last. But this day we saw no ibex at all. We ultimately descended from the heights to Nimu by way of a steep side-nullah with crags fashioned into all manner of odd shapes—a fantastic spot even for Ladak. The cliffs at the mouth of this gorge were of a sort of concrete of mud and pebbles, in which were embedded many large boulders. As the cliff had disintegrated, the concrete had fallen away all round these boulders, but had not been completely eaten through underneath, so that they were left standing on thin, isolated columns, twenty feet or more in height. Some of these curious natural monuments were to be seen in course of formation on the cliff-side, not having been yet separated by the disintegration. On all sides of us these columns stood up in their hundreds, supporting their top-heavy boulders, so that we seemed to be walking through a great plantation of Brobdingnagian yellow mushrooms. I am astonished that no lamas have perched their dwellings on these perilously-poised rocks, for they are just the sort of sites that these lovers of the grotesque in Nature would select as eligible building-land.

This day we encamped at Nimu, which felt oppressively hot after the greater elevation of Iamps, where it freezes every night, even in summer. On June 12 I reached Leh. Bower's preparations were now complete, and he and Thorold were to start in two days. The Doctor's services were no longer needed at Leh, for during my absence poor Dr. Redslop had died, and Shaw, the only remaining Moravian missionary, was in a fair way of recovery, and did not require medical assistance.

Bower's and Thorold's enforced delay at Leh enabled us to be spectators together of what is certainly one of the strangest religious festivals in the world, the far-famed fair of Himis Gompa, which I should have been very sorry to have missed.

This large monastery is two marches from Leh up the Indus Valley, close to the point where Bower's route was to diverge from the Indus to cross the mountains by the Chang La It was therefore settled that we should travel as far as Himis together, and see what we could of the proceedings there. Himis Gompa is the most important and wealthy monastery in Ladak, and, according to Duke's Guide, contains accommodation for 800 monks and nuns. The annual festival that is held here commences at a fixed date according to the Tibetan calendar, but on a variable date according to ours. In this particular year the opening day was to be on June 16, but it is often at least a week earlier. The proceedings continue for two days, and attract great numbers of Buddhists from Chinese Tibet as well as from Ladak, the Yellow lamas and nuns from Lassa mingling with their Red brethren of Western Tibet. This fair is naturally a great centre of intrigue between the Buddhist subjects of the Maharajah and the priests of Lassa, and is therefore not looked upon with great favour by the Kashmir authorities.

For these two days the lamas, disguised in grotesque masks, richly-embroidered robes of Chinese silks, and other masquerading garb, engage in a complicated mummery in the large courtyard of the lamasery, with strange symbolical ceremonies, chantings, and fantastic dances, the meaning of which, if there be any, it is difficult to discover.

But the Devil Dance, which is the most important

feature in the function, has at least one definite object. It seems that after a man has died his soul, on its way to its next sphere, is waylaid by demons with horrible faces and forms, who endeavour to terrify the soul out of its proper road. Should the demons succeed in this, that belated soul will wander about space for an indefinite period, in vain seeking its proper sphere. In order to lessen the risk of such mischance the lamas during this festival put on masks resembling the faces of these demons, and imitate their awful antics; in this way the spectators are familiarised with these sights and sounds of horror, and when they die their souls will not be so readily dismayed by the apparitions.

When Ladak was conquered by the Dogras, some fifty years ago, Himis was the one important monastery which escaped pillage. It is rumoured that the lamas purchased this exemption by proffering supplies to the invading army. However this may be, the fact remains that Himis Gompa is still in possession of great treasures, which, however, the Kashmir Durbar does not permit the lamas to dispose of as they please. Were it not for this control the Buddhists would naturally feel disposed to carry this wealth across the frontier into Chinese Tibet, and found another monastery under happier auspices in that sacred and inviolate land. The Naib Wazir, as representative of the Durbar, is in custody of one of the keys, without which the principal treasure-room cannot be entered, and the lamas are not permitted to visit it unless he be present.

Fortunate as is Himis Gompa in the possession of its hoarded riches, it is particularly unfortunate in one other respect: though the most important lamasery in Ladak, it lacks the one essential thing to crown its dignity—it can boast of no resident skooshok. Ramsey, in his book, explains that a skooshok does belong to this monastery, but that three or four births back he was re-incarnated at Lassa, and refused to go to his gompa in Ladak. Since then he has always been re-born in Lassa, and persists in his objection to his proper home. The present skooshok is now twenty-three years old, and is as obstinate as ever. The holy city of Lassa, where lamas are supreme, is a more agreeable residence to this man than Dogra-ruled Ladak. Surely it must be a very wicked thing to be an absentee skooshok, and he deserves to be re-born in an inferior sphere—as a cuckoo, for instance—and lose his skooshokship for his desertion of his poor monks and nuns of Himis.

So on Sunday, June 14, we set out for Himis Fair. We formed quite an imposing cavalcade; for the Naib Wazir, the Treasurer of Ladak, and other dignitaries who were to be present at the festival, accompanied us. The officers and others who had travelled with Bower in Central Asia on his last expedition rode down with us as far as the banks of the Indus, and there bade their old chief farewell. Many Asiatics are undoubtedly as faithful followers as one could desire, and often entertain a genuine affection for a sahib who has led them well, and whom they respect. These good fellows wept as they bade Bower good-bye, and one, a Mussulman, threw off his turban as he prostrated himself before him. With a follower of the Prophet, to thus bare the head is always a sign of vehement emotion, being either intended as a gross insult and a readiness to take all the consequences of it, or, as on this occasion, indicating a keen and reckless sorrow, and a desire to humiliate himself in despair before the object of his regard, from whom he is about to separate.

Great manis and chortens bordered our road down

LADAKI BUDDHISTS.

THE NAIB WAZIR OF LADAK.

KASHMIRI PUNDITS.

to the Indus, which we crossed by a wooden bridge.
In front of us, lying in a broad hollow in the mountains, was an irrigated oasis with several buildings, and one rather imposing edifice standing amid the orchards. This is Stok, the estate of the Gialpo, or Rajah of Ladak, the grandson of the ruler who was overthrown by the Dogras. Here the deposed monarch sulks in state, and looks across the Indus at the grand old palace of his ancestors dominating the city of Leh. The Gialpo is treated with the greatest respect by the Ladakis, who still look up to him as their prince. He enjoys a reputation for great piety and erudition in Buddhist literature. He is completely priest-ridden, and passes most of his time in solitary devotion and in theological converse with learned lamas.

We rode up the left bank of the Indus, and formed part of a great straggling crowd travelling in the same direction as ourselves. Nearly all these people were mounted, and were dressed in their gayest attire, making a great display of China silks and Tibetan turquoises. There were merry little family parties— a wife, her child, and her three husbands jogging along on small ponies, the minor husbands carrying with them the provisions and baggage; or a lady and her latest magpa astride of the same horse. There were plenty of red-robed lamas too, who were journeying to Himis from distant gompas, and a goodly number of stately turbaned merchants from Leh—Hindoos, and Mahomedans in white robes, or brightly-coloured chogas, looking remarkably clean and handsome by the side of the Mongolian Buddhists. These last formed the bulk of the crowd, and had no dignity about them. They were bent on enjoying their three days' holiday at Himis, and were in the highest spirits, and ready to crack a joke with us as we passed. The Ladakis thoroughly relish a bit of buffoonery on occasion, and indulged in rollicking horseplay. It was a motley and lively procession, a sort of Tibetan version of a Canterbury Pilgrimage.

As we neared Shushot, where we were to encamp for the night, we saw a large crowd awaiting us, and we were greeted by a wild music of gongs, surnais, drums, tomtoms, and trumpets. We found that the authorities had got up a polo-match for our amusement. The men of Shushot are famed for their skill in the game, and have an excellent polo-ground in the village. Carpets and cloths had been placed on a kind of grand stand in anticipation of our coming, and here we sat down, with the Naib Wazir and other notables, to view the game.

The polo was followed by a *nach* of Ladaki women. The ladies, who were not possessed of any charms, wore the usual clumsy national dress, reaching to their ankles, sheepskin cloaks, and very large boots of felt or raw hide, which would have done well for some gouty rajah, but were not what one expects to see on the dainty feet of a *coryphée*. There was no dancing in the strict sense of the word, nor were there any of the graceful undulations of the body which distinguish some Eastern naches. These well-wrapped-up creatures stepped in solemn figures to the strains of the band, gesticulating queerly with their hands, turning the palms, now up, now down, opening and shutting their hands, and extending or closing their fingers, in concert. They waddled about thus for some time, looking inexpressibly miserable, until the music suddenly stopped, when they formed themselves into a row, salaamed us by bowing their heads to the ground, and took themselves off. I can conscientiously say that by attending this nautch we were not in the slightest degree countenancing any impropriety. It was a respectably dull and sedate performance, that would not have raised a blush to the cheek of the most immaculate of London County Councillors.

Early the next morning we mounted our horses and resumed our journey. We found the road crowded with jovial pilgrims, as on the previous day. At last we came to where the nullah in which the Himis monastery is situated debouches on the Indus Valley; and here, in a little orchard, the Naib Wazir had arranged that we should have tiffin. The repast was set out in a large tent which the lamas had sent down for our convenience, and which was decorated with designs of devils, monsters, and prayers in Tibetan characters. The steward of the gompa was also here to bid us welcome, and escort us for the rest of our way.

Tiffin over, we set out again. At the entrance of the Himis nullah we passed through some good land with well-irrigated and carefully-cultivated terraces, promising abundant crops of grain and fruit. Struck by the prosperous appearance of this oasis, I made inquiry of my companions, and learnt that this was, as I had suspected, Church property, being held by zemindars of the monastery on the Metayer system, the tenants handing over one-half of the produce to the lamas, and being practically exempt from taxation and begar. We rode up the savage ravine, which formed a fitting approach to the sacred place. The scenery was barren for the most part; but the torrent was bordered by dense groves. The signs of Buddhist worship were everywhere around us: manis lined the steep path, and every prominent crag was crowned with chorten, altar, or hermitage. At last, on turning a corner, a most picturesque sight burst upon us. The vast lamasery stood before us, perched high up on the rugged rocks, with wild mountains forming a fine background to the picture. Himis is at a much greater

A CHORTEN AT HIMIS.

height above the sea than Leh, and in every shaded hollow of the gorge the snow was still lying.

As soon as our party was seen to approach, the monks on the battlements of the lamasery, high above, welcomed us with their weird music from long shawms and cymbals. We now dismounted, and ascended by steps hewn out of the rock to the outer precincts of the gompa, where many tents were pitched and merchants had opened booths to sell their wares to the crowds of chattering, laughing, pigtailed pilgrims.

We reached the main gate of the gompa; and here some monks took charge of us and led us to our quarters through that great rambling edifice of weird sights, across strange courtyards fantastically decorated, where huge and ugly Tibetan mastiffs of yellow colour, sacred creatures of the gompa, barked furiously at us as we passed, and strained at their stout chains, eager to fly at the intruders' throats; along dim, narrow alleys, where dripping water turned the praying-wheels, and where hand-wheels and other facilities for devotion met one at every turn; up steep, winding flights of stairs; across wooden galleries overhanging abysses. Everywhere we were surrounded by uncanny objects. The walls were covered with frescoes of grotesque gods and frightful demons; banners with monstrous designs waved over us; and, not the least uncanny, the Red lamas, with their dark rags and shaven heads, some of them scowling and hang-dog, with not a little *odium theologicum* and priestly hypocrisy in their expression, kept flitting by us with noiseless footsteps, whispering to one another after the peculiar manner of this country—so low a whisper that no sound was audible even when we were quite near; and it appeared as if they were conversing by watching the silent movements of each other's lips, as do our own deaf and dumb.

The Abbot of Himis treated us with great hospitality. Comfortable chambers were placed at our disposal in a high turret of the gompa, commanding a splendid view down the nullah, across the Indus Valley, to the snowy range beyond—a depression in which was pointed out to me by Bower as the Chang La, by which lay his road to China. The steward of the gompa also kindly sent us presents of provisions—sheep, rice, and sugar—and did not forget the jars of cheering chung.

From an overhanging gallery close to our quarters we could look down on what may be described as the chief quadrangle of the gompa, the one in which the religious mummery was to take place. In the centre of the flagged courtyard stood a lofty pole hung with gaily-coloured streamers, on which dragons and mystic signs were delineated. Banners and beautiful silk draperies, with similar quaint figures worked upon them, depended from the walls. On that side of the quadrangle which faced us was the porch of the temple, with steps leading up to it, its columns and friezes being painted in rich red, green, and brown tints. On the side to our right the building was only one storey high, and had a gate under it leading to the outer precincts of the monastery. Towering over this building could be seen the houses of the little town of Himis perched upon the bare crags. Praying-flags were fluttering everywhere on the roofs of the gompa and the houses.

As an undress rehearsal of the Devil Dance was taking place in the quadrangle when we arrived, all the galleries, windows, and roof-tops round it were crowded with spectators. The Ladaki women were conspicuous in their bright holiday dress: each had her dowry of turquoises on her head and shoulders, and her cloak of scarlet and sage-green cloth lined with snowy fleece. Many visitors from Chinese Tibet were present, lamas and nuns of the Yellow order, their robes and caps of dingy yellow contrasting with the dark red of the Ladak priesthood. The Yellow nuns had their heads shaven like the monks, and were not attractive-looking creatures. The lay Tibetans from across the frontier were much like the Ladakis, but had a wilder appearance. Many of them were wonder-

HIMIS TOWN.

fully hideous, with great misshapen heads and stumpy bodies. They seemed much given to clumsy buffoonery. Some of the women had no peyraks, but wore their masses of coarse black hair fastened up in a great straggling bunch. Nearly all the spectators were twisting their praying-wheels as they chatted to each other and contemplated the rehearsal.

It was an outlandish scene, and no fitter stage could be imagined for the strange ceremonies we were about to witness than the quadrangle, with its buildings of quaint architecture, the crowding people, the background of cliffs, and houses one above the other; and when the barbaric music arose, and the Devil Dance commenced, it was not only a very weird, but a really very impressive experience. Among these surroundings, one felt very far from the Western world and its nineteenth-century civilisation and beliefs.

Buddhists have few prejudices, and allow the stranger to penetrate the arcana of their temples and see their most sacred rites; but I was agreeably surprised when the Treasurer of Ladak, himself a Ladaki, and a strict Buddhist, came to me and said he knew I would like to take photographs of the ceremonies, that he had spoken to the Abbot on the subject, and that there was not the slightest objection to my using my camera whensoever and wheresoever I pleased. I accordingly secured a number of pictures in the course of the festival; but no photograph can do justice to a scene in which was present such an extraordinary wealth of colour—the orange robes of the Yellow lamas; the draperies of the Red lamas, of various shades from fiery red to purple black; the red, white, and green dresses of the thronging people; the numerous rich tones of the painted monastery, and the hanging banners; the mud-coloured town and crags behind, glaring in the sunshine; and lastly, above the whole picture, the beautiful blue of the Tibetan sky.

The undress rehearsal was itself a strange performance, and promised well for the interest of the next day's ceremony. When it was over, we took a stroll up the picturesque and chorten-studded nullah of Himis, and perceived several ibex not far from us on the crags above. These ibex are protected by the lamas, no one being permitted to shoot in this sacred preserve, a fact which is evidently well-known to the timid beasts, which are much bolder in this ravine than elsewhere, and venture close to the habitations of the harmless priests.

CHAPTER XIII

THE MYSTERY-PLAY AT HIMIS — FIRST DAY'S CEREMONIAL — THE LAMA MASK — THE DEVIL DANCE — THE TREASURES OF THE LAMASERY — THE IDOL CHAMBER — SECOND DAY'S CEREMONIAL — THE CONSECRATION OF ANIMALS — A HARLEQUINADE — RETURN TO LEH — THE LAMASERY OF TIKZAY — THE SKOOSHOK.

AT an early hour of the morning of June 16 we were awoke to a realisation of where we were by the sounding of the priestly shawms in different quarters of the great monastery. We arose, and found it had been snowing in the night, and the distant mountains were white almost down to the level of the Indus—an unfavourable circumstance for Bower's start on the morrow.

After breakfast we repaired with the Naib Wazir, the Treasurer, and other notables to the gallery overlooking the quadrangle, where seats had been prepared for us. The jovial Treasurer, finding that I appreciated the national beverage, produced at intervals flowing bowls of chung to cheer us as we gazed at the successive whirling troops of devils and monsters that passed before us.

The great crowd had already collected—men and women of Ladak and Chinese Tibet, lamas and nuns red and yellow, and a sprinkling of Hindoos and scornful Mussulmans, filling the galleries, covering the roofs, and squatting on the floor all round the quadrangle. Several sepoys of the irregular Ladaki levy—in the

Ladaki dress, and not in the least like soldiers—and lamas with scourges in their hands, kept the spectators in order, and prevented them from pressing on to the space reserved for the performers. In a state-box of the gallery opposite to us, hung with silken draperies, sat the Gialpo, or deposed Rajah of Ladak, with his suite and attendant lamas. Though of the same Mongolian stock as his people, he was of much fairer complexion; his features were highly refined, having much of the pure beauty of asceticism, contrasting strangely with the ignoble faces around. One could distinguish at once that he was of an ancient and well-bred race. He quite looked the Buddhist mystic and devotee absorbed in the contemplation of Nirvana. His expression was sad, resigned, and dreamy. He never smiled, and seldom spoke to those by him. His young son, equally conspicuous among his companions for his refined look and bearing, had been devoted by the Gialpo to the Church, and was one of the singing-boys who took part in the ceremony.

It is difficult to give an account of the ever-changing and very interesting mummery which was carried on for the whole of this long summer's day—a bewildering phantasmagoria of strange sights, a din of unearthly music, that almost caused the reason to waver, and make one believe that one was indeed in the magic realm represented by the actors, a dreadful world, affording but dismal prospects; being even as these Buddhists regard this present existence of ours, and of which, if it were thus, one would indeed be well quit. For the principal motive of this mystery play appeared to be the lesson that the helpless, naked soul of man has its being in the midst of a vast and obscure space full of malignant demons—the earth, the air, the water crowded with them—perpetually seeking to destroy him, harassing him with tortures and terrors; and that against this infinite oppression of the powers of evil he can of himself do nothing, but that occasionally the exorcisms or prayers of some good lama or incarnation may come to his assistance and shield him, and even then only after a fierce and doubtful contest between the saint and the devils. And only for a time, too, can this relief from persecution endure, for all the exorcisms of all the saints are of little avail to keep back the advancing hordes. The shrieking demons must soon close in upon the soul again. Such is the gloomy prospect of human existence as depicted by the Tibetan lamas.

The extraordinary resemblance between much of the pageantry and forms of Tibetan Buddhism and those of the Church of Rome has been observed by all travellers in these regions. The lamas, who represented the saints in this mummery, had the appearance of early-Christian bishops: they wore mitres and copes, and carried pastoral crooks; they swung censers of incense as they walked in procession, slowly chanting. Little bells were rung at intervals during the ceremony; some of the chanting was quite Gregorian. There was the partaking of a sort of sacrament; there was a dipping of fingers in bowls of holy water; the shaven monks, who were looking on, clad almost exactly like some of the friars in Italy, told their beads on their rosaries, occasionally bowed their heads and laid their hands across their breasts; and there was much else besides that was startlingly similar to things one had seen and heard in Europe.

I will only attempt the description of some of the principal features of this two days' complicated cere

THE MYSTERY PLAY, HIMIS.

mony, to rehearse for which is one of the chief occupations of the lamas throughout the year. Some of the sacred dances have intricate figures and gesticulations, and must need a great deal of preparation. The musical instruments employed by the lama orchestra on this occasion included shawms and other huge brazen wind instruments, surnais, cymbals, gongs, tambourines, and rattles made of human bones. The many-coloured and grotesquely-designed robes worn by the mummers were of beautiful China silk, while the masks exhibited great powers of horrible invention on the part of their makers.

The gongs and shawms sounded, and the mummery commenced. First came some priests with mitres on their heads, clad in rich robes, who swung censers, filling the courtyard with the odour of incense. After a stately dance to slow music these went out; and then entered, with wild antics, figures in yellow robes and peaked hoods, looking something like victims destined for an *auto da fe*; flames and effigies of human skulls were on their breasts and other portions of their raiment. As their hoods fell back hideous features, as of leering satyrs, were disclosed. Then the music became fast and furious, and troop after troop of different masks rushed on, some beating wooden tambourines, others swelling the din with rattles and bells. All of these masks were horrible, and the malice of infernal beings was well expressed on some of them. As they danced to the wild music with strange steps and gestures, they howled in savage chorus. These, I believe, were intended to represent some of the ugly forms that meet the dead man's soul in space while it is winging its way from one sphere to the next.

The loud music suddenly ceased, and all the

demons scampered off, shrieking as if in fear, for a holy thing was approaching. To solemn chanting, low music, and swinging of censers, a stately procession came through the porch of the temple and slowly descended the steps. Under a canopy borne by attendants walked a tall form in beautiful silk robes, wearing a large mask representing a benign and peaceful face. As he advanced, men and boys, dressed as abbots and acolytes of the Church of Rome, prostrated themselves before him, and adored him with intoning and pleasing chanting. He was followed by six other masks, who were treated with similar respect. These seven deified beings drew themselves in a line on one side of the quadrangle, and received the adoration of several processions of masked figures, some of abbots, and others beast-headed, or having the faces of devils. 'Those seven masks,' said the Treasurer to us, ' are representations of the Delai Lama of Lassa and his previous incarnations. They are being worshipped, as you see, by lamas, kings, spirits, and others.' A few minutes later the steward of the gompa came up to us and explained that these were intended for the incarnations of Buddha, and not of the Delai Lama; whereupon he and that other erudite theologian, the Treasurer, discussed the point at some length in their native tongue. The incident shows how little these people know of the original meaning of their traditional ceremonial.

Throughout the day, even during the above solemn act of worship, certain lamas masked as comic devils performed all manner of buffoonery, hitting each other unawares, tripping each other up, and bursting into peals of insane laughter each time that one played some monkey trick on another.

Again there came a change. The solemn chanting

MASK OF THE DELAI LAMA DESCENDING THE TEMPLE STEPS.

ceased, and then rushed on the scene a crowd of wan shapes, almost naked, with but a few dark rags about them, which they sometimes held up by the corners, veiling their faces, and sometimes gathered together round them, as if they were shivering with cold. They wrung their hands despairingly and rushed about in a confused way, as if lost, starting from each other in terror when they met, sometimes feeling about them with their outstretched hands like blind men, and all the while whistling in long-drawn notes, which rose and fell like a strong wind on the hills, producing an indescribably dreary effect. These I was told represented the unfortunate souls of dead men which had been lost in space, and were vainly seeking their proper sphere through the darkness. On seeing these poor shadows some lines I had read were vividly recalled to my mind. They run, so far as I remember, thus:—

> Somewhere, in desolate, wind-swept space,
> In Shadow-land, in No-Man's land,
> Two hurrying forms met face to face,
> And bade each other stand.
>
> 'And who art thou?' asked one, agape,
> Shuddering in the fading light.
> 'I know not,' cried the other shape;
> 'I only died last night.'

The sudden onrushing of these wildly-whistling shapes occurred at frequent intervals during the ceremony. The change from one phase of this curious mummery to another was always startlingly abrupt. One never knew when some peaceful anthem and stately dance of holy figures would be suddenly interrupted by the clashing discord of cymbals and trumpets and the whirling torrent of shrieking fiends.

For a time the Spirits of Evil ruled supreme in the arena. The variously-masked figures flocked in, troop after troop—oxen-headed and serpent-headed devils; three-eyed monsters with projecting fangs, their heads crowned with tiaras of human skulls; lamas painted and masked to represent skeletons; dragon-faced fiends, naked save for tiger-skins about their loins; and many others. Sometimes they appeared to be taunting and terrifying the stray souls of men—grim shapes who fled hither and thither among their tormentors, waving their arms and wailing miserably, souls who had not obtained Nirvana, and yet who had no incarnation.

The demons went through complicated evolutions—their dancing occasionally being like what a European ballet-step would be if performed to extremely slow time and very clumsily—accompanied by mystical rhythmical motions of hands and fingers. There were solo dances, too, while the other demons stood round beating gongs, clashing cymbals, and clapping hands.

Then the demons were repelled again by holy men; but no sooner did these last exorcise one hideous band than other crowds came shrieking on. It was a hopeless conflict.

At one period of the ceremony a holy man with an archbishop's mitre on his head advanced, to the beautiful chanting of men and boys, the basses, trebles, and tenors taking successive parts in solo and chorus. On listening with shut eyes one could well imagine oneself to be in a Christian cathedral. This holy man blessed a goblet of water by laying his hands on it and intoning some prayer or charm. Then he sprinkled the water in all directions, and the defeated demons stayed their shrieking, dancing, and infernal music, and gradually crept out of the arena, and no sound was heard for a time but the sweet singing of the holy choir.

But the power of the exorcism was evanescent, for

THE DEVIL DANCE.

the routed soon returned in howling shoals, and then lamas and spirits appeared to be contending with rival magic. Strange signs were made and rites performed on either side, all no doubt symbolical, but the meaning of which none could tell me; it was unknown to the people, and to the priests themselves, only the outward forms remaining to them of their ancient creed, the inward signification lost centuries on centuries ago.

A small black image representing a human corpse was placed within a magic triangle designed upon the pavement of the quadrangle. Figures painted black and white to simulate skeletons, some in chains, others bearing sickles or swords, engaged in a frantic dance around the corpse. They were apparently attempting to snatch it away or inflict some injury on it, but were deterred by the magic of the surrounding triangle, and by the chanting and censer-swinging of several holy men in mitres and purple copes, who stood beneath the temple porch. A more potent and very ugly fiend, with great horns on his head and huge, lolling tongue, ran in, hovered threateningly over the corpse, and with a great sword slashed furiously about it, just failing by little more than a hair's breadth to touch it with each sweep of the blade. He seemed as if he were about to overcome the opposing enchantment, when a saint of still greater power than he now came to the rescue. The saint approached the corpse and threw a handful of flour on it, making mystic signs and muttering incantations. This appeared from his mask to be one of the incarnations of Buddha. He had more control over the evil spirits than any other who had yet contended with them. The skeletons, and also he that bore the great sword, grovelled before him, and with inarticulate and beast-like cries implored mercy. He yielded to their supplication, gave each one a little of the flour he carried with him, which the fiends ate gratefully, kneeling before him; and he also gave them to drink out of a vessel of holy water.

And so on, hour after hour, the ever-changing mumming proceeded, until one was dazed by gazing at it, and began almost to believe oneself to be really in spirit-land. The ceremony did not come to a conclusion until sunset, when, after a hot day, the cold wind sprang up, and it commenced to snow lightly—a not unusual occurrence, even in mid-June, at the elevation of Himis.

After the performance the Abbot took us over the Idol Chamber and other portions of the lamasery. We were not able to visit the great treasure-room, which cannot be opened without permission of the Durbar; but wherever we wandered we saw a considerable display of wealth. In the temple were quantities of sacred vessels and ornaments of gold and silver. There were chortens of saints solidly plated with silver and inlaid with gold and jewels. There were also some fine wood carvings and silk hangings of wonderful workmanship in these strange, dimly-lighted halls. We were shown collections of Buddhist manuscripts and illuminated scrolls, some obviously of great antiquity, and the study of which might throw much light on the mysteries of the Tibetan belief.

The Idol Room was a weird place with pictures of aërial battles between hideous fiends and equally hideous Gods, many-headed and many-armed; of tortures of the damned, dreadful as only the Chinese imagination can evolve; of Gods and Goddesses on a gigantic scale, with cruel, callous eyes, sitting unmoved among the horrors, 'careless of mankind.' There were many idols in the chamber. Images of unclean and malicious deities stood in the niches of the walls. But among all these repulsive faces of degraded type, distorted with evil passions, we saw in striking contrast here and there an image of the contemplative Buddha, with beautiful calm features, pure and pitiful, such as they have been handed down by painting and sculpture for two thousand years, and which the lamas, with all their perverted imagination, have never ventured to change when designing an idol of the Great Incarnation.

This was a night of noise and revelry. From dusk to dawn monkish music resounded through the corridors and quadrangle of the gompa, whose doors appeared to be open to all who might choose to enter. Nautches of Ladaki women and festivities of different sorts were organised for the amusement of the visitors to the sacred precincts, who became boisterously merry, but not quarrelsome, over their copious draughts of chung.

On the following morning, June 17, Bower and Thorold, with their following, left Himis to cross the Chang La—which was visible from here as a gentle dip in the distant white mountain-range—to plunge, a few marches beyond, into the unknown world. I was the last European they were to see until they had crossed mysterious Tibet and had fallen in with the Christian missionaries in China proper. It was a doubtful thing whether we should ever hear of these two good Englishmen again. It was upwards of a year later that I received a letter from Bower, and was delighted to find that not only he and Thorold, but his faithful followers, the Rajpoot surveyor and the Pathan orderly, had got through safely to Shanghai. Even my old friends Benjamin and Joseph, the Kashmiri-baiting spaniel pups, were still hearty after their strange experiences.

P

We saw them well off down the nullah, and then the Naib Wazir, the Treasurer, and myself returned to our gallery in the monastery to witness the second day's ceremony, which is supposed to be the most important of the two.

At one stage three richly-caparisoned horses were brought into the quadrangle by some masked lamas, robed and hatted like Chinese mandarins. The fine cloths were taken off the horses, and the unfortunate beasts were then dragged hither and thither by the men, who also shouted and gesticulated before them, as if to scare and enrage them, while the whole crowd of spectators joined in with discordant howls and cheers. The lamas now poured buckets of red paint upon the horses and smeared their bodies over with it. Three large Tibetan dogs were also led in, and painted and worried in a similar fashion, until all six creatures were frantic with terror. I was told afterwards that these were like the scapegoats of the ancient Jews, and that the red paint symbolised the sin of the people, that was being transferred to the animals. The Naib Wazir explained to me that these creatures were now dedicated to the gompa, and would henceforth be exempt from any work and be considered as holy, the mastiffs to be chained up in the monastery passages and fret themselves into fury, the horses to live a life of contented ease in the adjacent paddock.

The masks were still more extraordinary on this than on the previous day, and defy description. Ceremonies of unknown meaning succeeded each other: there was a blessing of little pans of corn; a lighting of fires with mystic rites; there were dances of warriors, of savages in skins, of wild beasts, of fabulous monsters. At one time four masks came forward and placed a black cloth on the ground, danced round it with intricate steps, then, raising it, disclosed a prone black image of a man, like the one we had seen on the day before. But now, after a protracted conflict between rival spirits, the devils broke through the lamas' magic and rent the image to pieces with their claws; and, being filled with some red paste, it bled most realistically during the operation.

A sort of harlequinade terminated this extraordinary two days' pantomime, full of coarse and often obscene buffoonery, which hugely pleased the audience, and was received with peals of laughter even by the onlooking lamas. Clowns came on, and proceeded to burlesque the preceding sacred mysteries. A comic school was one of the chief features of this part of the performance. The schoolmaster was a fatuous old pantaloon. The bare-armed and bare-legged boys who represented the scholars wore large masks of moonshaped, grinning faces. They fought among each other; they chaffed their old pedagogue, pinched him from behind and ran away, threw things at him, stole his hat and writing materials, and played all manner of other tricks on him; while he tottered after them with his stick, trembling with rage, and unable to catch them. But he had an usher, or assistant, who was much more agile. Whenever the boys became over-obstreperous he would suddenly dart across the quadrangle harlequin-wise, buffeting the young rascals right and left as he went.

Last of all, the schoolmaster prostrated himself with comical action before the bowls of consecrated corn and the images of the Gods, and proceeded to ape the worship of the lamas. His scholars, imitating him, prostrated themselves in a row beside him, and engaged in mock prayer and ridiculous gestures and antics at the expense of their own religion. Thus, with an orgie of indecency and blasphemous caricature of all that these people are supposed to hold sacred the festival ended at dusk, when once again the cold wind sprang up after the sultry day and the snow fell lightly.

On the following morning, June 18, the large gathering began to break up, and the pilgrims set out by divers ways for their homes, some to Ladaki villages and Rupshu highlands, and some to far-off Lassa.

Though this festival is termed the Himis Fair, a very limited amount of trade was carried on, for few Tibetan caravans had crossed the passes at so early a season. On a small scale, however, the produce of the two countries was being bartered—the dried apricots of Baltistan. the saffron and sugar of India, being exchanged for the brick tea, the incense-sticks, the medicinal herbs, and the turquoises of China.

I returned to Leh with the Naib Wazir and his suite. He suggested that we should cross the Indus by a wooden bridge below Himis, and travel back by the right bank of the river. By taking this route we should pass the large and interesting Gompa of Tikzay, and be able to interview that nearest approach to a Mahatma, a real live skooshok; for this monastery, unlike unfortunate Himis, possesses a resident incarnation. We rode along the white sands of the Indus bed, and encamped not far from the monastery in a delightful bagh of birches and great rose-bushes covered with blossoms, where many wild flowers, too, were in bloom amid the long grass. This garden was surrounded by a sandy desert. In the evening, as is the rule here, a strong wind came up the Indus Valley, and a mist of granite dust obscured the sky andland.

On the following morning we halted at Tikzay on our way to Leh, and paid our salaam to the skooshok. The Monastery of Tikzay is built on the summit of an isolated peak, and is a most picturesque place, with the usual inleaning walls and overhanging, open galleries that characterise the Tibetan architecture.

We clambered up the steep path to the monastery gate, and were ushered into the presence of the

THE LAMASERY OF TIKZAY.

skooshok, who was sitting in a gallery at the very summit of the building. He is much looked up to by all the lamas of Ladak as being a man of great learning. While completing his education at Lassa he passed the highest examinations, and is an adept in all the Buddhist mysteries. He appeared to be a man of middle age, and had a gentle, intelligent face. He spoke but little, and had a dreamy, far-off look in his eyes. For most of the time that we sat with him he was abstractedly gazing at the immense landscape that was extended before him—deserts, oases, the far-stretching Indus Valley, and the snowy mountain-ranges. He pointed out this view to us with evident appreciation of its somewhat sterile beauties. His incarnations have been many here. He thoroughly believes that he was Skooshok of Tikzay at a date when we British were naked, painted savages, and has been gazing century after century over the same glaring wilderness from this high monastery top. At times he muttered prayers almost inaudibly as he sat by us, contemplating the scene with mild, sad eyes. He ordered a gift of sugar and dried apricots to be brought to us, and then we bade farewell to the incarnation, whom we left still praying and dreamily considering the world below.

Some of the lamas now took us over the monastery, where we saw the usual grotesque objects of Tibetan worship, and were snarled at by the sacred mastiffs as we passed by them. These savage brutes are securely chained, else a gompa would be a very unpleasant place to visit. We were brought to the mouth of a dark chamber, or chasm in the rock. I peeped into this, and could not see the limits of it; but perceived dimly the images of many grovelling demons, who were being trodden under foot by a black figure of gigantic dimensions. All that was visible of this figure was one huge foot, with a portion of the lower leg. The rest of the body was lost in the obscurity, and the likeness of the god was left to one's imagination; but the image was on so great a scale that, were it continued upwards in proper proportions to the foot, it would tower high above the monastery roofs.

CHAPTER XIV

A REVOLUTION—NATIVE CHRISTIANS IN LEH—BAZAAR RUMOURS—COMMENCE MARCH THROUGH BALTISTAN TO GILGIT—LINGUA FRANCA—THE TRUCULENT AFGHAN—DEFILES OF THE INDUS—SKIRBICHAN—GOMA HANU.

On returning to Leh I took up my residence again in the Joint-Commissioner's house. On the night of my arrival I was woke up by an extraordinary noise: gongs and tomtoms were being beaten in the city, people were shouting, and now and again men rushed by the European quarter shrieking words I could not understand. I naturally concluded that a fire had broken out, so went into the bungalow grounds to discover in what direction it might be. But I could distinguish no signs of a conflagration, and not being able to make anything of this hubbub, I turned into bed again. The din gradually subsided, and at last no sound was to be heard save the usual cry and challenge of the watchmen in the town and neighbouring villages. These watchmen, by the way, call out at intervals, 'Look out! Look out! all who do not carry lanterns are thieves,' and it is their duty to arrest anyone going about after dark unprovided with a light.

On the following morning, the Naib Wazir called upon me, and told me the story of the nocturnal disturbance. Nothing less than a revolution had taken place, a trumpery one, it is true, but it might have led to mischief had it not been promptly put down; and to some extent it was an anti-European demonstration. It appeared that the Mahomedans of Leh had worked themselves up to a high pitch of indignation because some poor men of their faith had carried the bodies of the dead Moravian missionaries to the cemetery for burial, and had received payment for doing so.

These angry Mussulmans, profiting by the absence of the Naib Wazir at Himis, had proceeded to take the law into their own hands. Their chief men had drawn up a list of regulations for the government of the city, to which the *mullah* affixed his seal. According to this proclamation, which had been posted up in the bazaar, no man was to eat with the outcasts who had touched the Christian dead. Punishments for various offences were instituted, and public floggings in the bazaar were to be inflicted on anyone who should disobey the injunctions of this self-constituted tribunal. A great meeting of Mahomedans had been convened on the previous night, and had ended in the riot which had disturbed my slumbers. But the Naib Wazir had now returned to his post, so he sallied forth with the handful of Gurkha sepoys which forms part of the small garrison at Leh, and in a very short time put an end to this *imperium in imperio*. He arrested the ringleaders, among whom were some of the leading merchants in the town, and confined them in the fortress, from which, I believe, they were not liberated until they had been handsomely fined and soundly flogged.

I was glad to find that the only other European man in Leh, the Moravian missionary, Shaw, though weak, was now well recovered of the fever: so we foregathered, and saw a good deal of each other during the few days I remained here awaiting my letters.

The postman and his family are, I believe, the only native Christians in Leh. Shaw and myself had tea with them one afternoon. Theirs was a regular Tibetan home, less the Buddhist shrines and idols, with a rough mud-stove at one end of the chamber and the cooking-vessels strewn about the floor. Here we found the host, his wife, his two grown-up, unmarried daughters, and his other children—for, as he is a Christian, his family is much more extensive than is usual in polyandric Ladak. One of his daughters had displeased him by marrying a Buddhist, and he seemed much perturbed because there were no Christian young men in Leh who could become husbands to these other two daughters, who are good-tempered, not uncomely, and well-dowered girls. This was a happy, jolly family, and no foolish attempts were made to ape European ways. The meal they put before us was quite Tibetan, consisting of cakes and bowls of China tea, in which clarified butter had been melted. This last mixture is by no means so unpalatable as one would imagine, and I think the simple people were pleased that I thoroughly appreciated and did justice to the delicacies they had so kindly provided.

About this time the bazaar at Leh was full of rumours of frontier troubles. It was reported that a Russian force had invaded Afghanistan, and that Colonel Durand, our Agent at Gilgit, was fighting the Kanjutis who had raided into Kashmir territory. My servant Babu Khan came to me one day with a tale he had heard in the bazaar to the effect that a sahib had just been murdered near Gilgit. A few days later further particulars came in. The sahib was said to be Mr. Lennard, who had been killed by Kanjutis on his way from Yarkand to Kashmir. How the story originated I do not know; but it spread through Kashmir, found its way into the Indian papers, and thence to the English, no doubt causing much groundless alarm to Mr. Lennard's relatives and friends. I met him alive and whole later on, and we took part together in the campaign which ended in the total defeat of his supposed murderers, the Kanjuti tribesmen.

This and other bazaar tales chilled the courage of Babu Khan. He took it upon himself to strongly recommend me not to march to Gilgit; it was a dangerous road, he said, to travel, with plenty of bad men on it, who might slay his master; as for himself he was an old man, and his life was of no value. When the poor old gentleman found that I had no intention of changing my plans, he promptly fell ill, or pretended to do so. He certainly appeared to have a fever of some sort, and, as is the habit of the Asiatic, at once threw up the sponge and came to the conclusion he was about to die. There was no doctor in Leh save a kind of Buddhist physician, or magician, who would have treated the case with incantations and charms, so that I had to physic him myself. Despite my care he would not get well, and I was forced to leave him behind at Leh, the Naib Wazir kindly undertaking to send him back to Srinagur as soon as he was convalescent. I subsequently learnt that two days after I had left him he arose from what he had assured me was his deathbed and started for home, his pockets well lined with his arrears of wages and the extra rupees that were to have met his hospital expenses. This rapid recovery, like that of Gil Blas, may have been due to the departure of his medical adviser; but my opinion is that the old humbug had simply malingered to avoid the journey to Gilgit. Gilgit certainly has a very bad name in this country, and servants often refuse to accompany their masters to the Kashmir Siberia.

On June 22 the letter from Spedding which I had been waiting for arrived. He told me he would be on the Gilgit road in the middle of July, and also that Major Cumberland was starting for the Pamirs, and was willing that I should accompany him, could I obtain leave to do so. This was very good news for me. To visit the Roof of the World with so experienced a traveller was an opportunity not to be lost; so I decided to set out for Gilgit forthwith.

I had a long journey before me, and as there was no place on the way at which stores could be procured, I had to make some purchases in the bazaar at Leh. I found that rice and sugar, the articles I was most in need of, were very dear here. Ladak is dependent on Kashmir for these, and it is the custom of the Leh people to travel to Srinagur in the autumn to exchange the produce of their own country with that of the lowlands. I was told that in the previous autumn numbers of these travellers had been kidnapped by pickets of Kashmir sepoys lying in wait for them near Gunderbal, and had been carried off for begar on the Gilgit road. At that late season the march to Gilgit would signify frostbite and possible death for many of these poor creatures. So the men of Leh, terrified at the fate that awaited them at the other end of the road, had declared that they would not undertake the journey to Kashmir this year to exchange their goods. Consequently rice and other Kashmir produce had already almost risen to famine prices in anticipation of the coming scarcity.

The distance from Leh to Gilgit by the road I decided to follow is, roughly, 370 miles, or thirty-two marches. On looking at the map the most obvious route would appear to be by the Indus Valley; but as I have already explained, the difficulties presented by the Indus gorges are so great that the road diverges from the valley twice, for several marches, to cross high snowy passes.

This road is a rough one at its best, and a very up and down one, varying from 4,400 to nearly 17,000 feet above the sea. As the track in many places is not practicable even for unladen animals, I decided to walk all the way. It was an interesting journey, in the course of which I came across some magnificent scenery, and traversed from end to end the province of Baltistan.

As I was leaving Babu Khan behind, my Kashmiri follower, the camera-bearing Subhana, to his great pride and delight, became my factotum, and for the first time in his life was elevated to the rank of khansamah. Having thus far been travelling in the company of fellow-countrymen, or with Babu Khan, who spoke a little English, I had made little progress in the acquisition of Hindostani. But now that I had to get on as well as I could with no one by me who understood a word of English, I of necessity rapidly picked up a sort of language by which I was enabled to make myself intelligible, but which, when I came across Spedding's staff on the Gilgit road, puzzled and amused those young men exceedingly. To my followers and the peoples through whose countries I was travelling Hindostani was almost as much a foreign tongue as it was to myself, and those who spoke it did so but indifferently, mixing with it a good many words of their own dialects. I thus acquired a sort of hodge-podge, which for a time I fondly imagined to be Hindostani, but which, in addition to Urdu, contained Tibetan, Kashmir, and Balti words, and also many Persian terms; for the higher classes in all these regions are acquainted with the 'French of Asia,' and often employ Persian when endeavouring to make themselves understood of the European traveller.

Between Subhana and myself this *lingua franca* at last developed into a regularly-organised language, each of us knowing the particular words of the divers tongues with which the other was conversant; and though my man never spoke a word of English, I found him most useful at first as an interpreter.

My road lay down the Indus Valley for six marches, the first four of which—Leh from Khalsi—I had already traversed on my way from Kashmir. I set out on the morning of June 27 with my little train of coolies, having first bid farewell to weeping Babu Khan—who gave me his dying blessing, the old ruffian—and to all my friends, who came outside the town to see me off, leading sheep and goats, and carrying baskets of vegetables for me, as parting gifts.

During these mid-summer days I found it much hotter work tramping over the sands and gravel of the Indus bed than it had been on our journey up; but the oases were lovelier and more refreshing than ever when we reached them after the long desert marches. The roses were now in full blossom, as, too, were many wild flowers familiar to a European eye—vetches, lavender, thyme, bluebells, iris, corn-flowers, delicate columbines, pink or pure white, while convolvulus wreathed trees and bushes with leaves of vivid green and large petals of various hue. At every halting-place the children were sent out to me with bunches of roses as presents. The apricots, too, had now formed, and were almost of full size in the lower grounds. I watched these with interest, for I looked forward to a great feasting on fruit later on during every hot day's march.

The Ladakis have a more manly bearing than the Kashmiris; still, they can scarcely be termed a brave people. When I reached Saspul I found a caravan from Yarkand encamped there for the night. Among the drivers was one Afghan—like many of his race, a truculent and quarrelsome fellow—who for some reason had thrown a large stone at a Ladaki's head and cut it open, had kicked the head-man of Nimu, and assaulted several others. His Turki companions took no part in the quarrel, and when I came up the Afghan, having satisfied his wrath, was standing, dignified and scornful, in the midst of a crowd of fifty agitated and chattering Ladakis, eager for vengeance, anxious to arrest him, but not one daring to lay hands on him.

When I approached, the blood stained men, who had been but slightly hurt, appealed to me, displaying their wounds and demanding justice, while their friends stood round lamenting, and, after the manner of the mild Buddhists, shuddering at the sight of the blood. I saw no reason to meddle in the matter, but when the terrified creatures asked me to see if their injuries were serious I did so, and recommended them to wash the wounds. They were evidently amazed to hear of this most unusual method of surgical treatment, and I do not think they carried out my instructions. Ladakis, I believe, never wash. In the winter it is too cold to do so; when summer arrives, they argue that having dispensed with ablution for so long it is hardly worth while beginning it.

By order of a sahib a Ladaki can summon some little courage, and had I given the word to seize and bind the Afghan these men would no doubt have obeyed me; but as I refused to act as magistrate, they did not venture to interfere with that terrible man. It is gratifying to observe in what extraordinary estimation the Englishman is held throughout these regions, and how he is always appealed to in every difficulty, and his fiat is accepted without question. 'The sahib has said it, it is enough,' a man will declare, bowing his head in submission to a decision given against himself. The natives of these districts have only seen English gentlemen—officers and Civil Servants from India for the most part—and have acquired an absolute confidence in the integrity and justice of our race, a confidence which is seldom, if ever, abused; for, happily, the mean white does not extend his travels here. The Asiatics do not understand us, neither do they love us, but they respect Englishmen as being straight and brave, and it is only because we have the right men in India, who maintain this reputation, that we are able to rule the land at all. This is all very trite, and has often been said before; but it would be difficult to convince those strange people at home (fortunately fewer than they were some years ago), to whom it appears to be an unpleasant reflection that the British breed should be respected beyond the seas, and to whom every gross misrepresentation which throws discredit on the English in India is more acceptable than the truth.

Those who know Russian Turkestan tell us that even there, should a dispute occur—over some trade transaction, for instance—between two natives, these, having no confidence in their own magistrates, and not much faith in Russian incorruptibility, will ask any English traveller who may be by to act as arbitrator in the case, his word being of higher authority to them than the decision of tribunals.

At midday on June 30 we reached Khalsi, and there, leaving the Srinagur road, plunged into what was to me a new country, following the rough cross-country track by which the Balti traders bring down their loads of dried apricots. This day we descended the Indus Valley for some ten miles below Khalsi, and halted for the night at Doomkha, a very pious village, if one may judge from the amazing number of chortens, manis, and *lhato* that are scattered all over the arid ground surrounding the oasis. 'Books in the running brooks,

SKIRBICHAN.

sermons in stones,' may be taken literally in this land of praying-waterwheels and praying-stones.

Now that I had left the Srinagur road I found no rest-houses at the stages, and so here my tent was pitched among the roses and wild flowers under the apricot-trees, close to a little cascade of ice-cold water. On July 1, passing picturesque Skirbichan, with its gompa-crowned rock, we arrived at the point where the Indus gorges commence to become difficult. In order to avoid the terrific precipices the track is carried high over the stony mountain-spurs. A *maidan* my servant called this portion of the way; for any land that does not slope at a steeper angle than forty-five degrees is considered a plain by the Kashmir mountaineer. We encamped this night at Acheenatang, a hamlet perched on a little ledge of the precipitous mountain-side. Its inhabitants, being away from the high-roads, evidently do not think it worth while to study appearances, for they were the raggedest and filthiest people I met on my whole journey, and that is saying a great deal; but, unlike the poor Baltis, they had at least a sufficiency of clothing, such as it was, and each individual was ingeniously and warmly swathed in a multitude of foul bandages and cloths. There was no water near our camp when we arrived, but the head-man of the village, when this was pointed out to him, walked into the irrigated land some fifty yards away, and by dint of throwing up a dam here and scraping out a hole in an embankment there with his hands, soon sent a nice little stream of clear, cold water babbling by my tent.

On July 2 we descended the Indus gorge through gloomy but magnificent scenery. The stupendous cliffs towered above us on one side of the narrow track, and fell beneath us to the raging torrent on the other side. There was no vegetation, not even a blade of grass to be seen, for a long distance; but at one point of the road we came across a single rose-bush, with one solitary red blossom on it, springing from the débris of a shattered mountain—a strange sight amid the surrounding desolation.

Then we reached the spot beyond which the Indus Valley becomes practically impassable; and it certainly looks it, narrowing to one of the most awful gorges imaginable. It is here that the road, as a reference to the map will show, leaves the Indus for ten marches, crossing the high mountain-range to the north by the Chorbat Pass, to descend to the banks of the Shayok River, a tributary of the Indus rising under the Karakoram Pass.

So here we turned up a side-nullah, down which the Hanu, a torrent of clear blue water, rushes into the dis-

GORGES OF THE INDUS.

coloured Indus. The Hanu has its source among the eternal snows of the Chorbat, and we now had to ascend its steep gorge for two days before reaching the foot of the pass. This night we encamped in a field of purple flowers near Goma Hanu, a hamlet of miserable dwellings honeycombing the cliff-side. This is the highest hamlet of the nullah, and there are no habitations for three days' journey beyond, that is, until the pass is crossed and the banks of the Shayok are reached. This is also the last

Buddhist village. Here I was to bid farewell to the queer land of the pigtailed Ladakis, and the next settlement I was to enter would be in Mahomedan Baltistan.

The inhabitants of this highland village were of a different type to the other Ladakis I had seen. They were of smaller stature—some might be described as dwarfs—and they were uglier and less-intelligent looking than the men of the Indus Valley. Several of them had goitres, and a few miserable creatures appeared to be cretin idiots. I do not know what is the elevation of Goma Hanu, but it must be considerable, for the wind was bitterly cold, and it froze at night. All the villagers who were suffering from any form of sickness came to my tent to be healed. It was in vain I told them I was no *hakim*. I was a sahib, and that in their eyes was a sufficient qualification for medical practice. There were many cases of old sores and wounds that had been neglected and poisoned by dirt. I distributed some Holloway's Ointment and explained its use, and also endeavoured to lecture on the beneficial effects of occasional ablution. I was often consulted by sufferers of this sort on the road, and gave away a good deal of the Ointment, a fact, I fear, which is quite useless as an advertisement, for I marched rapidly through the country, never saw any of my patients again, and cannot say what was the result of my treatment.

There were some other travellers encamped here for the night—a body of twenty Baltis, who were on their way to Ladak, laden with mill-stones. Their burdens were very heavy, for when carrying their own goods and bent on their private enterprise these little men will tramp along merrily under quite double the regulation load of the begar coolie.

At Hanu we exchanged our coolies for others who were to accompany us for the next three days' journey across the mountains. On July 3 we proceeded up the ravine to a camping-place at the foot of the Chorbat La. The embers of old fires under the rocks showed us that this was much used as a halting-ground by the Baltis, of which fact the fleas we picked up here afforded yet another proof. It was a dreary spot, exposed to all the winds of heaven; there were snowy downs all round us, and patches of snow were lying about our camp. It froze hard at night, and there was a strong and biting wind; but we had brought plenty of wood up with us from Goma Hanu, and the coolies had a roaring fire to sleep by.

It began to snow hard in the evening, and the jovial old lumbadar of Goma Hanu, who was accompanying us, shook his head doubtfully, and evidently did not relish the prospect of facing the pass on the morrow. He told us that the Chorbat La was in an exceptionally bad condition after the preceding hard winter, and that we should have to force our way for many hours through soft snow.

CHAPTER XV

THE CHORBAT LA — THE KARAKORAM RANGE — THE PROVINCE OF BALTISTAN — BALTIS — A MUSSULMAN COUNTRY — A DEPOSED RAJAH — KAPALU — ITS RAJAHS — A JOURNEY ON A SKIN RAFT — BRAGAR.

LUCKILY we were not delayed here by bad weather, else our supplies would have run short, and we should have had to send coolies down the valley for more. When I turned out of my tent at dawn on July 4 I found that it was freezing hard and snowing; but there was no wind, and the lumbadar said that we could cross the pass.

For the first part of the way we marched over undulating downs of snow coated with ice, and consequently fairly easy to walk upon; but for the last 2,000 feet or so to the summit of the pass it was very fatiguing travelling, as here we had to ascend a slope of forty-five degrees deeply covered in soft snow, into which we sank at every step.

At this elevation one began to realise that the air was considerably thinner, the atmospheric pressure, as a matter of fact, at 17,000 feet being little more than half what it is at the sea level, and I found that frequent halts were necessary while toiling up this incline; the laden coolies did not reach the summit till three hours after myself. I had my midday halt and tiffin at the extreme top of the pass, which is 16,700 feet above the sea.

The col is formed by a sharp ridge of rock, from

either side of which fall the steep snow-slopes. It had now ceased snowing, and the sky was clear, so that from here I could distinguish the details of the immense landscape that was spread before me—leagues on leagues of snow-fields, couloirs of stones and rocky pinnacles, range behind range of great mountains with glaciers glittering in the hollows of them, the white snow lying wherever the crags were not too steep—a weird and desolate scene, such as one imagines may exist on the Antarctic continent.

Looking to the north across the Shayok Valley, I perceived some stupendous mountains rising above the lesser ranges. These must have been peaks of the main Karakoram range, some fifty miles away, forming the frontier between Baltistan and Chinese Turkestan. I consulted my map, and found that there were several summits exceeding 25,000 feet in the direction I was looking, and one attaining 28,265 feet, the loftiest mountain in the world save Mount Everest. This is K 2, as it is called in the Survey; it is not visible from here, and, indeed, is so buried among huge peaks that it is not at all easy to obtain a glimpse of it from any point, and those who have gazed at it are very few in number.

A glance at a good map enables one to realise what an extraordinary region this is. Glaciers and snow-fields are delineated as covering thousands of square miles, the glaciers being far the largest known outside the Arctic regions, filling valleys forty miles in length. There are no really practicable passes across this awful range between the Karakoram and the head of the Hunza River.

The province of Baltistan, or Little Tibet, into which I was now about to descend, was conquered by the

VIEW FROM THE SUMMIT OF THE CHOBRAT PASS.

Sikhs in 1840. Before that it was ruled by the Rajah of Skardu and a number of subordinate rajahs, whose descendants still preserve their nominal titles and dignities, and, as is the case with the Gialpo of Ladak, are held in great respect by their faithful people, who, like all Orientals, value gentle blood.

Baltistan, lying between the Himalayas and the ranges of the Hindoo Koosh, the Karakoram, and Tibet, is thus hemmed in on all sides by the highest mountains in the world, and in the winter months, when the passes are closed, it is almost completely isolated. It has, indeed, one natural outlet to the lowlands, the valley of the Indus; but the route afforded by this is far more dangerous to the traveller than the highest pass, for that portion of the Indus Valley which lies between this country and India is inhabited by bloodthirsty and fanatical tribes, Mahomedans of the Suni sect. The Baltis for the most part are of the Shiah sect, and it is one of the pleasant customs of the above-mentioned tribesmen to cut the throat of every Shiah who ventures into their country, while they make slaves of strangers who happen to be of their own creed. These poor Baltis, robbed by the tax-farmers of their conquerors, hunted by Kanjuti robbers to be sold as slaves in Central Asia, dragged from their homes to do forced labour on the dreaded Gilgit road, and murdered by their Suni neighbours, have hitherto dragged on but an insecure and harassed existence among their wild hills and valleys.

But in every respect a better time is now coming for the Baltis, as they are already beginning to realise; and for this they have to thank our interference in the affairs of the Kashmir State. The Kanjutis, who sold them as slaves, will do so no longer since Colonel

Durand's successful expedition; the position we have taken up at Gilgit has put a stop to the raids of the Indus Valley tribes; an organised transport corps will now do away with the evils of the Gilgit road begar; and when our Settlement Officer has extended his work to this portion of the Maharajah's dominions, it is to be hoped that the poor persecuted Baltis will become the happy and prosperous people they deserve to be. For this is a blameless and innocent race of men. Europeans who have travelled through their country always speak well of and remember with kindly feelings these honest, simple, cheerful, and good-natured creatures, in whose character there is much that is pathetically attractive.

Dwelling in a country almost as barren as Ladak, and being polygamous Mussulmans, they are, as I have pointed out, far poorer than their well-to-do Malthusian neighbours. Polygamy is an expensive amusement in all lands, and is ill-adapted to these highlands. The signs of extreme poverty are, indeed, manifest all over Baltistan, and there is much positive distress. Numbers here have never known what it is to have a sufficiency of food, do not even possess the clothing necessary to withstand the rigours of the climate, and can be seen shivering in bitter winter weather, with bare limbs, and only thin rags about their bodies. It is marvellous how they exist at all; but this is a sturdy race, and the stern laws of the survival of the fittest have full play among the population. Rajah Ram Singh, Commander-in-Chief of the Maharajah's forces, recently travelled through Baltistan. On entering the country he was met by a large, doleful crowd of ragged creatures, all wailing, and carrying lit lanterns, though it was broad daylight. The Rajah demanded an explanation. 'O Maharajah!' replied the spokesman, 'our land is so darkened with suffering that we have brought lanterns, that your Highness may see how it is with us, and relieve us.'

The Baltis are of Mongolian stock, somewhat resembling the Ladakis, but have an admixture of Aryan blood, as there is a considerable intermarriage between them and the Astoris, Gilgittis, and others of the socalled Dard race. The Balti men wear skull-caps; the top of the head is shaven, but the long black hair hangs down over either cheek in wild, curling elf-locks. This is distinctly an ugly people; but the women are more comely than those in Ladak, and of fairer complexion. Some of the piquant Balti girls, with their funny little flat faces always wreathed in smiles, their snub noses, and eyes twinkling with fun, can almost be described as pretty, despite their unclassical type of feature, and have, at any rate, the pleasing expression which a cheerful disposition gives. Cheerfulness is the chief characteristic of the long-suffering Balti. He is always ready to laugh. He is the most easily-amused person in the world. At the end of a long day's march along the hot Indus sands, when the wearied coolies are inclined to grumble or sulk, any sort of feeble joke or encouraging remark will send them all stepping out again with cheery good-will. You have only to look in a good temper yourself, and your Balti followers will be contented and amiable under the most depressing circumstances.

After I had taken some photographs at the summit of the pass I commenced the descent. The Chorbat is an easy pass, presenting no difficulties, but it is weary work floundering up and down its steep, soft snows. At last we came to where the little Chorbat stream issues from the snow-field, and followed it down declivities of débris till we reached our camping-place, an exposed spot in a broad glen, where some grass and alpine flowers grew by the bank of the stream. It had been a long day's march, and the coolies did not come in till dusk.

There were no huts here, but we found some wild-looking, highland herdsmen, with their cattle. These hardy fellows were bivouacking through the summer on the bleak mountain-side, with but a scanty blanket each for covering at night. There was no firewood about, but the herdsmen had collected a quantity from the neighbouring mountain, and were willing to sell it to travellers. I could see that there was a little grass growing here and there on the hillsides, which made this appear quite a rich country after naked Ladak; but in most parts of the world it would be looked upon as little better than a howling wilderness.

It was snowing and cold when camp was broken up on July 5; but after abruptly descending for a few hours to lower altitudes, we escaped from a winter morning into a hot summer day. This was another long march, but it was all downhill. The glen narrowed to a gorge; in many places the road had been carried away by landslips, so that it was rough travelling over slopes of falling boulders. It was late afternoon when, between the crags that rose on either side of us, we opened out the broad sandy valley of the Shayok, backed by great precipices. At the mouth of the ravine we came upon human habitations again for the first time for three days, and entered the village of Chorbat, which was to be our halting-place for the night.

The *kotwal* came out to welcome me, and brought

me to a camping-ground among the apricot-trees. The village nestles snugly between the steep mountain-side and the sandy river-bed. I had not been at so low an elevation as this for some time; so that the crops were far more advanced than any I had yet seen. The barley was already turning yellow, and the mulberries were ripe. I had tasted no fresh fruit for months, and of late no fresh vegetables; but now I had come to a land of fruit, and during my progress through Baltistan was presented with apricots and mulberries in profusion at every halting-place. Large groves of apricots surround every hamlet in this province, and the dried fruit is the principal export, the *kabani* of Baltistan being famous in all the neighbouring regions.

This was my first Balti village, and that I had crossed the mountains into a country very different from Ladak was at once apparent. All the men and children gathered together to stare politely at the sahib. The men squatted round my tent in a ring, passing the *hookahs* solemnly from one to another; while the numerous half-naked and wholly naked children played in and out of the circle, laughing, romping, and shrieking after the manner of those of their years all the world over; but of women not one was to be seen. I was evidently in a Mussulman land again; in a Ladak village the crowd would have been of men and unabashed women, with a very small sprinkling of quiet children. On walking through the village the women —save the wrinkled beldams—scurried away into their homes when they saw me approach. I did not find here open-doored houses, as in Ladak, in which there is no attempt at privacy, and into which one can look freely as one goes by, but passed up alleys of bare walls, presenting no window on the road, with little wicket-gates kept well closed—the jealous habitations of the followers of the Prophet.

I sat for some time under the trees, enjoying the mulberries and conversing with the villagers, before I heard the clamorous chorus of my indefatigable coolies descending the gorge; and shortly afterwards they marched up with my baggage, cheery as ever after their three days' journey. The kotwal informed me that the road ahead was in a bad condition, and unfit for baggage-animals, so after dismissing my Ladak coolies I engaged others here.

The kotwal brought me the salaam of the rajah of the district, who had heard of my arrival and desired to visit me. This was a fine-looking old gentleman with white beard, white robe, and voluminous white turban, who came up accompanied by his *munshi* and several followers. He was one of those deposed rajahs who, as I have said, are permitted by their Dogra conquerors to preserve their nominal rank. He shook his head when he heard I was going to Gilgit. He said the road from here as far as Astor was a good one, but that from Astor to Gilgit it was a dangerous one, with many bad people about. As a matter of fact, the Gilgit road is now as safe as the road from Brighton to London; but the Oriental mind is slow at accepting new facts, and this old rajah had not forgotten the devastating raids of the men of Yasin and Chilas into the Gilgit district and the western valleys of Baltistan.

Here, as in every village in Baltistan, men came up to me to be treated for sores and wounds that would not heal. I was puzzled to find so many suffering in this way. I imagine that some of these ugly raws were the old galls of the burdens got while doing Gilgit-road begar.

On July 6, just as I was about to march, the lumbadar, who had been away, appeared on the scene and introduced himself to me. He had a good deal to say for himself. He showed me a number of chits that had been given him by passing sahibs, in which his virtues were wonderfully extolled ; one spoke of him as being the only official in all Baltistan worth his salt. I thought him too suspiciously good altogether, and was prepared for an exhibition of the cloven foot. He accompanied me outside the village, speaking all the while of his own extraordinary merits. When I was leaving him I offered him a little bakshish ; upon which he calmly informed me that it was the dastur for every sahib who passed through Chorbat to give him five rupees. He had done nothing for me, so I politely declined to follow the precedent. It is possible that some sahib did once give him five rupees, and consequently, Asiatic that he is, he looks forward to the same sum as his prescribed due from every other sahib who comes his way—a dastur to remain unchanged until some more generous globe-trotter happens to present him with ten rupees, when the higher sum will become the dastur, and so on. But I bade farewell to this blackmailing lumbadar who stands in wait for the white man at the gate of the Chorbat Pass, without having any such dealings with him as he will be inclined to impose on others as a precedent, and proceeded on my way.

The Shayok here appears to be of about the same volume as the Indus where I had left it in Ladak, but is not so furious a torrent, flowing smoothly for many leagues at a time between its broad white sands. The scenery is finer than in the Ladak valleys, the mountains being of more varied outline, while the oases are more frequent and more extensive. Now our road would follow the hot, flat sands, the river on one side of us, the sheer cliffs on the other; now we had to mount high up the cliffs, and descend again by the usual risky-looking scaffolded paths. In other places, where whole mountain-spurs had fallen down to the beach, we had to clamber across wastes of boulders.

It was here much hotter than in Ladak, and each day's journey brought us down to a sultrier land, until on the sandy plains of Skardu the temperature was as high as it is in India; but there was always ice-cold water to drink and fruit to feast on, so I had not much to complain of. On July 6 we passed the usual stage, and encamped at Lunkha. We were tormented during the latter part of this day's march by the strong wind that blew up the valley—as it generally does here in the afternoon—driving stinging showers of granite sand into our faces.

On July 6 we had a long march to the village of Kapalu. In consequence of some recent big landslips, the lower road could not be followed, so that we had to take a steep and difficult track, which zigzagged up the face of the cliff, until we were several thousands of feet above the river, and had reached the summit of the ridge. We now crossed an undulating plateau, on which were occasional patches of poor pasture; but for the most part it was a waste of stones, where the air was heavy with the sickly scent of boortsa, and whose only inhabitants were black lizards. It was a windless, sultry day, and the silent sand devils were constantly rising round us. From this elevation I obtained a grand view over the great range beyond the Shayok; for I was looking up the broad valley of Mushe, at the head of which, thirty miles off, some magnificent peaks towered above the rolling clouds—the glaciers filling the hollows between them—one of these summits, Mount Masherbrum, attaining 25,676 feet.

It was late in the afternoon when, on arriving at the edge of a high ridge, I looked down upon a most charming landscape. Far beneath was the valley of the Shayok, with its river winding among the sands, and enclosed by snowy ranges. And there at my feet lay an oasis far larger than any I had yet seen. It was an unbroken garden of rich vegetation which bordered the river for several miles, and which was also of considerable breadth, stretching from the river sands across the maidan, and climbing for some way up the lower slopes of the mountains—a succession of orchards of apricot, cherry, walnut, and other fruit-trees; fields of yellow corn, peas, and lucerne, most grateful to eyes that had been gazing all day on sand and stones glaring in fierce sunshine. This fair spot was Kapalu, the richest district in Baltistan, and regarded as a very Garden of Eden by the Balti people. Several little hamlets are scattered through the cultivated lands, in the principal one of which we were to halt for the night.

My tent was pitched, as usual, in an orchard, and soon some hundreds of villagers assembled, and sat in a respectful semicircle in front of me. A few of these were of the upper class, men of quite fair complexion, and of a very different type from the others; they had little of the Mongolian in their features, but were something like the modern Greeks, having the same worn, refined faces, while the skull-cap, black moustache, and long, black hair made this resemblance still more noticeable.

Subhana came to me and announced that the two

small Rajahs of Kapalu were about to call on me; and soon I perceived, through the fruit-trees, a number of men in white robes approaching. Then all the villagers who were squatting round my tent rose to their feet and respectfully made way for their chiefs. I had been told that the Rajahs were small, but was not prepared to see quite such juveniles as my two visitors. These were the two orphan sons of the late Rajah of Kapalu, the hereditary rulers of this fertile district, who, like the numerous other rajahs I came across in Baltistan, are treated with as much respect by their people as in the days when their power was absolute.

One of these boys was a fine little fellow of ten, clad in a snow-white robe, and with a huge white turban almost as big as himself on his head. His brother was a baby in arms, similarly attired, and looking an absurd little creature in his topheavy turban; he was brought to me, crowing and laughing, in the arms of a man belonging to the Rajah's retinue, for his female nurse could not, of course, appear in my presence. The baby was then induced to hand to me a dali of ripe cherries, to the intense delight and pride of his nurse and all the onlookers; his own mother could not have displayed greater pleasure than did all these poor people when I expressed my admiration of their infant Rajah's intelligence.

Then the other boy walked up, stately, quite at ease, the little gentleman all over. He took a seat on a cloth in front of my tent, and we conversed as well as we could for some time. He was a very handsome boy, of complexion fair as a European's, with intelligent, well-bred features. His family is a very ancient one, and is considered one of the most noble in this country. He had been told that I took photographs,

RAFT OF INFLATED SKINS, KAFALE.

and was anxious to see some of the pictures and the machine that produced them. He was chiefly interested in some groups I had taken of Ladaki men and women, but looked at them, I think, with some awe; for he had, no doubt, been educated to consider the Buddhists as an abominable people, idolaters of the most accursed sort, and powerful magicians. He was a thorough boy, inquisitive, and eager, in a polite and dignified way, to view all my possessions. 'Have you anything else to show me?' he would inquire of me as soon as he had sufficiently inspected each fresh article. There was an interchange of dalis between us—his consisting of dishes of dried apricots, mulberries, cherries, raisins, and rice —and then we separated.

Having tramped the eleven rough marches from Leh, on June 21 I had a pleasantly lazy journey for a change by another mode of locomotion. The more favourable route to Skardu crosses the Shayok at Kapalu, and follows its right bank to its junction with the Indus. We accordingly traversed the orchards that surround the village and descended to the river. The passage of the Shayok is effected on rafts of inflated skins, such as have been in use from time immemorial in the East. We found awaiting us a raft of forty goatskins supporting a framework of light sticks. To carry my baggage, myself, my servant, the thirteen coolies, and the two officials who were to do me the honour of escorting me for a few marches, necessitated two voyages of the raft and considerable delay.

The four men who composed the crew propelled the raft across the broad and rushing river with long poles, which were well enough for shoving her along in the shallows, but were very inadequate when employed as oars in the deeper water. It does not appear to be

R

the custom for the boatmen in Baltistan to employ paddles, as it is in Kashmir and other parts where watermanship is to some extent understood. The raft progressed but slowly in consequence of this senseless dastur, and by the time it had reached the opposite bank it had been swept nearly a mile downstream. Having disembarked the first cargo of baggage and coolies, the men, walking in the shallow water, towed their raft up stream again, and then re-crossed the river to carry the rest of us over.

The Shayok here divides itself into numerous channels, flowing between shoals and sandy islets, and is not much encumbered with rocks. It was a little rough when we reached mid-stream, but not dangerously so, and I could see no signs of difficulties lower down; I therefore suggested to the boatmen that they should take me to the next stage on the raft. At first they demurred to doing this, saying that there were rapids ahead, and raising other objections; but by promising them the enormous sum of two rupees I over-persuaded them, and they agreed to carry me as far as Bragar, a stage and a half below Kapalu. The coolies were accordingly sent off by road with the baggage, to meet me at Bragar, while I remained on board, with my servant and the tiffin kilta, to float down stream. The captain of the vessel explained to me that, being the Government ferryman at Kapalu, and bound to carry across any mails that might arrive—a rare event—it would be unlawful for him to abandon his post; but that he would get out of this difficulty by dividing his vessel into two portions, one of which he would retain here to serve as mail-boat, while he would despatch me with his crew on the other portion. It did not occupy a minute to break the raft into two bits;

it might have been disjointed into four or forty fragments with equal ease, as it was constructed in this convenient fashion, and each part would have lived upon the water and served as an independent boat, even as each morsel of a chopped-up medusa preserves its vitality and forms a new creature.

We kept well in the middle of the river, as a rule, where the stream was strongest; and as the men had but little control over their vessel with their bladeless poles, she was constantly revolving, which enabled me to admire all the scenery round without turning my head. The goatskins leaked a good deal, as was testified to by the constant bubbling and whistling sounds beneath us; but the crew stuck manfully to the pumps, or rather to what is the duty equivalent to pumping on a *mussuck* raft, and preserved us from foundering. The legs of the inflated goatskins pass upward between the framework of the raft, and serve as pipes, by which the air is replenished. Our men at intervals blew vigorously down these legs, deftly tied the orifices up again, and thus counteracted the gradual collapsing of the floats.

This was a great change after the dusty road. Being carried down at a rapid rate against the breeze, it struck our faces with the force of a fresh gale. When in the rapids we were whirled across waves of a considerable height, with their tops broken by the wind, so that we were tossed about in most exhilarating fashion, and were often partly under water, shipping seas and being drenched by showers of spray, till I was reminded of the seas and tidal river-mouths, the glories of which these poor inland people knew not of. Subhana, for his part, had no ambition to know more of navigable waters; he held on tightly to the frail framework of the raft, turned ever paler as we dashed on, and at last experienced the qualms of sea-sickness at an elevation of 9,000 feet above the sea.

On either side we saw the sands and rocks quivering in mirage, while columns of sand swept along the hot coast; but it was pleasantly fresh on our leaping bark. The scenery was ever rapidly changing as we flew by. Now a magnificent rocky cape would jut out from the mountains into the foaming breakers; now a long, low promontory of green orchards would shut in a bay of still, blue water, forming a charming foreground to the bare hillsides and snowy peaks that rose behind. Here and there I perceived on the cliffs curious little patches of barley or grass, perched high up on apparently inaccessible ledges—on every spot, indeed, where soil could be collected, and to which water could be led.

We beached our vessel for tiffin in a sandy bay on the left bank, close to an orchard of apricots, and halted while our crew thoroughly blew out again the leaky craft. Then we launched her once more, and swept rapidly by Karku, the regulation stage, and entered more boisterous water than we had yet seen, where rocks rose here and there above the foam and had to be carefully avoided. Then the village of Dowani flashed by us; and at last, just before a point where the river enters a narrow gorge and forms dangerous rapids, into which, had we ventured, shipwreck would have been our probable fate, our boatmen, encouraging each other with shouts, plied their poles, and, directing the raft out of the current, beached her on the sands of the right bank in front of our destination, Bragar.

I paid off and discharged the mariners—who, having broken their vessel up and divided it between them, proceeded to carry the fragments back on their heads by road to Kapalu—and we tramped over the sands and pebbles to the little village, which—arriving in the unexpected fashion we did—we took entirely by surprise. The men stared at us with astonishment as we approached, and the women scampered away to hide themselves. The ladies were very timid here, and I caught but the merest glimpse of them; but I observed that all wore short robes and scarlet trousers. It blew a strong gale of wind all this night, howling among the trees and obscuring everything with the driving clouds of dust. So fierce were the gusts that it was not possible to pitch my tent, and I had to bivouac under the lee of a wall.

CHAPTER XVI

SKARDU — KATSURAH — WEATHER-BOUND AT SHIKARTHANG — THE BANNOK LA — NANGA PARBAT — ON THE GILGIT ROAD — THE DARDS — ASTOR FORT — APPLEFORD'S CAMP.

THE journey from Bragar to Skardu occupied us three days. Each march brought us to a lower altitude and to a warmer climate. We had left the barley green in Ladak, but now found the grain all gathered in, while the wild vegetation of the irrigated land was that of a later season, numbers of field-orchids and other summer flowers being in blossom here, instead of the early spring plants we had seen in the highlands.

On July 10, after passing the junction of the Shayok and Indus, we were carried across the broad waters of the combined rivers on a small skin raft, which had to make four journeys, so that the passage occupied two hours—all for want of the paddle tabooed by dastur. Near the village of Gol we joined the dak road from Srinagur to Skardu, and saw once more that sign of civilisation, the telegraph-wire, stretching by the side of us.

On July 11 we came to the plain of Skardu. Here the mountains on either side of the Indus retreat, and leave a sandy basin five miles or more in breadth, the bed of an ancient lake, across which the river winds. This plain is 7,250 feet above the sea. Skardu itself stands on an alluvial plateau 150 feet above the sandy

THE OLD FORT, SKARDU.

waste, and is approached by long avenues of poplars. This plateau is well irrigated, and is extensively cultivated. Skardu, though the old capital of all Baltistan, is not an imposing town, consisting of scattered groups of low mud-houses, and possessing a very mean little bazaar, where I saw, sitting at their stalls, several foreigners to the land—insincerely-smiling Kashmiri merchants, more offensive-looking than ever now that I had not seen such rascal faces for some time, and had been travelling among the ugly but honest Baltis and Ladakis. The chief feature of Skardu is the old fortress, which picturesquely dominates it from a rocky eminence.

I marched in from Gol some miles ahead of my servants and coolies, and on reaching an open space outside the town, which is the customary camping-place for sahibs, I was surprised to see some Cabul tents pitched, and realised that I had come once more on white men. Here I found two Gunners on leave, who had been shooting in Baltistan nullahs. We foregathered, and after my long, hot tramp, I enjoyed the five-o'clock tea, for which I arrived just in time. The Naib Wazir of Skardu now called upon us, and invited us to witness a game of polo. We therefore adjourned to the polo-ground, and were spectators of a most aristocratic game; for all the players were hereditary rajahs of the neighbouring districts, good-looking fellows, rather showily dressed. It was curious to see the two teams squatting down, in separate rows, after the game was over, each team refreshing itself with its own hookah, which a small boy carried up and down the row, handing the long mouthpiece from one nobleman to the other.

I dined with the two English officers. As we had all been in the wilds for some time, we had run out of stores, but were able to supply each other's wants to some extent. I happened to have plenty of tea and sugar, which they were in lack of; on the other hand, they were well supplied with tobacco, whereas I had little left; so some mutually satisfactory bartering was done.

The Indus Valley affords the most direct route between Skardu and Gilgit; but the road is perhaps the worst in all Kashmir, and it is often spoken of as being only practicable for experienced cragsmen; the difficulties, however, have been somewhat exaggerated, as I discovered afterwards, when returning to Kashmir by this route.

On leaving Skardu on July 12, I followed an easier road, which, after ascending the Indus Valley for twenty-four miles to the village of Katsurah, crosses the mountains by the Bannok La, a high, snowy pass, and descends on the Gilgit road near the fortress of Astor. In consequence of bad weather, which delayed us at the foot of the pass, the journey to Astor occupied nine days.

The march to Katsurah is rather a trying one: for most of the way the traveller drags himself through the soft sands of the Skardu plain, and in the summer the heat and glare is intense on this desert. On July 13, leaving the Indus, we proceeded to ascend the rugged ravine of Shikarthang by a rough track, and encamped near the village of Stokchun, on the bank of the torrent, which here rushes through a jungle of roses and other flowering shrubs. Close by I saw a fine cascade, which, falling over a perpendicular cliff, disappeared in the midst of an immense accumulation of snow, the remains of an avalanche of the preceding winter, through which it had burrowed a great tunnel.

On July 14 we continued the ascent of the ravine.

There was a good deal of wild vegetation round us here: pines, elms, junipers, and roses grew on the hillside wherever they could get a hold among the crags, while harebells, orchids, wood anemones, and other wild flowers carpeted the ravine-bottom. We clambered still higher up the gorge, until we had left trees and flowers behind us, and reached the treeless waste on which Shikarthang, the highest village of the nullah, is situated. This is one of the bleakest spots imaginable, even in the Dog-days, and it makes one shiver to think what it must be like in winter. This miserable hamlet is in the centre of an open down at the junction of four converging nullahs, and is exposed to all the winds of heaven, which, concentrating in one or other of the four gorges, or, maybe, occasionally sweeping down all of them together, drive in icy blasts and whirlwinds among the low stone huts of the hillmen. There is good summer pasture here, and a certain amount of grim is grown, but the elevation is too great for fruit-trees or other crops.

When we got into camp the clouds were rolling low down on the surrounding mountains, and soon the wind rose, and it commenced to sleet. It was like a wild February day on the coast of the North Sea, whereas in the morning we had basked in the climate of the Algerian summer. We had to pass two days on this wind-swept plateau, the weather being far too bad to allow of our attempting the pass. As no supplies can be procured on the four marches between this place and Astor, I laid in a good stock of fowls here.

On July 15 the outlook was very dismal: each of the four nullahs was obscured with the rolling vapours, the sleet fell incessantly, and we only got occasional glimpses of the mountains, as they appeared through the rifts in the driving clouds. On July 16 there was no improvement in the weather. Our Skardu coolies had left us, and I had engaged Shikarthang men to carry the baggage as far as the Gilgit road. These exhibited the greatest reluctance to setting out for the pass, and explained that much fresh snow had fallen, and that it would mean death to them to make the attempt while so strong a wind was blowing. Whatever the coolies were afraid of, it was not rain; for, neglecting their homes, which were hard by, they sat about our camp all day, quite happy, though exposed to the chilly downpour and the biting wind; and I noticed that the other inhabitants, likewise, did not stay within doors, but were squatting on their flat roof-tops, rolled in their blankets, which, as well as their clothes and faces, were of the dirty mud-colour which prevails all over Shikarthang. In the evening of this day things looked even worse: the clouds descended to our level, and enveloped us with their chilly damp, and nothing round was visible. It rained all night, and occasionally I heard, above the howling of the wind, the rumbling of avalanches and landslips on the neighbouring mountains.

It seems that even the elements obey dastur in Asia; for on the morning of July 17, the weather being to all appearance as unfavourable as ever, the lumbadar of Shikarthang came up to see me, smiling, and said that we might now start. 'It is not the dastur here,' he explained, 'for foul weather to last for longer than three days in summer. To-day is the third day of wind and snow, so to-morrow will be fine. To-day you can march to the foot of the pass, and to-morrow you can cross the mountain in safety.' So, putting faith in this meteorological dastur, we set out; but hearing that there was no fuel to be found beyond this place, I engaged some extra men to carry up a quantity of wood, so that there should be ample bivouac-fires for the ill-clad coolies.

It was unpleasantly cold as we ascended the nullah; but the hardy coolies tramped along over the sharp stones and through the snowdrifts with bare feet and legs. Some of them, too, were naked to the waist; they had tied up their spare rags in bundles, and were reserving these for the pass on the morrow, where a sufficiency of covering would be absolutely necessary to ward off frostbite.

This night's encampment was just under the steep ascent leading to the col, where the stream issues from the snow-fields and glaciers. It was a dreary spot: snow and bare rocks surrounded us, and there was no vegetation, save a little rhubarb growing here and there in sheltered nooks. The coolies plucked the stalks of this, and ate them raw. I tried the experiment, and found this rhubarb not nearly so acid as our English variety.

Now that we had got into camp it began to snow hard, and we had to wait shivering an hour or so before the somewhat tardy coolies, who had been told off to carry the fuel from Shikarthang, arrived. In the evening the clouds cleared off, and as I sat smoking by my fire after dinner the scenery round me assumed a singularly impressive appearance under the moonlight. The snowy peaks around seemed vaster than by day, and the fields of snow on the heights appeared to extend to an immense distance. It was a night of frequent avalanches. I would often hear a dull roar, and, on looking up, perceive a great cascade of powdery snow pouring over a high cliff-edge, to fall perpendicularly some hundreds of feet, and then sweep down the lower mountain-slopes, in a succession of white billows, to the valley-bottom.

At dawn on July 18 it was snowing lightly, but the air was still, so the lumbadar, having looked round with a knowing air, declared that we might attack the pass, and having bade us farewell departed for his home, little thinking, unfortunate man, how soon he would see us again. I substituted grass shoes for the ammunition-boots in which I had been recently marching; the coolies also wrapped up their feet and legs with bandages, and placed all the rags they possessed upon their shoulders; while those who had them put on coloured goggles—and we commenced the ascent.

It was a long, weary climb up the steep snow-slopes to the summit of the col. Here I found no abrupt ridge and sudden descent on the other side, as on the Chorbat La, but saw before me undulating downs of snow stretching for a long distance, with craggy peaks rising above them here and there. I could now understand the necessity of our two days' halt at Shikarthang. To have crossed this exposed snowy waste in bad weather would have been extremely dangerous. I looked over the desolate white summits of successive ranges; but the mighty Nanga Parbat mountain, which should be visible from here, was unfortunately shut from my sight by a mass of black clouds; though now and then, through rifts in the vapour, I caught glimpses of distant snows at an immense height.

I had tiffin at the summit of the pass, photographed the desert of snow that lay before me, and then, at the importunity of the anxious tiffin coolie, hurried on, for there were signs of approaching bad weather. According to the map we were now crossing glaciers, but as everything was deeply covered in snow, these were not to be distinguished. As we floundered on through the soft snow, under the perpendicular cliffs that form the watershed, snow-cascades and small avalanches frequently fell across our path. One of these last overtook a coolie and swept him a long way down the slope, but without doing him any injury.

At last, having crossed the white downs, we reached the head of a profound nullah, by which lay our way down to the world of life again; and now we could see, far beneath us, some patches of grass among the snow. A rough descent of some thousands of feet brought us to the issue of the stream, and then to our camping-place, where, on the scanty soil between the great boulders of a landslip, grew a little grass with some violets and forget-me-nots in flower. Here my servant, the tiffin coolie, and myself warmed ourselves over a small fire of dry grass, and awaited the others with some anxiety; for a strong wind had risen again, and we saw the wreaths of dark storm-cloud rolling across the summit of the pass, while it began to snow thickly even at our camping-place. However, all the men turned up safely, but not until after dusk, looking weary and miserable, some of those who had not worn goggles suffering slightly from snow-blindness.

To my surprise, I saw among the coolies my old friend, the lumbadar of Shikarthang, whom I had bidden farewell to and duly presented with bakshish in the morning. 'What are you doing here?' I inquired. In reply he pointed sadly to two truculent-looking sepoys of the Maharajah who were with him. It seems that these soldiers were on their way from Skardu to Astor, and happening to meet the lumbadar just after I had dismissed him, they had at once impressed that unfortunate man to act as their guide across the pass.

These military gentlemen do pretty well as they like when journeying thus alone, with no officers to keep them in order, extorting transport and supplies from the peasants as they go along, and not infrequently insisting on being given money as well. Of old sepoys used to be sent tax-collecting, and realised plenty of plunder; but the Settlement reforms have deprived them of this privilege. Up till now it has been possible for the Kashmir State to raise mercenary troops without difficulty, despite the well-known fact that the pay of the soldiers was generally years in arrear, and that even rations were often not forthcoming. Now that the irregular advantages, which more than balanced these inconveniences, have been abolished, it is obviously necessary that the men should receive their pay as it falls due, and Colonel Neville Chamberlain, the Military Secretary to the Kashmir State, has energetically taken this matter in hand. It froze hard all this night, and in the morning I found my tent stiff as a board, so that we had to wait till the sun had thawed it before it could be taken down.

On July 19, after traversing some miles of boulders and patches of hard snow, we descended into a different climate and into a more pleasing country than any I had seen for some time. Pine-woods and flowery pastures covered the hillsides, save where some great landslip of débris, like an unsightly scar, clove the green vegetation from the mountain-top to the torrent-edge. Little tributary streams rushed down shady dells. There was no lack of water here; in places reedy swamps filled the valley-bottom, and it was indeed refreshing to see a nice damp morass again, after the arid countries I had left.

This day I enjoyed an experience not easily to be

NANGA PARBAT.

forgotten; for at last, at a turn in this fair valley, I saw before me, rising above the lower ranges into the cloudless blue sky, a huge white mass, such a mountain as I had never beheld before: not a solitary sharp pinnacle this, but shaped like a hog's back; a long, rolling height sloping steeply at either end; a prone Titan. The snowy domes were piled one on the other, and flashing glaciers leagues in length streaked the furrowed sides. This I knew could be no other than the mighty Diyamir, or Nanga Parbat (naked mountain), 26,629 feet in height, which was about twenty miles distant from where I stood. The range of which it is the culminating point forms the frontier of the Maharajah's territories, and also, it may be said, of the known world; for beyond is the unexplored country of the Chilas tribesmen, into which no stranger may venture. The appearance of the mountain was indeed wonderful, not to be described.

We encamped near a little hamlet where the habitations were built of logs, showing that we had reached a land of plentiful timber. For months I had only seen stone huts, and in Ladak it is no easy matter to procure even the wood of which to make one's house-door.

Here I found only one inhabitant, a sinister-looking and squint-eyed person, who gave me no favourable impression of the Dard race, into whose country I had now descended. He told me he was lumbadar of this place, but could supply me with no coolies, as all his villagers had been seized for begar on the Gilgit road. I sent him off with my servant to another village lower down, to collect coolies there if possible. They returned after some hours, having searched the villages, and even wandered to the pastures on the mountain-side, but were unable to get a single man. The peasants were no doubt hiding away, so as to avoid the journey to Astor. Now that I was but one march from it I was beginning to realise the difficulties of the Gilgit road.

Not being able to procure fresh coolies, I suggested to my Shikarthang men that they should accompany me as far as Astor, instead of leaving me here, as had

MY BALTI COOLIES COMING INTO CAMP.

been originally arranged, promising them ample bakshish. But no bakshish availed in this case; they knelt at my feet, and implored me with tears in their eyes to let them go. They urged that they were sorefooted after their three days' march. They made all manner of excuses, giving, indeed, every reason but the true one—which, being wrong-headed Orientals, was the last they would think of employing—namely, their fear lest they should be seized at Astor and sent on the road, probably not to return to their homes and families for months. They were naturally averse to marching into the lion's mouth; so I paid the poor wretches off, and discharged them, on which they were effusively grateful, and, bidding me farewell, hurried across their pass into a safer country.

I was thus left at this inhospitable spot with twelve coolie-loads of baggage and not a man to carry it; but it was only a day's march to Astor, so I decided to leave my property here, in charge of my servant, and walk on alone the next morning, to procure transport from the Astor authorities. The squinting lumbadar sat in front of my tent in a friendly manner all the evening, and smoked my tobacco with relish. But he would do nothing for me; he said he had no fowls or eggs, and could not even supply me with milk.

Indescribably beautiful as had been the aspect of Nanga Parbat by day, it was still more so by night. The air was perfectly clear, and the moon shone full upon the side of the mountain that faced me, revealing every detail of the pure snows, the steel-blue glaciers, the stupendous crags. The dark-shadowed chasms had an awful appearance. It was the barrier of the unknown world, and it might have been the wall of fairy-land itself, so mysteriously lovely did those lifeless wastes appear.

I set out for Astor early on July 20. It was a pleasant walk down this fair valley, across reedy flats thronged with doves, through pine-woods, over green pastures, and at many a turn opening out some fresh view of Nanga Parbat. I passed several small hamlets of log huts, where I again tried, in vain, to engage coolies. I met few men, but saw many women working in the fields, who were unveiled, and did not appear terrified at the aspect of the unbeliever, but stared boldly at him.

s

I was now in what is called Dardistan, among a people of different type and dress to any I had seen before. But the Dards who live in the vicinity of the Gilgit road are not favourable specimens of their race: they have been raided upon, oppressed, and enslaved for ages; for the most part they are miserably poor; their faces have a melancholy, and often a lowering, expression; they have little of the cheeriness of the Balti, and are not so patient under their misfortunes.

I do not know who is responsible for the present accepted signification of the terms Dard and Dardistan. There are no people who call themselves Dards, and there is no region known as Dardistan to its inhabitants. Dardistan appears to be simply a convenient, but somewhat misleading, name employed by our geographers to express a large tract inhabited by different Aryan races of somewhat similar type. It includes the districts of Astor and Gilgit in the Maharajah's dominions, the little kingdoms of Hunza and Nagar, Yasin, the independent republics of the Indus Valley, and other countries south of the Hindoo Koosh. On the west it is bounded by Kafiristan, to the south by the Pushtoo-speaking races, to the east by Kashmir.

The Dards are of Aryan race, a sturdy people, thickly-built, of rather dark complexion, and generally of roughly-hewn and homely features. Drew speaks of them as a people 'who are bold, and who, though not caring much for human life, are not bloodthirsty; a people who will meet one on even terms, without sycophancy or fear on the one hand, or impertinent self-assertion on the other.' When in happier circumstances than are the unfortunate wretches who live near Astor, the Dards are a cheery people, fond of dance and music. They are braver than their neighbours, and the Hunza-

Nagars especially have established a high reputation for valour. The dress of all the Dard men is much the same—woollen pyjamas, woollen choga, or gown, tied in at the waist, and a cloth cap like a long bag, which is rolled up outwards from the bottom till it fits the head tightly.

At last I came to where the nullah debouched upon the broad valley of Astor—not a pleasant green vale like the one I had been descending, but arid and dismal-looking. The Astor, a torrent of some volume, thundered several hundreds of feet beneath me. Beyond it was a hot, bare, dusty slope, with clumps of bluish wormwood scattered over it, and I saw extending up and down the valley along this slope what, from where I stood, appeared to be a mere irregular scratch on the dry earth—and I knew that I was looking at the dreary road of slavery, the hated track to Gilgit, of which I had heard so much; and even as I looked I perceived a long string of ragged men, bending under sacks of grain, toiling slowly down the valley, through the cloud of dust they raised, to the north.

A mile or so up the valley, on the farther bank of the torrent, stood the fortress of Astor, with its towered walls crowning an eminence, steep cliffs falling away from it on three sides. I crossed the river by a wooden bridge, ascended the cliff by a rough path, passed through the outer walls, and found myself among barracks and narrow streets of mud huts. These were crowded with Kashmir sepoys, begari coolies, trains of mules, and dingy camp-followers. Though one of the most important garrison towns of the State, Astor is but a dirty, ragged, disreputable place, that one does not care to stay in longer than one need.

I went to the post-office, and was informed that there

were no Englishmen in Astor itself, but that a gang of navvies under Mr. Appleford, one of Spedding's staff, was working on the new road four miles down the valley.

A number of begari coolies were sitting down in a row outside the post-office, awaiting orders. Someone in authority, to whom I explained my difficulties, at once sent twelve of these off under a sepoy to my last night's camp to bring my baggage down, and I then set forth to beg a dinner and a home from Appleford. It was a hot four miles walk down the valley. The Gilgit road is notorious for its sultriness in summer, despite the high elevation of a great portion of it; and some of the marches are very trying. At last I came upon the Pathans working with pick and shovel on the new road, and on turning a corner saw, to my delight, for I was getting very hungry, the white tents of the camp on a little maidan beyond the river. I crossed the torrent by an ancient cantilever bridge, found Appleford at home, and was made welcome.

I now heard all the news. Spedding was in Kashmir, and was not expected here for ten days. Colonel Durand was not at war, as I had been informed at Leh, but had very nearly been so. The Kanjutis had attempted a raid into Kashmir territory, and had threatened Chalt, which important frontier fortress would have probably fallen into their hands had not Colonel Durand promptly set out with a small body of Kashmir troops and anticipated them.

CHAPTER XVII

RAIDS ON THE GILGIT AND ASTOR DISTRICTS—THE GILGIT GARRISON—NATIVE MISMANAGEMENT—THE GILGIT AGENCY—SPEDDING AND CO.'S NEW MILITARY ROAD—DESERT CONDITION OF THE COUNTRY AND DIFFICULTIES OF TRANSPORT—STRATEGICAL IMPORTANCE OF GILGIT AND CHITRAL—SPEDDING AND CO.'S STAFF AND COOLIES.

I HAD travelled along the great trade-route of Kashmir, which leads to the Central Asian marts through Leh, and I was now to follow the other great road of the country, busier and more crowded than the first, not, however, with merchants and their caravans, but with moving troops and the endless trains of military transport—the war road to the extreme north corner of the regions that pay tribute to the Empress of India—that Gilgit road, whose history so far has not been uneventful, and of which we shall not improbably hear a great deal more in the future.

The Gilgit Valley and the districts south of it, through which the road from Kashmir passes, were not subjugated by the Dogras without severe fighting. The possession of this route was realised as being of the utmost importance to Kashmir, as enabling her to hold in check the raiding tribes that hang upon her northern frontier; so that, despite the great tax upon her resources and frequent repulses, the Maharajah's Government persevered in the conquest, which may be said not to have been really completed until within the last four years. On one occasion an entire Dogra army was cut to pieces near Gilgit, a fortress that was ever changing hands, to be re-lost and re-conquered again. The tribes of Yasin and the Hunza-Nagars were wont to make frequent raids upon the Gilgit Valley, both before and after the Dogra occupation, making slaves of all the people they seized, and it is calculated that when the Dogras first came quite 40 per cent. of the Gilgittis had passed their lives in captivity. The Astor Valley, on the other hand, was the more especial raiding-ground of the Chilas tribesmen, who occupy the valley of the Indus below Boonji, the crest of a lofty range forming the frontier between their territory and the Astor Valley. They were in the habit of carrying away the crops and cattle, killing all the men, and making slaves of the women and children. They entered the valley either at its junction with that of the Indus, or by the Mazeno, a high pass that crosses a shoulder of Nanga Parbat a few miles from Astor.

In consequence of the constant raids, these valleys were almost entirely abandoned by their inhabitants; so that the traveller on the Gilgit road now frequently comes across deserted villages, the walled terraces of bare earth and dead fruit-trees alone remaining to show where were once the green and laboriously-irrigated oases. The Chilas tribesmen received a severe punishment at the hands of the Dogra troops some years ago, and have since then not ventured to raid into Kashmir territory. They even, to some extent, acknowledge the suzerainty of Kashmir, paying a nominal tribute of goats and gold-dust, and giving hostages; but they are still very jealous of any strangers visiting their country, and put to death every Shiah they come across. They often treat the envoys of the Maharajah with contumacy, threaten to renew their raids, and are ever ready, should the Kashmir troops meet with a reverse on the frontier, to fall upon the Astor Valley and cut off the communication with Gilgit.

The more formidable Hunza-Nagars carried on their depredations till a much more recent date, and the field of their operations was far more extensive. I shall have a good deal to say concerning these people later on.

The Gilgit road up to now has been the scene of successive raids, little wars, and troubles of various sorts. Here one did indeed always dwell in the midst of alarms.

That the neighbouring tribes have for so many years been able to defy the power of Kashmir is due to the corrupt system of administration which has hitherto prevailed in this State. It is a far cry from Gilgit to Srinagur, twenty-two marches along a difficult and often dangerous road lying between the capital and the frontier outpost, so that it has been easy to hoodwink the Durbar as to the true condition of affairs on the borders. Thus, on occasions when it was understood at Srinagur that several thousands of sepoys had been marched to Gilgit, a large proportion of these had no existence save on paper, though the officers in charge did not fail to claim and embezzle pay and rations for the full number. And, again, the transport of grain for the troops, a difficult matter on the Gilgit road even with a good organisation, afforded an easy opportunity to certain officials for robbing the State on a large scale; with the result that a very insufficient supply of food used to reach Gilgit, and that the unfortunate sepoys stationed there were left to starve through the winter on the smallest possible rations of grain, and that most probably damaged and unfit for food, having been bought up cheap, while, as a natural consequence, their ranks were woefully thinned by fatal disorders. In the godowns of Astor I myself have seen what was called grain, but which for the most part consisted of empty husks of corn and the corpses of myriads of maggots that had devoured the contents. Had this not been condemned by the British officers, it would probably have been distributed in rations to the Balti coolies as quite good enough for them, at any rate. There were also quantities of a sort of mouldy round grain in a state of fermentation, generating such heat that it threatened to destroy the fort in which it was stored by spontaneous combustion. It is no wonder that soldiers fed on damaged canary-seed, as we used to call this appetising stuff, did not always fight well.

Discontented, badly officered, badly equipped, and utterly undisciplined, the troops of the Gilgit garrison were quite useless from a soldier's point of view, and never displayed much keenness in their desultory campaigns against the Hunza-Nagars. But the maintenance of this garrison, in consequence of the dishonesty and shameful incapacity of the servants of the State, has ever been an excessive drain on the Kashmir treasury; while the unnecessary inhumanity with which the begar has been conducted on the Gilgit road has driven the inhabitants to desperation, compelling them to fly from their homes, and thus still further diminishing the scanty population left by the Chilas raids.

Great loss of life, a fearful sum of human misery, a vast waste of the State funds, and all with no result— such was the history of the Gilgit garrison and the Gilgit road up to the inauguration of the wise policy by which the defences of Gilgit have been put into the hands of a British Agency. The evils of the old system are now doomed, and great improvements have already

BALTI TRANSPORT COOLIES ON THE GILGIT ROAD.

been effected. In the place of a large, useless rabble of Kashmir regulars, a small compact force of Kashmir Imperial Service troops now garrisons Gilgit; and though it is but recently that these men have been placed under the discipline of British officers, they already look a very serviceable body, and there is a remarkable contrast between their appearance and that of the slovenly State sepoys. For the future the Kashmir State will not be so outrageously plundered by its own servants; with a proper organisation and an honest expenditure of the funds provided for the purpose the frontier defences will, for the first time, be really efficient. Great credit is due to Lieutenant-Colonel Durand for initiating and so successfully carrying out these important reforms. For the last three years he has devoted his entire energies to this end, and has been well supported in his efforts by the late Resident, Colonel Parry Nisbet, and Colonel Prideaux, the present Resident, as well as by that enlightened statesman, Rajah Amar Singh, the President of the State Council.

The strategical road which Messrs. Spedding & Co. are now constructing between Srinagur and Gilgit will greatly facilitate the transport, and render the oppressive begar unnecessary. It is notorious, as I have before said, that numbers of the unfortunate coolies who are every year torn from their homes in different parts of the State to carry loads on the old road never return, but perish of cold or starvation by the wayside. Most important from an Imperial point of view, the new road will also confer a great boon on the country by doing away with this cruel system; an organised transport corps is being established, and beasts of burden will now take the place of the wretched peasants.

so entirely dependent as now on the countries beyond the passes for its supplies.

The value of Gilgit to the Kashmir State, commanding as it does the Indus Valley and the mouth of the Hunza River, and so holding in check the unruly tribes on either side, is obvious enough, but it is only recently that the great strategical importance to the Empire of this position has been fully realised. This region is now attracting some attention. The Russian expeditions are exploring the passes of the Hindoo Koosh on the northern side. They have crossed that range, too, at several points, and trespassed into the territories of our allies. Ianoff, for example, took his Cossacks across the Korabaut Pass into Chitral; another party, under Captain Gromchevtsky, descended from the Pamirs into the Hunza Valley, and, if report be true, stirred up those people against us; while we are ever hearing of fresh movements and gatherings of the Czar's forces on our frontier.

Now, whatever position we take up with regard to the debatable lands beyond the Hindoo Koosh, there can be no doubt as to what our course of action should be on the southern slope. Our influence should at least extend up to that great mountain-range which forms the natural frontier of India. It is necessary for the safeguarding of our Empire that we should at any rate hold our side of the mountain-gates; but unless we looked to it, Russia would soon have both sides under her control.

The Russians have broken all treaty regulations with impunity so far, and, by marching their troops into the territory of Chitral, a State under our protection, and subsidised by the Indian Government, have deliberately taken steps which are generally looked upon as equiva-

STRATEGICAL IMPORTANCE OF GILGIT 269

lent to a declaration of war. Some people in England affect to regard such incidents as trivial; the natives of these countries look upon them in a different light. Should we submit to this trespassing of Russian troops into States which we guarantee against foreign invasion, the natives cannot but lose faith in us; they will conclude that Russia is the stronger Power, to which we are afraid to offer resistance; and as with the Asiatic the strongest Power is the one to be friendly with, we must expect intrigue against us, if not more open hostility, as the result of our apathy.

To argue that the natural difficulties presented by these desert mountain regions render any invasion on a formidable scale from this quarter impracticable, is not to the point. That small bodies of troops can cross the Hindoo Koosh the Russians have proved, and here a very small body indeed could prove the nucleus of far-spreading mischief. If we neglected to keep under our influence the tribes south of the great watershed, these would undoubtedly place themselves on the side of the apparently stronger Power. Led by Russian officers, the tribesmen would fight well, and a diversion, which we might find very serious, would thus be brought about in the event of a war breaking out between the two Empires. How far the defection of our present friends would then extend it is difficult to foresee. Such an attack could be, no doubt, repelled, provided matters went well with us elsewhere—our Indian officers are not afraid of the ultimate result; but we should be compelled to send up to this country a considerable force, which we could ill spare, and possibly this is the only object the Russians hope to attain on this part of the frontier.

Now there is little doubt that the above risks can

be obviated by the simple expedient of locking the door on our side. A handful of British officers, such as we have at Gilgit, can effect this, if the proper steps are taken in time. This particular gate of the Empire is easily held and guarded. It is chiefly a question of inspiring the natives with a confidence in our power to protect them. A firm policy to this end will minimise the chances of a war, into which, however, it is so easy to drift by vacillation.

Gilgit, the northernmost outpost of the Indian Empire, covers all the passes over the Hindoo Koosh, from the easternmost one, the Shimshal, to those at the head of the Yasin River, in the west. It will be seen, on referring to a good map, that all these passes descend to the valleys of the Gilgit River and its tributaries. But the possession of the Gilgit Valley does more than this: it affords us a direct communication through Kashmir territory to the protected State of Chitral, which would be otherwise removed from our influence by the interposition of countries at present practically closed to us. We now guarantee the independence of Chitral against Afghanistan, as we do that of Afghanistan against Russian aggression. Our friendship with Chitral dates from the Lockhart Mission in 1886, when these regions were fully explored. The information that was then gathered concerning the routes and passes was not made public; but French and Russian explorers have recently gone over the same ground, so that the facts can no longer be kept secret.

During the reign of the late Mehtar of Chitral, a most sagacious ruler, who died a few months ago, this State was aggrandised by the absorption of several tribes which placed themselves under the protection of their powerful neighbour. It is of the utmost importance to us that Afghanistan does not acquire Chitral, and, of course, it is quite as urgent that Russian influence does not extend in this direction.

Constant relations are kept up between the Gilgit Agency and Chitral, and we have supplied the Chitralis with arms wherewith to defend their frontier-posts. But the valley of Chitral should be as completely under our control as is that of Gilgit, for it commands some of the lowest and easiest passes across the Hindoo Koosh, and affords a ready road to India from Bokhara *viâ* Badakshan. It is known that the Russian military authorities consider this a favourable route for the invasion of India; it avoids the great natural difficulties presented by the lofty and inhospitable Pamirs, and, moreover, there is an easy and much-used caravan road running direct from Chitral to Peshawar *viâ* Bajur.

The town of Chitral itself is situated at the junction of several valleys leading to the very passes which an invader would have to attempt, commanding them all. We should certainly maintain an Agency here, as at Gilgit. This has long been meditated, and the late Mehtar himself repeatedly expressed a wish that a resident British officer should be appointed to his State. The strategical road which will connect Gilgit with India is all but completed. Some authorities are of opinion that this road should be continued up the higher Gilgit Valley, through Yasin, to Chitral. Then we should have the key of the Hindoo Koosh, and, what is more, by commanding the lower Chitral Valley, be enabled to outflank a Russian army advancing from Herat. Such arrangements might be made with the native States on our frontier as to permit of our constructing still other strategical roads, and establishing outposts where necessary.

It is unfortunate that our road to Gilgit should be through Kashmir, across passes closed by snow for two-thirds of the year; whereas there is a direct natural route by the Indus Valley into British India, traversing no passes, and open all the year, but which is at present entirely closed, so far as we are concerned, by the hostility of the Shinaka and other tribes, who inhabit the country between Boonji and our territory.[1]

[1] Since this chapter was written disturbances have broken out both in Chitral and Chilas. A British Agency has been established in the former country, of which our friend Nizam-ul-Mulk is now master. The capital of Chilas is now occupied by Imperial Service troops; and a road will no doubt shortly be opened out through this country to India. Gilgit will then be ten days' nearer Abbotabad and the railway than it is at present, while the dangerous passes of the Kashmir route will be avoided.

The following forms part of a summary of an article in the Russian paper, the 'Svet,' which appeared in the 'Times' of December 9, 1892. Comment is unnecessary:

'Adverting to the Pamir question, the "Svet" strongly condemns Russian diplomacy for the Convention concluded with Lord Granville in 1872, whereby the Russian frontier in that region was formed by a line from Lake Sari-Kul to Pandja, crossing the Pamirs in such a way as to cut off Russia from access to the Hindu Kush. The newspaper describes this range as the key of Great Britain's Asiatic possessions, and points out that if Russia commanded the passes leading to Chitral, her troops would only have to march some 250 miles along a good route to enter Cashmere, their entry into which country would be the signal for a formidable insurrection against the British throughout India. This, pursues the "Svet," is the reason why Great Britain is so anxious to reach the southern slopes of the Hindu Kush, which she intends to render impregnable, and this is why Russia should take advantage of the short time left her to preserve this key to her power, and, since it is impossible for her to act against India by way of Afghanistan, to do so through Chitral. After declaring that the Convention of 1872 was not a formal treaty, and that owing to the change in the situation since it was concluded it has practically lapsed, the newspaper urges the Government to show no delay in securing the Khanate of Wakhan, extending Russian influence to the Hindu Kush, placing Chitral under Russian protection, and hoisting the Russian flag on the passes before Great Britain hoists the English colours. At the same time a military road should immediately be constructed from Marghelan across the Pamirs, and the passes of the Hindu Kush should be strongly fortified, so as to permit at any moment of a Russian descent into the Chitral Valley.'

I have here given but a bare outline of the advantages of Gilgit to the Empire, for the subject is a large one. The Gilgit Agency is a model of what a frontier outpost in a friendly and protected State should be. Colonel Durand was appointed British Agent at Gilgit in 1889, and is assisted by a handful of English officers—until last year there were only five of these. While training and rendering efficient the Imperial Service troops of the Maharajah, he has been skilfully carrying on the political work entrusted to him, conciliating neighbouring peoples, extending our influence and firmly establishing it, and has also proved that he is ever ready to punish with strong hand any offence on the part of a hostile or rebellious tribe.

I halted for several days at Appleford's camp to await letters. The engineers of Messrs. Spedding & Co.'s staff were now scattered over the 240 miles of road, each with a gang of coolies, working on the particular section allotted to him; and, to my inexperienced eye, the rapidity with which the road was being carried across this most difficult country was amazing. Some five thousand navvies were employed on it, men of various countries — Afridis, Kyberis, Peshawaris, Kabulis, Kashmiris, Swats, Punjabis, and others.

It needed a firm hand to keep all these in order. The Pathans, who formed the majority, were for the most part big, handsome men; but some of them looked thorough ruffians, as in fact they were—fugitives from justice, who had been robbers and murderers in their own land. But, with all his bloodthirstiness and general savagery, the jovial, courageous, independent Pathan is a more pleasing and respectable character than the effeminate Kashmiri, mild and harmless merely because

T

he is so complete a coward. The Pathan is brutal, but he is a man.

These wild aliens inspire great terror in the timorous natives hereabouts, who are ever trumping up charges of robbery and outrage against them, in order to obtain compensation. If a crime of any sort is committed on this road, it is invariably put down to the Pathans—very unfairly so, for the Maharajah's sepoys are far from being beyond suspicion; but the Pathan is a dog with such a very bad name that it is only natural he should be the object of calumny. It would lead to a great deal of mischief were these cases settled before the corrupt and rapacious native magistrates, who would mulct both parties, and probably by their injustice excite the angry Pathans to murderous riots. Spedding, therefore, and some of the staff, have been appointed magistrates by the Kashmir Durbar, with full powers to adjudicate in all disputes that may arise between the servants and coolies of the firm and the subjects of the Maharajah. The truculent Pathan places complete confidence in the justice of his sahibs, and accepts their decision, whatever it may be, without question.

High faculties for organisation are necessary to one who would contract to make strategical roads in these regions. The responsibilities attending such an undertaking are great. In the first place, the transport service is a matter for serious consideration. This country producing nothing, Spedding & Co. have to bring up from Kashmir all the grain and other supplies necessary for their host of coolies. Godowns have also to be established at various points, where the men can purchase clothes and other requisites. In this particular summer, when, in anticipation of the Hunza-Nagar expedition, all available coolies and baggage-animals were needed to carry the supplies for the troops at Gilgit, and when it was only·after the most strenuous efforts that a bare sufficiency of grain was brought across the passes before they were closed for the winter by heavy snows, it may be imagined that Spedding's transport was an anxious business, demanding his constant supervision. At one time it seemed as if it were impossible that enough grain could cross the passes in time, and it was feared lest the thousands of men who were about to be shut up for eight months in this desert region would suffer from actual famine.

The organisation of this energetic firm is certainly very complete; and as Mr. Spedding has now had much experience in the work, he can at very short notice appear with an army of coolies and his own commissariat at any point in the Himalayas, or elsewhere, where a road is urgently needed. His services are invaluable on any military expedition into the hills.

CHAPTER XVIII

ON THE SLOPES OF NANGA PARBAT — MARCH TO GILGIT — ASTOR COOLIES — THE HATTU PIR — RAMGHAT — THE INDUS VALLEY — THE SHINAKA REPUBLICS — HOME RULE — BOONJI — THE FLOOD OF 1840 — THE INDUS FERRY — CHAKERKOT — A DESERTED VILLAGE.

WHILE waiting for my letters I made some expeditions in order to obtain a near view of Nanga Parbat and take photographs of that white giant. On one occasion I clambered up a precipitous mountain behind Appleford's camp, some fourteen thousand feet or so in height, from which the view would have been magnificent were it not for a dust-haze that filled the still, sultry air—a most disagreeable phenomenon, not, like a cloudy, moisture-charged atmosphere, lending distance to the landscape, and producing soft and pleasing tones, but blurring all with its monotonous ashy veil.

On another occasion, accompanied by two or three coolies carrying bedding and provisions, I made a four days' most delightful trip to the glaciers that lie at the head of the nullah behind Astor. Here I found a charming Alpine valley, with grassy slopes and forests of pine, where, among the ferns and moss beneath the trees, one could gather as many ripe strawberries as one pleased. Higher up I crossed a slope of boulders and débris on which rose and other bushes were growing. I naturally concluded that I was walking on the solid surface of the earth, when, to my surprise, I suddenly came upon a great chasm, and, looking into it, saw dark caverns opening out under me, with walls of solid ice; while in places the ice had melted away, leaving the crust of moraine above unsupported. The water was fast dripping down from the roofs of these icy caverns, and rocks were continually tumbling in from above as the thaw proceeded. I now realised that I was walking on the top of a great glacier covered with the débris of the mountains it had brought down with it. I came across many others of these openings where there had been a recent subsidence of the moraine, and it was curious to see, far down, at the bottom of these dim chasms, the uprooted rose-trees, still covered with blossoms, lying among the blocks of ice and fallen boulders. In other parts the stony crust was thin, and crags of ice projected through it, whose gradual melting watered little surrounding gardens of grass and Alpine flowers.

Then I fell in with a lovely blue lake, called Sangosar, surrounded by snow-clad heights, which were reflected on its still surface, and having only a few dwarf birches growing on its shores. From here, after a long and arduous climb, I reached the summit of a snowy spur, the height of which above the sea must have been about seventeen thousand feet, and was rewarded by a spectacle than which it would be difficult to find a grander. Before me stood a buttress of Nanga Parbat. My vision could travel from the depths lying almost perpendicularly a mile beneath my feet, up awful wastes, to a white dome at an immense height above me, and about ten miles distant. The foot of this scene was formed by the snow-streaked moraine, and the little lake from which I had ascended. Above these was a long and very steep glacier, cloven by many crevasses, filling the hollow between two sharp projecting ridges of the mountain. Above the glacier were mighty slopes of snow, with great pinnacles and walls of rock springing from them, while what appeared to be glittering icicles of gigantic size hung over the outjutting ledges of the precipices. And at last, highest of all, topping this sublime desolation, was that vast dome of snow, rolling in soft outlines, with not a rock appearing through the pure white, standing out against the pale blue sky.

Occasionally an avalanche would thunder over some cliff on to the glacier below; but otherwise a wonderful stillness prevailed in this lifeless region. The gentle downs of unsullied snow that formed the horizon appeared in striking contrast to the savage ruggedness beneath, a mysterious region stretching out calm and solemn under the pure, thin air, in which no creature or plant could exist.

That white horizon so near me was the limit of the British Empire, the slopes beyond descending into the unexplored valleys of the Indus, where dwell the Shinaka tribesmen. Had I crossed the ridge with my followers, the first human beings we met would in all probability have cut our heads off.

On returning to Appleford's camp I found that Spedding had arrived, and was very busy superintending the construction of this section of the road. There was a disappointing message from Gilgit awaiting me. Major Cumberland was prostrated with fever, and our journey to the Pamirs had to be abandoned. On August 11 Colonel Durand passed through here on his way to Simla, and Spedding, who was compelled to return to Kashmir, to look to that ever-worrying transport and grain question, accompanied him as far as Srinagur.

I was anxious to see Gilgit before leaving this district, and decided now to march there. Had I known what would take place later on, I might have spared myself this trouble, and occupied my time in shooting in pleasant nullahs or in mountaineering; for I was destined to see a good deal of Gilgit, and to make three journeys along this particularly dreary and undelectable road.

It was not easy at this time to procure horses at Astor, either for myself or my baggage, so I decided to tramp it. I soon began to realise the difficulties that beset the traveller on this military road, which was now crowded with the trains of men and animals carrying supplies to the frontier outpost. It was not easy to obtain even the few coolies I required, and when some were at last raised for me in the neighbouring village of Los, they were very different men to the active and cheery Baltis and Ladakis with whom I had been travelling so many hundreds of miles hitherto. They toiled along slowly and reluctantly, with gloomy, sulky expressions, always lamenting and complaining when they passed me. But the life on the Gilgit road is well calculated to ruin the temper of the most amiable and contented people. The natives of the Astor district were having an especially bad time of it, the Kashmir authorities having this year imposed an excessive share of begar on them, so that many of the men were halt and worn with the hard labour.

The road from Astor to Gilgit is divided into nine marches, which I got over in six days. There are no rest-houses, so that the traveller has to encamp at night. Having sent my baggage on ahead, I set out on August 12, and marched to Doiun, a distance of twenty-four miles. Spedding's new road had not yet been completed beyond Appleford's camp, so that I had to follow the old native track. The new road will not only be far more easy, but it will also shorten the distance considerably; the construction of a gallery along the cliff-face opposite Appleford's camp, for instance, will avoid a long zigzag to the heights above.

At first I traversed a dreary country, over gravelly

DASHKIN.

downs glittering with mica, sparsely grown with ugly wormwood bush; then along gorges by the river-bed where, had it not been for frequent draughts of the ice-cold water, the heat would have been insupportable. The water of this torrent, like that of the Gilgit and other streams in this region, is very discoloured by the minute particles of mica it holds in suspension. It does not appear that ill-consequences follow the drinking of this prickly mixture. Then the road ascended, high above the river, to cross barren, hot plateaus to the village of Dashkin; beyond which it led for a time through a pleasanter country, traversing valleys well covered with pine-woods, and watered by many streams from the snows of the mountains above. At last, just before dark, I reached a point whence I overlooked the large valley of Doiun, where it opens out upon the ravine of the Astor River; and here I perceived, much to my joy, far below, a white spot, which I recognised as a sahib's tent—the present quarters of Mr. Wilkinson, another of Spedding & Co.'s busy staff. I clambered down the hillside, introduced myself, and was made welcome.

The village of Doiun is higher up the valley, and still higher is a Dogra fort containing a small garrison—an important position, for hard by is a pass into lawless Chilas. I did not see my baggage or coolies this night, and on the morrow I ascertained that they had reached Doiun Village at eleven o'clock, and that three of them had thrown down their loads and run away. This disappearance of one's coolies is of not infrequent occurrence on the Gilgit road.

Having with difficulty replaced the deserters with three Doiun men, I set out on the afternoon of August 13 for the next stage, Ramghat, the march that is the most dreaded of all by the coolies, and which is, not without reason, described in Ince's Guide-book as being a ghastly journey. There is not a drop of water to be obtained on the way, and the heat is always more intense here than on any other part of the road. The numerous bones of dead baggage-animals—not long since of men likewise—lying among these parched rocks testify to the horrors of this march.

There are two roads from Doiun to Ramghat, the lower and the upper. I went by the first and returned by the second, and there is little to choose between them. Close to its junction with the Indus the Astor torrent rushes down a narrow gorge with lofty, arid mountains rising on either side. The mountain on the left bank, where not precipitous, has gigantic slopes of débris, and boulders piled one on the other at a dangerously steep angle, down which landslips and showers of rock often sweep, while large portions of the mountainside at times fall away. The lower road winds and zigzags among these horrid slopes, now rising 1,000 feet, only to descend to its former level, and then rise once more in order to avoid the frequent precipices, and at last brings one to a high spur, from which there is a final very steep descent to Ramghat.

The upper road is easier, being carried along the top of the mountain till it reaches a point nearly 6,000 feet above the river—the spur of Hattu Pir—whence one looks down on Ramghat, lying at one's feet far beneath, and the thin, white line of the torrent, whose roar is scarcely audible. Seen from the Hattu Pir the Astor gorge is appalling for its nakedness and desolation, and the gigantic scale of its precipices. The steep descent from the Hattu Pir to the river is by a rough track, very bad for horses and fatiguing for men, zigzagging down these 6,000 feet of precipices and piled-up boulders.

The line of the new road will be somewhere between the two native roads. The engineering difficulties presented here are very great, and it must be almost impossible to construct a road that will not be repeatedly swept away by the falling rocks; while the loose mountain-side, ever ready, as it is, to slide away, affords the least secure of foundations. It was anticipated that there would be numerous accidents among the navvies employed on this section of the road while working on this perilous mountain; and I heard that upwards of thirty men had been killed here before I left the country, having been struck by falling rocks, or precipitated into the abyss by the crumbling away of their foothold. But when the road across this dangerous bit has been successfully finished, it will save a vast amount of suffering to man and beast.

After the long scramble up and down these miles of hot boulders under the fiery sun, every traveller rushes eagerly to the torrent-bank at Ramghat, and quenches his thirst in that delicious icy water. Ramghat itself is a spot as ghastly as is the road that leads to it. It is merely a little military post of caves and huts guarding the two bridges—one a rope bridge, the other a wooden cantilever bridge—which span the river. The post is an important one, for should an enemy seize it and destroy these bridges, all communication with Gilgit would be cut off.

There is no vegetation at Ramghat: on all sides rise the stupendous bare crags. The rocks here become so heated by the sun in the daytime that I found them almost too hot to touch for some time after the westering sun had left them in shadow. The air, heated by the rocks, felt like the breath of a furnace. Three times I visited Ramghat, and it was always the same. A man might almost as well pass his life in a stokehole as in this infernal oven of a place. I should imagine that the unfortunate sepoys who have to live here must develop livers like those of the similarly-treated geese of Strasburg.

The Gilgit road has been called the Siberia of Kashmir. It was once the custom of the Kashmiris to conduct their convicts as far as this Ramghat bridge, force them across the river, and leave them to shift for themselves on the farther bank, their usual fate being either to starve in the desert or to fall into the hands of the Yaghistanis, who killed them or sold them into slavery.

On crossing the bridge I felt a chilly breath on my face like that which meets one on opening the door of a cellar; for the air for a few feet over the surface of the river was deliciously cooled down by that icy water fresh from the snows and glaciers.

The camping-place was in a little nullah a mile or so farther on. Luckily some of the provisions came in; but the coolies, with the bedding and baggage, did not enter an appearance this night, having succumbed to thirst and weariness, and remained by the river at Ramghat. It was oppressively hot all night in this gorge: no dew fell, though the sky was quite clear; the gusts of wind that swept past occasionally still felt like the blast of a furnace, and though I slept coatless under the moon, I was uncomfortably warm. We purchased sufficient fuel to cook our food from some sepoys who were stationed in a little block-house that guarded this side of the Astor River.

The next day's march—August 14—was a waterless one, so I started at daybreak in order to get it over before the sun should gain full strength. A short distance beyond the nullah in which we had bivouacked the road enters the Indus Valley, which is broad at this point, but narrows again into gorges both above and below the plain of Boonji. The scenery round was wofully barren, the Indus flowing through an undulating waste of stones, while the enclosing mountains were destitute of vegetation.

It is here that the Indus leaves Kashmir territory to enter the Shinaka country. The maps indicate the course of the river from near this point to where it emerges into British territory by dotted lines, to signify that it has never been surveyed; while the word ' unexplored,' so tempting to a traveller's imagination, is written large across the region. From here one looks down the valley into the mysterious and forbidden land that is so near, and from the upper Hattu Pir road, by which I returned, the first Chilas village, Gor, with its surrounding orchards, is visible.

The district of Shinaka includes the Chilas, Darel, Tanger, and other valleys. The inhabitants are Dards, and resemble the Astoris, Gilgittis, and Hunzas in dress and appearance. One very curious feature of this district is that the form of Government is Republican, and that the principle of Home Rule has been carried out to its extreme limit. Each Shinaka valley is a small Republican State, and each village of each Republic manages its own affairs. There is one settlement, of twelve houses only, in this region which can boast of being the tiniest independent State in the world. The smallest village has its local Parliament, at which every male above a certain age has a voice; for not only is ' one man one vote' the law here, but everyone is a Member of Parliament. Drew gives a most interesting account of these federations. A Village Parliament, he tells us, manages all the internal affairs of the village; but questions of general policy are settled by the State Parliament, to which each village sends its representatives. If only one member of the House objects to a proposed measure, it cannot be carried out; Parliament is adjourned until the dissentient is talked over, or possibly bribed or bullied over, to the views of the majority. Here a majority is never allowed to dictate to a minority. Thus, if one village of a State differs from the others, it is at liberty to carry out its own policy; so that occasionally one village is in alliance with one foreign Power, while the other villages in the same State have thrown in their fortunes with a rival Power.

As may be imagined, it is not easy for a Government to have a strong definite foreign policy under such a system; while the obstruction of the minority prevents despatch in public business. It was perhaps well for us in the coming winter that the Shinaka valleys were not governed by despotic rajahs, like their neighbours; for it was known that the federated tribes meditated an attack on our line of communication when we were being held in check by the Kanjutis at Nilt. The local and general Parliaments met to discuss the question, and no doubt a good deal of talking was done by members, both of the war and peace parties. We heard of Jingo meetings at which there was some very fine blustering; but as, according to the ancient Constitution of the land, war could not be declared until all the peace party had been argued over by the eloquence of the bellicose, we had turned the enemy's position at Nilt and subdued our foes before the federal tribesmen had come to any decision—and then it was too late to take action. Thus, Home Rule has its decided advantages when put into practice by States hostile to us.

The Shinakas are, however, unanimous on one subject—the righteousness of cutting off the head of every Shiah who falls into their hands: they are intolerant of dissent.

Closed as this region at present is to us, the Gilgit merchants obtain their goods from India through Chilas by the Indus Valley route, despite the heavy tolls they have to pay to the tribesmen, so far preferable is this way to the Gilgit road, with its high passes and dangers.

I now followed the road across the stony plain to Boonji. The view both up and down the Indus Valley terminates in great snowy ranges. Looking down the valley towards Chilas I saw Nanga Parbat, with its leagues of snow, towering above all the lesser heights; while up the valley distant rugged peaks were faintly visible—the mountains that hem in the ravines of the Kanjuti robbers. For I was now approaching that extreme north-west strip of Kashmir territory which projects into Yaghistan, or Rebel Land, as the fearful Kashmiris term the wild countries on their frontier; and the traveller proceeding along this road has on either side of him more or less unknown or hostile tribes.

Boonji signifies fifty in the language of these parts; and the name, it is said, was given to this district because there were once fifty villages and considerable cultivation in the now desert vale of the Indus between the mouths of the Astor and Gilgit streams. An extraordinary flood in 1840, which is a striking example of the huge scale of the convulsions of Nature in this region of gigantic mountains, was no doubt the primary cause of the present desolation. Near the Hattu Pir a whole mountain suddenly fell into the Indus, forming a great dam across the river, and preventing all outlet. The waters rose behind this dam for six months, flooding all the plain of Boonji and the valley of the Gilgit River, till a lake was formed thirty five miles in length, and of great depth. At last the rising lake reached the top of the dam, overflowed it, forced a breach, and then, with irresistible power, the immense mass of water opened a broad, deep channel through the opposing mountain. The liberated Indus once more rushed down its gorges, and the vast lake was drained in one day.

Hundreds of miles away, the great wave of the flood overwhelmed a Sikh army that was encamped near Attock, and the loss of life and property all down the valley of the Indus was beyond computation.

The Chilas raids, and subsequently the Kashmir begar, have hitherto discouraged any attempts at again bringing these lands under cultivation, while a large proportion of the inhabitants fled into neighbouring countries to escape the unceasing oppression. But now that our active interference in the affairs of the State is putting a stop to the old abuses, and that the peasants, having confidence in our will and power to see that justice is done them, are ready to take up unoccupied lands and cultivate them, it is to be hoped that oases of green, irrigated fields and orchards will soon once more be scattered over this dreary desert. Colonel Durand is doing his utmost to promote the colonisation of all cultivable lands on the Gilgit road, and the country, I imagine, will present a very different aspect in a few years.

It was a short, easy, but very hot march to Boonji. I had not been at so low a level as this since I had been in Kashmir territory, for the Indus near Boonji is only 4,400 feet above the sea. Doiun is 8,720, and the Hattu Pir, 10,000 feet.

Boonji stands on an extensive plateau rising 250 feet above the river. This plateau is fairly well watered, and here, undoubtedly, more land could be brought under cultivation. The habitations are scattered, and few in number, but there is a good-sized Dogra fort, with barracks for the accommodation of a considerable garrison. Boonji, standing as it does at the gate of the valleys of Chilas, and commanding the passage of the Indus, is one of the most important positions on the Gilgit road.

I reached Boonji in advance of all my followers, and sat down under the shade of a walnut-tree to await them. A hospitable old man brought me out some welcome refreshment—a bowl of milk, cakes, and bunches of grapes. A crowd of courteous natives gathered round me, and I noticed that these men were of more dignified bearing and of a finer type than any I had of late seen. I was now on the frontier of Yaghistan, and these people were probably the descendants of bold robbers, and not of slaves.

The view from the plateau of Boonji is very fine, whether one looks down the hot valley into the land of the Shinakas, dominated by Nanga Parbat's snowy dome, or, in the other direction, over the plain where the Chakerkot and Gilgit rivers pour their tributary waters into the Indus. An immense panorama extends around one, a magnificent but melancholy waste of sands, rocks, and distant snows, basking in the fierce sunshine, at noon no shadows relieving the universal glare.

At last the coolies, many of whom I had not seen for two days, straggled into camp and my tent was pitched. Then these miserable men came up to me, with groans and supplications that would have been very pitiable did not one know how much of humbug there was in this demonstration, and begged me to dismiss them. They must have known that, had I let them go, they would have been probably pounced upon by Kashmir officials, to do begar under uncomfortable conditions. As it was, they were carrying light loads, had been promised bakshish in addition to their pay, and had been presented with a goat, rice, and other luxuries. Baltis would have made themselves very merry under such circumstances, but it was

U

difficult to content these Astoris. I told them I would discharge them here provided I could find other coolies to relieve them. The Dogra commandant, who now came up, informed me that this was not feasible, all available coolies having been requisitioned for the carriage of grain. My men had, therefore, perforce to accompany me for the few remaining marches to Gilgit.

They at once reconciled themselves to their fate, and the spokesman of the queer creatures declared that if I gave them a little tobacco to smoke this day, this would put them in a good temper, and they would grumble no more. Having learnt from personal experience that nicotine does possess properties of this nature, I complied with their request, with the result that they were very quiet and amiable for a while. They had no hookah with them, so contrived to make a pipe after the most primitive fashion known to smokers, and which prevails in wild parts of America, as well as in Asia. A little mound of earth was piled up, and then well patted down with the hands to make it firm. Into this mound a stick was then thrust horizontally for six inches or so. A hole was next bored with a finger through the earth just above the innermost end of the stick, and this hole formed the bowl of the pipe, and was filled with tobacco. Lastly, the stick was gently withdrawn, leaving behind a little tunnel that served as pipe-tube. Each coolie in turn applied his lips to the earthy mouth of this tube, and inhaled the grateful fumes. They had never before smoked such tobacco as I had given them, and expressed their high approval of it.

The next day's march was to Chakerkot. The road leads from the Boonji plateau down to the Indus, which has here to be crossed by a wooden raft. The river was now in full flood, and the breakers were tumbling ominously in the centre. Accidents are not infrequent at this passage. In the previous summer, Dr. Robertson, on his way to Kafiristan, lost nearly all his baggage, and some instruments most necessary for an explorer—which, of course, could not be replaced—by the capsizing of this raft, while nineteen coolies were drowned. A native officer, condoling with him after the accident, exclaimed, with the indifference to human life characteristic of his race, 'Ah, sahib, what a disaster! As for the coolies, we can easily find you others; but as regards the baggage, it is another matter.'

This passage is, of course, a position of vital importance to the Gilgit garrison, and while guarded by Boonji on one side, has the little fort of Sai on the opposite bank. A memorable night-surprise took place here some years ago. The Kashmir garrisons had been driven across the Indus by the Yaghistanis, and the latter were holding Sai in force. One dark night the Maharajah's troops stealthily came down from Boonji, swam the Indus with the aid of many hundreds of inflated goatskins (with the loss of numbers of men, who were numbed by the icy water and swept away), surprised the enemy, captured Sai, and secured once more the road to Gilgit—a most creditable performance; but the brave Dogra soldiers will do anything that is required of them when properly led, as I myself saw later on.

The dangers of the Boonji ferry will soon be a thing of the past, for a suspension-bridge is being sent from England to span the broad torrent.

We effected the passage on this occasion without accident. I observed that the ferrymen here were more skilled in their work than those in Baltistan, not attempting to paddle with bare poles, but employing broad-bladed oars and rullocks; which is just as well, for at this point, were the raft carried away by the current, it would soon reach rapids in which nothing could live.

We landed on the sandy shores of the right bank. As there are difficult cliffs at the junction of the Indus and Gilgit rivers, the road ascends the Sai nullah to the village of Chakerkot, and then crosses the intervening range to the Gilgit Valley. This nullah is a pleasant spot for this generally desert region, with clear running water and a good deal of vegetation. Our this day's camping-place was a grassy patch on the left bank of the little river, just opposite Chakerkot. The lumbadar came to me across the cantilever bridge that here spans the stream, with presents of grapes and apricots. Chakerkot is surrounded by orchards, and the wild vines festoon the trees.

But on our side of the river the aspect was a very melancholy one; for here was one of the deserted villages I have spoken of. It was evident that within recent years cultivated fields had extended for some distance up the valley, but of the former inhabitants there was not one left. In more favoured lands the nakedness of abandoned tillage would soon be hidden by rank weeds and bushes; but it is not so here. As the canals that tapped the streams above had been untended, and allowed to fall to ruin, this land, depending as it does so entirely on irrigation, had lapsed into desert. Save for a narrow margin of wild growth by the river-brink, there was no vegetable life to be seen. Where once the maize and lucerne had gladdened the eye, the stone walls now enclosed terraces of dry, yellow earth. Numbers of fine walnut, peach, and other valuable fruit-trees dotted the stony hillside, or stood thickly together in what had once been green orchards; but now all these trees were leafless, with stark branches, dead for want of the needful moisture.

On our side of the river all had been abandoned. Looking towards the other side, I perceived that though a good deal of land was still under cultivation and beautifully green, there were also sad signs of ruin and wasted labour; there, too, were ranged the dreary rows of dry terraces and the skeleton trees standing above them, where once the irrigation-streams had babbled down in miniature cascades, spreading fertility. Many of the inhabitants, I was told, had made an exodus into Chilas. It was scarcely necessary to inquire the cause.

My tent was pitched on a small flower-spangled plot of grass which the river often floods, shaded by an ancient walnut-tree, whose branches were smothered by a luxuriant vine covered with bunches of ripe grapes—a delicious islet of verdure amid this stony desolation.

In the evening it began to rain, a very rare occurrence here. The coolies, who had before declared themselves unable to support the heat of the sun, now complained bitterly of cold, and said they could find no shelter. Close by was a hut made of the branches of trees, so I asked them why they did not take up their quarters there. 'There are two sepoys in it' was the reply. 'We cannot go where sepoys are.' 'Then cross the river,' I suggested. 'There are plenty of houses?' 'We dare not,' said the spokesman. 'Those men are Yaghistani wallahs! We are afraid to go into their houses.' So, fearing the sepoys on one side, and the natives on the other, they had to content themselves with a bivouac under the trees; no great hardship, for their clothes were not thin and the weather was warm. The Astoris evidently regard all peoples who dwell beyond the Indus as Yaghistanis, to be avoided as dangerous.

CHAPTER XIX

THE GILGIT VALLEY—GILGIT—THE KASHMIR ARMY—REGULARS—IRREGULAR LEVIES — THE IMPERIAL SERVICE TROOPS — WORK OF THE GILGIT AGENCY—COSSACKS ON THE PAMIRS—HUNZA ENVOYS—MARCH TO SRINAGUR—A PATHAN DASTUR—IDGARH—SIRDARKOTE—THE BORZIL PASS—MINEMERG—THE VALLEY OF GURAIS.

From Chakerkot to Gilgit is three stages, which can be easily travelled by laden coolies in two days; but these are not agreeable marches, leading one through a very burnt-up country.

On leaving Chakerkot on August 15, we first traversed the ridge dividing the valley of the Sai from that of the Gilgit River. On reaching the summit of this stony pass, I looked down upon the Gilgit torrent rushing through a broad, completely barren valley, enclosed by mountains of monotonous outline. It was a hot tramp from here to the camping-place some miles up the valley. Luckily the road in two places approached the torrent, so that one could slake one's thirst in the cold, mica-discoloured water.

I passed numbers of coolies this day carrying military stores to Gilgit—Baltis; Astoris; and even some poor Ladakis, who greeted me with the familiar *jooly*, and were evidently suffering more than the others from an oppressive heat such as is unknown in their highlands. The camping-place was a cheerless spot, a dusty plateau high above the river, with not a blade of grass growing near. Here stood a small stone hovel used as a shelter by the dak wallahs, who were able to provide us with a little firewood, and who brought us up the water we required from the torrent in their *mushoks*.

Blood has been freely shed along all this dreary frontier road, and near this spot one is pointed out the scene of a massacre of Dogra troops by treacherous Yaghistani tribesmen.

POST-HOUSES, GILGIT ROAD.

The next day, August 17, we marched into Gilgit, another hot and desert journey for a great portion of the way; but on nearing our destination we passed through considerable cultivation, the villages of Minawar and Sakwar being surrounded by orchards and maize-fields, and presenting an appearance of prosperity rare on this road. Doubtless their proximity to the British Agency secures these villagers some immunity from the oppression which prevails elsewhere. At Sakwar I rested for tiffin, and was regaled by the people with grapes and milk. The men were much better looking here than those I had seen in the Astor district, while the girls, who were not particularly shy, but who, with unveiled faces, peeped at the stranger from round the corners of walls and trees, were really very pretty, having rosy complexions, good features, and lovely eyes.

I had heard so much of the desolation of the Gilgit district that I was much surprised, on reaching the plateau of Jutial, and looking down on the famous fortress, to find it surrounded by one of the largest and best-cultivated oases I had beheld since leaving fertile Kapalu. The mountains here recede from the river, leaving on the right bank a broad plain, well watered by little streams. I walked through orchards of ripe peaches, under clusters of purple grapes, across fields of rice, millet, maize and Indian hemp, past the Dogra fort and barracks, and reached the British Agency—a further surprise for me; for here I came upon signs of civilisation I had not anticipated, a pretty bungalow standing in the middle of well-kept grounds and gardens. Here I found four of the officers of Colonel Durand's staff, by whom I was made welcome: Lieutenant Manners Smith, the military secretary, and Lieutenants Townshend, Stewart, and Molony, the attachés to the Agency. Here, too, was Major Cumberland, still suffering from the effects of fever.

On this occasion I stayed at Gilgit for three days, and was enabled to form some idea of the excellent work this handful of British officers had already accomplished in putting this, the extreme outpost of the Empire, in a proper state of defence. A few years back a Kashmir garrison of 6,000 men was found inadequate to hold in check the Kanjuti tribesmen. The Hunza-

Nagar campaign has shown what the same troops can do since they have been taken in hand by our officers.

The Kashmir Army was supposed to consist of 20,000 men, but numbers of these only existed on paper. The total force now probably amounts to about ten thousand men, and is thus composed:—First, the regular army, recruited in India from Dogras and Gurkhas, men who, though not so carefully selected as the sepoys of our own regiments, are of fair material and good fighting-stock. These are still, for the most part, armed with muzzle-loaders—Enfields and others.

Secondly, the irregular levies that are raised in different parts of the State. Some of these men, the Punialis for example, are capable of being converted into useful soldiers; but most of them are recruits from the unwarlike races—Baltis, Ladakis, even Kashmiris—on whose prowess in fight it would not do to rely. These irregulars are armed with matchlocks and other primitive weapons, and some of them with the native sword and shield.

Thirdly, the Imperial Service troops, who compose the Gilgit garrison. It will be remembered that, according to a recently-organised scheme, the fundamental principles of which were settled by the present Foreign Secretary in India, Sir Mortimer Durand, some of the important native States now place a certain portion of their armies at the disposal of our Government for the purposes of Imperial defence, the drilling and training of the men being supervised by selected British officers. The State of Kashmir supplies three regiments of Imperial Service troops and a mule battery, in all about two thousand men, who, like the regulars, are Gurkhas and Dogras. They are well equipped, and are armed with Sniders. Thanks to the energy with which the officers of the Agency have taken them in hand, the men now know their duties as disciplined soldiers, and have a smart appearance, which is more than can be said of the sepoys of the other Kashmir regiments.

I saw that the work of these officers was no sinecure. Little time had they to go shikaring into the well-stocked nullahs of the neighbourhood. While they were drilling the garrison into shape and superintending the grain transport at Gilgit, Captain Twigg was doing the same work at Astor; and Colonel Neville Chamberlain was contending with the most anxious task of all, that of hurrying all necessaries across the Borzil Pass before it should be closed for the winter, with native supineness and ineptitude, and often deliberate obstruction, to overcome.

There were but thirty men of our own Indian Army at Gilgit when I was there, fine Pathans of the 20th Punjab Infantry, who formed the bodyguard of the British Agent in this remote corner of the world.

Surgeon Roberts, the Agency doctor, whose share of the hard work was not to come till later on, had time to ride about the country with me and show me the sights. On the evening of my arrival we went to the mouth of the Kargha nullah, up which there is a track leading into Yaghistan, to see a carving of Buddha on the face of a rock, a sign that this country, as well as Baltistan, had once been Buddhist. There is but one European grave in Gilgit, that of the intrepid explorer, Lieutenant Hayward, who was treacherously murdered near here, by order of the King of Yasin, in 1870.

At this time various disquieting rumours were brought down to Gilgit by native informants. It was reported that a body of Cossacks was on the Pamirs at a point only ten marches distant, and would probably enter the Hunza Valley, where the rulers, while hostile to us, were favourably disposed to the Russians. Then we heard that Captain Younghusband had promptly left Kashgar for the Pamirs, to discover what was going on.

Four Hunza notables, accompanied by some eight or nine followers, entered Gilgit while I was there, bringing some message from their king. These specimens of the robber tribe were strongly-built men, with bold eyes and rather jovial expressions. They all wore the Dard caps and cloth chogas, or robes, some of the chogas being thickly studded with little white feathers to add to their warmth. Their long black hair hung in knotted ringlets on either cheek.

They were most diplomatic in their talk, and prated of the blessings of peace, which, with these people, is generally a sign of warlike intention; and it was, indeed, well-known at Gilgit that, possibly at the instigation of the Russians, the tribesmen had been strengthening their defences at Nilt for two years, and making every preparation for a fight; while, with all their protestations of friendship for us, they intercepted letters which were being forwarded, at this critical period of the Russian imbroglio, from Gilgit to Captain Younghusband.

On August 20 the pleasant little party at the Gilgit Agency broke up. Lieutenant Stewart was sent off to the Pamirs, with four Pathan sepoys, to discover what tricks the Russian Bear was up to, Lieutenant Manners Smith accompanying him for some marches, in order to make arrangements with the Puniali rajahs for keeping up a dak communication across the Hindoo Koosh. Major Cumberland departed to a neighbouring nullah, while I reluctantly turned my face south, but, seeing

HUNZA ENVOYS.

that there were so many signs of disturbance in the air, not without hopes of returning later on.

I now decided to travel the twenty-two stages to Srinagur, replenish my kit, and await events there. I was seven days returning to Appleford's camp, for the heat was now so great that one could not call upon the coolies to double the marches. The traffic on the road was becoming denser every day, as the long trains of men and beasts of burden were bringing up the anxiously-expected grain. On bad parts of the road, and especially on the terrible Hattu Pir, we frequently passed the bodies or bones of horses and mules that had fallen by the way, to feed the vultures.

I crossed the Hattu Pir this time by the upper road, 6,000 feet of hard climbing through the suffocating air. My tiffin coolie, lightly loaded though he was, and whom I had allowed, contrary to my rule, to lag far behind me, fell ill of the heat by the way. So I sat down, and waited in vain on the top of the mountain for the cold fowl and bottle of tea which he was carrying; ultimately I had to tramp all the way to Doinn before I could get anything to eat or drink. The view from the Hattu Pir was very fine, but I should have enjoyed it more had water been procurable. I saw far beneath me the broad Indus winding for leagues, from Baltistan into Chilas. Far away, above the lesser mountains, rose the great snowy ranges, their lower slopes hidden in blue haze, so that they appeared to be separated from the earth, and I seemed to be gazing at a mountainous archipelago floating in mid-air. The barrenness and ruggedness of this region could be well appreciated from here. In all directions were ruddy rocks, couloirs of débris, stony plateaus, the cultivation of Boonji and Gor appearing like two tiny green patches in the vast waste.

On August 25 I reached Appleford's camp. While travelling on these roads, to arrive at a place like Gilgit, or enter the camp of one of Spedding & Co.'s engineers, is much like making a port after a sea voyage. As I came in I felt as if I had just completed a rather rough seven days' run from my last port, Gilgit, and was now putting into a snug and civilised harbour, where I was to see again the face of the white man, and where, too, soft tack and other luxuries awaited me.

Appleford was exercising his magisterial powers when I arrived in camp. The predatory instincts of the Pathans had broken out. The lumbadar of a neighbouring village complained that some of the Afghans working on that section of the road had forcibly seized a sheep, and had stolen out of a house a valuable olive-wood casket, twenty rupees, and a robe of honour which Colonel Durand had presented to the owner. Appleford ordered accusers and accused to appear before him in the evening. It is, of course, often impossible to bring a matter home to the individual offenders; but should it be proved that they belong to some particular gang, the gang as a whole has to suffer the penalty, or give up its guilty members. On this occasion representatives of the suspected gang begged Appleford to allow them to settle the matter among themselves, according to their own dastur, undertaking that the property should be found. They religiously carried out the custom of which they spoke that night. A deep hole was dug in the ground, and as soon as it was quite dark every man of the gang in turn went alone, unobserved of the others, and poured into the hole his lapful of earth. The next morning the villagers were instructed to search in the loose earth, and there, indeed, they discovered the casket, the money, the robe of honour, and the price of the sheep, no man knowing who it was that had restored the property.

I had now to find coolies or beasts of burden to carry my baggage down the road. The official at Astor whose business it was to supply transport had been informed by someone that the last coolies he had provided for me had run away, and that unless he made a better bandobast for me this time I might write about him, and give him a bad name in England, for I was a book-wallah as well as a picture-wallah. The threat of writing to the papers has little effect in these days with extortionate hotel-keepers and others in Europe; but in this more unsophisticated region the superstitious fears of the potency of printing-ink still appear to exist, for my informant told me that the awe-inspired official exclaimed in horror: 'Ah, no! surely his Highness would not give me a bad name in England!' 'Yes, he will do so if you anger him. He is quite that sort of man,' was the reply. 'Then I shall die,' he groaned, and forthwith he supplied me with five homeward-bound men of the Gurais district, with their horses—an excellent bandobast.

Gurais, which is seven marches, or eighty miles, from Astor, is a rich valley, whence come a great number of the hardy transport ponies employed on this road. The Gurais people are a cross between the Kashmiri and the Dard, of good physique, cheery fellows, and the pleasantest natives to travel with on the Gilgit road.

On August 29 I left Appleford, and made a very short march to Idgarh, a camping-ground a mile beyond Astor, where the titular rajah of the district has his mansion, and where the British officers on duty and travelling sahibs, avoiding dismal Astor, are wont to pitch their tents. Here I found one Englishman only, Captain Twigg, who was hard at work superintending the improvements in Astor Fort, the drilling of the troops, and that ever-worrying grain transport. As I arrived in camp I saw a stately Pathan of the Agency Bodyguard putting some Imperial Service recruits through their facings, the words of command, as in our Indian Army, being given in English; they are given in Sanscrit, I believe, in the other regiments of the Maharajah's service.

From Idgarh the road to the south ascends the Astor Valley for four marches. Each day brought me to a higher elevation and a cooler climate. It froze at night, and each morning my tent was stiff with ice. The country was far less barren than between Astor and Gilgit, and the road often crossed high spurs covered with breezy pastures and pine-woods.

It was not an entirely solitary journey for me, for at no less than five halting-places I found the camps of Spedding's engineers—one Englishman at each. My second day's march from Idgarh brought me to the village of Kurrum, where I found Mitchell, whom I had last seen at Srinagur, working with his gang of navvies. Mitchell had intended to travel down the road on the following day to meet Spedding, who was on his way north again; so we marched off together on September 1.

First we traversed a great slope of loose rocks, which was giving the road-makers a good deal of trouble. There had once been a large wood of cedars here, but now the trees only showed their heads above the débris that had overwhelmed them, while some had been crushed down or uprooted. Mitchell told me that this rocky chaos was the result of a severe earthquake-shock three years back, which had broken away whole spurs of the mountain, and sent them thundering down into the valley. Beyond this the road had been completed for some leagues, and after the tracks to which I had been accustomed for the last few months, I felt as if I could walk on for an indefinite time without getting tired on so easy a way. The breadth and the regularity of the road is curiously alarming to many of the hill-ponies, who look upon it as a very uncanny phenomenon. When first brought on to it, they sniff at it suspiciously, and insist on getting off it on to the rough hillside whenever this is feasible.

Higher we went, over grassy, snow-streaked downs, on which many pretty Alpine flowers were now blossoming, till we came to this day's destination, Sirdarkote, the last camping-place at the foot of the pass. Here, some 12,000 feet above the sea, are the roofless ruins of an old rest-hut, standing in the middle of a treeless, open plain, much exposed to the winds, where there is a little pasture and shrub. Here the numerous marmots were weirdly whistling round us, to the maddening bewilderment of the dogs, as usual. As we waited for our baggage to come up it began to hail, snow, and blow, while the chilly mists rolled about us. It looked and felt unpleasantly wintry; I could understand how perilous a place this Borzil Pass might be a little later in the year.

But this night we were comfortable enough here. Our followers had warm clothing, and bivouacked by the brushwood fires under the lee of the ruined hut. Mitchell made each man a present of a seer of fine rice, such as they had only before eaten at weddings

x

and at important feasts. This caused great satisfaction, and some of the coolies even commenced to devour it raw, so tempting was it to them. Rice and iced water does not appear much of a repast on which to conduct boisterous orgies, especially when the revellers have to sit on a bare mountain-side in frost and sleet; but these easily-contented men of Gurais contrived to do this. Warmed by the generous feast, they sang in loud choruses, and made a regular rollicking night of it.

September 2 was a frosty, sunny day. After breakfast Mitchell and myself, leaving our camp standing, went to the top of the pass to meet Spedding. The Borzil, 13,500 feet, is an exceedingly easy pass in summer, but it is practically closed for the greater part of the year, for at the summit one has to cross a long, exposed down for many miles, where to be overtaken by a snowstorm or by the deadly winds that sweep across the gap signifies probable death to the traveller. A large number of lives are lost here annually, and after the snow has melted in summer the dead bodies of men and animals are to be seen lying by the wayside.

The new road had been completed across the pass during the two or three weeks that it had been clear of snow. In a few weeks it would be covered again. From the summit the outlook was bleak, even at this season: we looked out upon rolling, snow-streaked pastures and stony slopes alone.

As we sat at the very top of the pass we saw a strange sight. There stalked by us, going north, regardless of the bitter wind, a gaunt, sunburnt man, naked save for a scant loin-cloth, carrying nothing with him, long-haired, wild and savage of eye, as if stupefied with *bhang*. He apparently did not observe any of us, and did not reply when addressed by our Mahomedan followers, but still stalked on, as if automatically, down the pass, until he was lost to sight. We made conjectures as to what this weird creature was doing here. He was evidently a Mussulman fanatic—a very unusual sight on this road. Was he bound for Chilas, to excite against us the slumbering fanaticism of that people? We could see that he was not a native of these regions, but had come from some distant part of India. And so he passed on by us a mystery, looking neither to the left nor right, but gazing straight before him into vacancy, hurrying steadily on, like one bent on an urgent errand.

He appeared to us like a portent of coming war; and he was not the only one we came across. Some time afterwards we met another stranger, also travelling north. 'And where are you going?' asked Mitchell. 'To Gilgit,' he replied. 'And what to do there?' 'I am a sharpener of swords,' he said, with a grim smile, showing his white teeth.

At last Spedding rode up to us. He was accompanied by Mr. Johnson, C.E., of the Kashmir Public Works Department, who was inspecting the completed portions of the road. We returned with them to Sirdarkote, at which high, wind-swept spot our united camp this night presented quite an imposing appearance. We four Englishmen dined together in Spedding's tent, while our followers feasted on goats' flesh and fine rice.

On September 3 the camp broke up, my friends to travel towards Astor, while I re-crossed the pass, and continued my journey south to Srinagur.

For nearly all the way from here to Bandipur I

was able to travel by the new road. Gangs of coolies, working with pick and shovel, or blasting on the cliffside, were to be seen on each march, while strongly-built cantilever bridges were being constructed to replace the rickety, often dangerous, old, native bridges.

The Borzil Pass had brought me over the same great Western Himalayan range which I had crossed farther east, in the spring, by the Zoji La. As I have before explained, this range forms the barrier between the moister and more fertile plains and valleys of Kashmir proper and the almost rainless and arid regions of Ladak, Baltistan, and Astor. No sooner did I cross the Borzil than I perceived, even as I had done on the Zoji La, though not here to so marked a degree, that I was entering a different climate, where the air was soft and the vegetation luxuriant—a land of woods and pastures and continued cultivation, instead of deserts and scattered oases as heretofore.

Even this, my first march beyond the pass, brought me into a delicious country, such as I had not seen for many months, where all the hillsides were covered with deep grass full of flowers—the beautiful mergs of Kashmir; and my this night's halting-place was at Minemerg, a tiny village of shepherd-huts, inhabited only in the summer, surrounded, as its name implies, by these pleasant meadows. Here I found the camp of Mr. Blaker, one of Spedding's staff.

Fertile as was all the country through which I was marching to Bandipur, it was far more difficult to obtain supplies here than on the most desert portions of the Gilgit road. Had I not made provision before leaving Astor, I might have almost starved in the rich valleys of the Borzil and Kishanganga rivers, and I should have fared but badly had it not been for the camps of the road-making engineers I passed on the way—true oases, well known for their hospitality to the sahib wandering in Kashmir.

There were numbers of wild Pathans at work on this portion of the road, who, as elsewhere, were being kept well in hand by the engineers, the only men they will obey; for these turbulent fellows despise the natives of the country, and will not recognise the officials. Their sahibs they respect. But it must be remembered that the Company selects its officers with care, and the pluck and tact with which these half a dozen young Englishmen control these thousands of half-savages affords a good example of the way our race has gone to work to create an empire.

Shortly before I arrived at Minemerg a really serious disturbance had seemed imminent. Navvies coming from different villages in Afghanistan had quarrelled over the distribution of some grain. They proposed to settle the question by fighting it out on the maidan of Minemerg with picks and crowbars, so many hundred men on either side, which would no doubt have been a most bloody and Homeric conflict, had not the engineer stepped in and prevented it.

On September 4 I marched down the flowery vale to the next halting-place, Bangla, where stood the camp of Mr. Maynard, another of Spedding & Co.'s hospitable staff. It was a pleasant march on September 5, across the green mergs, thick with scented blossoms, blue, purple, and yellow, tossing their heads in the fresh breeze, and through shady pine-woods, in which the strawberries were ripe, till I reached the junction of the Borzil stream with the Kishanganga River, and entered the valley of Gurais, than which even Kashmir can show few fairer spots. Meadows, corn-fields, and orchards cover the broad bottom across which the river winds, and which is bounded by fine crags and gently-sloping mountains clothed with forest. Several little villages of log huts are scattered over this verdant land, and there is a Dogra fort commanding the passage of the river.

I encamped in a wood of tall poplars noisy with many crows, called Bodwan, where McCulloch, another of the road-making staff, had his camp. My cheery Gurais men, who had brought my baggage down from Astor, and who had been engaged to travel with me thus far only, now volunteered to accompany me to Bandipur, four marches farther on; but they explained that the Thanadar of Gurais, a much-dreaded official, would impound them and their horses for begar if he came across them. So the horses were picketed close to my camp, to be under my protection, and the men themselves did not venture out of the wood to visit the neighbouring village, where were their homes and wives, until darkness had set in.

At this period the thanadar, though it was his duty to supply sheep and other necessaries to Spedding's engineers and to officers passing through his district, avoided doing this so far as he dared, and persistently boycotted travellers. The villagers of Gurais were quite willing to sell supplies, but dared not. They said they could not do so without the permission of the lumbadar. When the lumbadar was brought out, he declared that the village would be heavily fined if anything was sold without the sanction of the thanadar. But when the thanadar was sought for, that great man was never to be found. And all this fuss would be made, perhaps, over a hen or a dozen eggs. On my next visit to Gurais it was necessary for me to procure enough supplies to carry me across the Borzil Pass. I found a simple way out of my difficulty: I did not inquire for the boycotting official, but entered a village and seized all the fowls I needed as they ran about among the huts. The owners protested gently, and spoke of the thanadar. I explained that the thanadar was nothing to me, paid the villagers well for all I had taken, and departed with my loot. It was plain to see that the people, who loved not their tyrant, were delighted with my course of action. They had received more money than they would have done had the officials put a finger in the pie; while, as they would represent that I had taken the fowls by force, the baffled thanadar would be unable to fine them.

I noticed that my following had been gradually increasing in numbers as I advanced. I had left Astor with five men, and now saw some nine or ten working for me in the Bodwan Wood, unloading the ponies, preparing fires, pitching the tents, and making themselves generally useful. These were native travellers, bound south like myself, who were glad to attach themselves to a sahib's caravan as if they belonged to it, thus avoiding the risk of being robbed by Pathans, or being snapped up on the way by sepoys for begar.

CHAPTER XX

THE RAJDIANGAN PASS—VIEW OF THE VALE OF KASHMIR—SRINAGUR AGAIN—WAR RUMOURS—REINFORCEMENTS FOR GILGIT—RETURN TO ASTOR—AN EARLY WINTER—CLOSING OF THE PASSES—DIFFICULTIES OF A MOUNTAIN CAMPAIGN—COMMUNICATION INTERRUPTED—LOSS OF LIFE ON THE PASSES—CAPTAIN YOUNGHUSBAND—ARRIVAL OF THE GUNS AND 5TH GURKHAS—A BLIZZARD ON THE PASS.

On September 6 our march was through a country which, save for the mountainousness of it, might have been a richly-timbered park in England. Leaving the Kishanganga Valley, we ascended a tributary nullah to the dak hut of Zadkusa, the camping-place at the foot of the Rajdiangan Pass. The snows of the preceding winter were still lying piled up by the torrent, and there were frequent signs of the destructive avalanches which render this portion of the Gilgit road dangerous in the spring.

On September 7 we crossed the Rajdiangan Pass, which, though only 11,800 feet above the sea, is even more dreaded than the Borzil in the winter months; for at the top there is an extensive plateau, where the snow lies deep for a great part of the year, and which, like the Borzil summit, is swept by frequent violent winds of deadly coldness, that prove fatal to men and animals overtaken by them. It was here, in the preceding autumn, that 300 mules and their drivers perished on one day in a snowstorm.

After a long ascent of the steep forest-clad mountain, we reached this fatal plateau, treeless, and quite exposed to all the winds; but at this season it was uncovered of snow, and the grassy downs were affording pasture to numerous herds. This night's camp was near the village of Tragbal, among the woods on the other side of the pass, and some 2,000 feet below the summit.

The wonderful view that is obtained from this point has been described by many travellers. The whole Vale of Kashmir is spread beneath one like a map—a scene strangely stirring, for its immensity and freedom, to one who comes suddenly upon it, after travelling for months among the imprisoning gorges to the northward. From the camp the mountains fall steeply to the fertile plain, 4,000 feet below. There was a slight haze in the air when I reached this spot, and as I looked down over the woods and cliffs and gorges, I saw what appeared to be a boundless seashore, with vast ponds and many winding channels left by the tide, but which was the great cultivated alluvial plain, with its lakes and rivers. Far away, hanging above the vague horizon of the plain, and separated from it by blue mists, lay what seemed to be a lone cloud, fringed with white at the top—the snow-capped mountain-ranges that divide Kashmir from India.

The whole Happy Valley, indeed, lay beneath me, and I could trace my former journeys, and those yet to come, for march after march. There lay the broad expanse of the Woolar Lake, with its little island in the middle, where is the ruined temple of the Serpent God, its winding bays and far-stretching promontories; and I could follow for leagues and leagues the sinuous reaches of the Jhelam, and the other rivers that bring fertility to this fat land from the surrounding mountain-snows. No wonder the old conquerors from over the desert northern highlands waxed enthusiastic when they looked down first upon the fair, well-watered vale, and hailed it as the earthly paradise.

The view at night was of magical beauty: the lake and the far snows gleamed in the moonlight; the plain stretched out, dim and blue, as if into infinite space. From this height it almost seemed as if I were gazing down upon some other world; and there was nothing to show that it was an inhabited plain beneath me save the scattered, flickering points of red light from the fires of travellers' camps or peasant farms.

September 8 was my last day's march for the present. After descending the mountain into the hot plain I walked along a broad high-road through the richly-cultivated land, by farmhouses with gabled, thatched roofs like Norman cottages, everything looking strangely civilised after the northern country, with its rough tracks, scanty vegetation, and wretched hovels. The scenery, too, was no longer alpine and contracted, but of gentle outlines and far horizons. On one side of me the Woolar Lake spread out like a great sea, while on the other side were low, wooded hills, which often projected in long promontories—purple in the distance—far out into the smooth, blue water.

Near the large village of Bandipur we selected one of the numerous passenger-doongahs that were brought up alongside the bank, got the baggage on board, paid off the cheery Gurais men, laid up provisions for the journey—not omitting the delicious water-melons, which are abundant in Kashmir at this season and are responsible for a good deal of sickness—and then we were poled, paddled, and towed to Srinagur, a voyage which occupied twenty-four hours, including a short halt at night.

First we traversed the hot, windless lake, in places now much overgrown with the nut-bearing *singhara*, through great floating fields of which the boatmen with difficulty forced the doongah; then we passed up a broad channel between malodorous swamps, where the clouds of midges or mosquitoes proved very troublesome, and at sunset entered the river, which we followed through a densely-inhabited land, large villages lining the bank on either side. We passed some caravans of laden camels. At present camels cannot proceed along the Gilgit road beyond Bandipur; but when the new road is completed, it is possible that they will be employed for the grain transport.

On the morning of September 9 I saw before me once more the familiar landmarks of the Vale of Kashmir—Hari Parbat and the Takht-i-Sulieman—and after several hours' travelling along the much-winding Jhelam we entered the city, and were paddled up the waterways of the Asiatic Venice. All seemed more strange to me now that I had come from the colourless North, than when I had arrived here first from India and Europe. What little civilisation I had seen lately was not of India, but of Central Asia; but here a good deal of the gorgeousness and picturesqueness of the real East was observable. On either hand, above the ruined temples of a still older civilisation, rose stately houses, the domes of Hindoo fanes, the minarets of mosques. There was a colour and a bustling life around me to which I had long been a stranger. On the balconies and terraces overlooking the river sat the white-faced, white-robed pundits. The worn stone steps of the ghats, the bridges under which we passed, the galleys which rowed swiftly by us, all were thronged with people in white or richly-coloured garments. It was, indeed, quite exciting to come out of the wilderness into the movement, brightness, and noise of this gay city.

I found the Chenar Bagh crowded with the tents of camping sahibs; for Srinagur was now full, the European society having returned from the summer station of Gulmerg. I did not remain in the bachelors' camping-place, but took up my residence in Spedding's capacious house-boat in the Munshi Bagh, where I found Mr. Beech and Mr. Lennard, who had returned from their travels in Central Asia, the latter not having been murdered by Kanjuti robbers, as had been reported.

Here I awaited the news that would determine my movements. Various rumours were about: the Russians were on the Pamirs; Cossacks had arrested British officers on neutral territory; the Hunzas were preparing to attack Gilgit, and an expedition against them was probable. But so far there was nothing certain known. At Srinagur people were making preparations to receive the Viceroy, who was to visit Kashmir in a few weeks.

All this while the grain was being hurried over the passes to Gilgit, and the resources of the officials were being taxed to the utmost to get it across before the first heavy snowfall. Colonel Neville Chamberlain was unceasingly at work. Had it not been for his energy and supervision, there would have been famine among the frontier garrisons that winter.

At last paragraphs in the Indian papers announced that several officers were repairing to Gilgit, and that the garrison there was to be reinforced by 200 men of the 5th Gurkha regiment from Abbotabad, and two guns of the No. 4 Hazara Mountain Battery. Seeing how difficult it was to send up a sufficient supply of grain for the existing garrison, it was obvious that such a force would not be despatched to Gilgit at so late a season unless a winter campaign were anticipated. I therefore decided to postpone my return to England and to re-cross the passes, though to do so would possibly involve my being locked in by the snow until the following spring.

Having obtained the necessary permission, I set out on September 22 to retrace my steps along the twenty-two marches of the Gilgit road. Spedding had written to me to bring up two of his servants and a quantity of stores, and had given me an order on his agent at Bandipur to supply me with all the necessary animals, so that I should have no difficulty about my transport. I had had enough of tramping it on that dreary road, so decided to ride all the way on this journey.

After a last dinner with Lennard on the house-boat, I set out for Bandipur at midnight in my doongah. We glided gently through the water-streets of the city, by palaces, temples, and houses looming indistinctly in the darkness, a few lights glimmering here and there from lattices above or from the watchmen's lanterns in the narrow streets. At one corner we passed a garden hung with coloured lamps, in which people were holding revelry to the music of tomtoms and mandolines; but elsewhere there was no sound to be heard, save the splashing of our boatman's paddle—a strangely still and peaceable departure this, through the sleeping capital, for the bloodshed and battle-din of the northern frontier.

On the following morning, when on the Woolar Lake, a tremendous storm swept down upon us from the heights of Rajdiangan, accompanied by heavy thunder and brilliant forked lightning. The wind blew with such fury that, had we been in open water, we must have been swamped by the waves; but the tangled singharas effectually prevented any sea from getting up, even as do the floating fields of kelp in the Southern Ocean.

At Bandipur I presented Spedding's order, and was supplied with fifteen horses. My horse-wallahs were Gurais men again, good-natured fellows, with whom it was a pleasure to travel.

I now began to realise that the summer was done, and that the brief autumn season was rapidly changing to winter. On the bleak top of Rajdiangan we passed through freezing mists, and encountered a slight snowstorm, accompanied by a most biting wind. On reaching the forests on the farther side of the pass I saw that the foliage, which I had left green a few days back, was now red and yellow, and that the leaves were falling fast. The weather remained fine during our journey to Astor: each day there was a blue sky overhead; but each night it froze, and each morning I woke to find the ground covered with hoar frost. There were but a few inches of snow on the Borzil Pass, and we effected the passage without difficulty.

The road was now more crowded than ever with bullocks from the Punjab, horses, and coolies, either journeying north laden with grain and military stores, or returning for fresh burdens. The news that the 5th Gurkhas were coming here from India had, of course, travelled up the road, and natives I met gravely informed me that the Empress of India had sold 200 of her sepoys and two hill-guns to the Maharajah. To my surprise I encountered Spedding again near the Borzil. He was yet once more marching down to Srinagur, the anxious grain question necessitating his stimulating presence among the dilatory contractors.

I reached the bagh of Idgarh, by Astor, on October 1, and there found Lieutenant Manners Smith and others of the Gilgit staff hard at work, as, too, was Blaker, of Spedding's staff, who had nearly completed this section of the road.

Here I had to wait for some time for further news or instructions. Each day the snow was lying lower on the mountain-side, and one morning we woke to find it some inches deep in our camp. It was evident that the winter was about to set in at an exceptionally early date this year, and matters began to look very serious; for, despite all efforts, but a small portion of the necessary grain had yet reached the granaries of Astor. There now came a succession of heavy rains and snowstorms on the hills; so that we frequently heard the booming of distant landslips and avalanches in the narrow valley of the Astor, and the newly-made road was swept away in several places. On October 9 news came that the Kamri Pass, over which lies the most favourable summer route between Kashmir and Gilgit, was completely closed, and that there were three feet of snow on the Borzil. For many days no grain-coolies arrived at Astor, communication being—at least temporarily—interrupted already.

At last, on October 13, Colonel Durand, Captain Colin Mackenzie, of the Seaforth Highlanders, and Captain Aylmer, R.E.—two of the officers who had been sent to Gilgit in view of the threatened disturbances—and Mr. Lennard, arrived at Idgarh. They had experienced rough weather on the Borzil, had lost a horse, while one of their followers had been badly frost-bitten. On the summit of the pass they had come across a poor woman searching distractedly for the frozen body of her child, herself on the point of death. They put her on a horse and brought her down to the first rest-house, where they found her particularly brutal husband, a Kashmiri contractor, I believe, who had hurried off to the refuge, leaving her to die, when the storm had overtaken his party. He expressed some regret at the loss of his child, but when his conduct was being strongly commented upon by the Englishmen, he excused himself by saying, 'It was wrong of me to forget the child; but as for the zenana, she is of little account, being but an old woman.

We learnt that the Gurkhas were not expected at Bandipur until the 14th, and would be accompanied by 1,200 transport mules and 400 drivers. They would have arrived at Astor before this had it not been for cholera, which had broken out during the march from Abbotabad, killing sixteen men; so that a long halt had to be made before the force could enter Kashmir. This enforced delay and the unusually early winter were most unfortunate events. So far luck seemed to be against Colonel Durand. The crossing of the passes would now be attended with great danger, and not only the troops, but the treasure-convoy, with the pay for the Gilgit garrison, and a large quantity of grain and other indispensable supplies, were still on the other side of the mountains. Of grain alone a quantity equivalent to 25,000 coolie-loads was necessary for the Gilgit troops; and when it is borne in mind that all this had to be carried, during the few months that the passes were open, for twenty-two marches through a country which, as I have explained, is incapable of supporting men or animals, so that the coolies had to carry their rations and the animals their fodder in addition to their loads, and along a road which only permits of very slow travelling in single file, some idea may be formed of the organisation necessary to control such a traffic. Those at home who speak of our Indian hill-campaigns as trumpery expeditions cannot realise the difficulties of conducting war in these regions. Moltke was wiser when, hearing some of his officers talk in this disparaging strain of the little wars of the British, he said: ' You must remember, gentlemen, that the British officers in India do not go to the front in first-class railway carriages.'

On the following morning the officers proceeded to Gilgit, Captain Twigg alone remaining at Idgarh to perform his many onerous duties. The life of the British officer was anything but an idle one on the Gilgit road about this time.

We were now surrounded by snow. We received no more news from beyond the Borzil for days, and still no grain-convoys arrived. Some hundreds of Spedding's Pathans, who had completed their contracts and wished to return home, were now waiting here, unable to set out in consequence of the condition of the pass, and had to be fed, to Blaker's dismay, on the grain that was intended for the men who were to remain at work on the road near Boonji throughout the winter.

On October 21 we were again put in touch with the outer world, and reassured as to the safety of some more of our friends; for on this day Spedding, Beech, and Mitchell arrived in camp from the south. The Borzil had already commenced to levy its annual tribute of life, for they had seen several men and many horses lying dead in the snow on the pass, and the number of victims was increasing daily.

On October 24 we had visitors from the other direc-

Y

tion. Captain Younghusband and Lieutenant Davison arrived from Gilgit, on their way to India. They had crossed the Pamirs and were the bearers of startling news. How these officers were arrested by the Russians on neutral ground, and how Captain Ianoff and his Cossacks trespassed not only into China and Afghanistan, but even crossed the Hindoo Koosh, by the Korabaut Pass, into the territory of Chitral, is an old story now, and need not be retold here.

At last we heard tidings of the expected force. It had arrived at Bandipur, and was coming up in three detachments. It was not till October 27 that the first detachment, having safely crossed the Borzil in an interval of fine weather, marched into Astor. For the first time I saw the smart, merry little Gurkhas, looking very business-like in their khakis, and in the highest spirits at the prospect of a fight. On October 28 the first detachment marched on and the second detachment arrived, accompanied by the treasure-convoy and the two little 7-pound guns of the Hazara Mountain Battery, with the Sikh gunners, the subadar-major being a magnificent old white-bearded warrior, covered with medals, who had fought for us through the Mutiny, and had been fighting for us nearly ever since. The little 5th Gurkhas, too, were not wanting in medals to show what they had done, for the 5th is a well-known fighting regiment. The doctors' mule train, with the boxes of drugs and implements, and the ominous *doolis*, or ambulance palanquins, each borne by two men, also arrived with this detachment.

On the following day the third and last detachment was expected, but it did not come in for some days, and then in a pitiable condition. A blizzard had overtaken it on the Borzil, and about 100 men, most of whom were of the transport service, had been frostbitten, several losing hands and feet. Many of these poor fellows died at Astor of tetanus and gangrene, the usual sequelæ of frostbite. The mule-drivers had been supplied with warm clothing before leaving India, but

SEPOYS OF THE FIFTH GURKHA REGIMENT.

in their short-sighted folly had sold much of it on the road. Captain Barrett, who was in command of the Gurkhas, had also been frostbitten on this fatal day while urging on the numbed and despairing men, who would otherwise have lain down to die in the snow. Poor Barrett lost several of his toes, and was invalided at Gilgit for many months, the expedition thus losing the services of a most valuable officer. It was reported that the Borzil was now strewn with corpses, and the campaign itself was attended with far less loss of life and fewer horrors than were the preparations for it, a not unusual experience in mountain warfare.

While waiting for orders at Idgarh camp I employed most of my time in playing at golf, with Beech and others, on the polo-ground. We taught the fine old Rajah of Astor this game, and it was funny to hear the flattering exclamations of his subservient followers on every occasion that the aged chief distinguished himself. The Rajah was very well disposed to all sahibs. His backbone, as he put it, had been broken by the recent murder of his son-in-law by the King of Hunza, and seeing the signs of warlike preparation around him, he was in hopes that we were about to wreak vengeance on the cruel tyrant of the robber valley.

It was held to be of importance that our Gurkhas and supplies should be well on their way to Gilgit before our enemies in Chilas or Hunza should suspect what was doing. Had they known of the coming reinforcements for Gilgit, they would probably have anticipated us, and attacked the Kashmir garrisons; and, what is more, the Russian adventurers on the Pamirs might have taken it into their heads to lead their Cossacks across the Hindoo Koosh into the Hunza Valley, as they did once before, to be ostensibly rebuked, of course, for their forwardness by their superior officers, but still, no doubt, to remain in possession of those impregnable positions, and to be rewarded with medals, swords of honour and promotion. The secret of the Indian Government was well kept, and even the Indian papers at about this time spoke cursorily of this advance of British Indian troops into Kashmir territory as the 'strengthening of the Agent's Bodyguard at Gilgit.'

We on the road knew but little more, though we shrewdly guessed a good deal. Having arrived at this stage of the narrative, I will give a short history of the Hunza-Nagar country, and of the causes that led to Colonel Durand's expedition.

CHAPTER XXI

DESCRIPTION OF HUNZA-NAGAR—DEFENCES OF THE VALLEY—KANJUT RAIDS ON CARAVANS—SLAVE-DEALING—THE THUMS—THE MAULAI SECT—RELATIONS BETWEEN HUNZA AND CHINA—RUSSIAN EXPEDITION TO THE VALLEY—CAUSES OF COLONEL DURAND'S EXPEDITION—OUR ULTIMATUM—FORMER KANJUT VICTORIES—SPEDDING'S SAPPER AND MINER CORPS.

THE allied States of Hunza and Nagar, as will be seen on reference to the map, comprise the valleys draining into the upper portion of the Kanjut, or Hunza River, which flows into the Gilgit River two miles below Gilgit Fort. This region is extremely difficult of access, to which fact is due the impunity with which the tribesmen have hitherto been able to carry on their raids into the countries of their neighbours. These valleys are buried in a gigantic mountain system containing some of the highest peaks in the Himalayas, Mount Rakaposhi, which towers above Chalt, being 25,560 feet above the sea-level, while several other summits exceed 24,000 feet. Immense glaciers descend into the ravines, the Nagar River itself rising in the vastest of known glaciers, covering hundreds of square miles.

Surrounded thus by granite precipices and huge wastes of ice and snow, affording only a hazardous passage during a few summer months into the neighbouring countries, Hunza-Nagar has but one vulnerable point on the southern side of the Hindoo Koosh, the ravine of the Kanjut River; while the junction of that torrent with the Gilgit River is the one gateway of the country assailable for an invading force. Even this entrance is practically closed during the summer months; for then the river, swollen by the melting snows, becomes an unfordable and raging torrent, overflowing the whole bottom of the valley at many points, so that the only way left by which one can ascend the gorge is a rough track high upon the cliff-side, carried along narrow ledges, and overhanging frightful precipices—a road fit only for goats and cragsmen, which could be easily held by a handful of determined men against a large force; while at this season the river can only be crossed by means of the frail twig-rope bridges, which will support but two or three men, and can be cut adrift with a knife in a few moments.

Such is the road into Hunza-Nagar from our side; but at the head of the Kanjut Valley there is a group of comparatively easy and low passes, leading across the Hindoo Koosh on to the Tagdambash Pamir, in Chinese territory, which are used by the Kanjuts on their raiding expeditions, and by one of which, a short time since, Gromschevtsky and his Cossacks entered the valley.

After ascending the Hunza Valley for thirty miles from its junction with the Gilgit Valley, the fort of Chalt is reached, the furthest outpost of the Kashmir State in that direction. Thirty miles above Chalt are the villages of Hunza and Nagar, the first on the right, the second on the left bank of the river, almost facing each other, the respective capitals of these two little robber States, which, despite all the trouble they have caused, can turn out between them not many more than

5,000 fighting-men. In name they were tributary to Kashmir, the King of Hunza paying a yearly tribute of twenty ounces of gold-dust, two horses and two hounds, the King of Nagar a certain quantity of gold-dust and two baskets of apricots. These rulers received for some years small subsidies from the Government of India and from the Maharajah of Kashmir. But till now both States have been practically independent; for though the Kashmir Durbar made repeated efforts to reduce them to submission, these proved entirely unsuccessful, and only resulted in puffing up the Hunza-Nagaris with an implicit confidence in their own power and prowess, and encouraging their insolent aggressiveness. On several occasions the tribesmen have repulsed the regiments of the Maharajah and attempted to invest Gilgit; and in 1888 they captured Chalt Fort, held it for some time, and were not driven out again without considerable difficulty, though no less than 6,000 Kashmir troops were then stationed at Gilgit. The tribesmen succeeded in carrying away the guns of the fort with them, which were employed against us later on.

It is strange to find two rival nations existing in one narrow ravine, occupying the opposite sides of a torrent; but this is the case in the Kanjut Valley. The torrent forms the frontier, and its precipitous banks, which can only be scaled at certain points, are carefully guarded on either side. For thirty miles up the valley the forts of Hunza face those of Nagar, the defences being evidently intended as against each other; whereas, at the strong position which forms the gate of their country, by Nilt and Maiun, a strong line of fortifications faces down the valley, ready for resistance to an invader from below. Hunza and Nagar, though they were at other times almost constantly at war with each other, always united their forces against a foreign enemy.

These Hunza-Nagaris, generally known to their neighbours as the Kanjutis, though this name strictly applies to the Hunzas alone, have for centuries been the terror of all the people between Afghanistan and Yarkand. Inhabiting these scarcely accessible defiles, they have been in the habit of making frequent raids across the Hindoo Koosh and earning their livelihood by a well-organised brigandage, the thums, or kings of these two little States deriving the greater portion of their revenue from this source. So great was the dread inspired by these robbers, that large districts have been abandoned by their inhabitants, and land formerly cultivated has lapsed into wilderness, under the perpetual menace of the Kanjut raids. The most profitable hunting-ground of the Kanjutis was the great trade-route between Leh and Yarkand over the Karakoram Pass, and many a rich caravan on its way from India to Central Asia has been waylaid and pillaged in the neighbourhood of Shadulah. The thums used to maintain their regular agents at Yarkand, who gave them notice of an expected caravan. On one memorable occasion a caravan of fifty laden camels and 500 laden ponies was captured. The Kashmiris and the Chinese found themselves powerless to put a stop to these raids, and the Kanjutis acquired a great prestige, and were considered as quite invincible. The Hunzas, indeed, had never known defeat before Colonel Durand's successful campaign.

But this wholesale brigandage, bad as it was, was only a minor offence when put by the side of the systematised slave-dealing in which these scourges of the frontier have been engaged from time immemorial. All prisoners of any commercial value—men, women, and children—captured in these raids were driven across the mountains, to be sold, either directly to the slave-owners in Chinese Turkestan, or to Kirghiz dealers, who served as middlemen in this trade. The forced marches across the snowy ranges that these unfortunate captives were compelled to undertake, thinly clad as they were, and provided with but a minimum of food, caused the death of a considerable proportion; and the abominable cruelty with which the Kanjutis treat their prisoners has been remarked by most travellers on the Pamirs. Numbers of the subjects of the Maharajah of Kashmir are at this moment slaves in Central Asia—these are for the most part poor, honest, harmless Baltis—while entire outlying garrisons of Kashmir sepoys have been surprised and carried off into captivity by these daring ruffians. This intolerable state of things has at last been put an end to once and for all.

The rulers of these two States were, as might be expected, ignorant and bloodthirsty scoundrels, faithless to their treaty obligations, and incapable of respecting anything but force. They were absolute monarchs, and murdered or sold their subjects into captivity at their own sweet will. The royal families of Hunza and Nagar are descended from two brothers who lived in the fifteenth century, but they trace their ancestry further back, to a divine origin. The Thum of Hunza, whom we were now about to depose, for his part boasts of being the descendant of Alexander the Great—a common claim hereabouts —by a fairy of the Hindoo Koosh; certainly a very respectable pedigree. It is said that it was a point of etiquette in his savage Court, on certain occasions, for a

Wazir to ask in the thum's presence, 'Who is the greatest king of the East?' and for another flatterer to reply, 'Surely the Thum of Hunza; unless, perhaps, it be the Khan of China; for these without doubt are the two greatest.' This monarch has a very high opinion of his own importance. When asked by Captain Younghusband why he did not visit India, he replied haughtily, 'It is not customary for great kings like myself and my ancestor Alexander to leave their own dominions.' Later on, however, he did undertake a journey to foreign lands; for after his stronghold had been stormed, he took to his heels and fled to China, with a somewhat undignified speed for so great a prince.

Patricide and fratricide may be said to be hereditary failings of the royal families of Hunza and Nagar. Safdar Ali Khan murdered his father, the Thum of Hunza, in 1886, usurped the throne, and put two of his brothers to a cruel death, in order to assure to himself the sole sovereignty over his country; while Rajah Uzr Khan, heir-apparent of Nagar, actuated by a similar policy, had two of his younger brothers assassinated in 1891, and would have also removed the others could he have got them within his power. And so, too, acted their forefathers before them for many generations. Thus, the old thum who was murdered by his son Safdar Ali, had himself succeeded to the throne by the assassination of his father. In this instance the method of removal was somewhat ingenious. The sister of the heir-apparent, entertaining great affection for her brother, sent as a New Year's present to the aged king a robe of honour, in which a man had died of confluent smallpox. The gift proved as fatal as the shirt of Nessus. These family arrangements of the

Hunza-Nagar royalties have at any rate had the advantage of sparing their countries from those bloody wars of succession so frequent in other Mussulman States.

The Hunzas and Nagars cordially hate each other. They are of the same type of the Dard race, but the Hunzas have the greatest reputation for courage. The Nagars are of the Shiah sect, and do not drink wine; whereas the Hunzas are of that curious sect known as the Maulai, and are abhorred as Kafirs by stricter Mahomedans for their wine-bibbing propensities and their generally irreligious way of living. The Hunzas, indeed, appear to be entirely free from any Mussulman prejudices or bigotry. Agha Khan, of Bombay, is the present spiritual head of the Maulais, and is supposed to be the descendant of the original Assassin, or Old Man of the Mountains. The Maulais proselytise a good deal in secret; an emissary of the faith will travel into a Suni or Shiah country, work himself into the confidence and affection of a man, undermine his religion with subtle suggestions, and finally, when the time is ripe, will confess that he is a Maulai, and make a convert of his friend. The Maulais reject the Koran, and have a Holy Book of their own. If a Maulai makes due presents to his Pir or spiritual chief, and obeys his orders, he need be restrained by no other considerations. It is not necessary for him to pray or fast, or lead a moral life; he need not busy himself about religious observances in the slightest degree, One has no religious fanaticism to contend with when dealing with this liberal-minded people. No one could preach a Holy War among Maulais.

Ignorant as they have hitherto been as to our real power in distant India, the rulers of Hunza-Nagar have apparently regarded China as the greatest empire in the world, and Russia the second, the poor British Empire coming far behind either. Relations have been carried on for ages between China and these States. The Kanjutis often visit Yarkand, to them a magnificent place, and the Thum of Hunza has a *jagir*, or grant of land, near that city—a recognition of the assistance Hunza gave to China during an insurrection in Turkestan in 1847. The Hunzas have naturally been. amicably disposed towards China ; for not only did the Chinese authorities wink at the slave-hunting and caravan-raiding of the tribesmen, but they used even once to pay a subsidy to the dreaded thum, and allowed him to levy toll on the Kirghiz shepherds of the Tagdambash Pamir.

While bitterly hostile to British influence, Safdar Ali Khan of Hunza, and Rajah Uzr Khan of Nagar—the latter ruling Nagar for his aged father—were known to be well-disposed to Russia. Captain Gromschevtsky, who visited this region with one of his usual exploring parties of armed Cossacks a few summers ago, boasts of this fact. That harmless, scientific traveller, as we discovered later on, undoubtedly left an impression in the valley that the Russians were ready to help the Kanjutis against us, for after the fighting was over, and we were on friendly terms with our recent foes, they used frequently to tell us that they would never have fought us had it not been for the Russians, who had deceived them and left them in the lurch.

About half a dozen Europeans only had thus far visited the Kanjut Valley—Colonel Lockhart ; Colonel Durand, in 1889 ; Captain Gromschevtsky, and, last of all, Captain Younghusband ; so that there was a great fascination in the idea that we were about to explore the robber fastnesses.

The immediate causes of the expedition may be summarised as follows. A full report of them has been published and presented to the Houses of Parliament.

A HUNZA RAJAH AND TRIBESMEN.

In 1889 the Hunza-Nagar chiefs entered into a treaty with Colonel Durand. They undertook to put an end to the raiding on the Yarkand road, and promised to allow properly accredited British officers to travel through their territories when necessary. On the other hand, the Government of India agreed to grant small yearly allowances to both thums. It was not long before the thums broke their engagements, and the old disturbances commenced afresh. The Thum of Hunza told Captain Younghusband that unless a larger subsidy was allowed him he would resume his caravan raids, as that was his legitimate source of income; later on, at a critical time, he would not allow letters to be carried through his territories to Captain Younghusband, then on the Pamirs.

In May, 1891, Rajah Uzr Khan murdered his two brothers, partly because he was jealous of their friendship with the British, and wrote an insolent letter to Colonel Durand announcing what he had done. News was now brought to Gilgit that the Kanjut raids had recommenced, and that people had been kidnapped near Chalt and sold into slavery. At last this defiant attitude was changed for active hostilities, and in the middle of May, as I had heard in Ladak, the Hunza and Nagar chiefs gathered their fighting men and marched upon Chalt with the intention of capturing that fortress. Colonel Durand, having had timely information of the intention of the tribesmen, made a forced march to Chalt with only 200 of his men and one British officer, and reinforced the garrison. The tribesmen, disconcerted by this prompt step, after some hostile demonstrations, having exhausted their supplies, withdrew to their own country.

It was, of course, impossible for Colonel Durand to bring the insolent descendant of Alexander the Great to reason at that time, as he only had the lately-organised Dogra Imperial Service troops at his disposal, men who had never seen real service, and could scarcely be relied upon in the case of severe fighting. It is only possible to manœuvre a small body of men in the difficult defiles of the Hunza River, and it is, therefore, essential that that body should be composed of soldiers of whose steadfastness there can be no doubt.

It will be seen that the position of the Gilgit garrisons was somewhat precarious. It was more than probable that, in the autumn, when the closing of the passes on the Gilgit road by snow had cut off the possibility of reinforcements from Kashmir, the tribesmen, elated at their immunity from punishment for their misconduct, would renew their disturbances and act vigorously on the offensive.

It was to discuss this position that Colonel Durand had been summoned to Simla, and the result was that the 200 Gurkhas and the two hill-guns were despatched to Gilgit, and that the Agent's staff was strengthened by fourteen officers.

Considering the provocation the tribesmen had given, the terms that were now to be offered to them were exceedingly lenient. The Indian Government was ready to condone previous offences, and Colonel Durand was instructed to take no punitive action unless it was forced upon him by further misbehaviour. But, at the same time, no more nonsense on the part of these turbulent petty monarchs was to be tolerated; and, in order to insure the safety of our garrisons for the future, a new fort was to be erected at Chalt, while a military road, practicable for mules, would be made from Gilgit to Hunza and Nagar—or beyond, should this be deemed necessary for the defence of the Hindoo Koosh passes. These roads were to be taken in hand at once, and should the thums offer any opposition, our troops would enter their country and the roads would be made in spite of them. Such were, practically, the terms of Colonel Durand's ultimatum.

To judge from their antecedents, the Kanjutis were

likely to offer resistance, and, in all probability, we should find them a foe not to be despised. So far unconquered, they had on several occasions inflicted defeat on armies composed of some of the best fighting-men in India. In 1848 Nathu Shah, the first Sikh governor of Gilgit, attacked them, but, falling into an ambuscade, was slain himself, and his whole army was massacred. In 1866 a Dogra invasion was repelled, and the army of the Maharajah fled precipitately back to Gilgit. Then there was the capture of Chalt Fort, and many other victorious records might be cited. That our force would be annihilated was evidently the idea of all the countrymen between Astor and Gilgit, and their dismal tales and forebodings cast a gloom over our Kashmir servants, whose long faces were amusing to behold.

As soon as Spedding was informed that an expedition into the Kanjut Valley had been decided upon, he volunteered to withdraw a number of his men from the Gilgit road work and place them, together with some of his staff, at the disposal of Colonel Durand as a sapper and miner corps. His offer was gladly accepted.

CHAPTER XXII

GOLF—PILGRIMS FROM MECCA—CAMP AT CHAKERKOT—ATTITUDE OF THE NATIVES—COMMISSARIAT DIFFICULTIES — A HUNZA SPY CAUGHT—THE ENEMY'S PLANS—COLONEL DURAND'S FORCE — THE PUNIALI LEVY—A COUNTRY OF MAGICIANS—THE FAIRY DRUM.

On October 29, Beech and myself, having with some difficulty procured horses with Ladaki drivers for our baggage, rode off towards Gilgit. The unfortunate third detachment was still behind, and, as we afterwards learnt, had to halt for a week at Astor, the hospital being full of the frostbitten men.

I had never played at golf before, and, like most novices, had been severely attacked for the time by golfomania. We took our clubs and balls with us and established links at every halting-place on the Gilgit road during our march to the front. As we passed through this rocky mountain region we contemplated and discussed the country solely from the point of view of its golfing capacities. A spot suitable for a putting-green would arouse more enthusiasm in us than the far more common sight of some sublime mountain peak. As may be imagined, it was rare indeed that we found any comparatively flat space where the game might be attempted. Whenever we came to a village polo-ground, we used to impress the little boys as caddies, and their fathers stood by smiling and wondering at our strange pastime.

Manners Smith once took a Gilgitti servant to Srinagur, who there saw golf played for the first time. He was overheard describing it to his friends on his return to Gilgit. He spoke of it as a sort of very poor polo, played without ponies. 'It is the truth I am uttering,' he said, to his doubting audience. 'It was polo on foot; sahibs and memsahibs played it together; and when a sahib hit the ball he paced the distance to see how far he had sent it. Polo indeed! What polo!'

On October 30, having ridden through Dashkin, we overtook the second detachment of Gurkhas, the mule-battery, and a great portion of the transport corps. We found it difficult to get by this slowly-travelling line of men and laden mules, which extended for several miles. Spedding's engineers had not carried their work so far as this, and the old road had to be followed, only practicable here for the passage of animals in single file, except at a few points, of which we availed ourselves to push ahead.

We heard mule drivers and sepoys growling at this abominable track, from which they were able to form a good idea of what the whole Gilgit road had been like only a year before, and to appreciate the new military road by which they had travelled thus far. The delays and blocks were frequent on these last marches. The mules were driven and dragged with difficulty over the bad bits. Occasionally a baggage or ammunition mule would lose its footing and tumble over the precipice. The Gatling gun once fell into the torrent, but was rescued; while one officer lost nearly all his baggage in the Astor River. Dead mules and horses lying among the rocks were now a more frequent sight than ever, and the vultures had gathered in quantities for the feast prepared for them daily.

At Doiun we found Spedding, who had preceded us, selecting from among his navvies the two hundred men who were to do the road-making in the Hunza Valley. Rejecting Kashmiris and men of other timid races, he enlisted Afghans alone. These were all, of course, anxious to volunteer for the front, and were keen to get a bit of fighting. There was a considerable chance of their having to show what they were made of while constructing the Hunza road. The tribesmen were likely to attack them, probably by rolling down avalanches of rocks upon them from the mountains above—a favourite method of Kanjut warfare. It had, therefore, been decided that the greater number of these 200 men should be armed at Gilgit, so that they might defend themselves when necessary. Those who had been selected were in high spirits; they did not know against whom they would be asked to fight, neither did they much care; they regarded fighting of any description as a big piece of fun. 'It must be the Russians we are going to war with,' they were heard to say to each other, and they evidently relished the idea of having a brush with the Cossack.

On November 1 we descended the frightful steep of Hattu Pir, which was proving very fatal to mules and ponies, and where the hideous gorged vultures were perched upon the crags all along the track. At Ramghat—hot as ever, though it was cold elsewhere—we found that Captain Aylmer had thrown a temporary wooden bridge across the river, the old one now being very unsafe. A continuous stream of sepoys, coolies, and beasts of burden, was now pouring along the dreary road; and even at midnight, as we bivouacked at my old camp in the Miskhin nullah, we saw flickering lights moving high above us on the Hattu Pir, showing where belated men were slowly crawling down the precipice by torchlight to the necessary water below.

At Boonji, Captain Aylmer had just completed a flying bridge over the Indus to facilitate the transport during the winter. He had slung a stout wire-rope across the river, and a large ferry-boat travelling on this was readily directed from one bank to the other by steering it at the requisite angle to the current. We accompanied Aylmer on the trial voyage of this vessel to the other side, and she was found to be a complete success. The Indus was now much lower than when I had seen it in August, and there were no dangerous breakers in the middle.

Among those who made this first passage with us was a family travelling north, consisting of a white-bearded patriarch, his son, the son's wife, and their little daughter. They were rosy-cheeked and handsome people, of a type I had not yet seen. On enquiry I learnt that they were natives of Badakshan, who were returning home after a pilgrimage to Mecca. The son said their eyes had been opened by the wonders of the world beyond the mountains, the railway, the city of Bombay, the sea, the steamer on which they had taken passage. A Mussulman pilgrim can undertake an immense journey, such as this was, at a very small outlay. A few weeks before this, one of our officers met some men of Nagar on the Borzil Pass, who were bound on the pilgrimage to Mecca. One of these was very sorrowful; he had no money for the journey, and he feared lest his richer companions should send him back. On being asked what his expenses would amount to, he replied that six rupees would take him to Mecca, as that, he understood, was the steamer fare from Kurrachee; the Mussulmans he met by the way would supply

For our part we were still quite unprepared for an advance in force from Gilgit. Nothing could be done until our commissariat arrangements were complete. The transport service of the contractor employed by the Kashmir Durbar had altogether broken down. Not a tenth of the grain required for the winter supply of the troops had reached Gilgit by the end of October; no greatcoats for the Imperial Service sepoys had yet arrived; there was an insufficiency of boots; there was no ghee; 1,200 coolie-loads of necessary stores were still lying at Bandipur beyond the passes. Matters, indeed, looked serious, and a well-informed and bold enemy might have made it exceedingly uncomfortable for us about this time.

We ought, of course, to have advanced long since; the campaign would now have to be undertaken in midwinter, when to bivouac at the high elevation of Hunza, in this rigorous climate, was likely to be attended with great suffering and loss of life, should the season prove severe. Our officers had done their very utmost to get all ready in time, but it was late in the year when Colonel Durand had received his instructions from Simla, while the delay caused by the cholera outbreak, the early winter, and the inefficiency of the arrangements made by the Durbar, were matters beyond his control.

On November 14, Beech and myself set out for Gilgit with our limited baggage. As we rode off, Spedding's Indian khansamah, who was left behind to guard our property, wished us good-luck, and smilingly said, 'I will have a very good tiffin ready for you when you return from the wars.' But the Kashmiris shook their heads sadly; I do not think they expected to see us again. We reached Gilgit in two days. The road, as hitherto, was encumbered with transport trains, and the natives of the scattered villages were at their wits' end to supply maize-straw, grass, borsa, or what other fodder they could collect. The oasis of Minawar, so green when I had last seen it, with the clusters of grapes hanging from the fruit-trees round which the vines were twining, was now leafless and of wintry aspect, and the dreary country looked more than ever like a hopeless desert.

We found Gilgit presenting a very lively appearance. Here all the troops were now encamped; the grain-trains were flowing in; there was a perpetual drilling of men, a bustle of preparation; the sounds of the bugles from reveille to lights-out ever kept us in mind that we were now really engaged in a military expedition. Officers and men seemed to have plenty of work on their hands, and all were in the highest spirits, though the grain question must have still been causing much secret anxiety to the leaders.

We learnt the latest news from Colonel Durand. A Hunza spy had been captured, prowling on our side of the frontier. He confessed that he had been sent to discover with what force we were holding a very strong position known as the Chaichar Pari, on the road between Gilgit and Chalt, a night attack on which was contemplated by the Hunzas. This position commands the road at a point where it is but a narrow ledge along the face of dangerous precipices, and so perpendicular are the cliffs falling away from it on all sides, that a small force holding this natural fortress with resolution, could not be dislodged without considerable difficulty and loss of life. Once before the Kanjuts seized this position, and, by thus isolating it, captured Chalt. The spy also revealed another scheme of the tribesmen, by which they hoped to surprise Chalt. A number of men concealing their arms about their persons and carrying loads on their backs, so that they might be taken for coolies from Gilgit, were to march up to the unsuspecting sepoys, and fall upon them when they had gained admittance within the fort. Seeing that the Kanjutis in dress and appearance are exactly like Astoris and Gilgittis, and that the garrison of Chalt at that time was composed of Kashmir troops alone, it is not impossible that they would have successfully carried out this ingenious plan.

Colonel Durand had, however, taken measures to anticipate the tribesmen, and the intended surprises were not attempted. Chalt had been reinforced, and British officers had been sent there; the Chaichar Pari was well guarded, while posts were established at other points between Gilgit and Chalt. We had signal stations on conspicuous hills, and Gilgit was kept in constant communication with the farthest outposts by the flag-waggers. On the evening of our arrival, the signal came that armed tribesmen had been rolling down rocks on the road near Nomal, from the mountains above.

On the following morning, November 16, we were awoke by martial music, and on turning out saw 100 men of the 5th Gurkhas, under Lieutenant Boisragon—on whom the command of this detachment devolved after poor Captain Barrett's accident—and the two 7-pound guns, under Lieutenant Gorton, setting out for Nomal, followed by a long string of Balti coolies carrying the baggage. They crossed the Gilgit River by a temporary winter causeway which Captain Aylmer had constructed—a series of stone islands connected by planks. The sole means of communication from bank

ENCAMPMENT OF SPERKING'S PATHANS.

to bank had hitherto been by a twig-rope bridge. Aylmer proved that he was a capital engineer, and had been well-selected for such an expedition; he was always working away with his own hands, and by his example making others work too, with energy and cheeriness. If all our R.E.'s are of this sort we shall do well, so far as this branch of the service is concerned.

On this afternoon, while I was walking with Lieutenant Molony, a very brown and weather-stained Englishman rode up, whom my companion at once recognised and greeted. This was Surgeon-Major Robertson, who for the last fifteen months had been exploring Kafiristan, and whose travels and strange adventures in that mysterious region will prove deeply interesting, if published to the world. He had but that moment come in, and we two were the first Europeans he had spoken to since leaving Gilgit in August, 1890. He had brought six Kafirs with him, queer savages, who much astonished the natives of these parts by their outlandish habits and Pagan rites.

This same day Spedding's 200 Pathans arrived, swaggering up in a body, shouldering their picks, shovels, and jumpers, and carrying five days' rations of rice, under Appleford, McCulloch, and Maynard, having tramped from Boonji in two days. These tall, wiry natives of Afghanistan marched in with a springy stride, looking very businesslike, in splendid training after their many months' heavy work on the road. They had procured a tomtom somewhere, which one of their number beat at their head. They seemed very pleased with themselves, like a lot of boys out for a holiday; excellent raw material for soldiery. But raw is hardly the word to apply to these men, for nearly all had seen fighting in their own tribal wars; many had fought against us; many, too, had obviously served as sepoys under us—deserters doubtless—for these often unwittingly revealed the fact that they quite understood all the English words of command. There was but one man with a grievance among them; he had been bugler to the Ameer, and was now very put out because he could not be supplied with a bugle.

The entire force now at Colonel Durand's disposal consisted of 188 men of the 5th Gurkha regiment (the remainder of the 200 having been frostbitten or otherwise incapacitated); two guns of the Hazara Mountain Battery; thirty men of the 20th Punjab Infantry (the Agency Bodyguard); three regiments of Kashmir Imperial Service troops; a Kashmir Mountain Battery; a few sappers and miners; and 160 irregulars from Punial, a semi-independent little Dard State in the upper Gilgit Valley, on the frontier of Yasin, who had been armed with Snider carbines, but who also carried their native swords and shields.

These Punialis are excellent mountaineers, and proved of use when heights had to be crowned during our advance. Being in appearance and dress exactly like the Hunza-Nagars, they were provided with black scarfs, so that they might be easily distinguished and not be shot by mistake. Their military training had not been extensive, having consisted, I believe, of one day's musketry practice at the Gilgit ranges. The Rajah of Punial, Akbar Khan, accompanied his men. The rajah receives a subsidy from Kashmir, in return for which he binds himself to guard the frontier forts of his country, and render military service in war time.

The total force under Colonel Durand thus amounted

to about 2,000 men; but with these he had to garrison Gilgit, Boonji, Astor, and hold all the posts on our long line of communication, which for many marches, as I have explained, was exposed to the attacks of the Shinaka tribes and had to be well-guarded. Consequently, only 1,000 men could be spared for operations beyond Chalt.

The weather was now perfect here, still, mellow and with unclouded skies—a true St. Martin's summer. We were congratulating ourselves on our luck in this respect, when the highest Dogra official in Gilgit shook his head: 'When we march, bad weather will at once come,' said he. 'That *badmash* Hunza Thum will send it to us.' The Hunzas are credited by all their neighbours, even by Kashmiris of the highest education and position, with supernatural powers. Hunza is dreaded as a city of magicians. The thum has but to throw a bit of ox-hide into a certain stream to raise hurricane, blinding snow, and killing frost wherewith to confound his enemies. On the topmost tower of Hunza castle a magic drum is suspended in the sight of all men, which is beaten by invisible fairy hands whenever a war in which the thum is about to engage is destined to prove successful to his arms. It so beat, I believe, on this occasion; in which case the fairies must have either been afraid to reveal the truth or have been sadly mistaken in their forecast. It is doubtful whether the Dogras, thoroughly believing all this as they do, would have the temerity to wage war with such necromancers, were it not that they, too, have their own methods of reading the future. The Maharajah himself would not undertake a journey without consulting his astrologers as to the lucky day on which to set out.

CHAPTER XXIII

SPEDDING CONSTRUCTS A TEMPORARY ROAD TO CHALT—SCENERY OF THE KANJUT VALLEY—NOMAL—GUETCH—THE CHAICHAR PARI—CHALT FORT—CHAPROT—MOUNT RAKAPOSHI—OUR TROOPS REACH CHALT—THE REPLY TO COLONEL DURAND'S ULTIMATUM—THE THUM'S CORRESPONDENCE—THE HUNZA-NAGAR FIELD FORCE—OCCUPATION OF THE KOTAL—OUR FORCE CROSSES THE FRONTIER.

Now that all the assailable positions between Gilgit and our further outposts up the Kanjut Valley were well guarded by our men, it was necessary, before Colonel Durand could advance with the remainder of his force, that a comparatively easy line of communication should be established between Gilgit and Chalt. Spedding was accordingly sent forward to construct a rough temporary road, practicable for mules, with the utmost expedition. The river being now low he would be able to avoid the difficult cliffs in many places and carry the winter road along the dry, boulder-encumbered bed of the torrent, while Captain Aylmer would find little difficulty in constructing temporary bridges across the shrunken stream.

So, on November 17, the Pathan navvies were taken down to the fort, and arms were distributed among them —Sniders and Enfield muzzle-loaders. They also got hold of a lot of old accoutrements and helped themselves, each man buckling about himself as many belts and pouches as he could lay hands on. It was amusing to observe the childish pride and excitement of these half savages as they marched off thus equipped, presenting a wild and ragamuffin, though also formidable, appearance.

Beech and myself, having witnessed the above strange scene in the fort, set out on foot together for Pilche, the first camping-place in the Kanjut Valley. We were armed, in case of accidents; for though there was small chance of encountering any of the enemy on this day's march, they were known to be on the watch on the heights above the road in places, ready to pick off stragglers. It would have suited them well to have carried off a sahib into Hunza as hostage; so orders were issued that no one should travel without escort between Nomal and Chalt.

We crossed to the farther bank of the Gilgit River by the rope bridge. This, like the other bridges in this region, is formed of three stout ropes of plaited birch twigs, one serving as a foot-rope, the other two as hand ropes, slighter guy-ropes of the same material connecting the former with the latter. A rope bridge cannot be stretched taut without breaking; so it is always slung slackly, forming a deep curve. Many men who have excellent heads on a hillside are nervous on a rope bridge, swinging dizzily as it does to every breeze, high over the foaming torrent. But no one accustomed to going aloft at sea finds any difficulty on one of these; whereas many a seaman would feel uncomfortable when crawling along some of the so-called roads of this country.

After following the left bank of the Gilgit River for about two miles, we came to the jaws of the Kanjut defile, and found ourselves amid scenery still more wild and desolate than that of the Gilgit Valley. Ruddy cliffs rose on either side of us to a great height; the bottom of the ravine was fairly broad, sandy, and strewn with boulders, producing no vegetation save scattered alkaline and desert herbs. The Kanjut River rushed by us in dark discoloured waves, breaking into white foam.

There was something peculiarly dreary in this gateway of the robber country. There were no signs of life; this, indeed, bore the appearance of a debatable land, the scene of frequent border forays, where no man dare cultivate the soil, knowing not who may reap what he has sown. It is thus all the way to Chalt, except round the fort-protected village of Nomal, and some time since the entire population of that place was surprised and carried away into captivity. At frequent intervals on the road we saw ruined *sangas*, or stone breastworks, and other defences, showing that we were in a country that had seen much fighting and had never known security. We overtook our servants and baggage-coolies and reached our destination long after dark. We found no habitations at Pilche, which is merely a camping-place were dwarf tamarisks supply a little fuel. Here we bivouacked on the sand for the night, as did McCulloch, Maynard, and the Pathans, who came in some hours after us.

The next day we all marched off together to Nomal, up to which point the road was good, having been much improved by Colonel Durand's sappers in the spring.

We found the river sands hereabouts to be full of small garnets and iron pyrites; while in several places the earth was yellow with sulphur. The natives manufacture their own powder, as the soil of the valley contains saltpetre as well as sulphur; but they have to depend on the outside world for the lead of which to make their bullets. The Hunza River is famous for its gold-washings; and the villagers, even with their rude appliances, extract quantities of the precious metal from the river sands.

At Nomal we found a good deal of cultivation and a Dogra mud fort, on whose battlements were some *sher bachas* (little tigers), cannon of native manufacture and apparently of little service. The garrison consisted of forty Imperial Service sepoys under a Dogra officer.

Spedding and Appleford here joined us, and the road-making was vigorously conducted at the first *pari* behind Nomal. A pari is a projecting spur of the mountain falling sheer into the river. Between the paris it was possible, as a rule, to carry this winter road along the dry margin of the torrent bed; but at a pari —often a perpendicular wall of very hard rock—much blasting and gallery work was necessary before the roughest mule track could be made. The old native road as usual avoided these obstacles by climbing high over the cliffs by steep scaffoldings, impassable for mules and even difficult for men. The first spot at which the road-makers had to work was very cheerless and chilly: the cliffs rose to a great height on either side, shutting out the sun's rays for all but half an hour or so at mid-day.

On November 21 the first pari having been overcome, our camp was moved on to Guetch, a horrid defile, such as Salvator Rosa might have painted. Here we found a block-house and a small sepoy guard. Houses or inhabitants there were none; but high above the camp, and not visible from it, we discovered a small ruined village of fifteen stone huts packed close together and rising one above the other like a flight of steps to a stone fort in the centre. This had been the village of Guetch, deserted for thirty years, we were told; a wonderfully-situated place, practically unassailable; for the little terraced ledge on which it stood, where now the gaunt dead fruit-trees alone remained to show the former cultivation, was surrounded on all sides by perpendicular precipices. There was but one narrow, difficult approach to it up the cliff side, and that could have been broken away and rendered inaccessible in a few minutes. This impregnable fastness was situated amid the wildest scenery; and behind it was an awful and seemingly impassable gorge leading steeply up to the eternal snows It was the sort of robber stronghold that one's imagination would conjure up while reading some tale of Albanian brigands.

Beech and myself, taking some Pathans with us, climbed up to this spot and usefully employed ourselves in cutting down the dead trees and pulling the rafters out of the houses, which we threw over the precipice; a goodly supply of fuel for our men below. From this point we could see, on the opposite side of the Kanjut River, high up a tributary ravine, a flat space, whereon was a village and some cultivated land. This we knew to be Jaglot, where it was reported that 200 of the enemy were now stationed observing our movements. From Jaglot there is a track across the mountains, affording a short cut to the Nagar fortress of Nilt; and there is also, opposite Guetch, an easy ford across the river; so we were warned to be on the look-out for a night surprise, and Lieutenant Taylor, who was guarding the Chaichar Pari, sent a few sepoys to protect us.

While some of Spedding's men were cutting through the pari near Guetch, the rest were at work on the Chaichar, the stiffest pari of all. On seeing the old road at this point I could readily understand how an enemy, holding the position above, could have given us much trouble. By pulling a few sticks out of the scaffoldings here and there, they could have sent great portions of the road tumbling into the river, and left sheer walls of rock.

The desolation of the frontier ravine was more remarkable as we advanced; there was no vegetation, there were no inhabitants, the only life being that we brought with us in our preparations for war—the sepoys, the road-makers, and the transport coolies; while the challenges of sentries, and the booming of the blasting on the road were the most familiar sounds at this time.

On November 23 we saw a Hunza envoy accompanied by a guard of Kashmir sepoys, on his way to Gilgit, with a message from the thum to Colonel Durand. An amusing conversation took place between him and the Dogra major in charge of Nomal Fort, a bit of a wag in his way. 'Can you tell me,' inquired the major, 'when this war of ours is going to begin?' 'We Hunzas are men of peace,' replied the diplomatic envoy; 'we don't want to fight at all.' 'That is very foolish of you,' exclaimed the major; 'you have made all your *bandobast* for a war; so have we. After having taken all this trouble we must have a fight.' 'You appear to be speaking wisdom,' said the Wakil. 'How ridiculous we should look,' continued the major, 'if we did not fight after all this palaver. Let us fight. Besides, if you beat us, you could go farther and conquer all the Punjab, a rich country that, I assure you.' The Wakil's language was very pacific, but not so, I believe, were the contents of the thum's letter he was bearing.

An order came this day from Colonel Durand to

the effect that Spedding's Pathans, when on the march and in camp, should be divided into separate bodies, each under one of Spedding's staff, as officer; the object being to avoid confusion in the event of a surprise. Six little companies were therefore formed, of which Beech and myself, who were now attached to Spedding's staff, were each given one to command. I had two gangs under me, thirty-three men in all, natives of Cabul. The contractor of one of my gangs, whose name was Kussim Ali, was known to his companions under the pleasant nickname of 'The Murderer.' To have earned such a distinctive title among so many cut-throats, he must indeed have been a man with a record.

The Pathans always had their numerous belts and pouches about them and their rifles by their sides, as they plied pick and jumper. They could not bear to be separated from their new toys. I think that the men of one gang mistrusted those of another, and feared that their weapons would be stolen if once out of their sight. There were, doubtless, blood feuds between some of these men, coming as they did from different tribes in Afghanistan; but these quarrels were in abeyance while they were working on the road. Admirable discipline was maintained by Spedding and his staff among these truculent outlaws, who have some fine qualities, and whom one comes to like, despite all their faults.

The road progressed rapidly, and we were neither surprised by night nor attacked by avalanches of rocks by day; the tribesmen observed our doings from distant heights, but so far took no steps to oppose us.

On November 26 I pushed on to our farther outpost, and our advanced base for the coming operations

—the fortress of Chalt. The gloomy gorge I ascended on this day's journey appeared—even more so than did the country below—to be a place devoted to the God of Battles. There was not a single peasant's hut; there was no vegetation; but stone breastworks were to be seen all round, and every big rock was topped by a miniature fort capable of holding two or three men, affording refuge in case of surprise.

Just below Chalt the narrow gorge suddenly broadens out. The fortress stands on an extensive maidan, high above the river, and is surrounded by cultivated fields. It is square, with towers at intervals, and within its walls there is a camping-ground for some hundreds of men.

The Kanjut Valley is here joined by that of Chaprot, a few miles up which there is a fort and a considerable village. Chaprot is a separate little State that has been fought for and has changed hands several times. The present rajah, Sekandar Khan, a fine young fellow, who accompanied us on the campaign, is a son of the Thum of Nagar. Two of his brothers, as I have said, had been murdered in the previous spring by the eldest brother, the ferocious Uzr Khan, who also threatened the life of Sekandar. The latter consequently bears no good-will to his royal relatives, and was as anxious as anyone else for the success of our arms.

Chalt was a busy place for the next four days, our numbers ever swelling, as troops and grain coolies poured in in an almost constant stream. A sufficient quantity of grain had now reached Gilgit to allow of a forward movement; and, from the reports that reached us, there was little doubt that the tribesmen had no intention of acceding to Colonel Durand's terms, and that there was some severe fighting before us.

I ascended the heights above Chalt, in order to obtain a view of that magnificent mountain, Rakaposhi, which is well seen from here. Unlike Nanga Parbat, it has one sharp, prominent peak—25,560 feet above the sea, and nearly 20,000 above the Kanjut River—whose granite crags tower high over the surrounding vast glaciers and snow-fields. Surely no military ex-

THE KANJUT VALLEY NEAR CHALT—THE TEMPORARY BRIDGE AND THE KOTAL.

pedition ever before penetrated into so sublime a mountain region as that which now lay before us.

It was Colonel Durand's intention to cross the river at Chalt, and advance up the valley by the Nagar or left bank. The indefatigable Captain Aylmer was, therefore, employed in constructing a temporary winter bridge across the torrent.

Two miles or so above Chalt the river is hemmed in by precipices, so that the river bed cannot be followed, and it would be necessary for our force to surmount a formidable ridge known as the Kotal, some eight or nine hundred feet in height, the summit of which was held by the enemy. Thus there was some chance of our first fight taking place almost within rifle-shot of Chalt fort.

On November 27 Colonel Durand and his staff arrived at Chalt. Dr. Robertson also came in with his six Kafirs, great men in their own land, who were first to be shown our fashion of making war, and then to be carried round India; so that they could return to their country and tell their friends what they had seen of the British Raj; a wise policy, which in other cases has done much to assist the establishment of diplomatic relations with the tribes on our frontiers.

On November 28, having taken a walk back to the Chaichar Pari, I met the remainder of our force tramping up the road—first the Gurkhas; then the Maharajah's troops; and, lastly, the picturesque Punialis, those hereditary defenders of the frontier, with the tomtoms beating at their head, armed with swords and brass-studded shields of ox-hide, like Homeric warriors, as well as with Sniders, scampering like cats along the difficult track, and even taking short cuts by leaping from ledge to ledge to avoid the zigzags. Their rajah was with them—a stout, good-natured looking ruler, who appeared to be popular with his people.

The Dogra General, Suram Chand, who commands the Gilgit Brigade, arrived this day with his staff. The somewhat anomalous system under which the Imperial Service troops are employed in the field was now on its first trial. We had with us Dogra officers of high rank, but in action, at any rate, they were practically superseded by the British officers, generally subalterns attached to the Kashmir regiments, who led the men. No friction or other difficulty apparently resulted, and it seemed to me that great tact and sense were displayed on either side in dealing with these delicate relations.

On this night we saw numerous beacon fires up the valley and on the mountain-side beyond the river, a sign that the tribesmen meant fighting. A strong picket was now stationed by Aylmer's bridge, which was all but completed, and which, it was expected, would be attacked. Spedding finished the work at the Chaichar Pari this day, and the temporary road was thus ready. News arrived that the Hunza-Nagars had burnt all the stacked grass between this and Nilt, so as to prevent our obtaining fodder for our mules.

On November 30 the reply to Colonel Durand's ultimatum came in. It appears that the Nagaris assembled at Nilt had half a mind to come to terms with us, when, suddenly, there rushed over from the Hunza fortress of Maiun, on the other side of the river, the ferocious hereditary Wazir of Hunza—Safdar Ali's agent in the murder of his father, the late thum— who broke in upon the council, threatened to cut off the head of anyone who ventured to speak of peace, and, overpowering all present by the violence of his eloquence, brought the Nagaris to throw in their lot with the Hunzas. He insulted, maltreated, and was about to slay Colonel Durand's envoy, a native of Nagar, but eventually contented himself with robbing him of his horse and sending the man back to us on foot.

The envoy reported that the enemy had so strengthened Nilt fort (we learnt that they had been at work on it for two years) that they were confident they would have no difficulty in holding it against us until the spring, when the Russians, it was asserted, had promised to come to their assistance with many breechloading guns and a supply of ammunition, if not with Cossacks. The written reply of the allied chieftains to Colonel Durand's ultimatum stated that they would have no roads in their territories, and boasted of their capacity to resist us. Like the other messages they had sent, it was couched in the most insolent terms.

Curious Oriental imagery was employed in these documents. In one of his earlier letters the thum asked why the British strayed thus into his country 'like camels without nose-rings.' In another letter he declared that he cared nothing for the womanly English, as he hung upon the skirts of the manly Russians, and he warned Colonel Durand that he had given orders to his followers to bring him the Gilgit Agent's head on a platter. The thum was, indeed, an excellent correspondent about this time. He used to dictate his letters to the Court munshi, the only literary man, I believe, in the whole of his dominions, who wrote forcible, if unclassical, Persian. In one letter the thum somewhat shifted his ground, and spoke of other friends. 'I have been tributary to China for hundreds of years. Trespass into China if you dare,' he wrote to Colonel Durand. 'I will withstand you, if I have to use bullets of gold. If you venture here, be prepared to fight three nations—Hunza, China, and Russia. We will cut your head off, Colonel Durand, and then report you to the Indian Government.' One of the strangest expressions employed by this scribe occurred in a letter that had been written long since, in which the thum demanded the evacuation of Chalt by the

Kashmir troops, as that place, he argued, belonged properly to himself. 'This fortress of Chalt,' he pathetically put it, 'is more precious to us than are the strings of our wives' pyjamas.'

Negotiations having thus broken down, and all being now ready on our side, the welcome orders were issued that we should advance across the frontier on the following day, December 1. As we had left the greater portion of our little army behind to hold the different forts and posts between Chalt and our base, the Hunza-Nagar Field Force, as it was henceforth called, was thus constituted:—188 men of the 5th Gurkhas; 28 men of the 20th Punjab Infantry; 76 men of the Hazara Mountain Battery; 7 Bengal Sappers and Miners; and 661 Imperial Service troops (257 from the Ragu Pertab, or 1st Kashmir Infantry Regiment, and 404 from the Body Guard, or 2nd Kashmir Rifles): in all, about 1,000 regular troops. In addition to these were the Irregulars—the Punialis and Spedding's Pathans. Two thousand Balti coolies performed the bulk of the transport service. Sixteen British officers accompanied the Field Force.

On the eve of our advance, Surgeon Roberts gave us each an ominous little packet to put in the pocket, labelled 'First Field Dressing,' so that we might be able to apply preliminary bandages to our own or others' wounds. It recalled to mind the handing round of basins by a Channel-steamer steward before the commencement of an unpleasant voyage.

In the Order Book of this same evening Spedding was instructed to make a practicable road over the Kotal on the following day, the ridge to be previously occupied by fifty men of the Ragu Pertab regiment, under Lieutenant Widdicombe; while, later on in the day, the whole Field Force was to cross the river and bivouac on the Nagar side.

Our baggage had been cut down considerably before we left Chakerkot. It was here cut down still further, one coolie only being allotted to each officer. So the few tents and extra impedimenta that had been brought on were now stored in Chalt Fort; and one had to limit oneself to one's sleeping sack, a spare flannel shirt, and such-like absolute necessaries, which included, so far as Beech and myself were concerned, a few golf clubs, as we intended to complete the conquest of the country by the introduction of that absorbing game.

Early on the morning of December 1 Lieutenant Widdicombe crossed the river with his fifty men under cover of our guns, scaled the Kotal, and occupied the ridge without encountering any resistance. As he came up, the enemy retired. He found their stone breastworks at the summit empty, their fires still smouldering, and saw several men running towards Nilt by rough tracks across the mountains. It was evident that the Kanjuts had not held the Kotal in any force, and had employed this strong position merely as a post from which to observe our movements, having no intention of defending it.

Then Spedding, his staff, and the Pathans set out. We crossed Aylmer's bridge, and were now over the frontier, and had set foot on the soil of Nagar. I do not know to how many of our young officers this day the original idea suggested itself of calling out, 'Now we have crossed the Rubicon!' as they sprang from the bridge planks on to the Nagar shingle. I myself heard two make this remark, and I was told that several others were guilty of it.

We found it a stiff climb up the Kotal. A determined enemy above might, by the rolling down of rocks, have made the storming of this position a very awkward task for our men. Spedding's Pathans set to work with a will, and in the course of the day carried a rough zigzag path up the precipitous slopes, practicable for the battery mules; but the sort of road that is considered good enough for an Indian Hill Battery would rather astonish some people at home. Our two seven-pounders were, unfortunately, of old pattern, not screw-guns, and, therefore, not so portable as they might have been; but it was wonderful to see these tough, sure-footed mules, scrambling over the cliffs with their heavy loads, one carrying the gun, another the wheels, others with the ammunition cases.

From the top of the Kotal, 800 feet above the river, there is a magnificent view up the Kanjut Valley. Some eight miles away we saw the towers of the fortress of Nilt, which we hoped to capture on the morrow. Beyond it, far off, at the head of the valley, we perceived dimly, rising above the clouds, a beautiful snowy dome of immense height, an unknown mountain in the midst of unknown wilds. Since the time I am writing of, the Conway Expedition, which visited these regions last summer, has carried on most interesting explorations among the glaciers, snow-fields, and awful peaks that hem in the valley of the Kanjuts.

From the Kotal we saw that the valley as far as Nilt was bordered on both sides by great bare mountains, culminating in snowy pinnacles, but that no paris projected into the river to bar our advance. On either side of the river extended a narrow maidan or flat, forming a terrace between the foot of the mountains and the top of the cliffs that hung over the river. The maidan on our side, along which our force was to march on the following day, was stony and barren save for scattered wormwood scrub, until near Nilt, where cultivation commenced. Two side-nullahs clove this maidan, but the difficulties presented by these could not be ascertained from the Kotal.

The sepoys gazed with interest at the distant towers of the reputedly impregnable fortress, from which the smoke could be seen rising, and passed rough soldiers' jests on the chances of the morrow. We could see no human beings in the valley beyond us, even with the aid of glasses, though, doubtlessly, keen eyes were watching us from the crags above.

But on looking back we could see life in plenty. The whole force of 1,000 soldiers and 2,000 coolies was slowly streaming down the cliffs by Chalt, then across the bridge in single file to the camping-place beneath us, where a zereba was being thrown up.

At sunset the numerous bivouac fires below had a cheery look, and, having done our work, we descended the Kotal and found our way to the space allotted to us within the zereba, where our welcome dinner was ready.

The mules, which were fastened up close to us, favoured us with a tremendous concert during our meal, and all around was an orderly bustle of preparation for the night. We read the Order Book to see what our duties would be on the morrow, and turned into our sacks to sleep, the 200 Pathans snoring round us. And so ended the first day of the campaign.

CHAPTER XXIV

THE FIGHT OF DECEMBER 2—ADVANCE ON NILT—STRENGTH OF NILT FORT—THE GURKHAS AND GUNS COME INTO ACTION—THE RIDGE CROWNED BY THE PUNIALIS—COLONEL DURAND WOUNDED—A FORLORN HOPE—THE MAIN GATE BLOWN UP AND THE FORT TAKEN BY ASSAULT—LOSSES ON BOTH SIDES—TWO V.C.'S—CAPTURE OF ENEMY'S SUPPLIES.

Long before daybreak on December 2 there was a bustle within the zereba, fires were lit, and coffee was prepared. At five the bugles sounded the reveille, and shortly afterwards, it being still dark, we fell into our positions and marched towards the Kotal through the frosty air.

Spedding's men came after the main body in the line of march; but twenty of his picked Pathans, under Appleford, accompanied Captain Aylmer and his seven sappers, and marched with the advance guard of fifty Gurkhas, to clear away the obstructions on the road, in front of the force.

The day broke before we reached the steeper portion of the Kotal, and here the ascent in single file for our 3,000 soldiers and coolies, and I know not how many mules, was, of course, a very tedious undertaking. For us who were behind, this portion of the march was pretty well as dangerous as being in action; for every now and again some battery or ambulance mule would make a false step, dislodging rocks which, gathering others on the way, would come rolling down upon us and had to be nimbly dodged. The Pathans were well-accustomed to this game and appeared rather to like it.

The descent on the farther side of the Kotal was steep and difficult, and when the troops had reached the maidan below they were halted for a short time, while the Pathans improved the track so that the battery mules could get by. By this time it was broad daylight; the weather was lovely, with not a cloud in the pale blue sky; a splendid day for a fight, as some of the youngsters said. As we looked down from the Kotal summit our little force massed below had a peculiarly insignificant appearance, a tiny patch set in the midst of this gigantic landscape. From here, too, we could now see through our glasses numbers of men hurrying about in the fields near Nilt, as if they were driving the cattle within the fort.

At last the march was resumed, now in line of columns, across the stony plain, until we came to the first of the side nullahs I have mentioned. This nullah clove the maidan like a gigantic trench, a chasm with perpendicular walls of conglomerate some hundreds of feet in height. The very narrow track ran steeply down one side and up the other. A sanga commanded the further side, but was not held by the enemy, though this was a formidable position; but the Kanjuts had broken away the path in places, so that there was no way of getting by until our sappers and navvies had been at work for some time.

As soon as Aylmer and Appleford had made the track practicable, the force crossed; but not without one accident at least, which happened just in front of me as I commenced the descent. An ammunition mule made a false step, and rolled over the precipice to the bottom of the nullah, bringing down with him an avalanche of large rocks, which scattered men and mules, and caused terrible confusion. Cases of ammunition and shells were thundering down the cliff. The mule that caused the mischief was, of course, killed instantaneously by his fall; but, strangely enough, though there must have been some cuts and hard knocks received, there was no other serious damage done.

Then we crossed an easy maidan for awhile, until we came to the second nullah, another frightful place, the track across which had also been broken away, and which, like the first, was undefended. In fact, we now saw no trace of the enemy, the whole country had been deserted before our advance, and the stacked grass had all been burnt, as our spies had reported. Here again there was a long delay while the road was being repaired. Our advance, I need scarcely say, was being conducted with all due precautions, and there was no chance of our falling into an ambuscade, a method of attack at which the Kanjuts are known to be clever. A party of Gurkhas and the Punialis, under Lieutenant Manners Smith, crowned the heights as we moved on, and having found a way to scramble round these nullahs, held the farther sides of them while the sappers and Pathans cleared a rough way with pick, shovel, and gunpowder, as rapidly as possible. The sound of the blasting appeared at last to stir up the enemy, and we could hear the beating of their tomtoms and their shoutings in the distant forts.

Once across the second nullah and on the maidan beyond, the road presented no more difficulties, and we soon reached the cultivated terraces of Nilt, across which the force advanced in quarter columns. All was now absolutely quiet again, not a human being

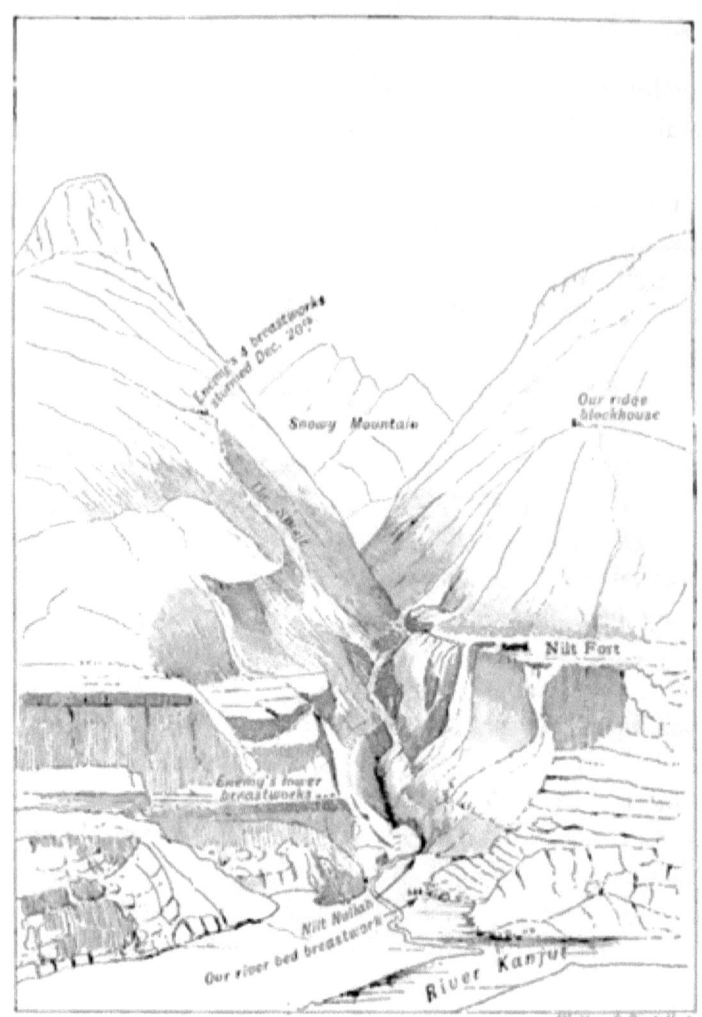

NILT NULLAH FROM MAIUN

was to be seen; and, even when we were close up to the fort itself, there was nothing to show that it was occupied, save the flags waving on the walls and the smoke rising from the fires within.

The strip of cultivated land along which we were now marching is narrowed considerably, a little distance below Nilt, by a projecting spur of the mountain, which covers the fort and makes it even impossible to see it until one has rounded the foot of the spur and is almost under the walls, at a distance of about two hundred yards. Thus, though the towers of the fortress had been visible to us in the morning from the distant Kotal, they were afterwards hidden from us, and we saw nothing more of Nilt until we suddenly opened it out on turning this corner.

The position will be better understood on referring to the illustration which represents Nilt as seen from Maiun, on the opposite bank of the Kanjut River. That river is in the foreground of the picture, while, hanging on the precipitous edge of the tributary Nilt nullah, and at the end of the maidan I have described, stands the fortress itself.

Nilt is, indeed, a very formidable place. As is the case in all Kanjut villages, the villagers live within the fort, which is a very rabbit-warren of strongly-built stone houses, two or three storeys high in places, with narrow alleys between, the whole enclosed within a great wall, carefully built of stones, and strengthened with massive timbers. This wall is fifteen feet to twenty feet in height, and is twelve feet thick in most places, with large square towers at intervals. The flat roofs of this fortified village are covered with stones, and are so well constructed that they were proof against our shell when dropped upon them, while guns of very

The best marksmen among the enemy had been told off to fire at the British officers, of whom there could not have been one who did not have some narrow escape on this day. For instance, Lieutenant Williams was shot through the helmet, and Lieutenant Boisragon's revolver was struck by a bullet as he was about to fire it during the final struggle within the fortress. One curious incident occurred. The old Sikh subadar-major had given the word for No. 1 gun to fire. No report followed, but the gunner laughed. A bullet had cut the lanyard in two just as he was about to pull it.

The two guns did not remain long on the bluff, but were moved across the maidan to another equally exposed position.

Spedding, who had accompanied Colonel Durand throughout the day as galloper, shortly after this came across the maidan to the bluff. He was the bearer of the bad news that Colonel Durand had just been severely wounded. Spedding had received an order to take his Pathans up to the height which the Punialis were holding, as they would be useful in cutting off the retreat of the enemy. So we collected our men and scrambled up the steep hillside as fast as we could go, the Pathans greatly pleased at the chance of doing a bit of fighting on their own account, instead of standing by as idle spectators.

While we were still climbing we heard a tremendous explosion sounding above the din of guns and musketry, and perceived volumes of smoke rising high into the air. We put this down to the blowing-up of one of the powder magazines in the fort, or to the bursting of the enemy's big sher bacha. We attained the ridge, rushed over it, and came to the dip where the Punialis were, and from here suddenly looked right down into the heart of the fort, the flat roofs and alleys being spread out beneath us like a map.

And now a fascinating spectacle met our eyes. In the narrow lanes there was a confusion of men, scarcely distinguishable for the dust and smoke; but in a moment we realised that fighting was going on within the fort itself—that our sepoys had forced their way into it; and then, as the atmosphere cleared somewhat, we saw that the Kanjut stronghold was won.

There appeared to be but a handful of the little Gurkhas within the fort; but it was certainly theirs. It was evident that the force below, outside the walls, did not at once realise what had happened, and the fort was shelled and the loopholes were fired at for some little time after our sepoys had effected an entrance. But the tidings soon spread, and we heard our men below raising lusty cheer upon cheer, in which we joined with what breath we had left in us after our hard climb.

We now saw our men pouring into the fort, while the defenders were rushing out of the gates at the back to escape beyond the nullah, many to be shot ere they got far. We did not rest a moment on the ridge, but clambered down with our Pathans to the fort, the men only stopping now and then to fire at the fugitives—with little effect, for it is no easy matter to hit a running man—while we, in our turn, were being fired at with similarly small results from the numerous breastworks, filled with Kanjut marksmen, that lined the opposite side of the Nilt nullah.

The whole stirring story of the taking of Nilt we did not learn for some hours later. In fact, I believe our entire force—with the exception of the handful of gallant men who did the deed—was in the dark as to what had happened. I will now explain how Nilt was stormed.

Any other method of attacking so strong a place being evidently unavailing, Colonel Durand just before he was wounded had given the order that the fort should be taken by assault. How this was done will long be remembered as one of the most gallant things recorded in Indian warfare. Captain Aylmer, as our engineer, was now instructed to blow up the main gate of the fort, so as to admit the storming-party. This gate, the only assailable one, did not face the direction from which our force had advanced, but was on the side of the fort which is under the mountain, and was difficult of approach.

First our guns and rifles opened a very heavy fire upon the fort, under cover of which 100 of the 5th Gurkhas, led by Lieutenants Boisragon and Badcock, made a rush at the outer wall, and began to cut their way through the abattis with their kukris, the garrison the while firing steadily into them. A small opening having thus been made, the three officers, closely followed by about half a dozen men, pushed their way through it. They then made for the wooden gate of the outer wall, which they soon hacked to pieces. They now found themselves in front of the main wall, and while his companions fired into the loopholes—the officers using their revolvers—Captain Aylmer, accompanied by his Pathan orderly, rushed forward to the foot of the main gate, which was strongly built, and had been barricaded within with stones in anticipation of our coming. The enemy now concentrated their fire upon this gallant little band, and it is marvellous that any escaped death. Captain Aylmer placed his slabs of gun-cotton at the foot of the gate, packed them with stones, and ignited the fuse, all the while being exposed to the fire from the towers which flanked the gate, as well as from some loopholes in the gate itself. He was shot in the leg from so short a distance that his clothes and flesh were burnt by the gunpowder. He and his orderly then followed the wall of the fort to a safe distance, and stood there awaiting the explosion. But there came no explosion, for the fuse was a faulty one, so Captain Aylmer had once more to face an almost certain death. He returned to the gate, readjusted the fuse, cut it with his knife, lit a match after two or three attempts, and re-ignited the fuse. While doing this he received another wound, his hand being terribly crushed by a stone that was thrown from the battlements.

This time a terrific explosion followed, and at once, before even the dust had cleared or the stones had ceased dropping from the crumbling wall, the three British officers, with the six men at their back, clambered through the breach and were within Nilt Fort. Enveloped in dense smoke and dust, their comrades, who had been cutting their way through the abattis, could not find the breach; indeed, they did not realise that one had been effected and that their officers were within the gates; so for many minutes that little handful of gallant Englishmen and Gurkhas was engaged in a hand-to-hand fight with the garrison in the narrow alley leading from the gate. Having gained this position, they held it resolutely, but soon two were killed and most of them were wounded, and it was obvious that not one of them would be left alive unless they were soon supported. Accordingly Lieutenant Boisragon went outside the gate once more to find his men, and thus exposed himself not only to the fire of the enemy at the loopholes, but to that of our own covering party.

In a very short time he was back again, at the head of a number of little Gurkhas eager to avenge the comrades they had lost. The Gurkhas poured into the narrow alleys of the fort and fought as they always do fight. The Kanjuts defended themselves like fanatical dervishes at first, but soon lost heart before the fierce attack. While this was going on a fire was still kept up from the loopholes on our supports, the detachment of the Ragu Pertab Regiment (Imperial Service), which now came up, led by Lieutenant Townshend. The fort was soon swarming with our men, who hunted the Kanjuts through the intricate alleys and holes. The Wazir of Nagar himself was killed, but the principal leaders escaped, as did most of the garrison, who, availing themselves of their knowledge of the maze which was their home, found their way to a small gate opening on to a steep nullah behind the fort.

Thus was Nilt Fort taken after a daring rush which, perhaps, has not had its equal since Umbeyla. As is so often the case, the boldest course of action here proved to be the safest: our total loss was only six killed and twenty-seven wounded, a number which would have been much exceeded had what some might consider a more prudent course of action been adopted. The loss of the enemy was uncertain; but it was estimated that over eighty were killed in the course of the action. Of the gallant handful of men who followed the three officers through the breach, two were killed and nearly all were wounded. Lieutenant Badcock was severely wounded, and Captain Aylmer received no fewer than three severe wounds, which may be considered as a very lucky escape when it is remembered what he did. Captain Aylmer and Lieutenant Boisragon have both been decorated with the Victoria Cross, which they so thoroughly deserved, while Lieutenant Badcock, who in the opinion of his brother-officers had also earned that highest reward of valour, received the Distinguished Service Order.

Many of our men, lying down at the edge of the cliff above the Nilt nullah, now attempted to pick off the fugitives, who were bolting from cover to cover like rabbits to the distant forts; while the enemy's marksmen, who still held all the sangas beyond the nullah, fired at us occasionally, and their sher bachas—roughly-constructed cannon, some of which, however, were heavier than our seven-pounders—propelled shot and shell at us from seemingly inaccessible ledges high up the mountain-sides. This desultory interchange of fire went on till sunset, producing a good deal of noise and little else.

It had been intended by Colonel Durand that a portion of our force should make a dash across the Nilt nullah and carry the sangas beyond as soon as Nilt Fort had fallen, and before the enemy had recovered from their confusion. But Captain Bradshaw, on whom the command devolved after Colonel Durand was wounded, found that the Kanjuts had taken steps to render this plan impracticable, the road across the precipitous ravine having been broken away.

The road up the valley after leaving Nilt zigzagged down our side of the Nilt nullah, and up the other side to a strongly-built sanga, through the middle of which it passed by a narrow gateway. This gateway the Kanjuts had barricaded with stones, and the approach to it was little better than a sheer precipice. This sanga I will always speak of as the enemy's 'lower sanga,' the name by which it was known to us. It stood at a much lower level than Nilt Fort. It had a long, loopholed wall facing us, about ten feet in height and of great thickness, and a stout roof of timber covered with large, flat stones, but, like most of these sangas, it was open and unprotected at the back. It was garrisoned, as we afterwards discovered, by about 100 men, and gave us, as I shall show, far more trouble than any other of the enemy's defences. Its position is indicated in the illustration facing page 368.

After the fort had fallen Gorton brought up his two guns to the edge of the cliff and proceeded to drop shot and shell on to the roof of this little wasp's nest. Some of the shot appeared to pierce the roof, and the defenders began to bolt, many of them to be shot down by our riflemen. At last the sanga seemed to be empty of men, and we were congratulating ourselves that on the morrow, after Spedding had repaired the road, we should be able to make a forward movement and pass through this breastwork without encountering any opposition, save from the fortifications on the heights above or the forts on the plain beyond, which could be easily turned did we once establish a footing on the farther side of the nullah. In this impression, which, I imagine, was shared by most of us, we were grievously mistaken; we did not yet understand how stubborn and skilled in the defence of their positions are the tribesmen of the Kanjut Valley.

Shortly after descending from the ridge I passed through the breach and entered the captured fortress. Across the ruined gateway lay the dead body of a Gurkha, one of Boisragon's gallant handful, and close to him was the corpse of Mahomet Shah, Wazir of Nagar, and one of the enemy's best leaders, who had been shot by Badcock as the storming-party rushed in. Many dead Kanjuts were lying in the narrow alleys and behind the loopholes of the walls; and though most of the garrison had escaped, there were several tribesmen still hiding away in the numerous dark holes and crannies of this curious place. The whole labyrinth of lanes was full of our sepoys, who were busy hunting up these men, and a shout was raised whenever another poor wretch

PRISONER IN NILT FORT, CAPTURED GUN, AND DOGRA SEPOYS.

was dragged out into the light. The Gurkhas, exasperated at the sight of their dead comrades, were like little tigers: their faces had lost all the jolly expression habitual to them; their savage passions were up, and, had they been allowed, they would doubtless have avenged their friends by cutting the throat of every Kanjut they could catch with their murderous kukris. The Pathans and Dogras would have been no more merciful. But all these were disciplined troops, and the three or four officers who were within the fort effectually prevented outrage of any description; the sepoys were soon drawn up outside the fort, and all was order and quiet routine again after the momentary excitement that naturally followed the successful assault.

One woman only was found in the fort, the others, as usual in time of war, having been removed to the mountains. Her husband was among the killed, and, I believe, had been a man of some importance. I saw the poor creature weeping and lamenting on a housetop, with two sepoys guarding her. The Punialis and Hunzas intermarry a good deal, and it turned out that both the brother and uncle of this woman were with Rajah Akbar Khan's contingent; so these men undertook the care of her, and sent her to the house of some relative in their own valley.

As I was wandering through the streets I suddenly came across Aylmer, covered with blood, staggering along on the arm of one of his men, but jolly as ever despite his three ugly wounds, and he gave me a cheery greeting. When he set out for that gateway he must have known that he was going to meet an almost certain death. His gallant deed produced a great impression in both camps, and he was spoken of by the natives as the *bahadur sahib*. The Puniali rajah who, from the ridge above, witnessed the assault on the gate, raised his hands and cried out, 'This is the fighting of giants, not of men.'

Our surgeons, doctors Roberts and Luard, had plenty of work on their hands this evening. We heard that Colonel Durand's wound was a very severe one; he had been hit in the groin by a jezail bullet, and at first it was feared that his injuries would prove fatal. This bullet, when extracted, was found to be a garnet enclosed in lead. There were sacks full of similar bullets within the fort. The cliff-sides here are studded with hard garnets of convenient size and shape; so the tribesmen, by employing them thus in their projectiles, economise the lead, with which they are not too well provided.

On rummaging the fort we found a considerable quantity of grain and ghee stored in granaries and buried under some of the chambers. The question of our supplies was still a cause of much anxiety, so this

NILT FORT IN JANUARY, 1892, AFTER THE TOWERS HAD BEEN BLOWN UP.

was a very welcome find. We captured a sher bacha in Nilt, and took nine prisoners. We discovered a quantity of native matchlocks, swords, shields, and gunpowder, also some of the bows of ibex horn, which of old were the war-weapons of the tribesmen, but are now only employed in the chase. We found ammunition for Winchester, Berdan, Martini-Henry, Snider, and other rifles; but the defenders had succeeded in carrying all their rifles away with them. So intricate is the arrangement of chambers and cellars within the fort walls, that for three weeks fresh discoveries were made almost daily, and several valuable caches of grain were unearthed.

In the course of this day I occasionally came across Dr. Robertson's six Kafirs, who were generally huddled up in a group under cover, apparently stupefied. This sort of fighting was quite new to them. The stalking of an enemy until one can stab him unawares with a dagger is the Kafir's idea of warfare, and very clever and daring he is at it.

A small garrison was left to guard the fort, but the greater portion of the force encamped at about half a mile from it, among the cultivated fields of the maidan. The broken irrigation-canal was repaired, and we were then well supplied with water from the Nilt stream. We saw the flickering fires of the enemy's pickets scattered all over the mountain-side beyond Nilt; but sher bachas and muskets became silent at sunset, and we had a quiet night's rest in camp after the exciting day.

CHAPTER XXV

THE FIGHT OF DECEMBER 3—WE ARE REPULSED WITH LOSS—ROAD-MAKING UNDER DIFFICULTIES—DETERMINED STAND OF THE KANJUTS—AN EIGHTEEN DAYS' CHECK—DESCRIPTION OF THE ENEMY'S LINE OF DEFENCE—LIST OF OFFICERS WITH FIELD FORCE—HUMOURS OF THE CAMPAIGN—VIGILANCE OF THE ENEMY—WORK OF SPEDDING'S ENGINEERS.

WE were up at dawn on December 3. We understood that Spedding's Pathans were to make a road across the Nilt nullah, under cover of the guns, and that the whole force was to then advance and attack the large Nagar fortress of Thol, and the other defences on the maidan ahead. So it was proposed; but the programme was not carried out, and as we were this day distinctly repulsed with loss, I think the enemy can fairly claim the skirmish I am about to describe as a victory to their account.

There is a small flat space of ground between the walls of Nilt fort and the edge of the cliff over the Nilt nullah. It was here that the guns were to take up their position and cover the road-makers. From this point the road descends a little gully for some distance before zigzagging down the exposed face of the cliff. I set out with some others of Spedding's staff, and the Pathans selected for this work, not long after daybreak; and we came upon this flat space of ground at the same time that Gorton's two guns and a guard of the 5th Gurkhas appeared on the scene. No sooner were we all collected together, somewhat crowded up, on this narrow place, none of us, I imagine, having any idea of danger, than suddenly, from a dozen or more rifles in the breastworks opposite to us, not more than eighty yards distant, a volley was poured into the thick of us; and then the whole hillside was covered with the ominous flashes and wreaths of white smoke, as the Kanjut marksmen, with jezails and Winchesters, opened a steady, well-directed fire upon us, which would have proved fatal to a large proportion of our men in a very short time had not the order at once been given to retire from this deadly corner, an order which was obeyed with considerable alacrity.

There was little confusion considering the circumstances. The terrified mules that had broken loose and were plunging about in the midst of us were got together, and the guns were carried off; while the Pathans, and many of the sepoys, took refuge at the mouth of the little gully I have mentioned. In the very short space of time during which we were exposed to the enemy's fire we had three men killed and five wounded, Lieutenant Gorton himself receiving a severe wound. Some of the battery mules were also hit.

Mitchell, who was in command of the Pathan roadmakers, now carried out his instructions, and set his men to work in the gully, the side of which protected us from the enemy's fire—though even here one sepoy was killed, probably by a bullet that had ricocheted. At last a rough track was cleared down to the mouth of the gully, where it opens out on to the face of the cliff. Here the Kanjuts were ready for us; for no sooner did we attempt to turn the last protecting corner, than bullet after bullet from a sanga, not more than seventy yards off, flattened itself against the rocks. Mitchell himself was hit in the chest by a jezail bullet, which, luckily striking him over the pocket in which he was carrying one of the thick little packets of first field dressings that Dr. Roberts had served out, did not penetrate. He was not disabled, and did not appear to be hurt. It was not till some days afterwards that he discovered one of his ribs had been broken by the impact.

The Pathans were perfectly cool under fire, and would have continued their work cheerfully round this dangerous corner, despite the Kanjut marksmen; but our loss would necessarily have been very heavy, so Mitchell withdrew them, and despatched me to the fort to explain matters to Captain Bradshaw and ask for orders.

One's progress from point to point on this day, and on many days afterwards, was rather like that of a rabbit bolting from cover to cover when fowling-pieces are about. Thus, to go between this gully-head and the fort, I had to cross the open space which the enemy had so effectually cleared with their rifles an hour or so before. It must have been grand sport for the Kanjut marksmen, who invariably gave each one of us a volley as he hurried by. There were also some exposed corners in the fort itself, and on the road between the fort and the camp, which we soon came to know, and across which we used to travel as if bent on some extremely urgent business. There were some less dangerous places, again, only exposed to the fire of distant sangas, by which we walked in a somewhat more dignified manner, though without loitering. Day after day each of us was individually fired at but never hit, and one began to realize what a very small percentage of bullets really have their billets.

On hearing my report, Captain Bradshaw gave

orders that the road-making in the gully should be discontinued; so Spedding withdrew his men, and they were employed in opening a new road between fort and camp, which would be more under cover than the existing one.

It was now obvious that the Kanjuts, having abandoned to us without a blow all the country below Nilt, were about to make a very determined stand here. Under cover of the darkness they had crowded the lower sanga and their other defences beyond the nullah with their marksmen, and had been busily employed the whole night in so strengthening these rough breastworks with timbers and stones, that from this day we found our seven-pounders produced practically no effect whatever upon them—every sanga was quite bomb-proof.

That the tribesmen should have returned in the night to that lower sanga, right under the fort as it was, with the intention of holding it against us by daylight, after the tremendous shelling we had given it on the previous evening, showed us that our foemen were anything but destitute of pluck. They were evidently not discouraged by the fall of Nilt; and, indeed, we afterwards discovered that it had been quite a question with them whether they should attempt to hold it against us at all; some of the leaders having been in favour of destroying this fort, and relying solely on the stronger positions beyond the nullah. It was Mahomet Shah who overruled this opinion, and insisted that Nilt was impregnable; as it indeed might have been had we not Aylmers and guncotton. The plucky old Wazir of Nagar fell a victim to his own theory; he died fighting, and it was over his corpse, stretched across the gateway, that our men entered the fort.

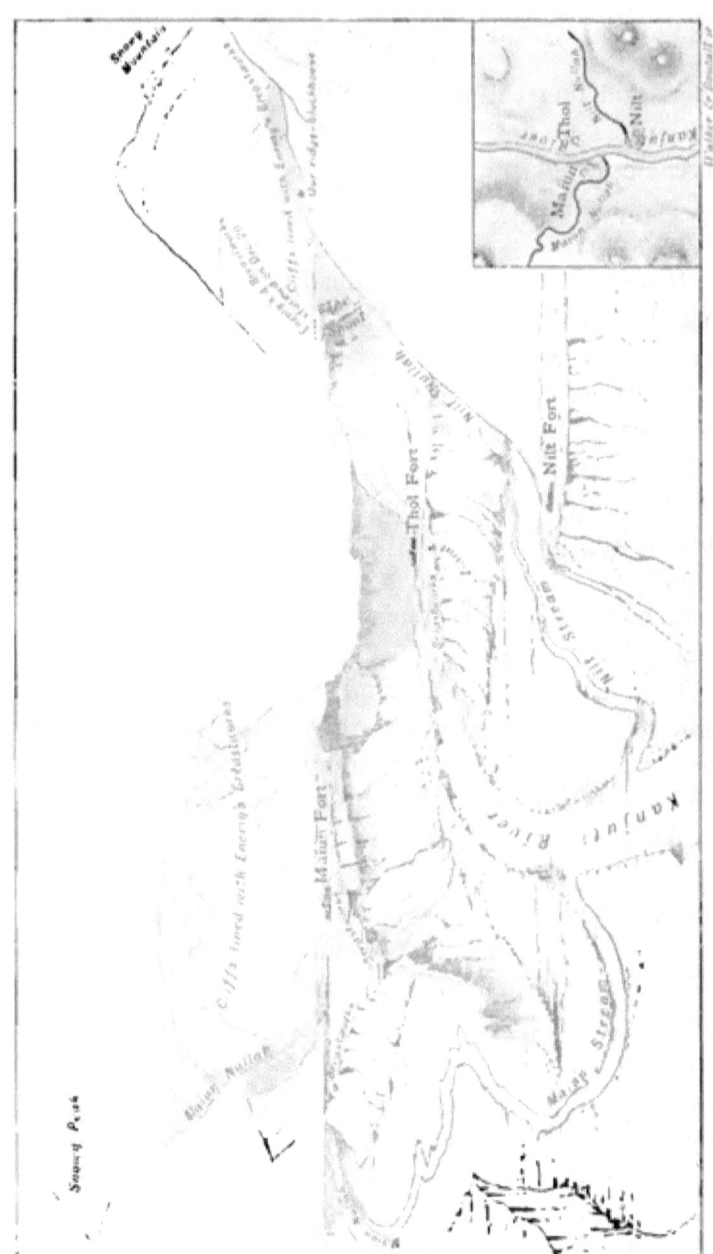

BIRD'S-EYE VIEW OF THE ENEMY'S LINE OF DEFENCE.

EXPLANATION OF THE POSITION

Before carrying this narrative further, it will be well to explain the nature of the extraordinary position which now confronted us, than which it would be difficult to imagine a stronger, and before which, despite all our efforts, we had now to remain for eighteen days; a check which, as will be easily understood, was attended with serious danger; for the hostile tribes of the Indus Valley, encouraged by our failure, were actually preparing to fall upon Boonji, while the Kanjuts themselves were about to act on the offensive, and attack our long line of communication. Seeing how small our available force was, and how we were cut off by the snow-covered passes from all possibility of reinforcement until the following summer, it is quite possible that a disaster would have occurred had the enemy been able to hold us in check much longer.

The bird's-eye view, in conjunction with the illustrations of Nilt and Maiun, will render the following description intelligible.

The Kanjut Valley, between the bases of the mountains, is here about fifteen hundred yards wide. On the Nilt side of the river, the precipitous tributary Nilt nullah, descending from the glaciers of Mount Rakaposhi, barred our advance; the opposite side of this nullah was defended by numerous sangas and sher bachas, the enemy's defences, indeed, extending up the mountain-side to the edge of the deeply crevassed glacier.

On the other side of the Kanjut River, another tributary nullah, equally precipitous, and with its farther side defended by the cliff-encompassed fortress of Maiun, also formed a seemingly insuperable obstacle. Here, too, the sangas lined the cliffs from the glaciers to the river bed.

R. St. G. Gorton, wounded. Lieutenant C. V. F. Townshend, Central India Horse, Lieutenant F. Duncan, 23rd Bengal Infantry, and Lieutenant G. T. Widdicombe, 9th Bengal Infantry, were attached to the Ragu Pertab Regiment of the Imperial Service troops; while Lieutenant J. McD. Baird, 24th Bengal Infantry, and Lieutenant F. H. Taylor, 3rd Sikh Infantry, were attached to the Bodyguard Regiment of the same force. Captain W. H. M. Stewart commanded the detachment of the 20th Punjab Infantry, and superintended the transport service. Two good officers had to be spared from the front to guard our long line of communication, Captain Kembell remaining at Boonji, in view of a Chilas raid; while Lieutenant C. S. Williams, 43rd Bengal Infantry, after the fight at Nilt, was given the command of our advanced base at Chalt, and acted as Commissariat officer.

So that the remaining officers might be relieved of the heavy work now thrown upon them, the civilians in camp were invited to volunteer to undertake outpost and other duties. We were all, of course, very glad to do this, and were forthwith placed upon the roster as officers. Lennard had already been attached to the guns, having had experience of that branch of the service. Beech was made Provost-Marshal. I was attached to the Ragu Pertab Regiment. Spedding was appointed Chief Engineer to the Force, with the local rank of Captain, and Appleford was Assistant-Engineer. Blaker, of Spedding's staff, was not with us at the front, but was made commander of Ramghat, near which place he was superintending the construction of the road.

All idea of taking the enemy's defences by assault on this day was at last reluctantly abandoned. Several officers had examined the approaches to the lower sanga from as close as it was possible to venture, and all brought back the same report as to the apparent absence of any practicable track up the opposite cliff. I was myself sent to inspect a lower path by which the enemy had fled on the previous evening, and found that it had been broken away in the night.

I crawled down a small gully, in which several of the enemy's dead were lying, and availing myself of the cover of rock and brushwood, worked my way along the cliff till I could plainly distinguish the details of the position I had been sent to reconnoitre. The sharp eyes of the marksmen in the sangas soon detected me, and a couple of bullets whistled uncomfortably near my head. The tribesmen were ever on the look-out for us.

Appleford this day made a path to the ridge which had been crowned by the Punialis, and as soon as it was completed Molony took the two guns up and opened fire on some sangas on the opposite side of the Nilt nullah, which had been rendering themselves particularly objectionable to us. A body of Ragu Pertabs who accompanied the guns also exchanged rifle-shots with the garrisons of the sangas, while the sher bachas, still higher up the mountain, added their quota to the din. It was strange to see this little artillery duel high above us on the seemingly inaccessible sky-line. Our shot and shell produced little effect on these sangas, for they were of great strength, like all the others along this line of defence. Occasionally Molony would turn his attention to the fortresses on the maidan below him, and send his shell over our heads into the heart of Maiun, or into Thol or the Ziarat. The Kanjuts soon discovered how to dodge our fire. They used to remain secure in the corners of their alleys till a shell had burst, and then rush out to scramble for the shrapnel bullets; for though powder was plentiful they had but little lead. Stones were sometimes fired from their sher bachas, which made a peculiar humming noise as they passed overhead, very distinguishable from that of shot.

For the eighteen days we remained here the Kanjuts and ourselves were always firing at each other from our respective sides of the nullah. Our guns and rifles at any rate compelled the enemy to keep within their fortified villages by daylight. On the other hand, their marksmen made it unadvisable for any of us to show his head above the parapets of Nilt Fort. They had men among them who evidently knew how to use the Martini-Henry or Berdan at long range. The Hunza general himself was wont to station himself all day at the summit of the Ziarat Tower, with a long telescope and a Berdan rifle, spying and shooting at us. Now and then a sher bacha would drop a shot into the middle of our camp. There was one very bold Kanjut who crossed the Maium nullah one day, took up a position on the farther side of the river, just opposite to our camp, and made most excellent practice with a Berdan, until he suddenly disappeared on a shell from Molony's gun bursting over him; so it was conjectured that he had been killed.

A campaign always has its humours, and these were not wanting here. To be perpetually under fire was little to the taste of some of our baboos, whose complaints on this subject were sometimes very amusing. One day a commissariat baboo came up, with clasped hands, to the commanding officer. 'Ah, sir!' he cried in his queer English, 'I indeed think this is no good place for the commissariat. Many cartridges are flying overhead. I have, of course, no fear for myself, but I dread lest the lead spoil our ata (meal), of which we have not too much.' This same thoughtful gentleman, when we were about to serve out the grain captured in Nilt Fort, begged us to proceed with due caution : 'The enemy may have poisoned this grain,' said he. 'Taste it not yet, sirs; but first give some to our Balti coolies, and watch if they thrive on it.'

Another baboo conceived the idea that he was a great military genius, and he was always devising and propounding to anyone who would lend ear to him some ingenious plan for circumventing the Kanjuts and capturing their positions. These schemes were invariably of blood-curdling atrocity and treachery. Unscrupulous cunning was his favourite weapon. Here is one of his precious suggestions. 'Let us parley with the enemy and pretend we wish to treat of peace. Let a sahib and six or seven Punialis go over to the big lower sanga to talk to the enemy. Then while the Punialis, who, of course, must not be in the secret, are still talking with the garrison and diverting their attention, the sahib will insert gun-cotton and a lit fuse into the wall, and retire with careless slowness, as if nothing was up and he were merely strolling to and fro during the talk. Then enemy and Punialis and fort will blow up, our sepoys will rush on, and the thing is done.' This strategist, it will be seen, did not stick at trifles. In his military ardour he had studied all the books he could pick up that taught the soldier his duties. Later on we took upwards of a hundred prisoners, and grain being scarce with us, it was a question what we should do with them. Our friend was at once ready with one of his ghastly suggestions. 'Why not tie these vagabonds up in a bunch,' he said, 'and slay them with shrapnel shell? I have carefully looked through the sangas, and the throwing up of sandbag breastworks in the very bed of the Nilt nullah, could only be carried on under cover of the night, and was even then attended with considerable risk. Spedding was assisted by Appleford, McCulloch, and Aylmer. Mitchell had been sent back to that important position on our line of communication, the Kotal, to construct a block-house there and hold it with fifty of the Pathans. Great credit is due to these young engineers, and it should be recognised that they contributed to no small extent to the success of this expedition.

CHAPTER XXVI

RECONNAISSANCES—THE ABORTIVE ATTACK OF DECEMBER 8—A NOISY NIGHT—A LETTER FROM THE THUM—FOOTBALL UNDER FIRE—ANOTHER FRUSTRATED ATTACK ON DECEMBER 12—A HALF-HOUR'S TRUCE—NAGDU'S DISCOVERY—DEPARTURE OF SPEDDING'S PATHANS.

DAY after day we woke to the noise of firing, which continued from dawn to dark, and occasionally throughout the night as well. So, on December 6, all the wounded men were carried away from this perpetual din to the quiet of Chalt Fort.

As there seemed small chance of an immediate forward movement, steps were taken to make our men as comfortable as possible in camp. The tents which had been left behind at Chalt were brought up; and very welcome they were, for it was chilly weather for a bivouac. Our sepoys put up some snug little huts of stones and branches of trees, and securely intrenched the camp. The enemy, seeing all these preparations, must have come to the conclusion that we were very deliberate people, in no hurry to advance, and were going into winter quarters.

The life was not monotonous, for each day brought its own little excitement. Our officers made frequent reconnaissances. Lieutenant Baird, on one dark night, descended into the Nilt nullah and clambered along the cliff right under the enemy's lower sanga, to discover the exact condition of the broken track. Captain Colin

Mackenzie and others made a reconnaissance up the river-bed by daylight; but the marksmen at the Ziarat prevented this from being carried far. The Pathans of the 20th Punjab Infantry—by the way, the only Mahomedan troops we had with us—had no respect for this holy shrine, and did not scruple to fire into it; indeed, I think they took a malicious pleasure in doing so; for, strictly orthodox Sunis as they were, they loathed these Shiahs and Maulai schismatics, especially the latter, who, they declared, were worse Kafirs than the unbelieving savages Dr. Robertson had brought from Kafiristan.

The result of these reconnaissances was a decision of Captain Bradshaw to make another attempt at forcing the enemy's position, at the lower end of the Nilt nullah, on the morning of December 8. At daybreak we were to open a tremendous fire, both from Nilt Fort and from the ridge, on the enemy's breastworks beyond the ravine, so as to cover Spedding and his men while they rapidly made the road across the nullah practicable for our troops.

On the evening of December 7 I was sent with a strong body of 5th Gurkhas and Ragu Pertabs to relieve the ridge picket, and was instructed to silence any of the enemy's sangas opposite me that should open fire on our storming-party and road-makers on the morrow. The enemy's lower sangas were at the same time to be dealt with by our marksmen and our two seven-pounder guns from the fort. It was arranged that as soon as the road had been opened out and all was ready for the advance, Molony was to signal to me with a flag from the gun bastion, and that then, leaving the Ragu Pertabs and Punialis to keep up the fire into the opposite sangas, I was to bring the Gurkhas down to the fort (as they would be required to guard the guns during the advance) and join the Ragu Pertab regiment, to which I was attached, and which, under Lieutenant Townshend's command, was to attack the Ziarat and the sangas near it, while the rest of the force was to assault Thol Fort.

Such was the programme; and as I clambered up the hill to the ridge, I thought that the following day promised to be a sufficiently exciting one for us all.

I found that the ridge blockhouse had now been completed, and though it had no roof, it afforded a welcome shelter against the cold wind that used to make a bivouac on this exposed hillside somewhat uncomfortable.

In the middle of the night, which was very black, just as I was about to set out on visiting-rounds, and all having been quite still so far, a fearful din suddenly broke out below, which for a moment led me to think that the enemy had attempted a night surprise on our camp. Tomtoms were loudly beaten; men were shouting in Thol, the Ziarat, and in Maiun; a heavy and unceasing fire was opened in every direction from sher bachas and muskets; while avalanche after avalanche of rocks thundered down the side of the nullah facing the picket.

On walking to the edge of the cliff, whence I could command a view of the situation, I saw by the flashes of fire that pierced the darkness below that the greater part of this tremendous demonstration came from the enemy's lower sangas, the defenders of which, at intervals, rolled large fireballs of resinous wood down the hillside, which fitfully illuminated the bottom of the nullah. It was as if the Kanjuts were repelling an attack on our side, or had engaged in this wild firing in some sudden panic of apprehension. But I could not arrive at any certain conclusion as to what was going on. From where I stood it was a curious and fascinating spectacle. So dark was it that I appeared to be looking down into some bottomless black gulf, for nothing was to be seen save the momentary flashes of flame—as from invisible combatants in mid-space—and the phantom-like, faintly-gleaming wreaths of smoke; for it was only when the blazing fireballs were set rolling that one could distinguish anything of the solid earth.

The firing and rock-rolling were carried on through the night with little intermission. At dawn I looked down from the ridge and saw that our two seven-pounders were shelling the lower sanga, and that the whole of the little gully in which Spedding's men had commenced to make a road on the morning of the 3rd, was packed with sepoys—Gurkhas and Ragu Pertabs—sitting as close as they could together. This led me to suppose that Spedding was working out of sight lower down, and that the advance would soon be made.

The enemy on the opposite ridge now opened fire both on my picket and on the fort below; so, in accordance with the orders I had received, I set my men to fire volleys at the loopholes of these sangas in order to silence them.

It was a bitterly cold morning, and we were glad when the sun rose to give us a little warmth. The air was very clear and the snows of Rakaposhi were not veiled by mists, as they had been for days, but gleamed in unsullied whiteness, towering in solemn peace above this noisy valley, where the men were so busy killing each other, or, to speak more accurately, trying to do so; for so far we were only firing at each other from behind our respective stone walls, and this is not a very sanguinary business.

Hour after hour passed by, and still the signal I was anxiously looking out for did not appear on the gun-bastion. The firing became intermittent, at last ceased altogether on both sides, and a complete silence followed. Our sepoys, several hundreds strong, were still crouching motionless in the gully; but no other men, friends or foes, were anywhere visible.

We waited thus, shivering in the freezing air on the ridge, until the afternoon, when Captain Stewart came up with some sepoys to relieve me, and I was at last able to obtain information as to the meaning of the mysterious doings below.

The men I saw in the gully were to have led the attack, and were provided with scaling-ladders for the assault of the enemy's lower sanga. They had been placed in the gully, under cover of the night, ready to push forward as soon as a track had been opened below. It was clear that information of our preparations had been carried over to Maiun by spies in our camp, and from Maiun forwarded to the sangas of the Nilt nullah. The enemy, no doubt under the impression that our attack was to be made by night, had strongly reinforced these sangas, and had proceeded to oppose the passage of the nullah by the firing and rock-rolling I had heard. They had thus anticipated us, and to such an extent had they strengthened the sangas at this point that our guns had this morning proved quite ineffectual to silence them. It was obvious that the projected advance would be attended by heavy losses, and that our already too small body of British officers would be still further reduced. Under these circumstances Captain Bradshaw abandoned his intention, and the attack was postponed until the conditions should be more favourable.

Between the top of the gully and the fort extended

that open flat, exposed to the raking fire of several sangas, from which we had been repulsed with loss on December 3. Our sepoys could not be taken back in broad daylight across that fatal place without something approaching to a massacre ensuing; and they consequently had to remain some fourteen hours altogether in this freezing hollow, to which the sun's rays could not penetrate, before they were able to silently creep away in the darkness.

The next day, December 9, some men were observed upon the opposite bank of the Kanjut River, upon whom our sepoys opened fire, until it became evident that these people had no hostile intention, but wished to communicate with us. One of our officers accordingly walked down to the river-bank, and made signs to them that they could come on with safety. All firing ceased on both sides, and one of the men swam across the river on a *mushok*, and was escorted to our headquarters.

He brought a letter from the Thum of Hunza, which stated that His Majesty was quite prepared to make peace, but that he would not accede to our demands as expressed in Colonel Durand's ultimatum, and was as determined as ever to have no roads made through his country. He pointed out that the capture of Nilt was but a small affair, of which we had no cause to boast, and had been more or less anticipated by his generals; but that we must know that it would be impossible for us to advance any farther, so impregnable were his defences. The envoy carried back our Political Officer's reply, in which the thum was informed that it was useless for him to send us letters unless he was prepared to do as the Government of India had ordered. Half an hour after the envoy had left our camp hostilities were renewed, and an exceptionally lively little artillery and rifle fire was exchanged, as if to make up for the time wasted in the futile truce.

The cold increased daily, and the steep mountain behind us so shut us in that the sun's rays could only reach our camp for about half an hour a day. The snow came ever lower down the hillsides; but, luckily, so far, none fell in the valley; the thum's enchantments had not yet sent us any bad weather.

This long check in the face of the enemy, and our repeated failures to turn their position, did not exercise such a depressing effect upon the troops as might have been expected, and the men seemed cheery enough. There was a good deal of work to do, and amusements were found to occupy spare time. Footballs had been brought from Gilgit, and now sepoys and officers used to play together every afternoon. The Gurkhas were very fond of the game, and threw themselves into it with great energy and boisterous laughter, evidently enjoying themselves thoroughly. It was funny to see one of these little men kick the ball. His sturdy leg would never bend in the least, but he would jerk it up quite straight from the hip, as if there were no joint in his knee. The enemy either looked upon football as some dangerous magic rite, or objected to our enjoying ourselves, for whenever the game commenced they would drum on their tomtoms, and open fire upon the football-ground from the numerous sher bachas that were posted on the mountains. It was an original experience to play football under an artillery fire; but the sher bachas made such very bad practice that our players and spectators paid not the slightest attention to them. We had an opportunity once of retaliating on these would-be sport-spoilers. Some men began to play at polo on a maidan beyond Thol, under the impression that they were out of range; but our marksmen with Martini-Henrys at the loopholes of Nilt showed them that they were mistaken, and made the players scurry away. Now that it was freezing hard we formed slides, and used to 'keep the pot boiling' to keep our circulation up. Beech and myself would occasionally make an attempt to establish golf-links, but we discovered that the ground was hopelessly bad. We constructed an amphitheatre, one side of which was guaranteed to be bullet-proof, and here, round a huge fire, the officers would sometimes sit at night to enjoy a jolly smoking-concert, for we had plenty of musical talent in the camp, and no less than two banjoists.

Each night our engineers were at work at the bottom of the Nilt nullah building sangas, the most advanced of which was in the torrent-bed, right under the enemy's lower sanga. From the shelter of these it was possible for us to closely inspect the river-cliffs for a way to surmount them, an examination which could not otherwise have been conducted by daylight under the enemy's fire. And not only did these sangas form posts of observation, but our industry in pushing forward breastwork beyond breastwork at this point puzzled and alarmed the enemy, made them concentrate their forces here, and distracted their attention from those other portions of their long line of defence which our scouts were diligently exploring in hopes of discovering the weak spot. There is little doubt that our final assault occurred where it was least expected by the enemy, else our losses would have been very heavy. To the uninitiated our proceedings at this time must have appeared mysterious, and even objectless. As a matter of fact, the game was being cleverly played.

MAIUN NULLAH FROM SILT.

On December 12 a force crossed the river by night and attempted to surprise Maiun; but the Kanjuts were on the alert, and the difficulties met with were so great that our men had to return without a shot having been fired.

On December 13 it was my turn to be in charge of the river-bed picket. To reach this one had to crawl along the precipices beneath Nilt Fort, somewhat to the risk of one's neck; for this picket could only be relieved under cover of the darkness. By daylight the marksmen in the enemy's lower sangas could have easily picked off every man of us as we descended the crags in front of them.

It was 3 A.M. when I set out through the darkness with twenty Gurkhas. I heard a good deal of firing in the direction I was going, as if the enemy were attacking the picket. Isolated as it was, the Kanjuts might have cut off this outpost without difficulty had they set themselves about it. After climbing along the steep rocky ledges for some way, we came to a long, vertical cleft in the cliff, and at the bottom of this I found the sanga which we were to occupy. It was made of sandbags, and there was only room in it for seven men standing or sitting in a cramped position, an unpleasant place to pass a day and night in in this bitter weather. I left the bulk of my men in a sheltered corner at the top of the cleft, and held the sanga with six sepoys.

When I arrived I found Lieutenant Duncan with some Sappers and Miners constructing another sanga in the bed of the Nilt nullah. This one was never completed, for it was recognised that it would be too risky to leave a handful of men in so exposed a place. Sanga-making in the nullah was a somewhat perilous business. Duncan and his men had frequently to abandon the work, and hurry for shelter to the cliff; for at short intervals the enemy rolled down their fireballs, lit up the scene, and opened a tremendous fire upon the party. After several interruptions of this sort Duncan had to leave the sanga unfinished and set out for the fort shortly before dawn.

Then all became quiet, and my six men and myself had to sit patiently in this cramped position until it was our turn to be relieved. At daybreak I had breakfast to warm myself up—cold tea and meat I had brought with me, both partly frozen. Wishing to survey my surroundings, I raised my head above the sandbags for a moment; but a bullet that whizzed by me from the lower sanga and flattened itself on the rock behind abated my curiosity, and I contented myself with such observation as was possible through the loopholes.

The hours went by without incident until some time in the afternoon, when I heard a shouting in the enemy's sangas, as if they were holding communication with men at a distance. Next, from the cliff on our side of the nullah, I heard a voice calling, 'Khabardar! khabardar!' (Have a care; be on your guard!), as if one of our men were endeavouring to warn us of an approaching danger. We stood ready, not knowing what was about to happen, and I half-expected to be attacked by a body of the enemy from round the corner of the nullah, when suddenly a man appeared, standing on the crags above us, in whom I recognised one of Spedding's Pathans. He clambered down to us, and delivered some written instructions to me. In these I was informed that a half-hour's truce had been arranged to give the enemy an opportunity of burying their numerous dead, who were scattered all over the side of the nullah, and that I was therefore not to allow my men to fire during that period.

We took advantage of this suspension of hostilities to step out of the confined sanga, and stretch our legs a bit on the sands of the river-bed. The Kanjuts observed the truce faithfully, and did not open fire upon us; the defenders of their near sangas did not venture to show themselves, but I perceived that the walls of Maiun were crowded with people. Not having a watch with me, and not having any idea when the stipulated half-hour was supposed to commence and when it would be over, I did not allow my men to stay outside many minutes. Besides, to promenade thus within seventy yards of so many of the enemy's rifles might prove too strong a temptation for some of them, so we soon retired once more to the security of our uncomfortable little breastwork.

I saw nothing of the burial-party, and afterwards learnt that the object of the truce had fallen through. Through the Puniali interpreters we had informed the enemy that they could carry off their dead without fear of molestation. The Kanjuts replied that they would do so by night. To this we objected. We could not have the tribesmen prowling about the nullah in the darkness, when they might have attempted to seize our river-bed sanga, or been up to some other mischief. So they were told that they must carry off their dead by daylight, or not at all. 'Then keep our dead' came back the enemy's message. 'Throw them into the river if you like. Dead men are of no use to us.' They were evidently suspicious of our motives, and imagined that we were enticing them to come out of their sangas by daylight, and so disclose to us the paths by which they could be reached.

During the few minutes that I was outside the sanga I had a good look at the position opposite, but could see nothing like a feasible track. The easiest ascent appeared to be by the Ziarat; but it was here that the ingenious enemy had directed the watercourse over the cliff, and produced an unassailable slope of ice. Shortly after dusk another messenger came down to me with instructions that I should bring my men back to camp, as no picket would be stationed in the nullah that night. In fact, this little sanga was never afterwards held by us.

Still we remained day after day before these seemingly impregnable heights; but there were never wanting men to volunteer for the dangerous service of exploring the precipices by night to find a road. The sepoys of the Kashmir Bodyguard Regiment especially distinguished themselves at this work. A plucky Dogra in that regiment, named Nagdu, was engaged night after night in these reconnaissances, and, as I shall show, much of the credit for our victory of December 20 is due to this man's perseverance and heroism.

He was a skilled cragsman, and it was his idea that it would be possible to scale the high cliffs where they faced our blockhouse on the ridge. He suggested that he should take with him twelve good men accustomed to hill-climbing, and make the attempt on a dark night. He would himself go first, and lower a rope when necessary to assist the others. On reaching the summit they would surprise the little sanga that stood at the cliff-edge, and by holding it would prevent the enemy from rolling down rocks on our troops, who, according to his plan, were to ascend by the same route on the following dawn and carry the whole position.

It was a bold design, and it appeared to be practicable; so the brave Nagdu was allowed to try what he could do. One dark night he and a party of men of his regiment noiselessly ascended the Nilt nullah. But the watchful—or well-informed—Kanjuts were aware of the presence of our sepoys, and they had not gone far before the alarm was given. First a gun was fired as signal in the enemy's lower sanga, and at once a loud shout was carried up the mountain-side from sanga to sanga, the tomtoms beat, the fireballs and rock avalanches plunged down the precipices, and fire was opened from a hundred rifles and jezails. Nagdu and his men had to shelter themselves behind a rock for a time, and then to seize what opportunities they could to creep from cover to cover back to the fort. On the following day it was observed that two new sangas had arisen in the night just over the portion of the cliff that Nagdu had proposed to scale.

This did not discourage the indomitable Nagdu, who tried again and again, and at last his perseverance was rewarded. He succeeded in climbing alone, unobserved, to the foot of the enemy's sangas; and now, having satisfied himself that the thing could be done, he returned, and promptly thought out the outline of the scheme of attack which was afterwards adopted with success. Nagdu is a quiet, simple-looking young fellow, to whom no one at first sight would attribute the possession of many brains; but he proved himself to be an excellent soldier, as full of resource as he was brave. His portrait will be found on page 426. Of the two sepoys in the picture, he is the tall one on the left.

From information which we received later on, it appeared that this prolonged check in the face of the enemy, disagreeable as it was to us, was not without its advantages. Had we crossed the nullah on the 2nd or 3rd we should probably have encountered resolute resistance at the other strong natural positions between Nilt and Hunza, in which case there would have been heavy losses on both sides; and as our British officers would have had to do the leading at each assault, we should have had few left by the time we reached the Hunza capital. The tribesmen had been told that we intended to kill them all, and that it was therefore best for them to fight to the bitter end. But they now had time to realize the humane manner in which we treated the prisoners, and began to understand that if they laid down their arms they would receive no harm at our hands. They consequently were not so determined as they had been to prolong the resistance; they became anxious to return to the cultivation of their neglected fields, for it was now the season at which the crops are sown in the valley; dissensions, too, began to rise in their midst, for there was a strong party hostile to the Hunza thum, and friendly to the exiled princes of the royal family. So at last, when the thum fled the country and deserted his subjects, these were disposed to come to terms with us. The deliberation with which we proceeded must also have astonished and dismayed the tribesmen, who had never before had experience of a properly organised expedition. The Kashmir armies which had previously invaded the valley had never been able to keep the field for more than a week or so; no arrangements for commissariat having been made for a longer period, the troops had to return or starve. But now the Kanjuts saw the almost daily trains of grain and ammunition coming into our camp from Gilgit, and realized that there was small chance of our retiring.

The check, however, had lasted quite long enough, and was beginning to be attended with danger. Our spies informed us that the Kanjut captains were making arrangements to seize the Chaichar Pari and cut off our convoys of grain; while the numerous little village republics of the Shinaka valleys had at last, after the meeting of many tiny Parliaments, come to one mind, and, despite paralysing Home Rule and the small-pox, which was also raging in their midst, were rapidly mobilising their forces to attack us.

The road that had been opened out by our engineers between Gilgit and Chalt was, as I have explained, merely temporary, and the bridges that had been thrown across the Gilgit and Hunza rivers would be swept away by the swollen waters as soon as the mountain snows commenced to melt. It was, of course, of extreme importance that our communication should not be interrupted at the termination of the winter; so Spedding was employed for some days in making arrangements for the construction of a permanent bridge at Chalt—the most indispensable work of all, for the Kanjut River becomes an unfordable torrent in the spring.

On December 15 Spedding returned to Nilt. He had an interview with our Political Officer and others at headquarters, and the position was talked over. Spedding was told that it would be necessary for him to take his Pathans back to the Gilgit road, as the grain question was now causing great anxiety, and it would be difficult, if not impossible, to feed his men any longer. Their services, moreover, were not now needed at Nilt itself, whereas there was a great deal of most important work for them to finish on the road below. Spedding was also led to understand that there was very little chance indeed of our force making any further advance this winter. The very fact of his Pathans being sent away seemed to point to the same conclusion.

Spedding only remained a few hours with us, and then rode back to Chalt, whither he was followed the next morning by his staff of engineers and his Pathans. I was very sorry to part with my friends, who themselves would have been most loth to go had they the slightest idea that there was a possibility of further fighting.

Spedding had volunteered to place himself and his men at the disposal of the Government for the purposes of this expedition. Their work had been most arduous, their conduct under fire and their discipline had been admirable. It would be difficult, I imagine, to mention an instance, since the Mutiny days, of such splendid service rendered by civilians in time of war. Spedding, with his talent for organisation and his great experience in the transport and the feeding of large bodies of men in a desert country hundreds of miles from the base, was an invaluable aid to Colonel Durand. This good work was done in a patriotic spirit, not for pecuniary remuneration, but at a considerable cost to Spedding himself. Such men deserve well of their country, and the Indian Government ought to be especially grateful to him.

It was funny to observe the face of my Kashmiri servant, Subhana, on the morning of the 16th. Through the door of the little tent which I shared with Beech, as I lay in bed, I saw him gaily packing up my baggage, under the impression that I was going back with the rest. He was laughing and joking, in the highest spirits at the prospect of escaping from the perils and alarms of war so uncongenial to his Kashmir soul. I did not interrupt him for a few minutes, and then I gently called him. The poor fellow stood smiling in front of me. 'Do not pack up my things,' I said; 'I am not going away.' 'Not going away, your Excellency!' he cried, and his face fell with consternation. I am afraid that we took a malicious delight in watching this sudden revulsion of spirits. There were no more smiles and jokes for Subhana that morning. His happier fellow-servants, who were returning to peaceful lands, bade him be of good cheer, and plied him with the usual cheap philosophy. 'As a good Mussulman,' they said, 'you must be resigned to your fate. It is Kismet; it is not right to grieve about it. He whose fate it is to live, lives. He whose fate it is to die by the sword, dies by the sword,' which was all very well for them, setting out, as they were, for the security of the Vale of Kashmir, but was poor consolation for the unhappy Subhana.

Our little mess having now broken up, I was kindly invited to join the head-quarters mess for the rest of the campaign.

CHAPTER XXVII

THE FIGHT OF DECEMBER 20—THE STORMING-PARTY—THE CLIFF SCALED—CAPTURE OF THE FOUR SANGAS—THE ENEMY'S POSITION TURNED—FLIGHT OF THE GARRISONS—BEHAVIOUR OF THE IMPERIAL SERVICE TROOPS—ANOTHER V.C.

STILL our little force remained in front of the great gorge, reconnaissances, feints, and attempted night surprises following each other, until at last, as was certain to be the reward of such patient but determined trying, the day came when an admirably-designed plan of attack was carried out, and proved entirely successful.

Nagdu, as I have said, had scaled the cliffs by night, and demonstrated the practicability of the ascent so far as he himself was concerned; but so difficult was the way he had discovered, that it was held to be impossible to take a body of troops up these precipices in the dark. It was therefore proposed that the sangas should be stormed in broad daylight, under cover of a heavy fire from the ridge on our side of the nullah. Nagdu himself suggested this plan to our Political Officer when describing what he had ascertained of the nature of the ground. He said that the cliff fell away so steeply from the sangas that the defenders could not possibly see what was going on below, unless they came out of their cover and looked over the edge, and this our marksmen should be able to prevent them doing.

A careful examination of the position through glasses from our blockhouse on the ridge completed the information that Nagdu had brought. The accessibility of this portion of the cliff having been thus determined, it was obviously important that we should make our attack without delay, else the enemy, as they had invariably done hitherto, would get wind of our intention, and take steps to frustrate it.

At this time Captain Bradshaw happened to be at Gilgit, having been compelled to ride there in order to consult with Colonel Durand on the troublesome subject of supplies and other matters; the command therefore devolved on Captain Colin Mackenzie, who carried the above plan into execution.

Complete secrecy was observed, and the spies in our camp had no suspicion of what was about to happen. On the afternoon of December 19 I was called aside, and told that on that night Lieutenant Manners Smith and Lieutenant Taylor, with 100 men of the Kashmir Bodyguard Regiment, fifty of whom were Gurkhas, the other fifty Dogras, all hill-men and accustomed to clamber over difficult precipices, were to set out for the bottom of the Nilt nullah, with the object of ascending its bed till they came to the foot of the cliff at the point where it was intended to scale it, and there remain hidden until daylight, when our sharpshooters would line the ridge above and cover their advance. I was informed that I had been put in command of the detachment of the 20th Punjab Infantry, and that with these Pathans, the best marksmen in our force, it would be my duty on the morrow to silence one of the four sangas that were to be assaulted. I was instructed to take up a Martini-Henry that had belonged to one of our dead Gurkhas, and do my share of firing at the opposite loopholes, for anyone who could shoot straight would be of use on this occasion.

E E

The moon rose at ten o'clock this night, so it was necessary that the storming-party should reach their hiding-place in the nullah before that hour. While we were in the middle of our dinner at the headquarters mess, it being seven o'clock, Lieutenant Manners Smith left us; the little force under his command was paraded, and then noiselessly marched off under cover of the darkness. The men took with them their greatcoats, blankets, and cooked rations. Manners Smith has, as I have said, earned a reputation as a most intrepid cragsman among the mountaineers of the Gilgit district. No better officer than he could have been chosen to lead men up that rocky wall.

It was calculated that the best part of two hours would be occupied by the storming-party in reaching the hiding-place in the nullah; so it may be imagined how anxiously we others, sitting in the mess-tent, listened for every sound, knowing that not only might this attempt prove unsuccessful should the enemy detect the presence of our men in the nullah, but that a fearful havoc would not improbably be wrought amongst the latter by the deadly rock-avalanches from the sangas.

One hour had passed quietly, when suddenly there arose a loud noise of cheering and beating of tomtoms from the fortress of Maiun. We held our breath to listen, but no sound of firing or of falling rocks followed; all was still as ever in the Nilt nullah. This was very reassuring; for it was evident this was no alarm that the Maiun men had raised, but that, on the contrary, they were off their guard, and were engaging in one of the periodical orgies with which they were wont to keep their spirits up, while the noise of their festivity would probably distract the attention of the men garrisoning the sangas above the Nilt nullah. From our point of view the men of Maiun could not have chosen a more opportune night for their *tamasha*.

Two hours and more had passed since the two British officers and their one hundred men had left us, and still there was no sound in the nullah. All was well; the enemy had neither observed nor heard our men as they crept up under their defences. We went to bed that night relieved of our apprehensions and hopeful for the morrow. It seemed as if our luck had indeed turned at last.

Before daybreak on the 20th the covering-party paraded, ascended the ridge, and took up a position near our blockhouse, facing the four sangas that were to be stormed. We had 135 rifles, all selected shots, viz. fifty rifles of the 5th Gurkhas under Lieutenant Boisragon, twenty five rifles of the 20th Punjab Infantry under myself, thirty rifles of the Ragu Pertab Regiment under Lieutenant Townshend, and thirty rifles of the Bodyguard Regiment under Lieutenant Baird. Lieutenant Molony was also here with the two seven-pounders. Lieutenant Widdicombe was left in charge of Nilt Fort, all the loopholes of which were lined with rifles, so as to prevent the enemy from sending up any reinforcements from the lower sangas to those above.

A reference to the illustration facing page 368 will clear the description of this day's fight. Our position by the blockhouse is shown on one side of the nullah; the enemy's particular four sangas that were the object of our attack are also indicated on the other side. These sangas stood on the edge of the cliff, above the only part where it was not absolutely inaccessible. It was from these that the enemy used to roll down rocks so frequently at night that a regular shoot had been worn away, appearing like a light streak against the dark cliff. The storming-party was concealed at the bottom of the nullah, between these two positions. The cliff that had to be scaled by our men was 1,200 feet or more in height.

When we came on the ridge in the freezing mist of dawn the men on picket duty there, having no idea of what was intended, looked somewhat astonished to see so many of our officers and men appear. The men of the covering-party, lying down, lined the edge of the cliff on our side, and Captain Colin Mackenzie gave the order to commence firing. We were divided into four parties, each of which now opened a steady independent fire on one particular sanga. We paid no attention to the other numerous sangas which were scattered over the opposite mountains, though they fired at us occasionally; for they were not so situated as to be able to offer any opposition to our storming-party while it was scaling the cliff. We concentrated all our fire on the four dangerous sangas, the distance between which and ourselves was between four and five hundred yards; at this range the fire of our sharpshooters was so accurate that the return fire soon slackened, and then ceased altogether. It was evident that in the face of such a shower of lead as we were directing upon them no man dared stand behind his musket at a loophole, still less come out of cover to hurl down rocks. Our two guns were also busy throwing shot and shrapnel on the four doomed breastworks.

Captain Colin Mackenzie—who, by the way, had a narrow escape, a bullet glancing off some portion of his accoutrements—had brought us up to the ridge before there was sufficient light to disclose our advance to the defenders of the forts below. But now, as day-

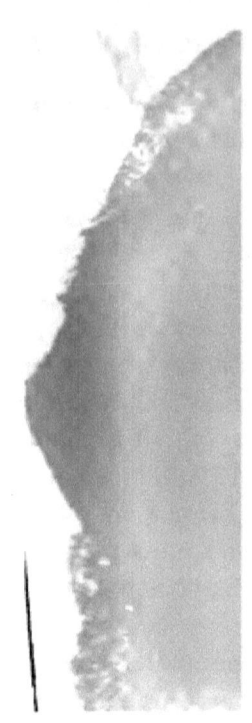

light broadened, the Kanjuts could see us from Maiun, and beat their tomtoms loudly when they heard the heavy firing, realizing that something beyond the ordinary was taking place. But so far the enemy had no suspicion of the presence of our storming-party in the nullah-bed.

It was certainly an extraordinary scene for a fight. From our ridge we looked down the crags on the far-stretching landscape of the Kanjut Valley, with its winding, rushing river, its belts of terraced cultivation, and its numerous fortified villages that lay beneath the stupendous cliffs; while, high above the lesser mountains that enclose the valley, the snowy summits of the Hindoo Koosh rose into the cloudless sky. Scarce had the first faint wreaths of smoke from the morning fires begun to rise above the houses than all the parapets and roofs of the towered fortresses below—Maiun, Thol, and the Ziarat—were crowded with spectators, anxiously watching the decisive action that was being fought on the mountain skyline high above them; while from every sanga and rough sher bacha battery all along the enemy's line of defences, from the mountains on one side of the Kanjut River to those on the other, the tribesmen looked on in their hundreds, awaiting the result.

Lieutenant Manners Smith had been instructed not to commence his ascent until we had carried on this fire for half an hour. Accordingly, after the specified time had elapsed, he with his fifty Gurkhas began to clamber up the steep rocks, Lieutenant Taylor following with the fifty Dogras. There were 1,200 feet of hard climbing before them; and from our ridge we could see the little stream of men gradually winding up, now turning to the right, now to the left, now going down again for a little way when some insurmountable obstacle presented itself, to try again at some other point, presenting very much the appearance of a scattered line of ants picking their way up a rugged wall.

At last Manners Smith, who had been scrambling up, active as a cat, ahead of his men, attained a point some 800 feet above the nullah-bed; and here he met with a check. After a thorough trial, it was obvious to him, and still more so to us who could see the whole situation from our ridge, that the precipice above him was absolutely inaccessible; it was therefore now necessary for him and his men to turn round and retrace their steps down to the nullah-bed.

Nearly two hours had thus been wasted. Looking on with some dismay, we began to fear lest this should prove yet another of our failures. But though this check had caused considerable delay, the attack was by no means to be abandoned yet. Lieutenant Manners Smith is not a man to be easily discouraged; he was determined to accomplish the scaling of the cliff somewhere, and he now flag-signalled to Captain Colin Mackenzie that he would make another attempt a little lower down the nullah; this he accordingly did, as soon as he had got his scattered party together again.

He now hit upon an easier route, probably the one Nagdu had originally taken in the night. As we fired over his head at the now silenced sangas, we saw him start from this fresh point and clamber higher and higher, till he and a handful of the more active and venturesome sepoys who immediately followed him were within sixty yards of one of the four sangas on the edge of the cliff.

It was, happily, not until this moment that the enemy had any idea that a party of sepoys was scaling the heights. The Maiun people first detected our men, and shouted a warning across the river, which was carried up the mountain-side from sanga to sanga until the men holding the four sangas with which we were immediately concerned realized that their position was being stormed, and that unless they bestirred themselves to make a resolute defence our sepoys would be amongst them, and their retreat would be cut off. Rocks were now thrown over the sanga walls, and showers of stones poured down the cliff. Happily, by this time most of the gallant little party had passed the points most exposed to this deadly method of defence, and the rocks either swept down the steep shoots to the left of our men, or bounded harmlessly over their heads. Several men, however, were more or less seriously wounded. Lieutenant Taylor himself was knocked down by a rock, but luckily received no injuries of any account.

The two British officers manœuvred their men admirably, watching their opportunities, working their way from point to point, with cool judgment, between the avalanches, and slowly gaining the heights foot by foot. It was a fearful thing to watch from our side. A little lack of caution or an unlucky accident might have so easily led to scores of our men being swept off the face of the cliff during this perilous ascent. We poured in a fiercer fire than ever to silence the sangas; but we could not prevent the defenders from throwing rocks from the inside of their breastworks, which, dislodging others, produced dangerous cataracts of stones.

Still our men pushed pluckily on up the steep slopes under the sangas; while the Kanjuts became desperate, knowing that there was no hope for them should the sepoys once attain the summit. Some of the enemy exhibited great bravery, boldly standing out in the open and rolling down the ready-piled up rocks as fast as they were able, until they were shot down by the marksmen on our side of the ridge.

At last—and it was a moment of intense suspense for the onlookers—we saw Lieutenant Manners Smith make a sudden dash forward, reach the foot of the first sanga, clamber round to the right of it, and step on to the flat ground beside it. A few sepoys were close at his heels, and then the men, having got to the back of the sanga, the rifles of the storming-party were for the first time brought into play. A few shots in rapid succession, a rush through the opening behind with bayonets and kukris, Lieutenant Manners Smith himself pistolling the first man, and the sanga was ours, those of the garrison who were not killed within being shot as they fled down the hillside by our marksmen on the ridge, and from the battlements of Nilt Fort.

More men having now rejoined Lieutenant Manners Smith, the other three sangas were rapidly cleared in the same way, Nagdu, bold as ever, rushing into one sanga, and fighting the defenders single-handed. The position being now secure, Lieutenant Manners Smith collected his men, and a short halt was called until the remaining Gurkhas and the Dogras under Lieutenant Taylor had come up. Then, dividing into parties, the sepoys attacked and carried the numerous sangas which studded the hillside, firing their roofs as they emptied each one. Some of our men swarmed high up the mountain-side, captured the sher bachas posted there, and rolled them down the precipices.

A determined resistance was offered by some of the enemy's marksmen, who fought to the death and asked no quarter; but seeing how desperate was their situation, between the storming-party on one side and our rifles on the ridge, the Kanjuts became flurried, their fire was unsteady, and the casualties on our side amounted only to four men wounded. Then the tribesmen lost heart and began to bolt precipitately from their defences; at least a hundred of them were shot down as they attempted to escape, and many of those who succeeded in getting away from the ridge were picked off by our riflemen in the fort.

And now the tomtoms that had been beating in the distance became silent, and suddenly we saw a strange sight beneath us, which made our men raise cheer upon cheer. The garrisons of the enemy's fortresses, realizing that we had effectively turned this position, on whose impregnability they had relied, that we had outflanked them, and that their retreat would be speedily cut off did they remain where they were, were seized with panic, and we looked down upon long streams of men hurrying up the valley on both sides of the river, the defenders of Maiun, Thol, and the Ziarat, hundreds upon hundreds of Kanjuts, racing up to Hunza and Nagar for their lives, and abandoning to us all the country within sight. Many horsemen, too, were galloping up the valley, evidently notables; and among them, as we afterwards learnt, were the leaders of the Kanjut forces, their general, the Wazir Dadu, and the infamous Uzr Khan of Nagar.

These terror-stricken people were not able to get away so fast as they would have liked; for just beyond Maiun the mountain falls precipitously into the river, and for some distance the path is very narrow and difficult. Here the hurrying fugitives were checked by a tremendous block of humanity. We were surprised to see what large garrisons these forts had contained. Our guns shelled the flying tribesmen, but with little effect from this distance.

The attack had thus proved a complete success. As one of our officers remarked, one might see many a bigger fight than this was, but never a prettier one. The whole affair was very cleverly planned and conducted; while the dash with which the Kashmir sepoys,

A DOGRA AND A GURKHA SEPOY OF THE KASHMIR BODYGUARD REGIMENT.

under their two British officers, rushed the sangas, evidently demoralised the bulk of the Kanjuts who held them; and to this must be attributed the extraordinary disparity between our casualties and those of the enemy.

The 5th Gurkhas had gallantly borne the brunt of

the first day's fight. It had now been the turn of the men of the Kashmir Bodyguard Regiment to prove of what stuff they were made; and they certainly acquitted themselves admirably in this assault, which was calculated to try the nerve of the staunchest soldiers that ever fought. It was grand to see the way they followed the two British lieutenants on this desperate venture. The Imperial Service troops distinguished themselves in this, the first campaign in which they have been employed, and have shown that, when properly led, they can be fully relied upon for the defence of our frontier.

In recognition of the gallantry he displayed while leading this attack, the Queen has conferred the Victoria Cross on Manners Smith. Thus, though this was but one of our little wars, no less than three of our officers won that coveted decoration, while another was appointed to the Distinguished Service Order. But this was a war of forlorn hopes. In an expedition such as this, when a handful of men is sent into a remote and difficult region to drive a well-armed foe, greatly superior in numbers, out of almost impregnable positions, it is only by such feats of individual heroism that victory is attained with so little loss of life. A show of indecision on our part before Nilt, a lack of fearless boldness in the hour of attack, would have led to far heavier losses on both sides and possible disaster on ours.

CHAPTER XXVIII

ADVANCE OF OUR FORCE—PRISONERS TAKEN TO CHALT—SUBMISSION OF NAGAR—FLIGHT OF THE THUM OF HUNZA—SUBMISSION OF HUNZA—OCCUPATION OF NAGAR.

It was about midday when we ceased firing from the ridge, and, led by our commander, we relieved our feelings with three ringing cheers. And now we had more work before us; for Captain Colin Mackenzie did not neglect the maxim which teaches that a flying foe should be followed up. It was not his intention to give the Kanjuts the opportunity to organise another stand. They were now 'on the run,' and they were to be most energetically kept 'on the run' by our troops, until their complete submission had been effected.

The guns and marksmen were now withdrawn from the ridge, and fell back on the camp. We had time to breakfast before the force was formed up and a general advance ordered.

It was about two o'clock when we reached the fort and proceeded to cross the foot of the Nilt nullah in order to effect a junction with Lieutenants Manners-Smith and Taylor, who had in the meanwhile been leading their men down the mountain-side to the river-bank, clearing the sangas before them as they went. Lieutenant Townshend led our advance-guard of Ragu Pertabs: then came the detachment of the 20th Punjab Infantry, and then the 5th Gurkhas.

Our Sappers and Miners were opening out a path between the fort and the enemy's lower sanga; but it was not yet practicable for mules, so Molony and his guns had to remain at Nilt until late in the evening, when the work was completed, and the battery was able to proceed.

The force now defiled down the steep path into the ravine which had given us so much trouble for the last eighteen days. We had to step over a number of bodies of the Kanjuts who had been killed in the action of the 2nd; the slaughter of the fugitives on that day had evidently been greater than we had supposed. All this while we heard firing on the hills above us, where desperate men, like wild beasts at bay, stuck to their sangas and shot at our men, until they themselves were bayoneted.

The path, after zigzagging up the precipitous farther side of the nullah, passes, as I have explained, under a gateway, through the centre of the enemy's large lower sanga. This gateway had been filled up with a barricade of stones eight feet thick, which had to be removed before our men could get by.

The sanga was known to be still full of the enemy's sharpshooters, from whom resistance was anticipated; but, as we came up, those loopholes from which for eighteen days a fire of dangerous precision had always been opened on any one of us who ventured to show himself within sight of them, remained quite silent. Our riflemen in Nilt Fort had made it impossible for the defenders to take to flight, and they now found themselves completely cut off. They had ceased all firing for some time; so it was supposed that they were ready to surrender, and by signs and shouts our willingness to give quarter was communicated to them. Then Lieutenant

Townshend cut his way through the abattis at the foot of the sanga, and clambered up the wall on to the roof. The Kanjuts made signs of submission, and helped him with their hands to descend into their works, where he found himself in the midst of ninety-two of the enemy. He ordered them to lay down their arms, and they at once obeyed him.

Lieutenant Manners Smith had by this time brought some of his men down the mountain-side to the back of the sanga, which was thus surrounded by our men.

These ninety-two were picked marksmen, fine-looking fellows most of them. They prayed for quarter by grovelling on the ground and eating grass, to indicate that they were no longer fighting-men, but as mere beasts of the field.

Our Sappers and Miners now made an opening through the stone barricade that blocked the gateway, our force ascended the steep cliff, and slowly defiled through the sanga. We found its walls and roof to be of immense strength; it looked as if it could have defied our little seven-pounders for ever.

The prisoners were sitting down in a long row outside, looking very disconsolate, poor wretches. Their arms were piled up in the sanga, a somewhat motley collection. Every man had been armed with a sword and shield, and a gun of some sort. We found a good many rifles, principally Sniders, cases of ammunition from our Government arsenal at Dum Dum—how did they get here?—and a large quantity of matchlocks, some of them handsome and well-finished weapons.

The Ragu Pertabs now marched across the cultivated maidan to Thol, clearing out the Ziarat and sangas on the way. In some of these little breastworks of stones and tree-branches a few Kanjuts still held out obstinately, and twenty-two were shot or bayoneted, while others asked for and were granted quarter. As soon as a sanga was taken its roof was fired, and columns of smoke were to be seen rising in all directions on the plain and on the mountain-sides.

In the meanwhile the Punialis crossed the river, occupied the abandoned fortress of Maiun, and then proceeded along the Hunza bank, having instructions to destroy the enemy's defences as they went. The main body of our force was now pushed on to the Nagar fortress of Pisan, some seven miles off, where a deep nullah formed one of the enemy's strongest positions, which it was advisable for us to seize before the Kanjuts should have time to recover from their panic and make another stand. Our troops encountered no resistance, found Pisan deserted, and encamped there for the night.

Captain Colin Mackenzie was determined to follow up the enemy to the Hunza and Nagar capitals as rapidly as was possible, and the forced march of the following day was a most creditable performance, when it is considered that this is possibly the most difficult country that has ever been traversed by troops, the rugged track up the valley beyond Nilt winding high up the precipitous mountain-side in places, crossing wearisome slopes of boulders, the couloirs of glaciers and frozen streams, and being generally as fatiguing a road as it is possible to imagine. The baggage, of course, could not keep up with the troops, and was, indeed, separated from them for two days, while the country had to be relied upon to supply food.

It was well for me that I had been marching for half a year, and was in good training, for while the troops were enjoying their well-earned repose I was set to travel two stages in the course of this night. One hundred and eighteen prisoners had been taken in the lower sanga and in the neighbouring defences. As we could not well feed or guard these men here, it was decided to send them at once to Gilgit; so while our force was advancing to Pisan, I was ordered to escort them as far as Chalt with my detachment of the 20th Punjab Infantry, and then overtake the main body without delay. This meant for me, as it turned out, a journey of forty-five miles—a forced march with a vengeance over such a rough country as this.

I had my prisoners searched and disarmed, sent some who were wounded into Nilt Fort, and had the remaining 114 lashed together in couples by the wrists with the rope matches of their jezails. I was unable to recross the nullah for a considerable time, as the long, slow stream of Balti baggage-coolies was now advancing and blocking up the narrow path.

It was dusk before we got away from Nilt Fort, and then my melancholy train of captives was formed into a long line, and marched two-and-two down the valley, the twenty-four sepoys of the escort guarding them with loaded rifles and fixed bayonets. It soon became very dark, and looking behind I could see the blaze of many burning sangas, while there was a glow in the sky to show that there were some more extensive conflagrations higher up the valley. The Thum of Hunza, as I afterwards learnt, had set fire to village after village as he fled up the valley with his followers, destroying the winter food-supplies and other property of his own subjects, who had fought too gallantly for such a miscreant. There was still to be heard the sound of occasional firing on the hills, where resolute Kanjuts were dying game in their sangas.

There was, as I knew, a chance of the enemy

making a last, determined stand at the capital of Hunza, a very strong position; so I was anxious to be back with the force as quickly as possible, fearing lest I should miss the storming of the thum's great castle, a wonderful place from all accounts, full of the spoils of a hundred pillaged caravans. But it was not possible to push along fast on this dark night, the crossing of the two defiles and of the Kotal ridge beyond proving especially difficult. I was ever tripping over the boulders I could not see, or jarring myself by suddenly dropping with all my weight into an unexpected hollow, making the journey a far more fatiguing one than it would have been by day.

On the Kotal and at the bridge across the Kanjut River we were challenged by the pickets stationed there, and the sepoys were delighted to hear the stirring news I brought. It was ten o'clock when we reached Chalt Fort. Lieutenant Williams, now in command at Chalt, and Wilkinson and Maynard, of Spedding's staff, who had been left here to construct the permanent bridge, turned out of bed, anxious to hear the story of the day's doings. Sekandar Khan was also here, beside himself with joy at the defeat of his bloodthirsty relatives.

I gave orders that we should set out from Chalt when the moon had risen sufficiently to afford us good light to find our way; and in the meanwhile we snatched a few hours' sleep. At 3 A.M. we were off again, and retraced our steps for the eight miles or so to Nilt, which we reached shortly after daybreak.

Here I found Lieutenant Widdicombe in charge of the fort. He told me the force was to have left Pisan at dawn, and would probably accomplish the double march to Nagar before night. It was seven miles from

F F

Nilt to Pisan; and another twenty-one miles from Pisan to Nagar; so I saw that I had little time to rest if I was to overtake the force this day.

I left my Pathans to follow me at a more leisurely pace under their native officer, and proceeded alone. It was a most interesting day's journey; but I was too fatigued to appreciate this as I toiled along. As I crossed the nullah, the signs of war were visible around me: dead men were lying on the frozen ground, and from the blackened roofs of Maiun and Thol rose dense volumes of smoke; every now and again there would be an explosion, and some fortress-tower would come tumbling down. I walked on and saw no natives; the whole country appeared to be abandoned.

I passed smouldering village after village, each a group of flat-roofed stone houses crowded together, and surrounded by lofty walls, with towers at intervals, and deep moats, like some city of mediæval Europe. These fortresses were much more solidly built than any of the Dogra forts I had seen in Kashmir; the houses, too, were well constructed, and had some pretensions to comfort; while extensive terraces of irrigated fields, beautifully tended, showed that the Hunza-Nagaris are industrious agriculturists as well as bold robbers. The whole country, indeed, presented an appearance of prosperity and civilisation that took me by surprise, and compared very favourably with those poverty-stricken regions of the Kashmir State in which I had been recently travelling. But the valley is much over-populated, and the supply of grain is so insufficient that during some of the summer months the people are compelled to subsist on apricots and other fruit alone, the harvest being stored for winter use.

After passing Thol I came to Gulmit Fort, then to

Pisan, outside which the ashes of bivouac-fires and the bones of goats that were strewn about showed where our force had encamped on the previous night. Pisan, its roof-trees still burning—the thum's malicious handiwork—looked woefully desolate. Not a human being was in sight; but a number of shaggy goats, sheep, and fowls were wandering about, disconsolately bleating and cackling among the ruins, evidently astonished and dismayed at the strange revolution that had occurred in their little world.

The scenery of the valley became more magnificent as I advanced. I passed the most picturesque forts perched on awful crags, such strongholds as Doré would have drawn to illustrate some mediæval legend. Great glaciers were visible at the head of every wild defile, and in one place a glacier descended right into the river, so that one had to walk for some distance over the ice and couloirs.

At last I overtook the Balti baggage-coolies slowly struggling along under their loads, but apparently very happy; for they, as well as the sepoys, had feasted royally on the previous night off the enemy's goats and sheep at Pisan; and a Balti, a wonderfully good-tempered creature at all times, is quite boisterously cheery, despite any amount of fatigue or hardship, when his stomach is full of meat. With them was a baggage-guard of Kashmir sepoys; and I also passed a party of 5th Gurkhas, who had been crowning the heights above Pisan during the night. But there were no British officers in charge of these, and I could not ascertain from the men how far ahead our main body was. It was evident that our energetic commander, leaving baggage and supplies behind, was hurrying up the valley as fast as his men could march, and it was very unlikely that I should come up with the force until I reached their night's camping-place, wherever that might be.

I only saw one British officer this day—Bradshaw, who overtook me, having hurried up from Gilgit without resting. He had picked up a horse by the way, and would have shared it with me; but knowing how anxious he must have been to rejoin the force, I would not hear of this, so he rode on. He was able to give me a stick of chocolate and a little whisky, the most delicious meal I think I ever had.

I passed all the sepoys, coolies, straggling camp-followers, and weary baboos, and found myself alone in the enemy's country. It was fatiguing work toiling up and down the precipitous paris of the defile, but I still tramped along, in the hopes of at last catching sight of our flying force; but though I could sometimes command a view of the road ahead of me for miles, I saw nothing of it.

I noticed that all the Nagar defences now faced the river-cliff, which was lined with sangas; so, too, was it on the Hunza side of the river, these two close neighbours, as I have explained, waging frequent war on each other when not allied against invaders from without.

I now came across crowds of natives, women and children as well as men, driving the cattle back from the mountains, to which they had been taken for safety, to the villages in the valley—a proof that peace had been restored in Nagar, if not in Hunza, and that the people had great confidence in us. They came up to me with demonstrations of friendship, and explained as well as they could that the ruler of Nagar had surrendered to our Political Officer, and that there was to be no more fighting on their side of the river. The poor people seemed delighted at the treatment they had received at the hands of their victors, and the security from all molestation which had been promised them. They brought me apples, which, with iced water, was my sole nourishment until the following day; and not a bad diet either is this to work on.

The Nagaris struck me as a particularly pleasant people, and there was an honest look in their rosy faces. Many of the women were distinctly pretty. It seemed strange to be thus marching alone through the midst of a tribe that had been fighting hard with us but a few hours before, and, after doing our best to kill each other one day, to be thus on the most amicable terms the next. There are no other Eastern countries that I know of, and I should say there are few in Europe, where one could venture on such an experiment as this; but I was, indeed, perfectly safe with our recent enemies, and it must be allowed that these tribesmen never exhibited the slightest treachery in their dealings with us. They fought well; they faithfully observed truces; and, as soon as they had come to the conclusion that they had had fighting enough, they most philosophically accepted the position, and to all appearance bore us no ill-will. That they have committed acts of atrocious treachery is well known; but I suppose they were wise enough to realize the policy of conciliating us by their excellent conduct on this occasion.

However it may have been, I was allowed to travel thus almost from one end to the other of the Nagar State unmolested. Looking across the river, I saw that the Hunza villages—of which there was one every two or three miles—were, like those of Nagar, enclosed within strong, towered walls. There were but very few houses among the fields, it being the custom for the cultivators in both these insecure States to retire to the protection of their fortifications every night. All the flat steps of soil which lay between the foot of the mountains and the edge of the river-cliff were under cultivation. Arid and bare as were the mountain-sides, the peasantry had utilized every glacier stream to make a fruitful land beneath. There were large orchards of peaches, apricots, apples, and mulberries, while the vines festooned all the other trees. In the spring this must be a lovely valley indeed, the blossoming fruit-trees and the green fields below contrasting wonderfully with the mountainous wastes and terrific peaks above. On entering the Kanjut Valley by the desert defiles below Nomal the traveller would never imagine that the ascent could lead him to so pleasant a region.

Though there was peace in Nagar, this did not appear to be the case yet in Hunza; the whole country seemed deserted, and the refugees were not flocking back with their cattle from the high nullahs, as they were doing on this side.

I tramped on, still seeing no signs of our force, until sunset, when it became difficult to find the right track along the cliffs. Arriving at last before a fortified village, with great towers looming through the darkness, I passed through the gate and came upon a group of tribesmen sitting in the gallery of a house and engaged in a discussion, no doubt upon the political situation. They not unnaturally appeared very surprised to see me. I contrived to explain to them that I required a man to guide me to the place where our force was encamped, and a young fellow was at once sent with me.

We proceeded along the narrow paths, abysses whose depths the eye could not gauge in the darkness yawning beneath our feet. Three more villages were passed, and at each one the guide was changed.

We crossed some deep nullahs, and then came to a bit of road worse than any I had yet experienced on the way. The high cliffs above shut out what little light there was in the heavens, and I found it impossible to see where I was placing my feet. I stumbled over boulders, and on one or two occasions nearly tumbled off the narrow ledges. To go on in this pitch-blackness over such ground was not only very risky but fearfully fatiguing; so I at last decided to wait until the moon rose before continuing my journey.

We had turned off from the Hunza Valley, and were ascending a side-nullah; but whether this was the ravine of the Nagar River, on which the city of Nagar stands, I was unable to ascertain from my guide, who could not speak a word of Hindustani. I sat down on a ledge of rock and made him sit close by me. Amiable so far as I had found the tribesmen, I of course could not be certain that treachery was not intended; so I conveyed to the Nagari by signs that he must not venture to move away from my side, as I should make him pay the penalty of his disobedience with the weapons I had with me.

We had to remain at this cheerless spot for about three hours before the moon rose. It was freezing very hard, and a biting, though light, breeze was blowing over the rocks. Our breath froze, and depended in large icicles from our moustaches. I had no great-coat with me, and my companion, who was much more thinly clothed than I was, shivered and groaned with cold, and his teeth chattered incessantly.

At last I heard footsteps and voices, and two men came down the path. I startled them a good deal by challenging them out of the darkness; but when they discovered that I was a sahib they were at once reassured. They said they were carrying letters to Hunza. The Nagaris, they explained, were now the friends of the British. As for the Hunzas, they thought their attitude was still doubtful.

The moon rose, and, shining brightly through the frosty sky, clearly disclosed the path; so I set off again with my guide, and after about an hour's walk, on suddenly turning a corner of the cliff I saw the square towers of a large castle rising before me, lit up by the flickering glare of numerous camp-fires which were burning at the foot of the walls. 'Nagar' said my guide; and glad indeed I was to learn that I had at last reached the capital of the little State and rejoined our force.

Very welcome to me was the challenge of the sentinels. I passed through the camp, where the weary sepoys were sleeping round their fires, and asked my way to the officers' quarters. I found all my friends together in one of the chambers of the castle, lying on grass and wormwood scrub round a little fire that was burning in the middle of the mud floor. They had no baggage or blankets, and had not dined that day. They were very pleased to see me, but could give me nothing to eat; so I lay down and slept soundly, rather exhausted after my exertions.

But before turning in I heard a *résumé* of the news. The troops had left Pisan at dawn, and had made a forced march to Nagar, which they had reached at about six in the evening. During their advance they had fired volleys at any Hunzas who ventured to show themselves on the other side of the river. Early in the day messages had come from Zafar Khan, the Thum of Nagar, who was anxious to come to terms. He awaited our force at the village of Fike, had an interview with our Political Officer, and submitted unconditionally. When our force was close to Nagar letters arrived from Hunza stating that the people of that State were also ready to submit. Their Thum, his general, Wazir Dadu, and a number of followers had fled the country, and were hurrying up the valley to cross the passes of the Hindoo Koosh and take refuge on the Tagdambash Pamir, in Chinese territory. The letters also informed our Political Officer that the tribesmen had sent a party of armed men to pursue these fugitives, the Hunzas being anxious to prove their friendship to us by delivering their tyrant, for whom they evidently bore little affection, into our hands.

It therefore appeared as if all opposition had come to an end; but it had been decided that our troops should cross the river and occupy the fortress of Hunza as early as possible on the following morning, before the Thum's party should regain the ascendency, or the tribesmen, changing their minds, should attempt any treachery.

The keen mountain air here is very appetizing, and I had had but little food for two days; so hunger drove me forth at dawn on December 22, and I set out to forage with two of the officers. On the previous night the chief men of Nagar, making lying excuses, had supplied a very insufficient quantity of *ata* to our troops; but large stores of food being now discovered in the castle, the natives were compelled to be more generous, and all our men breakfasted well. None of our servants having yet come up, we procured some ata cakes and lumps of cooked meat from the Gurkhas, which we ate with our fingers with great relish and washed down with iced water.

While exploring the castle, rather an imposing building, we came upon the Thum of Nagar, wandering aimlessly through the chambers, a weak and bewildered-looking old gentlemen, who has little voice in the government of his country. It had never been his wish to resist us; but he had been terrified into doing so by his blustering neighbour, the Thum of Hunza, and by his own villainous son and heir, the fratricide, Uzr Khan.

SAMAYA.

CHAPTER XXIX

OCCUPATION OF HUNZA—HUNZA CASTLE—THE ZENANA—HUNZA WINE—
LOOT IN THE THUM'S PALACE—THE ROYAL LIBRARY—THE THUM'S
CORRESPONDENCE—A TREASURE-HUNT—THE SECRET CHAMBER.

It was not considered necessary to leave any troops in occupation of Nagar; there was very little chance of our having further trouble on that side of the river. The Thum was therefore informed that all the weapons in his country must be collected and delivered to us within a certain time, and at 10 A.M. our force evacuated the town and marched five miles back down the valley to Samaya, a village on the Nagar bank of the Kanjut River, and exactly opposite to the capital of the Hunza State. Here we found encamped those of our troops who did not form part of the main body during the forced march from Pisan; here, too, were our servants and some of the commissariat, while the baggage-coolies and camp-followers were gradually coming in.

Fourteen men of influential families now arrived from Hunza to remain with us as hostages, and so to be responsible with their lives for the safety of the small body of sepoys that was to be sent across the river to occupy the Castle of Hunza.

Samaya is situated on a cliff some 600 feet above the river, and the view from here of the Kanjut fortress on the other side is exceedingly fine. Terraces above terraces of orchards and fields, broken here and there by abrupt cliffs, slope steeply up from the river-bed to the Hunza capital, which stands high on the mountain-side—a wall-surrounded city, covering a dome-shaped hill, and so forming a pyramid of buildings rising in steps to the imposing castle of the Hunza monarchs, which crowns the summit. Behind the town yawns the dark mouth of a narrow gorge hemmed in by precipices of immense height—an awful chasm in the mountains, at the head of which are glaciers of glittering green ice and stupendous snowy peaks.

This massive fortress, which has been for hundreds of years the secure stronghold of the robber kings, inviolate until that day, stands thus boldly out, set in the midst of a sublime landscape. It would be difficult in the world to find a situation more magnificent; but on looking from Samaya one does not even notice at first the distant Hunza capital—dwarfed as it is by the gigantic scale of the surrounding scenery, it appears merely as some insignificent mole-hill.

The Hunzas are a thorough people, and were now as energetically zealous in rendering us assistance as they had been in fighting us a day or two before. A party of tribesmen in the course of a few hours threw a capital temporary bridge across the Kanjut river to facilitate the passage of our troops; and as soon as it was ready Captain Twigg, Lieutenant Boisragon, and 100 men of the 5th Gurkhas were sent from Samaya to occupy Hunza Castle.

I obtained permission to go with them, and, taking Hunza guides to show us the road, we set out. All proper precautions to ensure us against surprise were observed. The tribesmen, notorious as they are for treacherous tricks, might have been leading us into a trap by a pretended submission. The ground below

CASTLE OF HUNZA FROM SAMAYA.

Hunza was admirably adapted for an ambuscade, and to have weakened our little force by cutting off 100 of our Gurkha detachment would have been a fine *coup* for the Kanjuts, who some years back, as we knew, had entrapped and massacred a whole Dogra army by a stratagem of this sort.

The two guns were brought into position on the cliff at Samaya to cover our advance; the troops were kept ready to come to our support if we were attacked, and our ascent of the opposite hills was watched with some anxiety from the camp, until it was seen that we had safely attained the fortress and commanded the position.

We descended the cliff to the river, crossed the new-made bridge, and stood on Hunza territory. We advanced with caution, twelve Gurkhas forming our advance-guard. We slowly mounted from terrace to terrace, the path being narrow, rugged, and steep, generally with high stone walls on either side—an awkward trap to be caught in should the enemy think fit to attack us. We saw no women or children—a somewhat suspicious circumstance; but the men came out in crowds to meet us, and we must have been surrounded by a dozen times our number. These citizens of Hunza were well clothed in warm chogas; their black ringlets were tied in knots on either side, and some were of quite fair complexion, with rosy cheeks. They were certainly fine, sturdy-looking men, with frank, fearless mien. The features of many of them were finely chiselled. The strength of their chins and the determined but rather cruel expression of their mouths was noticeable, and we were struck by the frequency with which the type of the Napoleonic countenance was repeated among them.

They had a rather more truculent air than the

Nagaris. They are, indeed, supposed to be the most warlike of the two peoples, and it is they who carried on the greater part of the caravan-raiding and slave-hunting in the valleys of the Hindoo Koosh. On the other hand, they have submitted to a far more oppressive form of tyranny than that which prevailed in Nagar, their thums grinding them down with heavy taxation, killing them out of mere wantonness, selling them into slavery, stealing their wives and daughters. When they realized that we were going to treat them with clemency they professed—and most probably in all honesty—to welcome us as their deliverers from this state of things. They spoke with loathing of their fugitive tyrant, who had dragged them from their homes and compelled them to fight against their own wishes, only to desert them at last, in a cowardly fashion very unbecoming in a monarch who claims descent from the mighty Alexander.

We reflected that if these men can bear themselves so stoutly when fighting against their will, it would be interesting to see what they would do when their heart was in the game.

The terraced cultivated land we were ascending to the castle stretches for seven miles up and down the valley, and is about two miles in breadth. Several fortified villages are scattered over it. Three or four deputations of natives came down to meet us. They awaited us on the open spaces, and received us with much salaaming and offerings of chapatis and ghee in signification of their submission. One of these deputations was weird to behold: it consisted entirely of elders, very old men with bowed backs, and long beards which should have been grey, but which had all been dyed scarlet.

The notables tried hard to dissuade us from entering the castle, explaining that it was very dirty, full of the fugitive thum's lumber, and that they had swept out and garnished a much nicer house for us in the town below, the mansion of some wazir or other big man who had accompanied the monarch in his flight.

These arguments naturally only served to make us the more keen to occupy the castle, and thither we insisted on being taken. We passed through the alleys of the town, and entered the gate of the thum's stronghold. We found it to be a curious, rambling old place, some five storeys high, well-built of sun-dried mud, stones, and timber. At the top were overhanging galleries of tastefully-carved wood. Some of the rooms were capacious and comfortable, but most of them were merely dark little cells. A ladder placed in the middle of the floor of a room, and passing through a square hole in the ceiling, afforded access from one storey to the next.

The Gurkhas were assigned certain rooms for their quarters, sentries were stationed, and we entered into possession of the thum's castle, signifying the fact from a broad platform at the summit by flag-signals to the officers at Samaya.

The view from the castle towers is superb, especially when one looks down the valley; for nearly the whole mass of Rakaposhi is visible, and the eye can follow the slopes of the mighty mountain right up from the glaciers that descend low down between the pine-woods and rocky ridges, past the immense undulating snow-fields, to the high, culminating peak of all.

The valley here, being broad and running east and west, is exposed to the sun's rays for the greater part of the day; and though Hunza is 8,400 feet above the sea, we found it much warmer here than in our cheerless camp at Nilt, where we enjoyed less than an hour's sunshine a day. The descriptions of this country, gathered I suppose from native information, appear to have exaggerated the rigours of the climate. For instance, we were led to expect nine feet of snow at Hunza at this season, and a far greater depth higher up the valley. June, July, and August were reported to be the only mild months; while for the rest of the year there was said to be perpetual wind and cold.

Twigg, Boisragon, and myself took up our quarters in the most comfortable chamber we could find, which we soon discovered to have been the apartment of the ladies belonging to the thum's harem. It was surrounded by a low, broad, wooden divan, on which our bedding was laid. Pillars of carved wood rose from the edge of the divan to the carved beams of the roof, blackened by the smoke of ages. There were several cupboards and niches in the walls. Grass and rushes were now strewed for us on the mud floor, and on the divan beneath our blankets. A fire was lit in the open fireplace at one end of the floor, the smoke escaping through a square hole in the roof. Save for the Oriental pattern of the wooden carvings it was just such a hall, I imagine, as King Canute might have lived in.

We found in this zenana many little feminine belongings that the poor creatures who had been dragged away by the flying thum, to suffer frightful hardships on the snowy wastes of the wintry Pamirs, had left behind them. There were a number of little workboxes and caskets of Chinese manufacture, containing cotton and needles from Manchester and Birmingham, artificial flowers, scissors, and bits of unfinished needlework. We also came across tooth-powder, boxes of

HUNZA CASTLE AND TOWN.

rouge, pots of pomade and cosmetics; all these from St. Petersburg shops. There were parasols too, scraps of silk, old robes and scarves, and other things of little value that women who had to pack up and fly in haste would be likely to leave. There were not wanting signs, too, of the children who had lived here: rough baby-drawings in charcoal on the walls, playthings of various sorts, little wooden toy sher bachas and jezails, to teach the young idea how to shoot. Two handsome and very tame cats roamed up and down the zenana, mewing in dismay at the disappearance of all their friends.

We enjoyed this night a dinner of most unwonted luxury, and for the first time for many months we tasted beef. Very good beef, too, is that of the sturdy buffalo-like cattle of these highlands. I have explained that to eat the flesh of the sacred ox is a most heinous crime in Kashmir under the Hindoo raj, and until quite recently was punishable with death. But now that we were beyond the frontier and among a beef-eating people we could do in Hunza as Hunza does. Not only are these Kanjuts beef-eaters, but being, as I have said, of the very easy-going Maulai sect of Mahomedanism, they are also wine-bibbers; and I accordingly expressed my desire to sample the thum's special vintages. The thum, we were informed, never drinks water by any chance, wine and spirit—when he can get this last—being his only beverages.

When Captain Gromchevtsky was in Hunza with his Cossacks he produced some vodka, of which the thum partook so freely one night that he was very unwell on the following morning. Gromchevtsky was suspected of having poisoned the monarch, and a wazir was sent to him to ask for an antidote. 'But I am no

G G

doctor,' urged the Russian. 'You gave our khan the stuff that made him ill,' said the wazir. 'You must now make him well again. If he dies, you and your men will be held responsible.'

The Hunza wine is not kept beyond a year, and is stored underground in earthen jars. Some of it was brought to me in a large gourd. It looked like weak cold tea with milk in it, and was not unpalatable, though sourish, tasting like Norman cider of the rough sort, and containing, I should say, about the same percentage of alcohol. For the benefit of travellers, I may mention that the vintage of Baltit is the best. The thum has a cellar in the fort there, wherein we discovered some jars of a wine held in high estimation by Hunza connoisseurs.

Not only was wine and beef brought to us, but we were kept supplied with excellent flour, milk, apples, pears, and walnuts; so we came to the conclusion that we had found a very Capua in Hunza. Our Gurkhas were provided with plenty of their favourite goat's flesh, and they appeared to appreciate the native wine. I may here mention that the animals in this high valley have been well furnished by Nature to withstand the inclemency of the climate: sheep, oxen, and goats have all very long hair, under which is a short, soft, silky wool, much used in the manufacture of Pashmina.

We had little time for exploring the castle on this day, and having completed our sybaritic supper, we enjoyed a delicious night's rest in this comfortable zenana after our late fatigues.

We were up betimes on December 23, and proceeded to rummage all the nooks and corners of the deserted palace. We had heard that the treasures of many a pillaged caravan, and the results of many a raid were stored here, so the search was an exciting one.

The tribesmen had been informed that, provided they gave up their arms, their property would be respected by us, and that they would be paid back in kind in the spring for the cattle, grain, and other supplies which were requisitioned by our forces subsequently to their submission; but the possessions of the fugitive thum were declared to be forfeited, so we set to work to collect together all the valuables that were to be found in the place, individual looting being of course forbidden.

As a matter of fact, few articles of any worth were discovered; these were afterwards sold by auction at Gilgit, and the proceeds were divided among the sepoys who had taken part in the campaign. We were informed that the thum had made all his preparations for flight long before his defeat at Nilt, and having impressed some hundreds of men as coolies, had carried off the bulk of his wealth with him across the Hindoo Koosh. It is also more than probable that his subjects had not neglected the splendid opportunity for appropriating the remainder of their monarch's personal property during the interval between his departure and our occupation of the castle.

Still, they had not taken all, and we raked together a curious and miscellaneous collection of odds and ends scattered about and secreted away in the various chambers and cellars.

To begin with the arms, of which we found a considerable quantity: there were Martini-Henry, Winchester, Spencer, Snider, Enfield, and Berdan rifles, with cases of Dum Dum and Russian ammunition. There were also some sporting-rifles, Express and others, shotguns of French and Russian manufacture, swordsticks, and Belgian revolvers. There were handsome jezails, talwars and shields of native workmanship, flags, tomtoms, and war drums; but we were not able to identify the famous fairy drum that had falsely foretold our defeat at the hands of the Kanjuts. The most interesting of our finds were some weighty antique suits of chain armour, such as mediæval knights might have

SEPOYS OF 20TH PUNJAB INFANTRY AND HUNZA GUN.

worn in Europe. Of native gunpowder there were considerable stores.

One of the sher bachas here was quite an imposing piece of artillery, weighing as much as our two sevenpounders put together. It has a characteristic history. Some years back a Chinese armourer from Yarkand came to Hunza and offered to cast so powerful a cannon for the defence of the thum's stronghold as to enable him to defy the world. The thum took him at his word, decreed a compulsory collection of all the brazen and copper cooking-pots and other vessels in the neighbourhood of the capital, and of this metal the big gun was forthwith made. The like of it had never before been seen in these highlands. The thum was delighted with it, graciously complimented the Yarkander on the excellence of his handiwork, and showed his sincere appreciation of his services by having him immediately decapitated, jealous lest this unique workman should betake himself to Nagar, Gilgit, or even to England, and construct similar ordnance for those rival Powers.

Next we collected a variety of articles, some of which had no doubt been sent to the thum as presents from Kashmir, China, and Russia; others had probably been looted from the caravans of Central Asia; while how some of the things we found had got here it was indeed difficult to conjecture. For instance, there was an European armchair, apparently of English manufacture, and two large mirrors with gaudy frames of flashing glass prisms, the sort of ornaments one would expect to see in some shady French *brasserie*. The following were some of our discoveries:—Several good telescopes and field-glasses; brazen lamps of elegant design; a large musical box from Paris; papier-maché writing-desks and workboxes; a coloured portrait of His Imperial Majesty the Czar, and another of the Czarevitch; a quantity of Russian prints and of old Dutch engravings in a portfolio; some packing-cases full of cheap looking-glasses—caravan loot probably; an extraordinary walking-stick, which could be pulled to pieces and converted into two knives, two forks, two spoons, and a corkscrew; a great many brazen bowls, ewers, and jars from Yarkand; Russian samovars; some China plates and cups of apparently good quality—there were, unfortunately, no judges of porcelain among us.

Of stores there were ample supplies, which proved of great use to us: granaries overflowing with grain; sugar, both loaf and candied; walnuts; dried apricots and mulberries; chillies; lucifer matches and candles from Russia, and several liqueur bottles, by the way, from the same country, all empty.

We scarcely anticipated that the most valuable loot to be found in the robber king's stronghold would take a literary form, but so it was. Though I believe the monarch cannot himself read, his library was extensive and interesting. There were in it many beautifully bound and illuminated Korans, and curious Hindoo books and manuscripts, some evidently of great age. There were the works of the Persian poets, and a book which one of our baboos recognised as being a copy of a famous Persian universal history—the 'Khilasset el Akhbar' of Khondimir, I believe, in which the thum might have read the doings of his ancestor, Alexander. This volume contained a number of well-painted pictures of battles, very realistic in their horrors.

There were masses of correspondence in Persian, letters from our Agent at Gilgit, from Kashmir, Russian and Chinese authorities. The illiterate thum must have made an unfortunate choice in his secretary, who, to judge from what we saw, is a very unmethodical person, and sadly neglectful of his duties. The greater portion of the letters addressed to the thum, some of which dated several years back, had never even been opened, and were scattered about all over the palace in corners of floors and disused cupboards.

Perchance this cunning munshi considered this calm indifference to the communications of neighbouring Powers to be the most diplomatic method of conducting the Foreign Secretaryship of the monarchy. Here, too, were the unopened letters which had been sent from Gilgit to Captain Younghusband during the imbroglio with the Russians on the Pamirs in the spring, and which the thum had intercepted.

I may mention that we came across some bottles of quicksilver and a little gold amalgam, a sample, no doubt, of the results of washing the sands of the Kanjut River.

Our quarters began to present quite a high-art appearance, for we arranged the copper vessels, weapons, old china, and the more valuable spoil, round the walls of the zenana. It looked quite the old baronial hall when lit up by night with the Russian candles we had appropriated.

Our exploration had been very complete, and I think but little escaped us. We were just about to abandon the search when a discovery was made that raised our highest anticipations: it seemed as if we had at last hit upon the secret treasure-room of the thum, and were about to feast our eyes on a very Ali Baba's cave of stolen riches. But having had some disappointing previous experiences of hunting for pirate treasure, I dared not feel over-sanguine.

Somebody's keen eye perceived that a space in one of the towers remained unaccounted for, showing that there must exist some secret chamber which had no windows, and the door of which had been walled up. This was very exciting. After probing about and knocking the mud plaster off the walls in several places, we at last discovered the artfully-concealed door, which our Gurkhas soon battered in, and then we found ourselves peering into the pitchy blackness of the mysterious vault. A candle was lit and we entered. The first glance did not dispel our hopes, but on the contrary rather reassured us. Banners and chain-armour hung from the roof-beams, and all round the walls were ranged in order large, strong, wooden chests, and sacks of canvas or leather. The first chest was carefully opened, and was found to be full to the brim—with gunpowder. One by one we examined all the others, with a like result. The sacks for their part contained garnet bullets.

So we had discovered no treasure-room, and this was evidently only the principal powder-magazine of the country. We came out laughing at our frustrated hopes, and had the door barricaded again, in case of accidents; for there was enough powder in this magazine to have brought the whole castle tumbling down upon the town below on the application of a spark.

CHAPTER XXX

A FLYING COLUMN IS SENT UP THE VALLEY—A CHRISTMAS NIGHT'S BIVOUAC—GULMIT FORT—FRIENDLINESS OF THE KANJUTS—PASSU—RETURN OF FUGITIVES—THE WAZIR HUMAYUN—KHAIBAR KHUSRU KHAN—GIRCHA—DIFFICULTIES OF THE UPPER KANJUT VALLEY.

On December 24 the rest of our force came over from Samaya, and as there was not sufficient accommodation in the castle, encamped on the polo-ground below.

Dr. Robertson had ascertained that Safdar Ali and Uzr Khan had been accompanied in their flight by some four hundred men, who had carried with them, not only the treasures of Hunza, but all the best rifles, and that it was their intention to cross the Killik Pass, at the head of the Hunza Valley, and proceed to Tash-kurghan, in Chinese Turkestan.

As it was desirable that these runaway princes should be captured, and prevented from causing further trouble later on, it was decided that a party of a hundred men of the Kashmir Bodyguard Regiment, under Lieutenants Baidr and Molony, and accompanied by Lieutenant Manners Smith as Political Officer, should set out for the foot of the Killik Pass on Christmas-day, with the object of overtaking the thum's party if possible, and also to report on the road, impress the remote villages with a military display, and effect the disarmament of that portion of the country.

I was anxious to see all I could of this interesting

and little-known region, so asked permission to join the flying column, and this was willingly granted.

There are several fortified villages between Hunza and Misgar, the highest inhabited place in the valley, so we were to dispense with tents, and even with commissariat, taking only a few stores, and rely on the country ahead to supply both food and shelter. Misgar, our destination, is six marches (about sixty miles) from Hunza; not far beyond is the Killik Pass, on whose slopes the Kanjut River has its source, flowing from here for 125 miles to its junction with the Gilgit River.

So on the morning of Christmas-day we left behind us the luxury of the royal palace for a fortnight's journey in the bleak high valley. We gathered from the descriptions that we should find this a very rough road. There were several high and difficult paris to cross, the freezing river had to be forded as many as twelve times in one day, and there was at least one broad glacier to be traversed.

As one ascends the valley beyond Hunza the country assumes a more dreary aspect, what cultivation there is becomes scanty and dwarfed, and each march takes one into a more rigorous climate. An elevation is soon reached at which fruit will not ripen; there are no pleasant orchards, as in the lower valley, and gaunt poplars are the only trees around the villages.

It is only at certain points, where passage along the cliffs would be otherwise absolutely impossible for the best cragsmen, that any steps have been taken to open a road, and then it is but the narrowest scaffolding thrown from ledge to ledge. One comes upon position after position of immense natural strength in this gorge, where the dangerous and only path passes under stout sangas, which could be held by a handful of men against a host. Even as the Kanjuts had left the approaches to their valley below Nilt as difficult of access as possible, so had they done here, at the outlet of their country on to the Pamirs, rendering it almost impossible for an enemy to invade them from either direction. On the other hand, the road between Nilt and Nagar is comparatively in excellent condition, and in places great labour has been expended upon it.

Our first day's march took us past the villages of Altit and Mahomedabad, and then across a long, high pari to the camping-place on the sands by the river. This night we had to bivouac (for the fort and village of Atabad were perched high above us) on a rocky summit, away from the road. But a messenger had been sent ahead to apprise the chief man of Atabad of our coming, and forty of the villagers were awaiting us by the river with the goats, meal, ghee, and firewood we had requisitioned for our force.

The ghee here, like all that was given to us in the valley, was of the consistence of cheese, had a most unpleasant odour, and, according to our ideas, it did not improve the flavour of food that was cooked with it. The older this so-called clarified butter is, the more is it to the taste of these highlanders. They bury it in holes in the ground, and it is often kept there for generations before it is used, one hundred years being quite an ordinary age for Hunza ghee. These people like their butter to be stale and their wine to be new, and would no doubt consider us coarse barbarians were they aware of our exactly opposite preferences. The men of Atabad supplied our sepoys with a very fine old brand of ghee, capital stuff to keep the cold out. It was exhumed in balls of about ten pounds weight each, packed in leaves and grass.

This looked a desolate place to pass our Christmas-night in. There was no vegetation around us; from the stony river-bed the precipitous, barren mountains rose high on either side of the gorge; the air was raw, to say the least of it, and the Kanjut torrent, rapid as it is, was frozen over in places, and rushed along under a roof of thick ice.

But the natives had brought down plenty of firewood for all, so a dozen and more camp-fires were soon blazing away. We four Englishmen, sitting round our own Yule logs, well rolled-up in our sheepskin coats and blankets, with the flaps of our Balaclava caps over our ears, enjoyed a capital dinner, and, indeed, had one of the jolliest Christmas evenings possible.

We had not forgotten to bring some stores with us for this occasion, and were provided with a fine quarter of Hunza beef; indeed, most of the orthodox delicacies of the season figured in our *menu*, which was as follows:—

Ox-cheek soup (tinned), roast beef, tinned plum pudding, chapatis.

We drank whisky and goat's milk for dinner, and mulled Hunza wine—a somewhat queer form of grog—with our pipes afterwards.

We had to dispense with vegetables during this little expedition—no hardship this in wintry weather—but always procured as much beef, milk, and chapatis as we required from the natives, so we fared very well.

Dr. Robertson had annexed the States of Hunza and Nagar pending the decision of the Government of India as to their disposal; so we congratulated ourselves on having our Christmas dinner on what was, at least temporarily, British territory — a rather rough and desert sample of the Empire, it is true, but still British— so we felt quite at home.

On December 26, turning out from under our blankets into a bitterly cold morning, we resumed our thum-stalking, and accomplished the next stage to Gulmit. This was a trying march across a howling wilderness, over frightful paris, up and down steep staircases and scaffoldings. We met several natives who were returning to their homes after having been impressed by the thum to carry his property to the Killik. They told us that he was five marches ahead of us, so there was small hope of our coming up with him, unless bad weather prevented him from attempting the pass, in which case we had him in a trap. One of these men, on being asked in what direction the thum intended to go, replied that he was about to cross the Bam-i-Dunya (the Persian for 'Roof of the World'), the first time any of us had heard the Pamirs thus designated by a native.

At last we saw before us the towered fortress of Gulmit, surrounded by cultivated fields; so we halted till all our men had come up, and marched in proper order to the gate of the fort. A number of men came out to greet us, bearing presents of chapatis, apples, and ghee. They had prepared our quarters for us. There was ample room for all in the fort, and to us four Englishmen a comfortable chamber was assigned in the house of a fugitive wazir, having the usual surrounding divan and carved columns. The fire was in the middle of the mud floor, the universal fashion here, and very trying, too, to unaccustomed eyes; for the greater portion of the smoke does not escape through the square hole in the roof, but rolls about the room to torment one.

Meal, goats, and ghee were requisitioned for our men, and the natives, in order to supply us with firewood, proceeded to pull down the upper storeys of the fortress towers, which were partly constructed of stout beams. 'For now that this country is yours,' they said, 'we have no need of forts. We shall have no

GULMIT FORT AND KANJUT TRIBESMEN.

more fighting; you will always protect us.' Considering that these were British subjects of only a few hours' standing, they had grasped the situation very completely. They appeared to think that the new *régime* would in many ways be greatly to their advantage. They realized that they themselves would be subject to no more oppression; but they scarcely approved of our curtailment of their prescriptive right to oppress others, and thought it hard that they would no longer be at liberty to support their families by practising the gentlemanly professions of caravan-raiding and man-stealing.

At each village we went through the chief men were called up and informed that they were now the subjects of the Angresi Sarkar. We had a Hunza guide and interpreter with us, one Abdullah, a cheery, shrewd old rascal, who was a great character in his way. He was a born orator, and used to make long harangues to the tribesmen on their new rights and obligations as British citizens. Abdullah had the intelligence to discover that one way to an Englishman's heart is by his stomach, especially when he is campaigning; so this wise man used to hurry ahead when we approached a village, advise the inhabitants as to what delicacies in the way of food were best calculated to conciliate the conquerors, and see to the immediate preparation of the same.

The chapatis of fine flour which were presented to us at each village were the best I had ever tasted. We heard that the fair ladies of the zenana had made these for us. It appears that there were many women in these forts; but we never saw a single one, and did not even catch a glimpse of a dark, inquisitive eye peeping through a lattice. The Hunzas do not keep their women in *purdah*, so this concealment was unusual. This distrust, which passed away when they had seen more of us, was no doubt due to the wild reports spread by the first fugitives who had come up the valley after the storming of Nilt; they declared that we were killing all the men we found, and sending all the women and children to London, where they were to be sold as slaves. The people in the remotest regions of the Hindoo Koosh have heard of London, just as they have heard of Alexander the Great, and know about as much of either. Many of these tribesmen imagine London to be a big fortified village, something like Hunza, and several days' march beyond Gilgit.

On December 27 we made a rather easy march—encountering no bad paris, but having to cross the couloirs of two glaciers—to Passu, another small but densely-populated rabbit-warren of a fort.

The people here, having recovered from their panic, had returned to their ordinary avocations, and received us in a friendly manner. As the religious prejudices which limit our intercourse with most other Mahomedan races do not exist in this Maulai country, we were quickly enabled to acquire some insight into the character and habits of these new British subjects. We found the Hunzas to be a jovial people, fond of boisterous merry-making over the flowing bowl, and possessed of a sense of humour rare among Asiatics. That strict Mussulmans consider these the vilest of Kafirs is not to be wondered at; for apparently the Hunzas are not only free from fanaticism, but are devoid of all religious sentiment whatever. They leave the care of their souls entirely in the hands of their spiritual masters, much in the same way as do the Buddhists of Ladak, and, like these, they deny the existence of a heaven or hell, and believe in re-incarnation.

At Passu, as elsewhere, the tribesmen stated that the Russians had advised them to resist us, and after having promised to lend them assistance, had left them in the lurch. If this be so—and there is little doubt that it is so—the over-zealous agents of Russia have kindly played into our hands, for the story of her faithlessness will be carried throughout all these regions. The Afghans have not forgotten how the Russians deserted them in similar fashion at Cabul; and there is no doubt that our rivals are earning for themselves a reputation for untruthfulness and deceitful dealing among the natives on both sides of the Hindoo Koosh. Some of our travellers in Turkestan can tell interesting tales in evidence of this.

We found that the men of Passu and of other villages higher up the valley were somewhat anxious to

KANJUT VALLEY NEAR PASSU.

ascertain whether they would still retain their ancient privileges beyond the Hindoo Koosh. It appears that the Chinese, for the last 200 years, have given the Kanjuts pasturage rights on the Tagdambash Pamir, and the Khirgiz nomads, who also graze their cattle there, have paid a regular toll to the thum.

The inhabitants of Passu discussed the recent war with us in a cheery way; they spoke of it as if it were some sort of tamasha, a merry little game that had been quite worth the playing. What tickled them immensely was the fact that by far the greater portion of the men who had been killed on their side had been Nagaris. 'The Nagaris did not want to fight,' said they, 'but our chiefs made them do so ; and yet, lo! we Hunzas have escaped with very little loss, while hundreds of those other foolish fellows were shot.'

In the frequent neighbourly little wars between the Hunzas and Nagaris, the former have invariably come off best. But when the two States are allied against a common foe, the shrewd Hunzas so contrive matters that the Nagaris shall bear the brunt of the fighting, and that the standing crops or winter stores of Nagar shall suffer most from a foreign foray. Once before the Hunzas quietly sat down on one side of the river at Maiun, and watched the Nagaris fight their battles against the Kashmir forces on the Nilt shore. The Hunzas evidently regard the Nagaris as an inferior people, to be put upon on every occasion. For instance, when we first occupied Hunza Castle the head-men there had the impudence to suggest that the Nagaris should be requisitioned to provide all the supplies for our troops in Hunza, as well as for those in Nagar, and that the Hunzas should escape scot-free from all the consequences of their rising. They would, no doubt, gladly have crossed the river and looted the grain of their allies for us had we suggested it.

I am afraid that the Hunzas, though a pleasant people to travel among now that they have been brought under subjection, are great rascals; but hypocrisy, at any rate, is not one of their faults. They are quite frankly unprincipled, will unblushingly confess to acts of abominable treachery, cruelty, and dishonesty; while there is a refreshing *bonhomie* in their wickedness that reminds one of the amiable villainy of the immortal Count Fosco. These hereditary robbers of the frontier are not even loyal to each other, and have no scruples in betraying and plundering their own friends and relations on occasion. We now began to understand how it was that the men of the upper valley were so well disposed to us, and accepted their defeat with such cheery resignation. We observed that within every fort the stones were sprinkled with fresh blood, and that the remains of recently-slaughtered cattle were lying on the ground. The thum and his companions in flight had left behind them large herds and stores of grain, to which the tribesmen were now obviously helping themselves very liberally, and were living a life of unwonted luxury, feasting on unlimited beef and choice meal. They were amicably dividing among themselves all the possessions of the runaways.

It is no wonder that they bore us no ill-will for having carried war into their valley; defeat had proved a blessing to them, while victory would have brought them no advantages. The supplies we requisitioned at each village were furnished from the property of the unfortunate runaways. Most of these men left the thum later on, and returned to their pillaged homes, and no doubt when they inquired about their missing cattle and grain, their fellow-villagers plausibly explained that our sepoys had eaten the lot, maintaining a discreet silence as to the far greater share of the good things they themselves had enjoyed.

We found it impossible to procure quarters for our Kashmir troops in Passu Fort. The blood and entrails of the cows on which the Hunzas had been feasting were strewn on the floor of every building; the Hindoo sepoys, horrified at a sight so repugnant to their reli-

gious feelings, would not stay in a place defiled by the
blood of a sacred creature, and so the poor fellows were
obliged to bivouac outside, despite the extreme cold.
But the upper storeys of the fortress towers were pulled
down, and the beams supplied them with an abundance
of firewood.

December 28 was a miserable day: the sky was
overcast, and a wind of deadly chilliness howled among
the rocks, driving clouds of freezing dust before it.
The country we marched through was bare of any
vegetation—a chaos of rock and ice and snow alone.
The mountains were of extraordinary steepness, and
terminated in sharp pinnacles. A short distance
beyond Passu we had to cross a large glacier that
descended to the river-bed, picking our way for two
miles among boulders of green ice. No description
would enable one to realise the awful desolation of the
upper Kanjut Valley in mid-winter.

Many of those who, of their own free will or by
compulsion, had accompanied the Thum of Hunza in
his flight, had now deserted him, and were returning
to their homes in Hunza and Nagar. On this day we
passed three parties of these refugees. One was escorting back two handsome, rosy-cheeked little boys, who
from their dress and high-bred features evidently belonged to a family of distinction. We found they were
the children of Humayun, who had been Wazir of
Hunza during the reign of the late Thum, Ghazan Khan,
the father of the gentleman we were now stalking.

Safdar Ali, it will be remembered, succeeded to the
throne after murdering his father; he then proceeded
to expel the Wazir Humayun from the country, and
appropriated his wife. The two boys remained with
their mother, while Humayun fled to Chitral and be-

KANJUT VALLEY NEAR KHAIBAR.

came a firm ally of ours. He is described as a man possessed of excellent qualities. It was known that he had many friends in Hunza, and that a large party in that country was ready to follow him. As such a man would be of service to us, he had been recalled from Chitral by our Resident; and his two boys, hearing of this, had left Safdar Ali and their mother, to rejoin their father. The little lads appeared very glad to see us, realizing that they had now got quite safely out of the tyrant's clutches. It is somewhat strange that he let them go. In one of his fits of rage he might have murdered them to revenge himself on their father, whom he hated; or he might have kept them with him as hostages. At the time I write this the exiled Humayun is once more in possession of his estates, and is Wazir of Hunza; while Safdar Ali, who had so wronged him, is a friendless wanderer on the wastes of Turkestan.

Our destination this day was the little village of Khaibar, a miserable place at the mouth of a grand gorge. The streams were here completely frozen up, so that, in addition to other supplies, baskets of ice had to be requisitioned, and melted in the cooking-pots to produce the water we required.

Here we met another refugee prince who had escaped the thum. This was Khusru Khan, who accompanied us during the remainder of this expedition. He is a bright boy of sixteen, and is closely related to both the royal houses of Hunza and Nagar. The Hunza Thum's sister was his mother, and the Thum of Nagar's son, Muhammad Khan, was his father. Uzr Khan had expelled Muhammad Khan from Nagar, and was therefore, of course, suspicious of the son, and hated the young Khusru. It was perhaps well for Khusru that he had placed himself in our hands; for his uncle, the heir-apparent of Nagar, would have probably added his name to the roll of the relations he had murdered. Khusru Khan was once a hostage at Gilgit, and was greeted as an old friend by some of our officers.

Twelve of our sepoys, who were ill or sore-footed, were left at Khaibar to await our return, and on December 29 the rest of us marched up the valley to the village of Gircha. It was a bleak, sunless day, and the grey clouds were low down on the desolate mountain-slopes. We had to cross to the left bank of the Kanjut River in order to avoid an inaccessible pari. There was an old rope bridge, by which some of us passed over, but it was very frail, and the few remaining strands of the foot rope began to give way one by one under even a single man's weight. Therefore most of the sepoys and all the Balti coolies had to ford the freezing stream, at this point broad and about three feet deep. Fires were lit on the farther bank, at which the men could dry their clothes and warm themselves before proceeding—an indispensable precaution in this weather.

It began to snow lightly as we advanced. We had, so far, been lucky in our weather. Had the snow fallen in earnest it would have made the narrow ledges of rock by which we had to cross the paris very dangerous; while we should certainly have had some cases of frostbite had a strong wind arisen.

At Gircha we as usual experienced no difficulty in obtaining supplies, while we annexed thirty sheep and a quantity of grain belonging to the thum.

The march of December 30 was our last and most arduous one. The paris on this stage are high and difficult, while the Kanjut River has to be crossed several times by deep and difficult fords. Under these circumstances we took only twenty-five sepoys on with us, leaving the rest of the column at Gircha.

With a cold, grey sky above us, we slowly toiled along through the gloomiest land imaginable. We had now attained a considerable elevation, and the temperature was very low, probably considerably below zero, but we had no thermometer with us to inform us how cold it was.

On this march huge pari after pari projects into the river with high, perpendicular cliffs. Consequently the road—it seems absurd to apply such a term to these Kanjut routes—is ever ascending and descending, the traveller having to scramble as best he can from crevice to crevice along the face of the precipices. Looked at from below, much of the way appears quite impassable for any creature, and it is, indeed, in places difficult even for hill-men.

In the summer, when the torrent, swollen by the melting snows, is unfordable, this dangerous track is the only one; but in the winter it is possible, though not particularly easy, to follow the river-bed on horseback, and avoid the paris by frequently fording the torrent. The upper road, like so many in this region, is much exposed to falling rocks, and a poor Balti who had been sent after us from Hunza with stores had one leg completely cut off by a large stone.

Manners Smith, Molony, Baird, and myself, having found three horses at Gircha, followed the lower route, and forded the river at twelve different points in the course of the day. The river was frozen over for a short distance from the banks, though open in the centre, and the ice was in that doubtful condition when it would bear a horse's weight at one step and break away under him at the next; so that the animals would not face the passage without much forcible persuasion. The Kanjut River is so discoloured that it is impossible to see what the bottom is like, and the horses, after alternately slipping over and floundering through the ice, tumbled about among the hidden boulders, occasionally falling into holes and drenching their riders. In a few places, where the torrent was deep, they were swept off their feet and had to take to swimming.

We soon began to present a curious appearance. The horses were covered with ice. From their shaggy coats and stomachs depended icicles, which grew larger after each ford, until they were some two feet in length, and clashed together at every movement. All our lower extremities, too, were encased in ice, while our frozen breath hung in masses of ice from our moustaches.

We were glad when we had accomplished our twelfth ford, and saw before us the towers of Misgar, our destination. The sepoys and coolies had followed the weary track across the mountains; but they, too, had to ford the river at least once.

CHAPTER XXXI

MISGAR—LITTLE GUHJAL—AN INDIAN ULTIMA THULE—A HUNZA MERRY-MAKING—THE KANJUT SWORD-DANCE—A HUNZA PANTOMIME—DISARMAMENT OF THE TRIBESMEN.

MISGAR is a poor little settlement, but is surrounded by a towered wall. It is the last inhabited spot of the Kanjut Valley, and is 10,200 feet above the sea. This curious robber valley, populated by an Aryan race which thrusts itself thus, like a narrow wedge, into the region of the Mongolians, practically terminates here. The traveller, on proceeding beyond Misgar, will encounter only the Khirgiz nomads and other peoples of Tartar type.

Our occupation of Misgar with our twenty-five sepoys now made this the extreme point to which British influence has extended into Central Asia. If the countries beyond are as cheerless as that which now surrounded us, they would be scarcely worth influencing one way or the other, were it not that this is one of the gates of our Indian Empire, and we cannot again allow the soldiers of that Power, in which to put any faith is suicidal folly, to pass through here and stir up the populations against us.

Here there are no trees or other vegetation save a little poor grass in places. The scenery is not even interesting. There are no grand peaks or cliffs; the bare mountains, of no great height, slope gently to the valley. The Hindoo Koosh at this point loses all its usual rugged sublimity, and the passes that lead from here on to the Tagdambash Pamir wind over stony downs, and are remarkably easy.

Thus, the Killik Pass hard by, about 15,000 feet, was still open and practicable for horses, and it remains so throughout the winter, save in exceptionally rigorous seasons. The road over this pass into China is undoubtedly less difficult and dangerous in winter than is the road we had left behind us leading across the Borzil and Tragbal passes into Kashmir. The snowfall is much heavier, and occurs at a considerably earlier date on the southern ranges than on the Hindoo Koosh. It is probable, now that merchants need no longer fear the Kanjut robbers, that the road up this valley, across the Tagdambash Pamir to Yarkand, may become a great caravan route between India and Central Asia, and supplant the longer and more difficult road by way of Leh and the Karakoram. But a good deal of blasting will first have to be carried on among the Kanjut paris, and the Indus Valley below Boonji must be open to us.

The higher portion of the Kanjut Valley, extending from near Gulmit to the passes of the Hindoo Koosh, is generally known as Little Guhjal. This district was colonised two centuries ago by refugees from the Afghan country of Wakkan. At Misgar especially one notices that the majority of the inhabitants are of a different type to that of the Hunza Dards, and here they still speak the Wakki language instead of the Burishki dialect of the Kanjuts. Nearly every man we met in Misgar also understood Persian.

On December 31 we took a holiday, and saw the old year out at this cheerless Indian Ultima Thule.

Our expedition up the valley, though successful in its other objects, had proved a failure so far as our thum-stalking was concerned. This we had anticipated, for the monarch had got too long a start of us; and now that we were at the foot of the Pamirs we could follow him no farther, our orders of course preventing us from crossing the passes into Chinese territory. A Russian officer under like circumstances would have had a freer hand, and would have troubled himself little as to whose lands he was trespassing over when in full chase of his quarry.

On this day Lieutenant Townshend joined us with five sepoys, having left at Gircha the rest of the small party with which he had marched from Hunza. He had been sent to penetrate some tributary nullahs of the Kanjut, to carry on the same work which had employed us in the main valley—the reconnoitring of the country and the disarmament of the natives.

It being New Year's Eve we got up a tamasha after supper. Several fires, forming a large circle, were lit outside in the clear frosty air, and we all—officers, sepoys, Baltis, and natives, the latter far outnumbering our party—sat round in a ring as spectators, while in the centre the Hunzas gave us an entertainment of a most interesting character.

For fourteen centuries, it is said, have these tribesmen lived as they do now, unchanging in manners or dress. The singing, dancing, and music of this evening's nautch were all traditional, and a thousand years ago a Hunza merry-making would have doubtless been little different from this one.

In this country women never dance, so men only took part in this performance. It is the custom here for every big man to maintain his band of musicians, which accompanies him when he makes a journey. Later on we requisitioned the thum's own orchestra for our nautches; but on this occasion we had to satisfy ourselves with the band of one of the fugitive wazirs, consisting of kettle-drums, tomtoms, mandolines, and strange wind instruments bearing some resemblance to clarionets.

These Kanjut musicians are really excellent in their way: the melodies, barbaric and in the minor key, are often singularly impressive; and the songs are not the melancholy lamentations of a subject and oppressed race, but the spirited war-chants of a conquering people, in which the bard triumphantly celebrates old fights, successful forays, and the raids on caravans of treasure; while to the furious beating of tomtoms all the tribesmen round clap their hands and energetically join, with flashing eyes, in the savagely exultant chorus, —the sort of thing to quicken the pulses of men and excite in them the lust of battle.

Various native dances, mostly graceful and stately, but sometimes fiercely energetic, filled up the intervals between the songs. Now one man alone, now two or four, would step into the ring and engage in the pleasing figures, which were entirely different from those of the tiresome nautches of most Oriental countries. There were some dances furious as those of hemp-intoxicated dervishes, when the drums and tomtoms would keep up a tremendous rolling, while the tribesmen shouted and clapped their hands to excite the dancers to still more frantic efforts.

We discovered that this was the very band that used to play in Maiun Fort during the campaign. When last we had heard these men raise this din of shouting and tomtoming, it was to inflame the tribesmen with warlike ardour and excite them to slaughter us; and yet, here we were having a merry smoking-

A HUNZA RAJAH'S BAND.

concert in the company of these late enemies, now fellow British subjects, and their head-men were sitting by us, showing a due appreciation of the cheroots and hot whisky-and-water we provided.

On looking at the wild, jovial, bold-eyed men around us, it was difficult to realize that these were Asiatics at all. The Hunzas are much like what one imagines the Northern Europeans to have been in the old savage days. Such hearty ruffians, careless of human life, cruel, fond of rough conviviality, must the Scotch Highlanders or Norse freebooters have been; and, indeed, many of these tribesmen, if dressed appropriately, could easily pass as weather-beaten fishermen of the Baltic or crofters of the Western Highlands. These Dards, with their strong, rugged features, stand quite apart from all other races of Asia. They claim descent from the armies of Alexander the Great; but, however that may be, their origin is somewhat of a mystery, and there is much interesting work to be done here by philologist and ethnologist.

It is the fashion in this country for men of the highest rank—even for the thums themselves—to excel in the dance. Thus, on this night Khusru Khan stepped into the circle and exhibited his skill; then Rajah Sekandar Khan and his faithful henchman and Prime Minister gave us a Hunza sword-dance. Each had sword and shield, and to warlike music they represented the various phases of a hand-to-hand combat with the traditional weapons of the Kanjuts. It was a most spirited performance. At times, when they pressed each other, they whirled their flashing blades, sharpened for war, with wonderful rapidity and accuracy, slashing away in what seemed alarming proximity to each other's ears.

Other natives engaged in sword-dances. Occasionally several men, following each other, each brandishing a sword in either hand, would rush round the circle with savage shouts and gestures, as if falling on an enemy, while the tomtoms rolled incessantly—a most picturesque spectacle, as seen by the flickering and uncertain light of the fires. In some of these dances a man would fall as if wounded, and would cut furiously about him in all directions with his two swords, as he rolled in the dust in his death agony, to keep his enemies at bay.

The Hunzas were the chief performers, but our own men took some share in the tamasha. Two Pathan sepoys who were with us danced the exciting sword-dance of the Afghans. Some Gurkhas of the Kashmir Regiment gave us some weird songs and dances of their own country, and even the Balti coolies were called upon to contribute to the evening's amusement. These last-mentioned poor fellows, who during this expedition had enjoyed their daily fill of the flesh of sheep or goats —an unique experience for them—were getting fatter and more cheery every day, and they now took the greatest pleasure in dancing to us the measures of Baltistan, their innocent, ugly faces beaming with smiles. Once we had started them dancing it was difficult to stop them, each coolie being eager to exhibit his skill. The dances of the harmless Baltis had nothing savouring of war in them, neither were they intended to be funny; but they were indeed ludicrous in the extreme, and convulsed the spectators with laughter. They daintily held up their ragged skirts on either side, as a ballet-girl does, and pirouetted and skipped around the circle with marvellous agility.

On our way back down the valley we had a similar

smoking-concert at nearly every night's halting-place, the Hunzas, pleased to find that we appreciated their attempts to amuse us, getting up the best tamashas they could for our benefit. At one fort the performance was varied with a pantomime which was really funny, and in which the Hunzas showed that they had a keen sense of the humorous. It was true pantomime: not a word was spoken, and the actors in clever dumb-show gave a burlesque version of a day's ibex-stalking. First there danced into the ring with ridiculous antics two huge ibex. Each was made up of a stick framework covered with cloths, two real ibex horns surmounting the head. Two men under the framework, their bodies concealed by it, supplied the quadruped with its proper number of legs. The animals having completed their *pas de deux*, had a butting-match, and then proceeded to graze quietly. Two sportsmen now crawled cautiously on, one evidently intended for a sahib, the other for his native shikaree. A boy on all-fours, got up as a comic and irrepressible dog of uncertain breed, accompanied them. The shikaree, lying behind a rock, scanned the whole horizon earnestly. Suddenly he started. Was that an ibex grazing on that far hillside yonder? (some four paces off). He shaded his eyes with his hand, straining his sight, but was unable to make sure; so, creeping up to the musicians, he took a clarionet from one of them, and applying his eye to it as if it were a telescope, he turned it in the direction of the ibex. He gave a low chuckle of satisfaction, put down the telescope, and with exultant smile signified by gestures to the sahib that there was the most magnificent ibex possible on the opposite mountain. He spread out his arms to indicate the extraordinary span of the horns from tip to tip. The sahib expressed

doubt, and in capital pantomime informed his attendant
that he was guilty of gross exaggeration. The shikaree
appeared hurt, handed the telescope to his master, and
pointed out to him the direction in which he should
look. The sahib then perceived the phenomenal beast,
and opened his mouth in wonderment. 'I told you so,'
nodded the shikaree. The stalking now commenced.
The sahib seized his rifle, a sepoy's Snider, and wriggled
over the ground on his stomach, in a snake-like fashion
no sahib could imitate, until he was within easy range—
two inches—of the larger ibex. He took deliberate aim,
and pulled the trigger. He was evidently an indifferent
rifle-shot, for the ibex, though considerably startled,
was not touched, but scampered away, and surveyed the
subsequent proceedings from a safe distance. Next
came a most natural bit of business, which showed
that the Kanjuts are keen observers of the ways of
men. The angry and disappointed sahib walked back
and kicked his shikaree. 'So like a sahib, that,' was
the remark of one of us. But the other ibex had not
yet taken alarm, so the sahib wriggled along once
more, made sure of his success this time by placing the
muzzle of his rifle against the animal's heart, and the
click of the trigger was followed by the fall of the huge
creature, which, with a wild shriek (from both of the
men beneath), collapsed into an indistinguishable heap
upon the ground. Then followed the exultation of the
sahib; flattering smiles of the shikaree, who put out his
hand for bakshish from his master, and received it;
and great delight of the comic dog, who, wagging his
tail vigorously, proceeded to devour the ibex until he
was whipped off.

The Hunza campaign over, I now bethought myself
how I was to get home without delay. It is possible

for small bodies of men to cross the Himalayas in midwinter, though so far as the transport of troops or supplies is concerned the passes are closed until the end of May, or sometimes later.

Spedding and Beech had already started for Srinagur, but instead of following the Kashmir road across the Borzil Pass, they had taken a circuitous route by the Indus Valley to Skardu, and thence to the Leh road and across the Zoji La. By going this way they would encounter only one pass, and that a comparatively easy one, instead of the two dangerous passes on the other road; while they would have little difficulty in obtaining supplies and transport, an almost impossible matter on the military road.

I decided to follow their example, more especially as by doing so I should visit a good deal of country that was new to me, and penetrate those wonderful gorges of the Indus above Boonji of which I had heard so much. The distance from Misgar to Srinagur by this route is 500 miles, or forty-eight marches; and Rawal Pindi, my nearest railway-station in India, was 700 miles off. Much of the road is very difficult, and quite impassable for horses: I was certain to find many marches under deep snow, while the cold would be intense, so that I had anything but a comfortable journey to look forward to.

On January 2 the flying column set out on its return march to Hunza, which we reached after six days' scaling of paris, clambering over glaciers, and wading across rivers. Ours was a curious-looking force now: the men's clothing had suffered a good deal after a campaign in so rough a country; boots, too, were falling to pieces, and were replaced by bandages; but the ragged uniforms were at times gaily bedecked with icicles, which rattled merrily as the sepoys marched along.

When we ascended the valley Manners Smith had ordered the head-men to collect the arms in their several districts, and these were now awaiting us, piled up, in each fortress. Our Balti coolies were laden with bundles of weapons, and we arrived at Gilgit with an interesting collection. We confiscated a number of ancient matchlocks, swords, and shields, but we found very few rifles. Several jingals of Chinese make were delivered to us—heavy wall-guns with rough, wooden stocks, firing bullets of the size of large chestnuts. Some of the curious shirts of mail were also brought to us, and we carried back with us a quantity of the thum's cattle and grain.

We reached Hunza on January 6. Six hundred men of the Imperial Service regiments were now left to occupy Hunza and Nagar, Lieutenant Townshend being appointed Military Governor, and the rest of the force marched to Gilgit on January 7.

A dak arrived at Hunza before we started, but when we went up to receive our expected letters from home, it was explained to us that this was the Chinese, and not the Indian mail. A postal service of a sort between Yarkand and Gilgit, by way of the Killik, had thus already been opened. The thum had not permitted letters to be carried through his country, but now the first letter that had come by the new route informed us that the fugitive monarch was in sore straits: his followers were rapidly deserting him, the Chinese had not received him with open arms, as he had expected they would, and the men who still remained with him had been divided into three parties, otherwise they could not have obtained a sufficiency of food on those desolate table-lands.

To show their loyalty to us the Hunzas now volunteered to carry the big cannon of Hunza Castle, which had been manufactured by the unfortunate Yarkander, to Gilgit, as a trophy for the Agency. It was dismounted, and 150 natives—three gangs of fifty relieving each other—actually succeeded in dragging this ponderous piece of artillery over the rough track to Gilgit in little over a week. Four other captured sher bachas were also brought in.

Our troops, followed by the Baltis laden with captured weapons and flags, made a triumphant entry into Gilgit on January 11. Crowds of natives were collected on the maidan to welcome the victorious army, and the band of Alidad Khan, Rajah of Gilgit, played stirring music in honour of our having overthrown that prince's father; for Alidad is the son of old Zafar Ali, the Thum of Nagar. Colonel Durand, we were glad to find, was sufficiently recovered to ride out and meet us, and the other wounded officers were also in a fair way of recovery.

When I left Gilgit it was not known what measures the Indian Government would take for the future control of the Hunza-Nagar States. Since then it has been decided to place Nazim Khan, half-brother to Safdar Ali, on the throne of Hunza, and to reinstate old Zafar Khan, who had fought us against his will, in Nagar. Zafar Khan's murderous son, Uzr Khan, who had escaped across the Killik, was arrested by the Chinese authorities, and was brought to Gilgit by an escort of Chinese soldiers. I do not think he will be let loose to work further mischief; the state prison of Hari Parbat, in Srinagur, will probably be his residence for the future. Many of the refugee tribesmen have now returned to their homes, the Chinese having disarmed them and conducted them across the frontier.

But the deposed thum, Safdar Ali, is still beyond the Hindoo Koosh.

The two States now recognise the Empress of India as their suzerain. Their country is open to us; but, provided that they remain loyal to the paramount Power, and abstain from slave-dealing and brigandage, the tribesmen will be permitted to manage their own affairs. This appears to be a most satisfactory arrangement for both parties, and our prestige on this frontier will gain as much by our unexpected clemency as by the success of our arms.

Thus were the operations in Hunza-Nagar brought to a close. The greatest credit is due to Colonel Durand, who so skilfully planned this expedition; to his officers, who conducted it so ably; and to the gallant sepoys, who fought so well under leaders worthy of them.

CHAPTER XXXII

FROM GILGIT TO RAWAL PINDI—A TROOP OF KINGS—THE INDUS VALLEY ABOVE BOONJI—SEVEN MARCHES IN SNOW—THE ZOJI LA IN WINTER— RAWAL PINDI AND HOME.

My long journey from Gilgit to Rawal Pindi, instead of being the dull and wearisome one I had anticipated, proved to be exceedingly interesting, and quite unique in some respects. I was, indeed, in luck's way, for Doctor Robertson, his services as Political Officer being no longer needed now that the campaign had terminated, was also travelling to India, and I was enabled to join his party.

The natives of our remote dependencies, of States allied to us, and even of countries with which we at present have no political relations, are often taken on a tour through India in order that they may realize the civilisation, the wealth, and the military strength of our Empire, and on their return to their homes be able to spread a report of what they have experienced.

This wise policy of the Indian Government was pursued on this occasion, and Doctor Robertson was instructed to bring to India as guests of the Viceroy, not only the six Kafirs who had accompanied him from Kafiristan, but some leading men of the hill-tribes who occupy the countries round Gilgit. It was certainly an aristocratic party, and included a few descendants of Alexander the Great, as well as other men of ancient family. We had with us two young princes of the royal houses of Hunza and Nagar, Sekandar Khan and Khusru Khan; other notables of the two States we had just brought under subjection, and several of their followers; and also Akbar Khan, Rajah of Punial, with some Punialis—in all about fifty men, who were to proceed to Calcutta, 'personally conducted' by Doctor Robertson, and pay their salaams to the Viceroy.

The long journey across the Himalayas with these half-savage hillmen, whom we always used to speak of as Robertson's kings, was a curious and instructive one, many humorous incidents occurring by the way. As one would expect in a travelling party of rival kings, there was a good deal of jealousy and bickering now and then; and the order of precedence, which was intimately connected with the commissariat, was a troublesome business. Each chief drew all the rations for his own party; but the amount he required depended upon his own particular rank, and not upon the number of mouths he had to feed. Thus, a rajah with only two followers expected more goats and ghee than an inferior rajah who had a dozen men with him. To have apportioned to one a half-pound too much or too little of salt or sugar would have been to ignore the delicate distinctions of rank between the rulers, a slight that would have caused much heart-burning. But it was impossible to entirely humour the caprices of these haughty village kings, for supplies were often too scarce to be wasted in observance of strict etiquette.

The party consisted entirely of fine young men, sturdy mountaineers full of energy, who got up a tamasha at every opportunity on the march; and the athletic Punialis and Hunzas, who had so recently been trying to cut each other's throats, now engaged in rivalry at polo whenever horses were procurable. They all behaved excellently as a rule, and thoroughly enjoyed their tour; but occasionally the hare-brained young kings, full of high spirits as they were, required a little looking after. Robertson is not only a venturesome explorer and a clever Political Officer, but he makes an admirable travelling tutor to youthful princes —parental in manner, not too severe, but maintaining due discipline.

The six Kafirs had weird ways, and as we marched through Baltistan they puzzled and terrified the timid natives of that country. The Kafir idolaters are looked upon with superstitious dread by their neighbours, and the Baltis believe that they are cannibals. One of the Kafirs, a boy of sixteen, who had picked up a little Hindustani, heard of this, and on entering a village it was a standing joke with him—to the huge amusement of his companions—to walk seriously up to the fattest Balti he could see—the lumbadar if possible—poke him with his finger as a butcher would a calf, and say, 'This one seems well fed; he will do for our supper.' As often as not the Balti, to judge from his scared expression, took the proposition quite seriously at first, and turned pleadingly to the sahib for protection. The religious belief of these heathen Kafirs appears to be curiously assimilative. They claimed the Gurkhas as co-religionists, because they killed their goats with somewhat similar rites; they also thought that the creed of sahibs must be the same as their own, because they too had no prejudices concerning what they ate or drank; and before they reached Rawal Pindi they exhibited an inclination to adopt Mahomedanism, and used to go off the road to pay their salaams to Mussulman saints and hermits.

It took us some days to get all ready for the start, and the kings, of course, had first to put the affairs of their several States in order, and appoint regents to rule for them in their absence.

We set out on January 23, and it was with regret that I left Gilgit and all the capital fellows there. In addition to the Viceroy's guests, we had with us two Pathan sepoys returning to India on leave, and four servants. On the bad parts of the road we sometimes had as many as 175 coolies to carry the baggage and supplies; so our party was rather a large one to attempt the Himalayan passes in winter.

I have already had so much to say on mountain journeys that I will give but a brief outline of this one. First we followed the Gilgit River, by the left bank, to its junction with the Indus, and then ascended the valley of the latter river to Skardu. It is 162 miles by this route from Gilgit to Skardu, and the road has the reputation of being the worst in Kashmir territory, so much so that it is spoken of as being only practicable for experienced cragsmen, and the descriptions one reads of it are enough to make one's hair stand on end. The reality is not quite so bad; but I should not have liked to attempt some portions of this road on my first arrival in this country. Nine months' scrambling among the Himalayas had naturally increased my confidence on a hillside.

The Indus here rushes between stupendous defiles, and for leagues at a time one sees nothing but almost perpendicular crags between the foaming water and the sky. The ever-recurring ascents and descents, sometimes of several thousands of feet, are very trying. In places one scales the cliff by rough ladders, by clambering up the trunks of trees standing up on end,

КАРТИНА.

from ledge to higher ledge, or with the assistance of pegs stuck here and there in little crevices in the rock. On one march a pari is avoided by an ascent to the height of 10,250 feet above the sea.

The weather was mild for the first few marches; but as we advanced higher up the valley it became colder; and when we reached the great sandy plain of Skardu, which I had last seen glowing under the fierce summer sun, it was covered in snow.

At Skardu we provided ourselves with leg-wraps, socks, and gloves of putto and sheepskin, sufficient for the whole party, so as to be well prepared to meet the great cold in front of us. We heard that Spedding and Beech had safely crossed the Zoji La some time back, and before any snow to speak of had fallen; but since then there had been a heavy fall, and the pass was in a dangerous condition, the snow, even at Dras, being five feet deep.

From Skardu we proceeded by what is the usual winter road to Srinagur, the summer one being over the plateau of Deosai. We continued the ascent of the Indus Valley for six marches above Skardu—the road often vile—and then went up the tributary Suru nullah to its junction with the Dras stream. This brought us on to the Leh road, and from here to Srinagur I retraced my route of the previous spring. We had now attained a considerable height, and the cold became more severe at each stage. On leaving the village of Gangani we had to traverse seven marches deeply covered in snow.

On February 13 we reached the serai of Dras, standing out dark against a world of snow. The snow was now falling steadily, and the cold was more intense than any I had ever experienced before. It would have been interesting to have had a thermometer with us. The weather-wise Thanadar of Dras, who had assisted Bower and myself across the pass in May, told us that all communication had been cut off, even for the dak, for two weeks, that the snow had been falling heavily for days, and that therefore all the tracks had been obliterated.

From here there was a four days' march over a snowy wilderness before us, on which no supplies were obtainable; and as with our large following we should soon have eaten up Dras, and consumed all the fuel there, it was absolutely necessary that we should push on at the very earliest opportunity. I need scarcely say that all arrangements for our journey had been made before we left Gilgit. Instructions had been sent ahead of us to the officials on the road to collect supplies, and Captain Trench, the acting Resident in Srinagur, was despatching a large party of coolies with all necessaries to meet us in the Sind Valley. But still our position was an anxious one should the bad weather continue, and it looked as if we should have to take our choice between the risks of famine and frostbite.

We had to remain at Dras during February 14, the snow still falling too heavily to allow of a start, and small quantities of fuel were served out. The aspect of the country round, the hard sky, the intensity of the cold, the stillness of the freezing air, impressed the imagination with an image of eternal and hopeless winter —so absolute a winter that one could not bring oneself to realize that it would ever yield to any summer sun, that it could ever be anything else than winter in this frightful place.

But at dawn on February 15 there was an improvement in the weather, so, after wrapping legs and hands well up in sheepskins, and putting on snow-glasses, we pushed on to the rest-house of Matayun. As I have explained in my description of the Leh road, the approach to the Zoji La from this side is by an almost imperceptible ascent; the traveller is practically on the summit of the pass for two marches, crossing bleak snowy downs and plateaus, often swept by fierce winds which are as fatal as those of the Rajdiangan.

We safely reached the rest-house of Matayun, and passed the night there. As good-luck would have it, the weather was favourable on the following morning, so we set out to face the pass.

The descent on the southern side is as abrupt as the ascent from the north is gradual. The winter road is down a steep gully blocked up with enormous masses of snow, which I have already described; and here there is a sudden drop of quite 2,000 feet. There was some appearance of bad weather in the sky, and our anxious guides hurried us on all day, permitting no halt of any duration. Just as we reached the edge of the plateau, and were about to commence the descent of the nullah, a strong wind suddenly sprung up, whirling clouds of frozen snow, like spray, into the air. It was well that it had not overtaken us before, for tired men could not long have contended with this icy blast, and we had been dragging ourselves through deep, soft snow for nearly ten hours.

An extraordinary stampede now took place. The coolies, knowing their danger, literally threw themselves down the almost precipitous snow slopes of the nullah, tumbling over each other, leaping, sliding, and rolling, hurrying for shelter to the bottom, far below, in any way they could, and as quickly as they could, almost regardless in their panic of the crevasses that opened out at the foot of the nullah into the torrent rushing under the piled-up snow. One man did fall through, but was hauled out at once, and we were soon all sitting safely round the fires in the rest-huts of Baltal, miserable holes that appeared very cheerful and comfortable to us now, and we cared no longer for the wind that howled outside.

It was a great relief to have got our large party here in safety; all anxiety was over now, the dreaded mountain had been crossed, there were no more difficulties ahead, and it was all easy-going from Baltal to London.

The Durbar sent a number of horses to meet us near Sonamerg; so that we were all mounted for the rest of the journey, and baggage-animals took the place of coolies.

The passage of the great mountain-range had brought us suddenly from the dreary northern deserts and an Arctic winter into the sweet Sind Valley. We rode through the soft air of the Kashmir spring-tide, crocus and other flowers blossoming at our feet, the fruit-trees budding in the orchards, the hills on either side of us, where not covered with fine pine-woods, green with young grass—a land where all, indeed, but the spirit of man was divine; for now around us once more were the false-smiling, jabbering Kashmiris, clad in their women's robes, looking contemptible wretches by the side of our manly Kanjuts and Punialis.

The practical-minded hillmen looked with gloating eyes at the rich vale they were descending. They had never seen the like in their mountains, and their mouths watered at the unlimited capacity of the country for the feeding of cattle and goats.

Many of the tribesmen rode well; but some had little or no experience of the saddle, and often, as we were cantering along, a riderless horse would be seen to break away from our troop, showing us that yet another king had tumbled off. The Kafirs were constantly being thrown, and appeared to enjoy it. In the whole of Kafiristan, it seems, there is but one horse, which was presented to a Kafir chieftain by the Mehtar of Chitral. It is considered a most valuable piece of property, and is much admired, but is never ridden, and wanders about the hillsides with the sheep and goats, living as it likes.

We rather astonished the citizens of Srinagur as we rode in a body into the capital, the kings having donned their most gorgeous raiment for the occasion. The tribesmen marvelled much at the thronged bazaars, the palaces, castles, mosques and temples, and the broad river crowded with boats and barges.

Their next excitement was the passage of the great Woolar Lake in doongahs. Several of them were sea-sick; and the Kafirs, who had never seen a boat before, seemed rather scared, and did not take nearly so readily to navigation as to horsemanship.

But it was when we had passed Murree, and looked down from the southernmost mountain-spur on the far-stretching, sunlit plains of India, that the hillmen expressed their greatest astonishment. Some of them had never before left their country, had lived all their lives between the narrow horizons of the Himalayan gorges, and so immense a landscape as this was a revelation to them.

But while the Dards were enthusiastic in their enjoyment of their new experiences, and took an intelligent interest in all they saw, the Kafirs, like most savages, looked with a stupid indifference at the marvels round them. Once, indeed, I saw them excited by an incident which opened their eyes to what appeared to them a most extraordinary and unnatural state of things. We were descending the Murree road, when a Kafir happened to remark that he was feeling hungry. Robertson bought him some chapatis at a wayside shop. The Kafir saw the money change hands. 'How is this?' he inquired in surprise. 'Do you have to pay for food in this country?' Robertson replied in the affirmative. 'What a country!' cried the Kafir in amazement. Then, after pondering awhile, he continued doubtfully, 'Supposing a man had no money in this country, he might starve.' On being told that this was quite possible, he shook with uncontrollable laughter. It was the best joke he had ever heard. He then explained this ridiculous system to his companions, and they roared in chorus.

On February 28 we reached Rawal Pindi, and on the same day I bade farewell to Dr. Robertson and his kings, who had months of wonderful experiences before them—trains, the ocean steamers, and the splendours of Indian cities—and travelled back to London as fast as Indian railways and the P. and O. vessels could take me.

Thus ended nearly a year's pleasant wanderings up and down the realm of the Maharajah Pertab Sing, in which I had lived in the midst of several interesting races—fantastic Ladakis, harmless Baltis, manly Dards, gallant Gurkha, Dogra, Pathan, and Sikh soldiery. And I was also fortunate enough to acquire the friendship of many of those soldiers and civilians of our own race who in the Far East maintain the glory of our Empire, working bravely and loyally. There one seems to live in a purer atmosphere, and old-fashioned patriotism takes the place of parochial-politics squabbling. It is in Asia, perhaps, that one realizes best what Great Britain is, and there one sees the pick of her sons living the larger and nobler life that men should live.

THE END.

A CATALOGUE OF WORKS
IN
GENERAL LITERATURE
PUBLISHED BY
MESSRS. LONGMANS, GREEN, & CO.

39 PATERNOSTER ROW, LONDON, E.C.
15 EAST 16TH STREET, NEW YORK.

MESSRS. LONGMANS, GREEN, & CO.

Issue the undermentioned Lists of their Publications, which may be had post free on application:—

1. MONTHLY LIST OF NEW WORKS AND NEW EDITIONS.
2. QUARTERLY LIST OF ANNOUNCEMENTS AND NEW WORKS.
3. NOTES ON BOOKS; BEING AN ANALYSIS OF THE WORKS PUBLISHED DURING EACH QUARTER.
4. CATALOGUE OF SCIENTIFIC WORKS.
5. CATALOGUE OF MEDICAL AND SURGICAL WORKS.
6. CATALOGUE OF SCHOOL BOOKS AND EDUCATIONAL WORKS.
7. CATALOGUE OF BOOKS FOR ELEMENTARY SCHOOLS AND PUPIL TEACHERS.
8. CATALOGUE OF THEOLOGICAL WORKS BY DIVINES AND MEMBERS OF THE CHURCH OF ENGLAND.
9. CATALOGUE OF WORKS IN GENERAL LITERATURE.

ABBEY (Rev. Charles J.), and OVERTON (Rev. John H.).
THE ENGLISH CHURCH IN THE EIGHTEENTH CENTURY. Cr. 8vo. 7s. 6d.

ABBOTT (Evelyn, M.A., LL.D.).
A SKELETON OUTLINE OF GREEK HISTORY. Chronologically Arranged. Cr. 8vo. 2s. 6d.
A HISTORY OF GREECE.
Part I.—From the Earliest Times to the Ionian Revolt. Cr. 8vo. 10s. 6d.
Part II.—500-445 B.C. Cr. 8vo. 10s. 6d.
HELLENICA. A Collection of Essays on Greek Poetry, Philosophy, History and Religion. Edited by EVELYN ABBOTT, M.A., LL.D. 8vo. 16s.

ACLAND (A. H. Dyke, M.P.), and RANSOME (Cyril, M.A.).
A HANDBOOK IN OUTLINE OF THE POLITICAL HISTORY OF ENGLAND TO 1890. Chronologically Arranged. Cr. 8vo. 6s.

ACTON (Eliza).
MODERN COOKERY. With 150 Woodcuts. Fcp. 8vo. 4s. 6d.

AMOS (Sheldon).
A PRIMER OF THE ENGLISH CONSTITUTION AND GOVERNMENT. Cr. 8vo. 6s.

ANNUAL REGISTER (THE). A Review of Public Events at Home and Abroad, for the year 1891. 8vo. 18s.
*** Volumes of the 'Annual Register' for the years 1863-1890 can still be had.

ANSTEY (F.), Author of 'Vice Versâ'.
THE BLACK POODLE, and other Stories. Cr. 8vo. 2s. boards; 2s. 6d. cloth.
VOCES POPULI. Reprinted from 'Punch'. With Illustrations by J. BERNARD PARTRIDGE. 1st Series. Fcp. 4to. 5s. 2nd Series. Fcp. 4to. 6s.
THE TRAVELLING COMPANIONS. Reprinted from 'Punch'. With Illustrations by J. BERNARD PARTRIDGE. Post 4to. 5s.

ARISTOTLE.
THE POLITICS: G. Bekker's Greek Text of Books I. III. IV. (VII.), with an English Translation by W. E. BOLLAND, M.A.; and short Introductory Essays by A. LANG, M.A. Cr. 8vo. 7s. 6d.
THE POLITICS: Introductory Essays. By ANDREW LANG. (From Bolland and Lang's 'Politics'.) Cr. 8vo. 2s. 6d.
THE ETHICS: Greek Text, Illustrated with Essays and Notes. By Sir ALEXANDER GRANT, Bart. 2 vols. 8vo. 32s.
THE NICOMACHEAN ETHICS: Newly Translated into English. By ROBERT WILLIAMS. Cr. 8vo. 7s. 6d.

ARMSTRONG (G. F. Savage-).
POEMS: Lyrical and Dramatic. Fcp. 8vo. 6s.
KING SAUL. (The Tragedy of Israel, Part I.) Fcp. 8vo. 5s.
KING DAVID. (The Tragedy of Israel, Part II.) Fcp. 8vo. 6s.
KING SOLOMON. (The Tragedy of Israel, Part III.) Fcp. 8vo. 6s.
UGONE: A Tragedy. Fcp. 8vo. 6s.
A GARLAND FROM GREECE: Poems. Fcp. 8vo. 7s. 6d.
STORIES OF WICKLOW: Poems. Fcp. 8vo. 7s. 6d.
MEPHISTOPHELES IN BROADCLOTH: a Satire. Fcp. 8vo. 4s.
ONE IN THE INFINITE: a Poem. Cr. 8vo. 7s. 6d.
THE LIFE AND LETTERS OF EDMUND J. ARMSTRONG. Fcp. 8vo. 7s. 6d.

ARMSTRONG (Edmund J.).
POETICAL WORKS. Fcp. 8vo. 5s.
ESSAYS AND SKETCHES. Fcp. 8vo. 5s.

ARMSTRONG (Edward), Queen's College, Oxford.
ELIZABETH FARNESE: The Termagant of Spain. 8vo. 16s.

ARNOLD (Sir Edwin, K.C.I.E.).
THE LIGHT OF THE WORLD: or, the Great Consummation. A Poem. Cr. 8vo. 7s. 6d. net.
Presentation Edition. With Illustrations by W. HOLMAN HUNT, &c. 4to. 20s. net.
SEAS AND LANDS. Reprinted letters from the 'Daily Telegraph'. With 71 Illustrations. Cr. 8vo. 7s. 6d.
POTIPHAR'S WIFE, and other Poems. Cr. 8vo. 5s. net.
ADZUMA, or the Japanese Wife. A Play. Cr. 8vo. 6s. 6d. net.

ARNOLD (T., D.D.), formerly Head Master of Rugby School.
INTRODUCTORY LECTURES ON MODERN HISTORY. 8vo. 7s. 6d.
MISCELLANEOUS WORKS. 8vo. 7s. 6d.

ASHLEY (W. J., M.A.).
ENGLISH ECONOMIC HISTORY AND THEORY. Part I. The Middle Ages. Cr. 8vo. 5s. Part II.

ATELIER (THE) DU LYS: or, An Art Student in the Reign of Terror. By the Author of 'Mademoiselle Mori'. Cr. 8vo. 2s. 6d.

BY THE SAME AUTHOR.

MADEMOISELLE MORI: a Tale of Modern Rome. Cr. 8vo. 2s. 6d.
THAT CHILD. Illustrated by GORDON BROWNE. Cr. 8vo. 2s. 6d.
UNDER A CLOUD. Cr. 8vo. 2s. 6d.
THE FIDDLER OF LUGAU. With Illustrations by W. RALSTON. Cr. 8vo. 2s. 6d.
A CHILD OF THE REVOLUTION. With Illustrations by C. J. STANILAND. Cr. 8vo. 2s. 6d.
HESTER'S VENTURE: a Novel. Cr. 8vo. 2s. 6d.
IN THE OLDEN TIME: a Tale of the Peasant War in Germany. Cr. 8vo. 2s. 6d.
THE YOUNGER SISTER: a Tale. Cr. 8vo. 6s.

BACON (Francis).
COMPLETE WORKS. Edited by R. L. ELLIS, J. SPEDDING and D. D. HEATH. 7 vols. 8vo. £3 13s. 6d.
LETTERS AND LIFE, INCLUDING ALL HIS OCCASIONAL WORKS. Edited by J. SPEDDING. 7 vols. 8vo. £4 4s.
THE ESSAYS: with Annotations. By RICHARD WHATELY, D.D. 8vo. 10s. 6d.
THE ESSAYS: with Introduction, Notes and Index. By E. A. ABBOTT, D.D. 2 vols. fcp. 8vo. price 6s. Text and Index only, without Introduction and Notes, in 1 vol. fcp. 8vo. 2s. 6d.

BADMINTON LIBRARY (THE). Edited by the DUKE OF BEAUFORT, K.G. assisted by ALFRED E. T. WATSON.
ATHLETICS AND FOOTBALL. By MONTAGUE SHEARMAN. With 51 Illustrations. Cr. 8vo. 10s. 6d.

[*Continued on next page*

BADMINTON LIBRARY (THE)— *continued.*

BOATING. By W. B. WOODGATE. With 49 Illustrations. Cr. 8vo. 10s. 6d.

COURSING AND FALCONRY. By HARDING COX and the Hon. GERALD LASCELLES. With 76 Illustrations. Cr. 8vo. 10s. 6d.

CRICKET. By A. G. STEEL and the Hon. R. H. LYTTELTON. With 63 Illustrations. Cr. 8vo. 10s. 6d.

CYCLING. By VISCOUNT BURY (Earl of Albemarle), K.C.M.G., and G. LACY HILLIER. With 89 Illustrations. Cr. 8vo. 10s. 6d.

DRIVING. By the DUKE OF BEAUFORT. With 65 Illustrations. Cr. 8vo. 10s. 6d.

FENCING, BOXING AND WRESTLING. By WALTER H. POLLOCK, F. C. GROVE, C. PREVOST, E. B. MICHELL and WALTER ARMSTRONG. With 42 Illustrations. Cr. 8vo. 10s. 6d.

FISHING. By H. CHOLMONDELEY-PENNELL.

Vol. I. Salmon, Trout and Grayling. With 158 Illustrations. Cr. 8vo. 10s. 6d.

Vol. II. Pike and other Coarse Fish. With 132 Illustrations. Cr. 8vo. 10s. 6d.

GOLF. By HORACE HUTCHINSON, the Rt. Hon. A. J. BALFOUR, M.P., ANDREW LANG, Sir W. G. SIMPSON, Bart., &c. With 88 Illustrations. Cr. 8vo. 10s. 6d.

HUNTING. By the DUKE OF BEAUFORT, K.G., and MOWBRAY MORRIS. With 53 Illustrations. Cr. 8vo. 10s. 6d.

MOUNTAINEERING. By C. T. DENT, Sir F. POLLOCK, Bart., W. M. CONWAY, DOUGLAS FRESHFIELD, C. E. MATHEWS, C. PILKINGTON, and other Writers. With 108 Illustrations. Cr. 8vo. 10s. 6d.

RACING AND STEEPLECHASING. By the EARL OF SUFFOLK and BERKSHIRE, W. G. CRAVEN, &c. With 56 Illustrations. Cr. 8vo. 10s. 6d.

RIDING AND POLO. By Captain ROBERT WEIR, J. MORAY BROWN, the DUKE OF BEAUFORT, K.G., the EARL OF SUFFOLK and BERKSHIRE, &c. With 59 Illustrations. Cr. 8vo. 10s. 6d.

SHOOTING. By LORD WALSINGHAM and Sir RALPH PAYNE-GALLWEY, Bart.

Vol. I. Field and Covert. With 105 Illustrations. Cr. 8vo. 10s. 6d.

Vol. II. Moor and Marsh. With 65 Illustrations. Cr. 8vo. 10s. 6d.

BADMINGTON LIBRARY (THE)— *continued.*

SKATING, CURLING, TOBOGGANING AND OTHER ICE SPORTS. By J. M. HEATHCOTE, C. G. TEBBUTT, T. MAXWELL WITHAM, the Rev. JOHN KERR, ORMOND HAKE and Colonel BUCK. With 284 Illustrations. Cr. 8vo. 10s. 6d.

TENNIS, LAWN TENNIS, RACKETS AND FIVES. By J. M. and C. G. HEATHCOTE, E. O. PLEYDELL-BOUVERIE and A. C. AINGER. With 79 Illustrations. Cr. 8vo. 10s. 6d.

BAGEHOT (Walter).
BIOGRAPHICAL STUDIES. 8vo. 12s.
ECONOMIC STUDIES. 8vo. 10s. 6d.
LITERARY STUDIES. 2 vols. 8vo. 28s.
THE POSTULATES OF ENGLISH POLITICAL ECONOMY. Cr. 8vo. 2s. 6d.

BAGWELL (Richard, LL.D.).
IRELAND UNDER THE TUDORS. (3 vols.) Vols. I. and II. From the first invasion of the Northmen to the year 1578. 8vo. 32s. Vol. III. 1578-1603. 8vo. 18s.

BAIN (Alexander).
MENTAL AND MORAL SCIENCE. Cr. 8vo. 10s. 6d.
SENSES AND THE INTELLECT. 8vo. 15s.
EMOTIONS AND THE WILL. 8vo. 15s.
LOGIC, DEDUCTIVE AND INDUCTIVE. Part I. 4s. Part II. 6s. 6d.
PRACTICAL ESSAYS. Cr. 8vo. 2s.

BAKER (Sir Samuel W.).
EIGHT YEARS IN CEYLON. With 6 Illustrations. Cr. 8vo. 3s. 6d.
THE RIFLE AND THE HOUND IN CEYLON. 6 Illustrations. Cr. 8vo. 3s. 6d.

BALL (The Rt. Hon. J. T.).
THE REFORMED CHURCH OF IRELAND. (1537-1889.) 8vo. 7s. 6d.
HISTORICAL REVIEW OF THE LEGISLATIVE SYSTEMS OPERATIVE IN IRELAND, from the Invasion of Henry the Second to the Union (1172-1800). 8vo. 6s.

BARING-GOULD (Rev. S.).
CURIOUS MYTHS OF THE MIDDLE AGES. Cr. 8vo. 3s. 6d.
ORIGIN AND DEVELOPMENT OF RELIGIOUS BELIEF. 2 vols. 7s.

BARRAUD (Clement William, S.J.).
SAINT THOMAS OF CANTERBURY AND SAINT ELIZABETH OF HUNGARY: Historical Dramas. Cr. 8vo. 5s.

BEACONSFIELD (The Earl of).
  NOVELS AND TALES. Cheap Edition.
  Complete in 11 vols. Cr. 8vo. 1s. each,
  boards; 1s. 6d. each, cloth.
      VIVIAN GREY.
      THE YOUNG DUKE, &c.
      ALROY, IXION, &c.
      CONTARINI FLEMING, &c.
      HENRIETTA TEMPLE.
      VENETIA.   TANCRED.
      CONINGSBY.   SYBIL.
      LOTHAIR.   ENDYMION.
  NOVELS AND TALES. The Hughenden Edition. With 2 Portraits and 11 Vignettes. 11 vols. Cr. 8vo. 42s.

BECKER (Professor).
  GALLUS: or, Roman Scenes in the Time of Augustus. Illustrated. Post 8vo. 7s. 6d.
  CHARICLES: or, Illustrations of the Private Life of the Ancient Greeks. Illustrated. Post 8vo. 7s. 6d.

BELL (Mrs. Hugh).
  CHAMBER COMEDIES: a Collection of Plays and Monologues for the Drawing Room. Cr. 8vo. 6s.
  NURSERY COMEDIES: Twelve Tiny Plays for Children. Fcap. 8vo. 1s. 6d.

BENT (J. Theodore, F.S.A., F.R.G.S.).
  THE RUINED CITIES OF MASHONALAND: being a Record of Excavation and Exploration in 1891. With a Chapter on the Orientation and Mensuration of the Temples. By R. M. W. SWAN. With 5 Maps and Plans, 13 Plates, and 104 Illustrations in the Text. 8vo. 18s.

BOYD (A. K. H., D.D.).
  TWENTY-FIVE YEARS OF ST. ANDREWS, 1865-1890. 2 vols. 8vo. Vol. I. 8vo. 12s. Vol. II. 15s.
  AUTUMN HOLIDAYS OF A COUNTRY PARSON. Cr. 8vo. 3s. 6d.
  CHANGED ASPECTS OF UNCHANGED TRUTHS. Cr. 8vo. 3s. 6d.
  COMMONPLACE PHILOSOPHER. Cr. 8vo. 3s. 6d.
  COUNSEL AND COMFORT FROM A CITY PULPIT. Cr. 8vo. 3s. 6d.
  CRITICAL ESSAYS OF A COUNTRY PARSON. Cr. 8vo. 3s. 6d.
  EAST COAST DAYS AND MEMORIES. Cr. 8vo. 3s. 6d.
  GRAVER THOUGHTS OF A COUNTRY PARSON. Three Series. Cr. 8vo. 3s. 6d. each.
  LANDSCAPES, CHURCHES AND MORALITIES. Cr. 8vo. 3s. 6d.

BOYD (A. K. H., D.D.).—continued.
  LEISURE HOURS IN TOWN. Cr. 8vo. 3s. 6d.
  LESSONS OF MIDDLE AGE. Cr. 8vo. 3s. 6d.
  OUR LITTLE LIFE. Two Series. Cr. 8vo. 3s. 6d. each.
  OUR HOMELY COMEDY: AND TRAGEDY. Cr. 8vo. 3s. 6d.
  PRESENT DAY THOUGHTS. Cr. 8vo. 3s. 6d.
  RECREATIONS OF A COUNTRY PARSON. Three Series. Cr. 8vo. 3s. 6d. each. Also 1st series. Popular Edition. 8vo. 6d.
  SEASIDE MUSINGS. Cr. 8vo. 3s. 6d.
  SUNDAY AFTERNOONS IN THE PARISH CHURCH OF A SCOTTISH UNIVERSITY CITY. Cr. 8vo. 3s. 6d.
  'TO MEET THE DAY' through the Christian Year: being a Text of Scripture, with an Original Meditation and a Short Selection in Verse for Every Day. Cr. 8vo. 4s. 6d.

BRASSEY (Lady).
  A VOYAGE IN THE 'SUNBEAM,' OUR HOME ON THE OCEAN FOR ELEVEN MONTHS.
      Library Edition. With 8 Maps and Charts, and 118 Illustrations. 8vo. 21s.
      Cabinet Edition. With Map and 66 Illustrations. Cr. 8vo. 7s. 6d.
      'Silver Library' Edition. With 66 Illustrations. Cr. 8vo. 3s. 6d.
      Popular Edition. With 60 Illustrations. 4to. 6d. sewed, 1s. cloth.
      School Edition. With 37 Illustrations. Fcp. 2s. cloth, or 3s. white parchment.
  SUNSHINE AND STORM IN THE EAST.
      Library Edition. With 2 Maps and 114 Illustrations. 8vo. 21s.
      Cabinet Edition. With 2 Maps and 114 Illustrations. Cr. 8vo. 7s. 6d.
      Popular Edition. With 103 Illustrations. 4to. 6d. sewed, 1s. cloth.
  IN THE TRADES, THE TROPICS, AND THE 'ROARING FORTIES'.
      Cabinet Edition. With Map and 220 Illustrations. Cr. 8vo. 7s. 6d.
      Popular Edition. With 183 Illustrations. 4to. 6d. sewed, 1s. cloth.
  THE LAST VOYAGE TO INDIA AND AUSTRALIA IN THE 'SUNBEAM'. With Charts and Maps, and 40 Illustrations in Monotone (20 full-page), and nearly 200 Illustrations in the Text from Drawings by R. T. PRITCHETT. 8vo. 21s.
      [Continued on next page.

BRASSEY (Lady)—*continued*.
THREE VOYAGES IN THE 'SUNBEAM'. Popular Edition. With 346 Illustrations. 4to. 2s. 6d.

BRAY (Charles).
THE PHILOSOPHY OF NECESSITY: or, Law in Mind as in Matter. Cr. 8vo. 5s.

BRENDA.
OLD ENGLAND'S STORY IN LITTLE WORDS FOR LITTLE CHILDREN. With 29 Illustrations. Imp. 16mo. 3s. 6d.
WITHOUT A REFERENCE. A Story. Cr. 8vo. 3s. 6d.

BRIGHT (Rev. J. Franck, D.D.), Master of University College, Oxford.
A HISTORY OF ENGLAND. 4 vols. Cr. 8vo.
   Period I.—Mediæval Monarchy: The Departure of the Romans to Richard III. From A.D. 449 to 1485. 4s. 6d.
   Period II.—Personal Monarchy: Henry VII. to James II. From 1485 to 1688. 5s.
   Period III.—Constitutional Monarchy: William and Mary to William IV. From 1689 to 1837. 7s. 6d.
   Period IV.—The Growth of Democracy: Victoria. From 1837 to 1880. 6s.

BUCKLE (Henry Thomas).
HISTORY OF CIVILISATION IN ENGLAND AND FRANCE, SPAIN AND SCOTLAND. 3 vols. Cr. 8vo. 24s.

BULL (Thomas).
HINTS TO MOTHERS ON THE MANAGEMENT OF THEIR HEALTH DURING THE PERIOD OF PREGNANCY. Fcp. 8vo. 1s. 6d.
THE MATERNAL MANAGEMENT OF CHILDREN IN HEALTH AND DISEASE. Fcp. 8vo. 1s. 6d.

BUTLER (Samuel).
Op. 1. EREWHON. Cr. 8vo. 5s.
Op. 2. THE FAIR HAVEN. A Work in defence of the Miraculous Element in our Lord's Ministry. Cr. 8vo. 7s. 6d.
Op. 3. LIFE AND HABIT. An Essay after a Completer View of Evolution. Cr. 8vo. 7s. 6d.
Op. 4. EVOLUTION, OLD AND NEW. Cr. 8vo. 10s. 6d.
Op. 5. UNCONSCIOUS MEMORY. Cr. 8vo. 7s. 6d.
Op. 6. ALPS AND SANCTUARIES OF PIEDMONT AND CANTON TICINO. Illustrated. Pott 4to. 10s. 6d.
Op. 7. SELECTIONS FROM OPS. 1-6. With Remarks on Mr. ROMANES' 'Mental Evolution in Animals'. Cr. 8vo. 7s. 6d.

BUTLER (Samuel)—*continued*.
Op. 8. LUCK, OR CUNNING, AS THE MAIN MEANS OF ORGANIC MODIFICATION? Cr. 8vo. 7s. 6d.
Op. 9. EX VOTO. An Account of the Sacro Monte or New Jerusalem at Varallo-Sesia. 10s. 6d.
HOLBEIN'S 'LA DANSE'. A Note on a Drawing called 'La Danse'. 3s.

CARLYLE (Thomas).
LAST WORDS OF THOMAS CARLYLE — Wotton Reinfred — Excursion (Futile Enough) to Paris — Letters to Varnhagen von Ense, &c. Cr. 8vo. 6s. 6d. net.
THOMAS CARLYLE: a History of his Life. By J. A. FROUDE. 1795-1835. 2 vols. Cr. 8vo. 7s. 1834-1881. 2 vols. Cr. 8vo. 7s.

CHESNEY (Lieut.-General Sir George).
INDIAN POLITY: a View of the System of Administration in India. New Edition, Revised and Enlarged.

CHETWYND (Sir George, Bart.).
RACING REMINISCENCES AND EXPERIENCES OF THE TURF. 2 vols. 8vo. 21s.

CHILD (Gilbert W.).
CHURCH AND STATE UNDER THE TUDORS. 8vo. 15s.

CHILTON (E.).
THE HISTORY OF A FAILURE, and other Tales. Fcp. 8vo. 3s. 6d.

CHISHOLM (G. G.).
HANDBOOK OF COMMERCIAL GEOGRAPHY. With 29 Maps. 8vo. 10s. net.

CLERKE (Agnes M.).
FAMILIAR STUDIES IN HOMER. Crown 8vo. 7s. 6d.

CLODD (Edward).
THE STORY OF CREATION: a Plain Account of Evolution. With 77 Illustrations. Cr. 8vo. 3s. 6d.

CLUTTERBUCK (W. J.).
ABOUT CEYLON AND BORNEO: being an Account of Two Visits to Ceylon, one to Borneo, and How we Fell Out on our Homeward Journey. With 47 Illustrations. Cr. 8vo. 10s. 6d.

COLENSO (J. W., D.D., late Bishop of Natal).
THE PENTATEUCH AND BOOK OF JOSHUA CRITICALLY EXAMINED. Cr. 8vo. 6s.

COMYN (L. N.).
ATHERSTONE PRIORY: a Tale. Cr. 8vo. 2s. 6d.

CONINGTON (John).
THE ÆNEID OF VIRGIL. Translated into English Verse. Cr. 8vo. 6s.
THE POEMS OF VIRGIL. Translated into English Prose. Cr. 8vo. 6s.

COPLESTON (Reginald Stephen, D.D., Bishop of Colombo).
BUDDHISM, PRIMITIVE AND PRESENT, IN MAGADHA AND IN CEYLON. 8vo. 16s.

COX (The Rev. Sir G. W., Bart., M.A.).
A GENERAL HISTORY OF GREECE, from the Earliest Period to the Death of Alexander the Great; with a sketch of the subsequent History to the Present Time. With 11 Maps and Plans. Cr. 8vo. 7s. 6d.

CRAKE (Rev. A. D.).
EDWY THE FAIR: or, The First Chronicle of Æscendune. Cr. 8vo. 2s. 6d.
ALFGAR THE DANE: or, the Second Chronicle of Æscendune. Cr. 8vo. 2s. 6d.
THE RIVAL HEIRS: being the Third and Last Chronicle of Æscendune. Cr. 8vo. 2s. 6d.
THE HOUSE OF WALDERNE. A Tale of the Cloister and the Forest in the Days of the Barons' Wars. Cr. 8vo. 2s. 6d.
BRIAN FITZ-COUNT. A Story of Wallingford Castle and Dorchester Abbey. Cr. 8vo. 2s. 6d.
HISTORY OF THE CHURCH UNDER THE ROMAN EMPIRE, A.D. 30-476. Crown 8vo. 7s. 6d.

CREIGHTON (Mandell, D.D., LL.D., Bishop of Peterborough).
HISTORY OF THE PAPACY DURING THE REFORMATION. 8vo. Vols. I. and II., 1378-1464, 32s.; Vols. III. and IV., 1464-1518, 24s.

CROZIER (John Beattie, M.D.).
CIVILISATION AND PROGRESS. Third Edition, Revised and Enlarged, and with New Preface. More fully explaining the nature of the New Organon used in the solution of its problems. 8vo. 14s.

CRUMP (A.).
A SHORT ENQUIRY INTO THE FORMATION OF POLITICAL OPINION, from the reign of the Great Families to the Advent of Democracy. 8vo. 7s. 6d.

CRUMP (A.)—continued.
AN INVESTIGATION INTO THE CAUSES OF THE GREAT FALL IN PRICES which took place coincidently with the Demonetisation of Silver by Germany. 8vo. 6s.

CURZON (The Hon. George N., M.P., late Fellow of All Souls College, Oxford).
PERSIA AND THE PERSIAN QUESTION. With 9 Maps, 96 Illustrations, Appendices, and an Index. 2 vols. 8vo. 42s.

DANTE.
LA COMMEDIA DI DANTE. A New Text, carefully Revised with the aid of the most recent Editions and Collations. Sm. 8vo. 6s.

DAVIDSON (W. L.).
THE LOGIC OF DEFINITION EXPLAINED AND APPLIED. Cr. 8vo. 6s.
LEADING AND IMPORTANT ENGLISH WORDS EXPLAINED AND EXEMPLIFIED. Fcp. 8vo. 3s. 6d.

DEAD SHOT (THE): or, Sportsman's Complete Guide. Being a Treatise on the Use of the Gun, with Rudimentary and Finishing Lessons on the Art of Shooting Game of all kinds, also Game Driving, Wild-Fowl and Pigeon Shooting, Dog Breaking, &c. By MARKSMAN. Cr. 8vo. 10s. 6d.

DELAND (Margaret, Author of 'John Ward').
THE STORY OF A CHILD. Cr. 8vo. 5s.

DE LA SAUSSAYE (Professor Chantepie).
A MANUAL OF THE SCIENCE OF RELIGION. Translated by Mrs. COLYER FERGUSSON (née MAX MÜLLER). Cr. 8vo. 12s. 6d.

DE SALIS (Mrs.).
CAKES AND CONFECTIONS À LA MODE. Fcp. 8vo. 1s. 6d.
DRESSED GAME AND POULTRY À LA MODE. Fcp. 8vo. 1s. 6d.
DRESSED VEGETABLES À LA MODE. Fcp. 8vo. 1s. 6d.
DRINKS À LA MODE. Fcp. 8vo. 1s. 6d.
ENTRÉES À LA MODE. Fcp. 8vo. 1s. 6d.
FLORAL DECORATIONS. Suggestions and Descriptions. Fcp. 8vo. 1s. 6d.
[Continued on next page

DE SALIS (Mrs.)—*continued.*
NEW-LAID EGGS: Hints for Amateur Poultry Rearers. Fcp. 8vo. 1s. 6d.
OYSTERS À LA MODE. Fcp. 8vo. 1s. 6d.
PUDDINGS AND PASTRY À LA MODE. Fcp. 8vo. 1s. 6d.
SAVOURIES À LA MODE. Fcp. 8vo. 1s. 6d.
SOUPS AND DRESSED FISH À LA MODE. Fcp. 8vo. 1s. 6d.
SWEETS AND SUPPER DISHES À LA MODE. Fcp. 8vo. 1s. 6d.
TEMPTING DISHES FOR SMALL INCOMES. Fcp. 8vo. 1s. 6d.
WRINKLES AND NOTIONS FOR EVERY HOUSEHOLD. Cr. 8vo. 1s. 6d.

DE TOCQUEVILLE (Alexis).
DEMOCRACY IN AMERICA. 2 vols. Cr. 8vo. 16s.

DOROTHY WALLIS: an Autobiography. With Preface by WALTER BESANT. Cr. 8vo. 6s.

DOUGALL (L.).
BEGGARS ALL: a Novel. Cr. 8vo. 3s. 6d.

DOWELL (Stephen).
A HISTORY OF TAXATION AND TAXES IN ENGLAND, from the Earliest Times to the Year 1885. (4 vols. 8vo.) Vols. I. and II. The History of Taxation, 21s. Vols. III. and IV. The History of Taxes, 21s.

DOYLE (A. Conan).
MICAH CLARKE. A Tale of Monmouth's Rebellion. With Frontispiece and Vignette. Cr. 8vo. 3s. 6d.
THE CAPTAIN OF THE POLESTAR: and other Tales. Cr. 8vo. 3s. 6d.

DUBLIN UNIVERSITY PRESS SERIES (THE): a Series of Works undertaken by the Provost and Senior Fellows of Trinity College, Dublin.
CODEX RESCRIPTUS DUBLINENSIS OF ST. MATTHEW. By T. K. ABBOTT. 4to. 21s.
EVANGELIORUM VERSIO ANTE-HIERONYMIANA EX CODICE USSERIANO (DUBLINENSI). By T. K. ABBOTT. 2 vols. Cr. 8vo. 21s.
SHORT NOTES ON ST. PAUL'S EPISTLES TO THE ROMANS, CORINTHIANS, GALATIANS, EPHESIANS AND PHILIPPIANS. By T. K. ABBOTT. Fcp. 8vo. 4s.

DUBLIN UNIVERSITY PRESS SERIES (THE)—*continued.*
GREEK GEOMETRY FROM THALES TO EUCLID. By G. J. ALLMAN. 8vo. 10s. 6d.
THEORY OF EQUATIONS. By W. S. BURNSIDE and A. W. PANTON. 8vo. 12s. 6d.
SEQUEL TO EUCLID'S ELEMENTS. By JOHN CASEY. Cr. 8vo. 3s. 6d.
ANALYTICAL GEOMETRY OF THE CONIC SECTIONS. By JOHN CASEY. Cr. 8vo. 7s. 6d.
EUMENIDES OF ÆSCHYLUS. With Metrical English Translation. By J. F. DAVIES. 8vo. 7s.
DUBLIN TRANSLATIONS INTO GREEK AND LATIN VERSE. Edited by R. Y. TYRRELL. 8vo. 6s.
LIFE OF SIR WILLIAM HAMILTON. By R. P. GRAVES. 3 vols. 15s. each.
ADDENDUM TO THE LIFE OF SIR WILLIAM ROWAN HAMILTON, LL.D., D.C.L. 8vo. 6d. sewed.
PARABOLA, ELLIPSE AND HYPERBOLA. By R. W. GRIFFIN. Cr. 8vo. 6s.
MEDICAL LANGUAGE OF ST. LUKE. By W. K. HOBART. 8vo. 16s.
ESSAYS IN POLITICAL ECONOMY. By T. E. CLIFFE LESLIE. 8vo. 10s. 6d.
ZOOLOGY AND MORPHOLOGY OF VERTEBRATA. By A. MACALISTER. 8vo. 10s. 6d.
MATHEMATICAL AND OTHER TRACTS. By JAMES MACCULLAGH. 8vo. 15s.
PARMENIDES OF PLATO, Text, with Introduction, Analysis, &c. By T. MAGUIRE. 8vo. 7s. 6d.
INTRODUCTION TO LOGIC. By W. H. S. MONCK. Cr. 8vo. 5s.
EXAMPLES ON THE ANALYTIC GEOMETRY OF PLANE CONICS. By R. A. ROBERTS. Cr. 8vo. 5s.
CORRESPONDENCE WITH CAROLINE BOWLES. By R. SOUTHEY. Edited by E. DOWDEN. 8vo. 14s.
HISTORY OF THE UNIVERSITY OF DUBLIN, from its Foundation to the End of the Eighteenth Century. By J. W. STUBBS. 8vo. 12s. 6d.
THE ÆNEID OF VIRGIL, freely translated into English Blank Verse. By W. J. THORNHILL. Cr. 8vo. 7s. 6d.
CICERO'S CORRESPONDENCE. By R. Y. TYRRELL. Vols. I., II., III. 8vo. each 12s.
THE ACHARNIANS OF ARISTOPHANES, translated into English Verse. By R. Y. TYRRELL. Cr. 8vo. 1s.

[*Continued on next page.*

DUBLIN UNIVERSITY PRESS SERIES 'THE'—continued.

GOETHE'S FAUST, Translation and Notes. By T. E. WEBB. 8vo. 12s. 6d.

THE VEIL OF ISIS: a Series of Essays on Idealism. By T. E. WEBB. 8vo. 10s. 6d.

THE GROWTH OF THE HOMERIC POEMS. By G. WILKIN. 8vo. 6s.

EPOCHS OF ANCIENT HISTORY.
Edited by the Rev. Sir G. W. Cox, Bart., M.A., and by C. SANKEY, M.A. Fcp. 8vo. with Maps, 2s. 6d. each.

The Athenian Empire from the Flight of Xerxes to the Fall of Athens. By the Rev. Sir G. W. Cox, Bart., M.A. With 5 Maps.

Rome to its Capture by the Gauls. By WILHELM IHNE. With a Map.

The Roman Triumvirates. By the Very Rev. CHARLES MERIVALE, D.D., Dean of Ely. With a Map.

The Spartan and Theban Supremacies. By CHARLES SANKEY, M.A. With 5 Maps.

Rome and Carthage, the Punic Wars. By R. BOSWORTH SMITH, M.A. With 9 Maps and Plans.

The Gracchi, Marius, and Sulla. By A. H. BEESLY, M.A. With 2 Maps.

The Early Roman Empire. From the Assassination of Julius Cæsar to the Assassination of Domitian. By the Rev. W. WOLFE CAPES, M.A. With 2 Maps.

The Roman Empire of the Second Century, or the Age of the Antonines. By the Rev. W. WOLFE CAPES, M.A. With 2 Maps.

The Greeks and the Persians. By the Rev. Sir G. W. Cox, Bart., M.A. With 4 Maps.

The Rise of the Macedonian Empire. By ARTHUR M. CURTEIS, M.A. With 8 Maps.

EPOCHS OF MODERN HISTORY.
Edited by C. COLBECK, M.A. Fcp. 8vo. with Maps, 2s. 6d. each.

The Beginning of the Middle Ages. By the Very Rev. RICHARD WILLIAM CHURCH, M.A., &c., late Dean of St. Paul's. With 3 Maps.

The Normans in Europe. By the Rev. A. H. JOHNSON, M.A. With 3 Maps.

The Crusades. By the Rev. Sir G. W. Cox, Bart., M.A. With a Map.

The Early Plantagenets. By the Right Rev. W. STUBBS, D.D., Bishop of Oxford. With 2 Maps.

EPOCHS OF MODERN HISTORY—continued.

Edward the Third. By the Rev. W. WARBURTON, M.A. With 3 Maps and 3 Genealogical Tables.

The Houses of Lancaster and York; with the Conquest and Loss of France. By JAMES GAIRDNER. With 5 Maps.

The Early Tudors. By the Rev. C. E. MOBERLY, M.A.

The Era of the Protestant Revolution. By F. SEEBOHM. With 4 Maps and 12 Diagrams.

The Age of Elizabeth. By the Right Rev. M. CREIGHTON, LL.D., Bishop of Peterborough. With 5 Maps and 4 Genealogical Tables.

The First Two Stuarts and the Puritan Revolution (1603-1660). By SAMUEL RAWSON GARDINER. With 4 Maps.

The English Restoration and Louis XIV. (1648-1678). By OSMUND AIRY.

The Fall of the Stuarts; and Western Europe from 1678 to 1697. By the Rev. EDWARD HALE, M.A. With 11 Maps and Plans.

The Age of Anne. By E. E. MORRIS, M.A. With 7 Maps and Plans.

The Thirty Years' War, 1618-1648. By SAMUEL RAWSON GARDINER. With a Map.

The Early Hanoverians. By E. E. MORRIS, M.A. With 9 Maps and Plans.

Frederick the Great and the Seven Years' War. By F. W. LONGMAN. With 2 Maps.

The War of American Independence, 1775-1783. By J. M. LUDLOW. With 4 Maps.

The French Revolution, 1789-1795. By Mrs. S. R. GARDINER. With 7 Maps.

The Epoch of Reform, 1830-1850. By JUSTIN MCCARTHY, M.P.

EPOCHS OF CHURCH HISTORY.
Edited by the Right Rev. MANDELL CREIGHTON, D.D., Bishop of Peterborough. Fcp. 8vo. 2s. 6d. each.

The English Church in other Lands. By the Rev. H. W. TUCKER.

The History of the Reformation in England. By the Rev. GEORGE G. PERRY.

A History of the University of Oxford. By the Hon. G. C. BRODRICK.

A History of the University of Cambridge. By J. BASS MULLINGER, M.A.

The Church of the Early Fathers. By A. PLUMMER, D.D.

The Church and the Roman Empire. By the Rev. A. CARR.

[Continued on next page.

EPOCHS OF CHURCH HISTORY—*continued.*

The Church and the Puritans (1570-1660). By H. OFFLEY WAKEMAN, M.A.

The Evangelical Revival in the Eighteenth Century. By the Rev. J. H. OVERTON.

The Church and the Eastern Empire. By the Rev. H. F. TOZER.

Hildebrand and his Times. By the Rev. W. R. W. STEPHENS.

The English Church in the Middle Ages. By the Rev. W. HUNT, M.A.

The Popes and the Hohenstaufen. By UGO BALZANI.

The Arian Controversy. By H. M. GWATKIN, M.A.

The Counter-Reformation. By A. W. WARD.

Wycliffe and Early Movements of Reform. By REGINALD L. POOLE, M.A.

EPOCHS OF AMERICAN HISTORY.

Edited by Dr. ALBERT BUSHNELL HART, Assistant Professor of History in Harvard College, U.S.A. Fcp. 8vo. 3*s.* 6*d.* each.

The Colonies (1492-1750). By REUBEN GOLD THWAITES, Secretary of the State Historical Society of Wisconsin.

Formation of the Union (1750-1829). By ALBERT BUSHNELL HART, A.B., Ph.D., the Editor of the Series. With 5 Maps.

Division and Re-Union (1829-1889). By WOODROW WILSON, Ph.D., LL.D., Professor of Jurisprudence in Princeton College. With 5 Maps. Fcp. 8vo.

EPOCH MAPS, Illustrating American History. By ALBERT BUSHNELL HART, Ph.D., Assistant Professor of History in Harvard College. 14 Maps. Oblong 4to. 2*s.* 6*d.*

EPOCHS OF ENGLISH HISTORY.

Complete in One Volume, with 27 Tables and Pedigrees, and 23 Maps. Fcp. 8vo. 5*s.*

*** For details of Parts *see* Longmans & Co.'s Catalogue of School Books.

EWALD (Heinrich).
THE ANTIQUITIES OF ISRAEL. Translated from the German by H. S. SOLLY, M.A. 8vo. 12*s.* 6*d.*
THE HISTORY OF ISRAEL. Translated from the German. 8 vols. 8vo. Vols. I. and II. 24*s.* Vols. III. and IV. 21*s.* Vol. V. 18*s.* Vol. VI. 16*s.* Vol. VII. 21*s.* Vol. VIII., with Index to the Complete Work. 18*s.*

FALKENER (Edward).
GAMES, ANCIENT AND ORIENTAL, AND HOW TO PLAY THEM. Being the Games of the Ancient Egyptians, the Hiera Gramme of the Greeks, the Ludus Latrunculorum of the Romans, and the Oriental Games of Chess, Draughts, Backgammon and Magic Squares. With numerous Photographs, Diagrams, &c. 8vo. 21*s.*

FARNELL (George S., M.A.).
GREEK LYRIC POETRY: a Complete Collection of the Surviving Passages from the Greek Song-Writers. Arranged with Prefatory Articles, Introductory Matter and Commentary. With 5 Plates. 8vo. 16*s.*

FARRAR (Archdeacon).
DARKNESS AND DAWN: or, Scenes in the Days of Nero. An Historic Tale. Cr. 8vo. 7*s.* 6*d.*
LANGUAGE AND LANGUAGES. A Revised Edition of *Chapters on Language and Families of Speech.* Cr. 8vo. 6*s.*

FITZPATRICK (W. J., F.S.A., Author of 'Correspondence of Daniel O'Connell').
SECRET SERVICE UNDER PITT. 8vo. 14*s.*

FITZWYGRAM (Major-General Sir F., Bart.).
HORSES AND STABLES. With 19 pages of Illustrations. 8vo. 5*s.*

FORD (Horace).
THE THEORY AND PRACTICE OF ARCHERY. New Edition, thoroughly Revised and Re-written by W. BUTT, M.A. With a Preface by C. J. LONGMAN, M.A., F.S.A. 8vo. 14*s.*

FOUARD (Abbé Constant).
THE CHRIST THE SON OF GOD: a Life of our Lord and Saviour Jesus Christ. With an Introduction by Cardinal MANNING. 2 vols. Cr. 8vo. 14*s.*
ST. PETER AND THE FIRST YEARS OF CHRISTIANITY. Translated from the Second Edition, with the Author's sanction, by GEORGE F. X. GRIFFITH. With an Introduction by Cardinal GIBBONS. Cr. 8vo. 9*s.*

FOX (Charles James).
THE EARLY HISTORY OF CHARLES JAMES FOX. By the Right Hon. Sir G. O. TREVELYAN, Bart.
　Library Edition. 8vo. 18*s.*
　Cabinet Edition. Cr. 8vo. 6*s.*

FRANCIS (Francis).
A BOOK ON ANGLING: or, Treatise on the Art of Fishing in every branch; including full Illustrated List of Salmon Flies. With Portrait and Coloured Plates. Cr. 8vo. 15s.

FREEMAN (Edward A.).
THE HISTORICAL GEOGRAPHY OF EUROPE. With 65 Maps. 2 vols. 8vo. 31s. 6d.

FROUDE (James A., Regius Professor of Modern History in the University of Oxford).
THE HISTORY OF ENGLAND, from the Fall of Wolsey to the Defeat of the Spanish Armada. 12 vols. Cr. 8vo. 3s. 6d. each.
THE DIVORCE OF CATHERINE OF ARAGON: the Story as told by the Imperial Ambassadors resident at the Court of Henry VIII. *In usum Laicorum.* 8vo. 16s.
THE SPANISH STORY OF THE ARMADA, and other Essays, Historical and Descriptive. Cr. 8vo. 6s.
SHORT STUDIES ON GREAT SUBJECTS. Cabinet Edition. 4 vols. Cr. 8vo. 24s. Cheap Edition. 4 vols. Cr. 8vo. 3s. 6d. each.
CÆSAR: a Sketch. Cr. 8vo. 3s. 6d.
THE ENGLISH IN IRELAND IN THE EIGHTEENTH CENTURY. 3 vols. Cr. 8vo. 18s.
OCEANA: or, England and her Colonies. With 9 Illustrations. Cr. 8vo. 2s. boards, 2s. 6d. cloth.
THE ENGLISH IN THE WEST INDIES: or, the Bow of Ulysses. With 9 Illustrations. Cr. 8vo. 2s. boards, 2s. 6d. cloth.
THE TWO CHIEFS OF DUNBOY: an Irish Romance of the Last Century. Cr. 8vo. 3s. 6d.
THOMAS CARLYLE, a History of his Life. 1795 to 1835. 2 vols. Cr. 8vo. 7s. 1834 to 1881. 2 vols. Cr. 8vo. 7s.

GALLWEY (Sir Ralph Payne-, Bart.).
LETTERS TO YOUNG SHOOTERS. (First Series.) On the Choice and Use of a Gun. With Illustrations. Cr. 8vo. 7s. 6d.
LETTERS TO YOUNG SHOOTERS. (Second Series.) On the Production, Preservation and Killing of Game. With Directions in Shooting Wood-pigeons and Breaking-in Retrievers. With a Portrait of the Author, and 103 Illustrations. Cr. 8vo. 12s. 6d.

GARDINER (Samuel Rawson, Fellow of All Souls College, Oxford).
HISTORY OF ENGLAND, from the Accession of James I. to the Outbreak of the Civil War, 1603-1642. 10 vols. Cr. 8vo. price 6s. each.
THE STUDENT'S HISTORY OF ENGLAND. Complete in 1 vol. With 378 Illustrations. Cr. 8vo. 12s.
Vol. I. B.C. 55—A.D. 1509. With 173 Illustrations. Cr. 8vo. 4s.
Vol. II. 1509-1689. With 96 Illustrations. Cr. 8vo. 4s.
Vol. III. 1689-1885. With 109 Illustrations. Cr. 8vo. 4s.
A SCHOOL ATLAS OF ENGLISH HISTORY. With 66 Maps and 22 Plans of Battles, &c. Fcp. 4to. 5s.

GOETHE.
FAUST. A New Translation chiefly in Blank Verse; with Introduction and Notes. By JAMES ADEY BIRDS. Cr. 8vo. 6s.
FAUST. The Second Part. A New Translation in Verse. By JAMES ADEY BIRDS. Cr. 8vo. 6s.

GREEN (Thomas Hill).
THE WORKS OF THOMAS HILL GREEN. Edited by R. L. NETTLESHIP. 3 vols. Vols. I. and II. Philosophical Works. 8vo. 16s. each. Vol. III. Miscellanies. With Index to the three Volumes and Memoir. 8vo. 12s.
THE WITNESS OF GOD AND FAITH. Two Lay Sermons. Fcp. 8vo. 2s.

GREVILLE (C. C. F.).
A JOURNAL OF THE REIGNS OF KING GEORGE IV., KING WILLIAM IV. AND QUEEN VICTORIA. 8 vols. Cr. 8vo. 6s. each.

GWILT (Joseph, F.S.A.).
AN ENCYCLOPÆDIA OF ARCHITECTURE. Illustrated with more than 1700 Engravings on Wood. 8vo. 52s. 6d.

HAGGARD (Ella).
LIFE AND ITS AUTHOR: an Essay in Verse. With a Memoir by H. RIDER HAGGARD, and Portrait. Fcp. 8vo. 3s. 6d.

HAGGARD (H. Rider).
SHE. With 32 Illustrations by M. GREIFFENHAGEN and C. H. M. KERR. Cr. 8vo. 3s. 6d.
ALLAN QUATERMAIN. With 31 Illustrations by C. H. M. KERR. Cr. 8vo. 3s. 6d.
MAIWA'S REVENGE: or, The War of the Little Hand. Cr. 8vo. 1s. boards, 1s. 6d. cloth.

HAGGARD (H. Rider)—*continued.*
COLONEL QUARITCH, V.C. A Novel. Cr. 8vo. 3s. 6d.
CLEOPATRA. With 29 Full-page Illustrations by M. Greiffenhagen and R. Caton Woodville. Cr. 8vo. 3s. 6d.
BEATRICE. A Novel. Cr. 8vo. 3s. 6d.
ERIC BRIGHTEYES. With 17 Plates and 34 Illustrations in the Text by Lancelot Speed. Cr. 8vo. 6s.
NADA THE LILY. With 23 Illustrations by C. H. M. Kerr. Cr. 8vo. 6s.

HAGGARD (H. Rider) and LANG (Andrew).
THE WORLD'S DESIRE. Cr. 8vo. 6s.

HALLIWELL-PHILLIPPS (J. O.).
A CALENDAR OF THE HALLIWELL-PHILLIPPS' COLLECTION OF SHAKESPEAREAN RARITIES. Enlarged by Ernest E. Baker, F.S.A. 8vo. 10s. 6d.
OUTLINES OF THE LIFE OF SHAKESPEARE. With numerous Illustrations and Fac-similes. 2 vols. Royal 8vo. £1 1s.

HARRISON (Jane E.).
MYTHS OF THE ODYSSEY IN ART AND LITERATURE. Illustrated with Outline Drawings. 8vo. 18s.

HARRISON (Mary).
COOKERY FOR BUSY LIVES AND SMALL INCOMES. Fcp. 8vo. 1s.

HARTE (Bret).
IN THE CARQUINEZ WOODS. Fcp. 8vo. 1s. boards, 1s. 6d. cloth.
ON THE FRONTIER. 16mo. 1s.
BY SHORE AND SEDGE. 16mo. 1s.
* Complete in one Volume. Cr. 8vo. 3s. 6d.

HARTWIG (Dr.).
THE SEA AND ITS LIVING WONDERS. With 12 Plates and 303 Woodcuts. 8vo. 7s. net.
THE TROPICAL WORLD. With 8 Plates and 172 Woodcuts. 8vo. 7s. net.
THE POLAR WORLD. With 3 Maps, 8 Plates and 85 Woodcuts. 8vo. 7s. net.
THE SUBTERRANEAN WORLD. With 3 Maps and 80 Woodcuts. 8vo. 7s. net.
THE AERIAL WORLD. With Map, 8 Plates and 60 Woodcuts. 8vo. 7s. net.
HEROES OF THE POLAR WORLD. 19 Illustrations. Cr. 8vo. 2s.
WONDERS OF THE TROPICAL FORESTS. 40 Illustrations. Cr. 8vo. 2s.
WORKERS UNDER THE GROUND. 29 Illustrations. Cr. 8vo. 2s.

HARTWIG (Dr.)—*continued.*
MARVELS UNDER OUR FEET. 22 Illustrations. Cr. 8vo. 2s.
SEA MONSTERS AND SEA BIRDS. 75 Illustrations. Cr. 8vo. 2s. 6d.
DENIZENS OF THE DEEP. 117 Illustrations. Cr. 8vo. 2s. 6d.
VOLCANOES AND EARTHQUAKES. 30 Illustrations. Cr. 8vo. 2s. 6d.
WILD ANIMALS OF THE TROPICS. 66 Illustrations. Cr. 8vo. 3s. 6d.

HAVELOCK (Sir Henry, Bart.).
MEMOIRS OF SIR HENRY HAVELOCK, K.C.B. By John Clark Marshman. Cr. 8vo. 3s. 6d.

HEARN (W. Edward).
THE GOVERNMENT OF ENGLAND: its Structure and its Development. 8vo. 16s.
THE ARYAN HOUSEHOLD: its Structure and its Development. An Introduction to Comparative Jurisprudence. 8vo. 16s.

HISTORIC TOWNS. Edited by E. A. Freeman, D.C.L., and Rev. William Hunt, M.A. With Maps and Plans. Cr. 8vo. 3s. 6d. each.
BRISTOL. By Rev. W. Hunt.
CARLISLE. By Mandell Creighton, D.D., Bishop of Peterborough.
CINQUE PORTS. By Montagu Burrows.
COLCHESTER. By Rev. E. L. Cutts.
EXETER. By E. A. Freeman.
LONDON. By Rev. W. J. Loftie.
OXFORD. By Rev. C. W. Boase.
WINCHESTER. By Rev. G. W. Kitchin, D.D.
NEW YORK. By Theodore Roosevelt.
BOSTON (U.S.). By Henry Cabot Lodge.
YORK. By Rev. James Raine.

HODGSON (Shadworth H.).
TIME AND SPACE: a Metaphysical Essay. 8vo. 16s.
THE THEORY OF PRACTICE: an Ethical Enquiry. 2 vols. 8vo. 24s.
THE PHILOSOPHY OF REFLECTION. 2 vols. 8vo. 21s.
OUTCAST ESSAYS AND VERSE TRANSLATIONS. Essays: The Genius of De Quincey—De Quincey as Political Economist—The Supernatural in English Poetry; with Note on the True Symbol of Christian Union—English Verse. Verse Translations: Nineteen Passages from Lucretius, Horace, Homer, &c. Cr. 8vo. 8s. 6d.

HOOPER (George).
ABRAHAM FABERT: Governor of Sedan, Marshall of France. His Life and Times, 1599-1662. With a Portrait. 8vo. 10s. 6d.

HOWITT (William).
VISITS TO REMARKABLE PLACES, Old Halls, Battle-Fields, Scenes, illustrative of Striking Passages in English History and Poetry. With 80 Illustrations. Cr. 8vo. 3s. 6d.

HULLAH (John).
COURSE OF LECTURES ON THE HISTORY OF MODERN MUSIC. 8vo. 8s. 6d.
COURSE OF LECTURES ON THE TRANSITION PERIOD OF MUSICAL HISTORY. 8vo. 10s. 6d.

HUME (David).
THE PHILOSOPHICAL WORKS OF DAVID HUME. Edited by T. H. GREEN and T. H. GROSE. 4 vols. 8vo. 56s. Or separately, Essays. 2 vols. 28s. Treatise of Human Nature. 2 vols. 28s.

HUTH (Alfred H.).
THE MARRIAGE OF NEAR KIN, considered with respect to the Law of Nations, the Result of Experience and the Teachings of Biology. Royal 8vo. 21s.

HYNE (C. J. Cutcliffe).
THE NEW EDEN: a Story. With Frontispiece and Vignette. Cr. 8vo. 2s. 6d.

INGELOW (Jean).
POETICAL WORKS. 2 vols. Fcp. 8vo. 12s.
LYRICAL AND OTHER POEMS. Selected from the Writings of JEAN INGELOW. Fcp. 8vo. 2s. 6d. cloth plain, 3s. cloth gilt.

JAMESON (Mrs.).
SACRED AND LEGENDARY ART. With 19 Etchings and 187 Woodcuts. 2 vols. 8vo. 20s. net.
LEGENDS OF THE MADONNA. The Virgin Mary as represented in Sacred and Legendary Art. With 27 Etchings and 165 Woodcuts. 1 vol. 8vo. 10s. net.
LEGENDS OF THE MONASTIC ORDERS. With 11 Etchings and 88 Woodcuts. 1 vol. 8vo. 10s. net.
HISTORY OF OUR LORD. His Types and Precursors. Completed by Lady EASTLAKE. With 31 Etchings and 281 Woodcuts. 2 vols. 8vo. 20s. net.

JEFFERIES (Richard).
FIELD AND HEDGEROW: last Essays. With Portrait. Cr. 8vo. 3s. 6d.
THE STORY OF MY HEART: my Autobiography. With Portrait and new Preface by C. J. LONGMAN. Cr. 8vo. 3s. 6d.
RED DEER. With 17 Illustrations by J. CHARLTON and H. TUNALY. Cr. 8vo. 3s. 6d.
THE TOILERS OF THE FIELD. With Portrait from the Bust in Salisbury Cathedral. Cr. 8vo. 6s.

JENNINGS (Arthur Charles, M.A.).
ECCLESIA ANGLICANA. A History of the Church of Christ in England, from the Earliest to the Present Times. Cr. 8vo. 7s. 6d.

JEWSBURY (Geraldine Endsor).
SELECTIONS FROM THE LETTERS OF GERALDINE ENDSOR JEWSBURY TO JANE WELSH CARLYLE. Edited by Mrs. ALEXANDER IRELAND. Prefaced by a Monograph on Miss Jewsbury by the EDITOR. 8vo. 16s.

JOHNSON (J. and J. H.).
THE PATENTEE'S MANUAL: a Treatise on the Law and Practice of Letters Patent. 8vo. 10s. 6d.

JORDAN (William Leighton).
THE STANDARD OF VALUE. 8vo. 6s.

JUSTINIAN.
THE INSTITUTES OF JUSTINIAN: Latin Text, chiefly that of Huschke, with English Introduction, Translation, Notes and Summary. By THOMAS C. SANDARS, M.A. 8vo. 18s.

KALISCH (M. M.).
BIBLE STUDIES. Part I. The Prophecies of Balaam. 8vo. 10s. 6d. Part II. The Book of Jonah. 8vo. 10s. 6d.
COMMENTARY ON THE OLD TESTAMENT: with a New Translation. Vol. I. Genesis. 8vo. 18s. Or adapted for the General Reader. 12s. Vol. II. Exodus. 15s. Or adapted for the General Reader. 12s. Vol. III. Leviticus, Part I. 15s. Or adapted for the General Reader. 8s. Vol. IV. Leviticus, Part II. 15s. Or adapted for the General Reader. 8s.

KANT (Immanuel).
CRITIQUE OF PRACTICAL REASON, AND OTHER WORKS ON THE THEORY OF ETHICS. Translated by T. K. ABBOTT, B.D. With Memoir. 8vo. 12s. 6d.

[Continued on next page.

KANT (Immanuel)—*continued.*
INTRODUCTION TO LOGIC, AND HIS ESSAY ON THE MISTAKEN SUBTILTY OF THE FOUR FIGURES. Translated by T. K. ABBOTT, and with Notes by S. T. COLERIDGE. 8vo. 6s.

KEITH DERAMORE: a Novel. By the Author of 'Molly'. Cr. 8vo.

KILLICK (Rev. A. H., M.A.).
HANDBOOK TO MILL'S SYSTEM OF LOGIC. Cr. 8vo. 3s. 6d.

KNIGHT (E. F.).
THE CRUISE OF THE 'ALERTE': the Narrative of a Search for Treasure on the Desert Island of Trinidad. With 2 Maps and 23 Illustrations. Cr. 8vo. 3s. 6d.

LADD (George T.).
ELEMENTS OF PHYSIOLOGICAL PSYCHOLOGY. 8vo. 21s.
OUTLINES OF PHYSIOLOGICAL PSYCHOLOGY. A Text-book of Mental Science for Academies and Colleges. 8vo. 12s.

LANG (Andrew).
HOMER AND THE EPIC. Cr. 8vo. 9s. net.
CUSTOM AND MYTH: Studies of Early Usage and Belief. With 15 Illustrations. Cr. 8vo. 7s. 6d.
BALLADS OF BOOKS, Edited by ANDREW LANG. Fcp. 8vo. 6s.
LETTERS TO DEAD AUTHORS. Fcp. 8vo. 2s. 6d. net.
BOOKS AND BOOKMEN. With 2 Coloured Plates and 17 Illustrations. Fcp. 8vo. 2s. 6d. net.
OLD FRIENDS. Fcp. 8vo. 2s. 6d. net.
LETTERS ON LITERATURE. Fcp. 8vo. 2s. 6d. net.
GRASS OF PARNASSUS. Fcp. 8vo. 2s. 6d. net.
ANGLING SKETCHES. With 20 Illustrations by W. G. BURN MURDOCH. Cr. 8vo. 7s. 6d.
THE BLUE FAIRY BOOK. Edited by ANDREW LANG. With 8 Plates and 130 Illustrations in the Text by H. J. FORD and G. P. JACOMB HOOD. Cr. 8vo. 6s.
THE RED FAIRY BOOK. Edited by ANDREW LANG. With 4 Plates and 96 Illustrations in the Text by H. J. FORD and LANCELOT SPEED. Cr. 8vo. 6s.

LANG (Andrew)—*continued.*
THE GREEN FAIRY BOOK. Edited by ANDREW LANG. With 11 Plates and 88 Illustrations in the Text by H. J. FORD. Cr. 8vo. 6s.
THE BLUE POETRY BOOK. Edited by ANDREW LANG. With 12 Plates and 88 Illustrations in the Text by H. J. FORD and LANCELOT SPEED. Cr. 8vo. 6s.
THE BLUE POETRY BOOK. School Edition, without Illustrations. Fcp. 8vo. 2s. 6d.
THE BLUE POETRY BOOK. Special Edition, printed on Indian paper. With Notes, but without Illustrations. Cr. 8vo. 7s. 6d.

LAVISSE (Ernest, Professor at the Sorbonne).
GENERAL VIEW OF THE POLITICAL HISTORY OF EUROPE. Translated by CHARLES GROSS, Ph.D. Cr. 8vo. 5s.

LECKY (William Edward Hartpole).
HISTORY OF ENGLAND IN THE EIGHTEENTH CENTURY.
Library Edition. 8 vols. 8vo. £7 4s.
Cabinet Edition. England, 7 vols. Cr. 8vo. 6s. each. Ireland. 5 vols. Cr. 8vo. 6s. each.
HISTORY OF EUROPEAN MORALS FROM AUGUSTUS TO CHARLEMAGNE. 2 vols. Cr. 8vo. 16s.
HISTORY OF THE RISE AND INFLUENCE OF THE SPIRIT OF RATIONALISM IN EUROPE. 2 vols. Cr. 8vo. 16s.
POEMS. Fcp. 8vo. 5s.

LEES (J. A.) and CLUTTERBUCK (W. J.).
B. C. 1887: A RAMBLE IN BRITISH COLUMBIA. With Map and 75 Illustrations. Cr. 8vo. 3s. 6d.

LEWES (George Henry).
THE HISTORY OF PHILOSOPHY, from Thales to Comte. 2 vols. 8vo. 32s.

LEYTON (Frank).
THE SHADOWS OF THE LAKE, and other Poems. Cr. 8vo. 7s. 6d.
Cheap Edition. Cr. 8vo. 3s. 6d.

LLOYD (F. J.).
THE SCIENCE OF AGRICULTURE. 8vo. 12s.

LONGMAN (Frederick W.).
CHESS OPENINGS. Fcp. 8vo. 2s. 6d.
FREDERICK THE GREAT AND THE SEVEN YEARS' WAR. Fcp. 8vo. 2s. 6d.

LONGMAN'S MAGAZINE. Published Monthly, 6d.
Vols. 1-20, 8vo. 5s. each.

LONGMANS' NEW ATLAS. Political and Physical. For the Use of Schools and Private Persons. Consisting of 40 Quarto and 16 Octavo Maps and Diagrams, and 16 Plates of Views. Edited by GEO. G. CHISHOLM, M.A., B.Sc. Imp. 4to. or Imp. 8vo. 12s. 6d.

LONGMORE (Surgeon General Sir T., C.B., F.R.C.S., &c.).
RICHARD WISEMAN, Surgeon and Sergeant-Surgeon to Charles II.: a Biographical Study. With Portrait and Illustrations. 8vo. 10s. 6d.

LOUDON (J. C.).
ENCYCLOPÆDIA OF GARDENING. With 1000 Woodcuts. 8vo. 21s.
ENCYCLOPÆDIA OF AGRICULTURE: the Laying-out, Improvement and Management of Landed Property. With 1100 Woodcuts. 8vo. 21s.
ENCYCLOPÆDIA OF PLANTS: the Specific Character, &c., of all Plants found in Great Britain. With 12,000 Woodcuts. 8vo. 42s.

LUBBOCK (Sir J., Bart., M.P.).
THE ORIGIN OF CIVILISATION, and the Primitive Condition of Man. With 5 Plates and 20 Illustrations in the Text. 8vo. 18s.

LYALL (Edna, Author of 'Donovan,' &c.).
THE AUTOBIOGRAPHY OF A SLANDER. Fcp. 8vo. 1s. sewed.
Presentation Edition. With 20 Illustrations by LANCELOT SPEED. Cr. 8vo. 5s.

LYDEKKER (R.).
PHASES OF ANIMAL LIFE, PAST AND PRESENT. With 82 Illustrations. Cr. 8vo. 6s.

LYDE (Lionel W.).
AN INTRODUCTION TO ANCIENT HISTORY: being a Sketch of the History of Egypt, Mesopotamia, Greece and Rome. With a Chapter on the Development of the Roman Empire into the Powers of Modern Europe. With 3 Coloured Maps. Cr. 8vo. 3s.

LYONS (Rev. Daniel).
CHRISTIANITY AND INFALLIBILITY—Both or Neither. Cr. 8vo. 5s.

LYTTON (The Earl of). (Owen Meredith.)
MARAH. Fcp. 8vo. 6s. 6d.
KING POPPY: a Fantasia. With 1 Plate and Design on Title-page by ED. BURNE-JONES, A.R.A. Cr. 8vo. 10s. 6d.

MACAULAY (Lord).
COMPLETE WORKS OF LORD MACAULAY:
Library Edition. 8 vols. 8vo. £5 5s.
Cabinet Edition. 16 vols. Post 8vo. £4 16s.

HISTORY OF ENGLAND FROM THE ACCESSION OF JAMES THE SECOND:
Popular Edition. 2 vols. Cr. 8vo. 5s.
Student's Edition. 2 vols. Cr. 8vo. 12s.
People's Edition. 4 vols. Cr. 8vo. 16s.
Cabinet Edition. 8 vols. Post 8vo. 48s.
Library Edition. 5 vols. 8vo. £4.

CRITICAL AND HISTORICAL ESSAYS, with *LAYS OF ANCIENT ROME,* in 1 vol.:
Popular Edition. Cr. 8vo. 2s. 6d.
Authorised Edition. Cr. 8vo. 2s. 6d. or 3s. 6d. gilt edges.
'Silver Library' Edition. Cr. 8vo. 3s. 6d.

CRITICAL AND HISTORICAL ESSAYS:
Student's Edition. 1 vol. Cr. 8vo. 6s.
People's Edition. 2 vols. Cr. 8vo. 8s.
Trevelyan Edition. 2 vols. Cr. 8vo. 9s.
Cabinet Edition. 4 vols. Post 8vo. 24s.
Library Edition. 3 vols. 8vo. 36s.

ESSAYS which may be had separately price 6d. each sewed, 1s. each cloth:
Addison and Walpole.
Frederick the Great.
Croker's Boswell's Johnson.
Hallam's Constitutional History.
Warren Hastings. (3d. sewed, 6d. cloth.)
The Earl of Chatham (Two Essays).
Ranke and Gladstone.
Milton and Machiavelli.
Lord Bacon.
Lord Clive.
Lord Byron, and The Comic Dramatists of the Restoration.

The Essay on Warren Hastings annotated by S. HALES. 1s. 6d.
The Essay on Lord Clive annotated by H. COURTHOPE BOWEN, M.A. 2s. 6d.

SPEECHES:
People's Edition. Cr. 8vo. 3s. 6d.

[Continued on next page.

MACAULAY (Lord—*continued*.
LAYS OF ANCIENT ROME, &c.:
  Illustrated by G. SCHARF. Fcp. 4to.
  10s. 6d.
  ——————————— Bijou Edition. 18mo. 2s. 6d. gilt top.
  ——————————— Popular Edition. Fcp. 4to. 6d. sewed, 1s. cloth.
  Illustrated by J. R. WEGUELIN. Cr. 8vo. 3s. 6d. cloth extra, gilt edges.
  Cabinet Edition. Post 8vo. 3s. 6d.
  Annotated Edition. Fcp. 8vo. 1s. sewed, 1s. 6d. cloth.
MISCELLANEOUS WRITINGS:
  People's Edition. 1 vol. Cr. 8vo. 4s. 6d.
  Library Edition. 2 vols. 8vo. 21s.
MISCELLANEOUS WRITINGS AND SPEECHES:
  Popular Edition. 1 vol. Cr. 8vo. 2s. 6d.
  Student's Edition. 1 vol. Cr. 8vo. 6s.
  Cabinet Edition. Including Indian Penal Code, Lays of Ancient Rome and Miscellaneous Poems, 4 vols. Post 8vo. 24s.
SELECTIONS FROM THE WRITINGS OF LORD MACAULAY. Edited, with Occasional Notes, by the Right Hon. Sir G. O. TREVELYAN, Bart. Cr. 8vo. 6s.
THE LIFE AND LETTERS OF LORD MACAULAY. By the Right Hon. Sir G. O. TREVELYAN, Bart.:
  Popular Edition. 1 vol. Cr. 8vo. 2s. 6d.
  Student's Edition. 1 vol. Cr. 8vo. 6s.
  Cabinet Edition. 2 vols. Post 8vo. 12s.
  Library Edition. 2 vols. 8vo. 36s.

MACDONALD (George, LL.D.).
UNSPOKEN SERMONS. Three Series. Cr. 8vo. 3s. 6d. each.
THE MIRACLES OF OUR LORD. Cr. 8vo. 3s. 6d.
A BOOK OF STRIFE, IN THE FORM OF THE DIARY OF AN OLD SOUL: Poems. 12mo. 6s.

MACDONELL (Arthur A., M.A., Ph.D., (Deputy) Professor of Sanskrit in the University of Oxford).
A SANSKRIT-ENGLISH DICTIONARY: being a Practical Handbook, with Transliteration, Accentuation and Etymological Analysis throughout. 4to. £2 2s.

MACFARREN (Sir G. A.).
LECTURES ON HARMONY. 8vo. 12s.

MACKAIL (J. W.).
SELECT EPIGRAMS FROM THE GREEK ANTHOLOGY. Edited with a Revised Text, Introduction, Translation and Notes. 8vo. 16s.

MACLEOD (Henry D.).
THE ELEMENTS OF BANKING. Cr. 8vo. 3s. 6d.
THE THEORY AND PRACTICE OF BANKING. Vol. I. 8vo. 12s. Vol. II. 14s.
THE THEORY OF CREDIT. 8vo. Vol. I. 7s. 6d. Vol. II. Part I. 4s. 6d. Vol. II. Part II. 10s. 6d.

MANNERING (George Edward).
WITH AXE AND ROPE IN THE NEW ZEALAND ALPS. With 18 Illustrations. 8vo. 12s. 6d.

MANUALS OF CATHOLIC PHILOSOPHY (*Stonyhurst Series*):
LOGIC. By RICHARD F. CLARKE, S.J. Cr. 8vo. 5s.
FIRST PRINCIPLES OF KNOWLEDGE. By JOHN RICKABY, S.J. Cr. 8vo. 5s.
MORAL PHILOSOPHY (ETHICS AND NATURAL LAW). By JOSEPH RICKABY, S.J. Cr. 8vo. 5s.
GENERAL METAPHYSICS. By JOHN RICKABY, S.J. Cr. 8vo. 5s.
PSYCHOLOGY. By MICHAEL MAHER, S.J. Cr. 8vo. 6s. 6d.
NATURAL THEOLOGY. By BERNARD BOEDDER, S.J. Cr. 8vo. 6s. 6d.
POLITICAL ECONOMY. By CHARLES S. DEVAS. Cr. 8vo. 6s. 6d.

MARBOT (Baron de).
THE MEMOIRS OF THE BARON DE MARBOT. Translated from the French. 2 vols. 8vo. 32s.

MARTINEAU (James, D.D., LL.D.).
HOURS OF THOUGHT ON SACRED THINGS. Two Volumes of Sermons. 2 vols. Cr. 8vo. 7s. 6d. each.
ENDEAVOURS AFTER THE CHRISTIAN LIFE. Discourses. Cr. 8vo. 7s. 6d.
THE SEAT OF AUTHORITY IN RELIGION. 8vo. 14s.
ESSAYS, REVIEWS AND ADDRESSES. 4 vols. Cr. 8vo. 7s. 6d. each.
  I. Personal: Political.
  II. Ecclesiastical: Historical.
  III. Theological: Philosophical.
  IV. Academical: Religious.
HOME PRAYERS, with Two Services for Public Worship. Cr. 8vo. 3s. 6d.

MATTHEWS (Brander).
A FAMILY TREE, and other Stories. Cr. 8vo. 6s.

[*Continued on next page.*

MATTHEWS (Brander)—*continued.*
PEN AND INK: Papers on Subjects of more or less Importance. Cr. 8vo. 5s.
WITH MY FRIENDS: Tales told in Partnership. With an Introductory Essay on the Art and Mystery of Collaboration. Cr. 8vo. 6s.

MAUNDER'S TREASURIES.
BIOGRAPHICAL TREASURY. With Supplement brought down to 1889. By Rev. JAMES WOOD. Fcp. 8vo. 6s.
TREASURY OF NATURAL HISTORY: or, Popular Dictionary of Zoology. With 900 Woodcuts. Fcp. 8vo. 6s.
TREASURY OF GEOGRAPHY, Physical, Historical, Descriptive and Political. With 7 Maps and 16 Plates. Fcp. 8vo. 9s.
SCIENTIFIC AND LITERARY TREASURY. Fcp. 8vo. 6s.
HISTORICAL TREASURY: Outlines of Universal History, Separate Histories of all Nations. Fcp. 8vo. 6s.
TREASURY OF KNOWLEDGE AND LIBRARY OF REFERENCE. Comprising an English Dictionary and Grammar, Universal Gazetteer, Classical Dictionary, Chronology, Law Dictionary, &c. Fcp. 8vo. 6s.
THE TREASURY OF BIBLE KNOWLEDGE. By the Rev. J. AYRE, M.A. With 5 Maps, 15 Plates and 300 Woodcuts. Fcp. 8vo. 6s.
THE TREASURY OF BOTANY. Edited by J. LINDLEY, F.R.S., and T. MOORE, F.L.S. With 274 Woodcuts and 20 Steel Plates. 2 vols. Fcp. 8vo. 12s.

MAX MÜLLER (F., Professor of Comparative Philology in the University of Oxford).
SELECTED ESSAYS ON LANGUAGE, MYTHOLOGY AND RELIGION. 2 vols. Cr. 8vo. 16s.
THE SCIENCE OF LANGUAGE, Founded on Lectures delivered at the Royal Institution in 1861 and 1863. 2 vols. Cr. 8vo. 21s.
THREE LECTURES ON THE SCIENCE OF LANGUAGE AND ITS PLACE IN GENERAL EDUCATION, delivered at the Oxford University Extension Meeting, 1889. Cr. 8vo. 3s.
HIBBERT LECTURES ON THE ORIGIN AND GROWTH OF RELIGION, as illustrated by the Religions of India. Cr. 8vo. 7s. 6d.
INTRODUCTION TO THE SCIENCE OF RELIGION: Four Lectures delivered at the Royal Institution. Cr. 8vo. 3s. 6d.

MAX MÜLLER (F.)—*continued.*
NATURAL RELIGION. The Gifford Lectures delivered before the University of Glasgow in 1888. Cr. 8vo. 10s. 6d.
PHYSICAL RELIGION. The Gifford Lectures delivered before the University of Glasgow in 1890. Cr. 8vo. 10s. 6d.
ANTHROPOLOGICAL RELIGION: The Gifford Lectures delivered before the University of Glasgow in 1891. Cr. 8vo. 10s. 6d.
THE SCIENCE OF THOUGHT. 8vo. 21s.
THREE INTRODUCTORY LECTURES ON THE SCIENCE OF THOUGHT. 8vo. 2s. 6d.
BIOGRAPHIES OF WORDS, AND THE HOME OF THE ARYAS. Cr. 8vo. 7s. 6d.
INDIA, WHAT CAN IT TEACH US? Cr. 8vo. 3s. 6d.
A SANSKRIT GRAMMAR FOR BEGINNERS. Abridged Edition. By A. A. MACDONELL. Cr. 8vo. 6s.

MAY (Sir Thomas Erskine, K.C.B.).
THE CONSTITUTIONAL HISTORY OF ENGLAND since the Accession of George III. 1760-1870. 3 vols. Cr. 8vo. 18s.

MEADE (L. T.).
DADDY'S BOY. With Illustrations. Cr. 8vo. 3s. 6d.
DEB AND THE DUCHESS. With Illustrations by M. E. EDWARDS. Cr. 8vo. 3s. 6d.
THE BERESFORD PRIZE. With Illustrations by M. E. EDWARDS. Cr. 8vo. 5s.

MEATH (The Earl of).
SOCIAL ARROWS: Reprinted Articles on various Social Subjects. Cr. 8vo. 5s.
PROSPERITY OR PAUPERISM? Physical, Industrial and Technical Training. 8vo. 5s.

MELVILLE (G. J. Whyte).
THE GLADIATORS.
THE INTERPRETER.
GOOD FOR NOTHING.
THE QUEEN'S MARIES.
HOLMBY HOUSE.
KATE COVENTRY.
DIGBY GRAND.
GENERAL BOUNCE.
Cr. 8vo. 1s. each boards. 1s. 6d. each cloth.

MENDELSSOHN (Felix).
THE LETTERS OF FELIX MENDELSSOHN. Translated by Lady WALLACE. 2 vols. Cr. 8vo. 10s.

MERIVALE (The Very Rev. Chas., Dean of Ely).
HISTORY OF THE ROMANS UNDER THE EMPIRE. Cabinet Edition. 8 vols. Cr. 8vo. 48s.
   Popular Edition. 8 vols. Cr. 8vo. 3s. 6d. each.
THE FALL OF THE ROMAN REPUBLIC : a Short History of the Last Century of the Commonwealth. 12mo. 7s. 6d.
GENERAL HISTORY OF ROME FROM B.C. 753 TO A.D. 476. Cr. 8vo. 7s. 6d.
THE ROMAN TRIUMVIRATES. With Maps. Fcp. 8vo. 2s. 6d.

MILL (James).
ANALYSIS OF THE PHENOMENA OF THE HUMAN MIND. 2 vols. 8vo. 28s.

MILL (John Stuart).
PRINCIPLES OF POLITICAL ECONOMY.
   Library Edition. 2 vols. 8vo. 30s.
   People's Edition. 1 vol. Cr. 8vo. 3s. 6d.
A SYSTEM OF LOGIC. Cr. 8vo. 3s. 6d.
ON LIBERTY. Cr. 8vo. 1s. 4d.
ON REPRESENTATIVE GOVERNMENT. Cr. 8vo. 2s.
UTILITARIANISM. 8vo. 5s.
EXAMINATION OF SIR WILLIAM HAMILTON'S PHILOSOPHY. 8vo. 16s.
NATURE, THE UTILITY OF RELIGION, AND THEISM. Three Essays. 8vo. 5s.

MOLESWORTH (Mrs.).
SILVERTHORNS. Illustrated. Cr. 8vo. 5s.
THE PALACE IN THE GARDEN. Illustrated. Cr. 8vo. 5s.
THE THIRD MISS ST. QUENTIN. Cr. 8vo. 6s.
NEIGHBOURS. Illustrated. Cr. 8vo. 6s.
THE STORY OF A SPRING MORNING, &c. Illustrated. Cr. 8vo. 5s.
STORIES OF THE SAINTS FOR CHILDREN : the Black Letter Saints. Illustrated. Royal 16mo. 5s.

MOORE (Edward, D.D., Principal of St. Edmund Hall, Oxford).
DANTE AND HIS EARLY BIOGRAPHERS. Cr. 8vo. 7s. 6d.

MULHALL (Michael G.).
HISTORY OF PRICES SINCE THE YEAR 1850. Cr. 8vo. 6s.

NANSEN (Dr. Fridtjof).
THE FIRST CROSSING OF GREENLAND.
   Abridged Edition. With numerous Illustrations and a Map. Cr. 8vo. 7s. 6d.

NESBIT (E.) (Mrs. Hubert Bland.)
LEAVES OF LIFE : Verses. Cr. 8vo. 5s.
LAYS AND LEGENDS. First Series. New and Cheaper Edition. Cr. 8vo. 3s. 6d. Second Series. With Portrait. Cr. 8vo. 5s.

NEWMAN (Cardinal).
APOLOGIA PRO VITÂ SUA. Cabinet Edition. Cr. 8vo. 6s. Cheap Edition. Cr. 8vo. 3s. 6d.
DISCOURSES TO MIXED CONGREGATIONS. Cabinet Edition. Cr. 8vo. 6s. Cheap Edition. Cr. 8vo. 3s. 6d.
SERMONS ON VARIOUS OCCASIONS. Cabinet Edition. Cr. 8vo. 6s. Cheap Edition. 3s. 6d.
THE IDEA OF A UNIVERSITY DEFINED AND ILLUSTRATED. Cabinet Edition. Cr. 8vo. 7s. Cheap Edition. Cr. 8vo. 3s. 6d.
HISTORICAL SKETCHES. 3 vols. Cabinet Edition. Cr. 8vo. 6s. each. Cheap Edition. 3 vols. 3s. 6d. each.
THE ARIANS OF THE FOURTH CENTURY. Cabinet Edition. Cr. 8vo. 6s. Cheap Edition. Cr. 8vo. 3s. 6d.
SELECT TREATISES OF ST. ATHANASIUS in Controversy with the Arians. Freely Translated. 2 vols. Cr. 8vo. 15s.
DISCUSSIONS AND ARGUMENTS ON VARIOUS SUBJECTS. Cabinet Edition. Cr. 8vo. 6s. Cheap Edition. Cr. 8vo. 3s. 6d.
AN ESSAY ON THE DEVELOPMENT OF CHRISTIAN DOCTRINE. Cabinet Edition. Cr. 8vo. 6s. Cheap Edition. Cr. 8vo. 3s. 6d.
CERTAIN DIFFICULTIES FELT BY ANGLICANS IN CATHOLIC TEACHING CONSIDERED. Cabinet Edition. Vol. I. Cr. 8vo. 7s. 6d. Vol. II. Cr. 8vo. 5s. 6d. Cheap Edition. 2 vols. Cr. 8vo. 3s. 6d. each.
THE VIA MEDIA OF THE ANGLICAN CHURCH. Illustrated in Lectures, &c. 2 vols. Cabinet Edition. Cr. 8vo. 6s. each. Cheap Edition. 2 vols. 3s. 6d. each.
ESSAYS, CRITICAL AND HISTORICAL. Cabinet Edition. 2 vols. Cr. 8vo. 12s. Cheap Edition. 2 vols. Cr. 8vo. 7s.

[Continued on next page.

NEWMAN (Cardinal)—*continued.*
ESSAYS ON BIBLICAL AND ON ECCLESIASTICAL MIRACLES. Cabinet Edition. Cr. 8vo. 6s. Cheap Edition. Cr. 8vo. 3s. 6d.
TRACTS. 1. Dissertatiunculæ. 2. On the Text of the Seven Epistles of St. Ignatius. 3. Doctrinal Causes of Arianism. 4. Apollinarianism. 5. St. Cyril's Formula. 6. Ordo de Tempore. 7. Douay Version of Scripture. Cr. 8vo. 8s.
AN ESSAY IN AID OF A GRAMMAR OF ASSENT. Cabinet Edition. Cr. 8vo. 7s. 6d. Cheap Edition. Cr. 8vo. 3s. 6d.
PRESENT POSITION OF CATHOLICS IN ENGLAND. Cabinet Edition. Cr. 8vo. 7s. 6d. Cheap Edition. Cr. 8vo. 3s. 6d.
CALLISTA: a Tale of the Third Century. Cabinet Edition. Cr. 8vo. 6s. Cheap Edition. Cr. 8vo. 3s. 6d.
LOSS AND GAIN: a Tale. Cabinet Edition. Cr. 8vo. 6s. Cheap Edition. Cr. 8vo. 3s. 6d.
THE DREAM OF GERONTIUS. 16mo. 6d. sewed. 1s. cloth.
VERSES ON VARIOUS OCCASIONS. Cabinet Edition. Cr. 8vo. 6s. Cheap Edition. Cr. 8vo. 3s. 6d.
FABULAE QUAEDAM EX TERENTIO ET PLAUTO AD USUM PUERORUM ACCOMMODATAE. With English Notes and Translations to assist the representation. Cardinal Newman's Edition. Cr. 8vo. 6s.
*_** For Cardinal Newman's other Works see Messrs. Longmans and Co.'s *Catalogue of Church of England Theological Works.*

NORTON (Charles L.).
A HANDBOOK OF FLORIDA. With 49 Maps and Plans. Fcp. 8vo. 5s.

O'BRIEN (William, M.P.).
WHEN WE WERE BOYS: a Novel. Cr. 8vo. 2s. 6d.

OLIPHANT (Mrs.).
MADAM. Cr. 8vo. 1s. boards. 1s. 6d. cloth.
IN TRUST. Cr. 8vo. 1s. boards. 1s. 6d. cl.

OMAN (C. W. C., M.A., F.S.A.).
A HISTORY OF GREECE FROM THE EARLIEST TIMES TO THE MACEDONIAN CONQUEST. With Maps and Plans. Cr. 8vo. 4s. 6d.

PARKES (Sir Henry, G.C.M.G.).
FIFTY YEARS IN THE MAKING OF AUSTRALIAN HISTORY. With 2 Portraits (1854 and 1892). 2 vols. 8vo. 32s.

PAUL (Hermann).
PRINCIPLES OF THE HISTORY OF LANGUAGE. Translated by H. A. STRONG. 8vo. 10s. 6d.

PAYN (James).
THE LUCK OF THE DARRELLS. Cr. 8vo. 1s. boards. 1s. 6d. cloth.
THICKER THAN WATER. Cr. 8vo. 1s. boards. 1s. 6d. cloth.

PERRING (Sir Philip).
HARD KNOTS IN SHAKESPEARE. 8vo. 7s. 6d.
THE 'WORKS AND DAYS' OF MOSES. Cr. 8vo. 3s. 6d.

PHILLIPPS-WOLLEY (C.).
SNAP: a Legend of the Lone Mountain. With 13 Illustrations by H. G. WILLINK. Cr. 8vo. 3s. 6d.

POLE (W., F.R.S.).
THE THEORY OF THE MODERN SCIENTIFIC GAME OF WHIST. Fcp. 8vo. 2s. 6d.

POOLE (W. H. and Mrs.).
COOKERY FOR THE DIABETIC. With Preface by Dr. PAVY. Fcp. 8vo. 2s. 6d.

PRAEGER (Ferdinand).
WAGNER AS I KNEW HIM. Cr. 8vo. 7s. 6d.

PRATT (A. E., F.R.G.S.).
TO THE SNOWS OF TIBET THROUGH CHINA. With 33 Illustrations and a Map. 8vo. 18s.

PRENDERGAST (John P.).
IRELAND, FROM THE RESTORATION TO THE REVOLUTION. 1660-1690. 8vo. 5s.

PROCTOR (Richard A.).
OLD AND NEW ASTRONOMY. By RICHARD A. PROCTOR and A. COWPER RANYARD. With 31 Plates and 472 Woodcuts. 4to. 36s.
THE ORBS AROUND US: a Series of Essays on the Moon and Planets, Meteors and Comets. With Chart and Diagrams. Cr. 8vo. 5s.
OTHER WORLDS THAN OURS: The Plurality of Worlds Studied under the Light of Recent Scientific Researches. With 14 Illustrations. Cr. 8vo. 5s. Silver Library Edition. Cr. 8vo. 3s. 6d.
[*Continued on next page.*

PROCTOR (Richard A.)—*continued.*
THE MOON: her Motions, Aspects, Scenery and Physical Condition. With Plates, Charts, Woodcuts, &c. Cr. 8vo. 5s.
UNIVERSE OF STARS: Presenting Researches into and New Views respecting the Constitution of the Heavens. With 22 Charts and 22 Diagrams. 8vo. 10s. 6d.
LARGER STAR ATLAS for the Library. In 12 Circular Maps. With Introduction and 2 Index Pages. Folio 15s. Or Maps only 12s. 6d.
THE STUDENT'S ATLAS. In 12 Circular Maps on a Uniform Projection and one Scale. 8vo. 5s.
NEW STAR ATLAS for the Library, the School and the Observatory. In 12 Circular Maps. Cr. 8vo. 5s.
LIGHT SCIENCE FOR LEISURE HOURS. Familiar Essays on Scientific Subjects. 3 vols. Cr. 8vo. 5s. each.
CHANCE AND LUCK: a Discussion of the Laws of Luck, Coincidences, Wagers, Lotteries and the Fallacies of Gambling, &c. Cr. 8vo. 2s. boards, 2s. 6d. cloth.
STUDIES OF VENUS-TRANSITS. With 7 Diagrams and 10 Plates. 8vo. 5s.
HOW TO PLAY WHIST: WITH THE LAWS AND ETIQUETTE OF WHIST. Cr. 8vo. 3s. 6d.
HOME WHIST: an Easy Guide to Correct Play. 16mo. 1s.
THE STARS IN THEIR SEASONS. An Easy Guide to a Knowledge of the Star Groups. In 12 Maps. Roy. 8vo. 5s.
STAR PRIMER. Showing the Starry Sky Week by Week. In 24 Hourly Maps. Cr. 4to. 2s. 6d.
THE SEASONS PICTURED IN 48 SUN-VIEWS OF THE EARTH, and 24 Zodiacal Maps, &c. Demy 4to. 5s.
STRENGTH AND HAPPINESS. With 9 Illustrations. Cr. 8vo. 5s.
STRENGTH: How to get Strong and keep Strong, with Chapters on Rowing and Swimming, Fat, Age and the Waist. With 9 Illustrations. Cr. 8vo. 2s.
ROUGH WAYS MADE SMOOTH. Familiar Essays on Scientific Subjects. Cr. 8vo. 5s. Silver Library Edition. Cr. 8vo. 3s. 6d.
OUR PLACE AMONG INFINITIES. A Series of Essays contrasting our Little Abode in Space and Time with the Infinities around us. Cr. 8vo. 5s.
THE EXPANSE OF HEAVEN. Essays on the Wonders of the Firmament. Cr. 8vo. 5s.
THE GREAT PYRAMID, OBSERVATORY, TOMB AND TEMPLE. With Illustrations. Cr. 8vo. 5s.

PROCTOR (Richard A.)—*continued.*
PLEASANT WAYS IN SCIENCE. Cr. 8vo. 5s. Silver Library Edition. Cr. 8vo. 3s. 6d.
MYTHS AND MARVELS OF ASTRONOMY. Cr. 8vo. 5s.
NATURE STUDIES. By R. A. PROCTOR, GRANT ALLEN, A. WILSON, T. FOSTER, and E. CLODD. Cr. 8vo. 5s.
LEISURE READINGS. By R. A. PROCTOR, E. CLODD, A. WILSON, T. FOSTER, and A. C. RANYARD. Cr. 8vo. 5s.

RANSOME (Cyril, M.A.).
THE RISE OF CONSTITUTIONAL GOVERNMENT IN ENGLAND: being a Series of Twenty Lectures on the History of the English Constitution delivered to a Popular Audience. Cr. 8vo. 6s.

RAWLINSON (George, M.A., Canon of Canterbury, &c.).
THE HISTORY OF PHŒNICIA. With numerous Illustrations. 8vo. 24s.

READER (Emily E.).
VOICES FROM FLOWER-LAND: a Birthday Book and Language of Flowers. Illustrated by ADA BROOKE. Royal 16mo. cloth, 2s. 6d.; vegetable vellum, 3s. 6d.

RIBOT (Th.).
THE PSYCHOLOGY OF ATTENTION. Cr. 8vo. 3s.

RICH (A.).
A DICTIONARY OF ROMAN AND GREEK ANTIQUITIES. With 2000 Woodcuts. Cr. 8vo. 7s. 6d.

RICHARDSON (Dr. B. W.).
NATIONAL HEALTH. Abridged from 'The Health of Nations'. A Review of the Works of Sir Edwin Chadwick, K.C.B. Cr. 4s. 6d.

RILEY (Athelstan, M.A., F.R.G.S.).
ATHOS: or, the Mountain of the Monks. With Map and 29 Illustrations. 8vo. 21s.

RILEY (James Whitcomb).
OLD-FASHIONED ROSES: Poems. 12mo. 5s.

RIVERS (Thomas and T. F.).
THE MINIATURE FRUIT GARDEN; or, The Culture of Pyramidal and Bush Fruit Trees. With 32 Illustrations. Cr. 8vo. 4s.

RIVERS (Thomas).
THE ROSE AMATEUR'S GUIDE. Fcp. 8vo. 4s. 6d.

ROBERTSON (A.).
THE KIDNAPPED SQUATTER, and other Australian Tales. Cr. 8vo. 6s.

ROGET (John Lewis).
A HISTORY OF THE 'OLD WATER-COLOUR' SOCIETY (now the Royal Society of Painters in Water-Colours). With Biographical Notices of its Older and all its Deceased Members and Associates. 2 vols. Royal 8vo. 42s.

ROGET (Peter M.).
THESAURUS OF ENGLISH WORDS AND PHRASES. Classified and Arranged so as to Facilitate the Expression of Ideas and assist in Literary Composition. Recomposed throughout, enlarged and improved, partly from the Author's Notes, and with a full Index, by the Author's Son, JOHN LEWIS ROGET. Cr. 8vo. 10s. 6d.

ROMANES (George John, M.A., LL.D., F.R.S.).
DARWIN, AND AFTER DARWIN: an Exposition of the Darwinian Theory and a Discussion of Post-Darwinian Questions. Part I. The Darwinian Theory. With Portrait of Darwin and 125 Illustrations. Cr. 8vo. 10s. 6d.

RONALDS (A.).
THE FLY-FISHER'S ENTOMOLOGY. With 20 Coloured Plates. 8vo. 14s.

ROSSETTI (Maria Francesca).
A SHADOW OF DANTE: being an Essay towards studying Himself, his World and his Pilgrimage. With Illustrations. Cr. 8vo. 10s. 6d.

ROUND (J. H., M.A.).
GEOFFREY DE MANDEVILLE: a Study of the Anarchy. 8vo. 16s.

RUSSELL (Earl).
A LIFE OF LORD JOHN RUSSELL (EARL RUSSELL, K.G.). By SPENCER WALPOLE. With 2 Portraits. 2 vols. 8vo. 36s. Cabinet Edition. 2 vols. Cr. 8vo. 12s.

SEEBOHM (Frederic).
THE OXFORD REFORMERS—JOHN COLET, ERASMUS AND THOMAS MORE: a History of their Fellow-Work. 8vo. 14s.
THE ENGLISH VILLAGE COMMUNITY Examined in its Relations to the Manorial and Tribal Systems, &c. 13 Maps and Plates. 8vo. 16s.
THE ERA OF THE PROTESTANT REVOLUTION. With Map. Fcp. 8vo. 2s. 6d.

SEWELL (Elizabeth M.).
AMY HERBERT.
THE EARL'S DAUGHTER.
THE EXPERIENCE OF LIFE.
A GLIMPSE OF THE WORLD.
CLEVE HALL.
KATHARINE ASHTON.
MARGARET PERCIVAL.
LANETON PARSONAGE.
URSULA. GERTRUDE.
IVORS.   HOME LIFE.
AFTER LIFE.
Cr. 8vo. 1s. 6d. each cloth plain. 2s. 6d. each cloth extra, gilt edges.

SHAKESPEARE.
BOWDLER'S FAMILY SHAKESPEARE. With 36 Woodcuts, 1 vol. 8vo. 14s. Or in 6 vols. Fcp. 8vo. 21s.
OUTLINES OF THE LIFE OF SHAKESPEARE. By J. O. HALLIWELL-PHILLIPPS. With numerous Illustrations and Fac-similes. 2 vols. Royal 8vo. £1 1s.
A CALENDAR OF THE HALLIWELL-PHILLIPPS' COLLECTION OF SHAKESPEAREAN RARITIES Enlarged by ERNEST E. BAKER, F.S.A. 8vo. 10s. 6d.
THE SHAKESPEARE BIRTHDAY BOOK. By MARY F. DUNBAR. 32mo. 1s. 6d. cloth. With Photographs. 32mo. 5s. Drawing-Room Edition, with Photographs. Fcp. 8vo. 10s. 6d.

SHERBROOKE (Viscount).
LIFE AND LETTERS OF THE RIGHT HON. ROBERT LOWE, VISCOUNT SHERBROOKE, G.C.B., together with a Memoir of his Kinsman, Sir JOHN COAPE SHERBROOKE, G.C.B. By A. PATCHETT MARTIN. With 5 Copper-plate Portraits, &c. 2 vols. 8vo.

SHIRRES (L. P.).
AN ANALYSIS OF THE IDEAS OF ECONOMICS. Cr. 8vo. 6s.

SIDGWICK (Alfred).
DISTINCTION: and the Criticism of Belief. Cr. 8vo. 6s.

SILVER LIBRARY (THE). Cr. 8vo. 3s. 6d. each volume.
Baker's (Sir S. W.) Eight Years in Ceylon. With 6 Illustrations. 3s. 6d.
Baker's (Sir S. W.) Rifle and Hound in Ceylon. With 6 Illustrations. 3s. 6d.
Baring-Gould's (Rev. S.) Curious Myths of the Middle Ages. 3s. 6d.
Baring-Gould's (Rev. S.) Origin and Development of Religious Belief. 2 vols. 7s.
Brassey's (Lady) A Voyage in the 'Sunbeam'. With 66 Illustrations. 3s. 6d.
[Continued on next page.

SILVER LIBRARY (THE)—continued.

Clodd's (E.) Story of Creation: a Plain Account of Evolution. With 77 Illustrations. 3s. 6d.

Conybeare (Rev. W. J.) and Howson's (Very Rev. J. S.) Life and Epistles of St. Paul. 46 Illustrations. Cr. 8vo. 3s. 6d.

Dougall's (L.) Beggars All: a Novel. Cr. 8vo. 3s. 6d.

Doyle's (A. Conan) Micah Clarke. A Tale of Monmouth's Rebellion. 3s. 6d.

Doyle's (A. Conan) The Captain of the Polestar, and other Tales. Cr. 8vo. 3s. 6d.

Froude's (J. A.) Short Studies on Great Subjects. 4 vols. 3s. 6d. each.

Froude's (J. A.) Cæsar: a Sketch. 3s. 6d.

Froude's (J. A.) Thomas Carlyle: a History of his Life. 1795-1835. 2 vols. 1834-1881. 2 vols. 7s. each.

Froude's (J. A.) The Two Chiefs of Dunboy: an Irish Romance of the Last Century. 3s. 6d.

Gleig's (Rev. G. R.) Life of the Duke of Wellington. With Portrait. 3s. 6d.

Haggard's (H. R.) She: A History of Adventure. 32 Illustrations. 3s. 6d.

Haggard's (H. R.) Allan Quatermain. With 20 Illustrations. 3s. 6d.

Haggard's (H. R.) Colonel Quaritch, V.C.: a Tale of Country Life. 3s. 6d.

Haggard's (H. R.) Cleopatra. With 29 Full-page Illustrations. 3s. 6d.

Haggard's (H. R.) Beatrice. 3s. 6d.

Harte's (Bret) In the Carquinez Woods and other Stories. 3s. 6d.

Howitt's (W.) Visits to Remarkable Places. 80 Illustrations. 3s. 6d.

Jefferies' (R.) The Story of My Heart: My Autobiography. With Portrait. 3s. 6d.

Jefferies' (R.) Field and Hedgerow. Last Essays of. With Portrait. 3s. 6d.

Jefferies' (R.) Red Deer. With 17 Illustrations by J. CHARLTON and H. TUNALY. Cr. 8vo. 3s. 6d.

Knight's (E. F.) The Cruise of the 'Alerte': the Narrative of a Search for Treasure on the Desert Island of Trinidad. With 2 Maps and 23 Illustrations. Cr. 8vo. 3s. 6d.

Lees (J. A.) and Clutterbuck's (W. J.) B. C. 1887, A Ramble in British Columbia. With Maps and 75 Illustrations. 3s. 6d.

Macaulay's (Lord) Essays and Lays. With Portrait and Illustration. 3s. 6d.

Macleod's (H. D.) The Elements of Banking. 3s. 6d.

Marshman's (J. C.) Memoirs of Sir Henry Havelock. 3s. 6d.

Max Müller's (F.) India, what can it teach us? Cr. 8vo. 3s. 6d.

Max Müller's (F.) Introduction to the Science of Religion. Cr. 8vo. 3s. 6d.

Merivale's (Dean) History of the Romans under the Empire. 8 vols. 3s. 6d. each.

Mill's (J. S.) Principles of Political Economy. 3s. 6d.

Mill's (J. S.) System of Logic. 3s. 6d.

SILVER LIBRARY (THE)—continued.

Newman's (Cardinal) Historical Sketches. 3 vols. 3s. 6d. each.

Newman's (Cardinal) Apologia Pro Vitâ Sua. 3s. 6d.

Newman's (Cardinal) Callista: a Tale of the Third Century. 3s. 6d.

Newman's (Cardinal) Loss and Gain: a Tale. 3s. 6d.

Newman's (Cardinal) Essays, Critical and Historical. 2 vols. 7s.

Newman's (Cardinal) An Essay on the Development of Christian Doctrine. 3s. 6d.

Newman's (Cardinal) The Arians of the Fourth Century. 3s. 6d.

Newman's (Cardinal) Verses on Various Occasions. 3s. 6d.

Newman's (Cardinal) The Present Position of Catholics in England. 3s. 6d.

Newman's (Cardinal) Parochial and Plain Sermons. 8 vols. 3s. 6d. each.

Newman's (Cardinal) Selection, adapted to the Seasons of the Ecclesiastical Year, from the 'Parochial and Plain Sermons'. 3s. 6d.

Newman's (Cardinal) Sermons bearing upon Subjects of the Day. Edited by the Rev. W. J. Copeland, B.D., late Rector of Farnham, Essex. 3s. 6d.

Newman's (Cardinal) Difficulties felt by Anglicans in Catholic Teaching Considered. 2 vols. 3s. 6d. each.

Newman's (Cardinal) The Idea of a University Defined and Illustrated. 3s. 6d.

Newman's (Cardinal) Biblical and Ecclesiastical Miracles. 3s. 6d.

Newman's (Cardinal) Discussions and Arguments on Various Subjects. 3s. 6d.

Newman's (Cardinal) Grammar of Assent. 3s. 6d.

Newman's (Cardinal) Fifteen Sermons Preached before the University of Oxford. Cr. 8vo. 3s. 6d.

Newman's (Cardinal) Lectures on the Doctrine of Justification. Cr. 8vo. 3s. 6d.

Newman's (Cardinal) Sermons on Various Occasions. Cr. 8vo. 3s. 6d.

Newman's (Cardinal) The Via Media of the Anglican Church, illustrated in Lectures, &c. 2 vols. 3s. 6d. each.

Newman's (Cardinal) Discourses to Mixed Congregations. 3s. 6d.

Phillipps-Wolley's (C.) Snap: a Legend of the Lone Mountain. With 13 Illustrations. 3s. 6d.

Proctor's (R. A.) Other Worlds than Ours. 3s. 6d.

Proctor's (R. A.) Rough Ways made Smooth. 3s. 6d.

Proctor's (R. A.) Pleasant Ways in Science. 3s. 6d.

Stanley's (Bishop) Familiar History of Birds. 160 Illustrations. 3s. 6d.

Stevenson (R. L.) and Osbourne's (LL.) The Wrong Box. Cr. 8vo. 3s. 6d.

[*Continued on next page.*

SILVER LIBRARY (THE)—*continued.*
  Weyman's (Stanley J.) The House of the Wolf: a Romance. Cr. 8vo. 3s. 6d.
  Wood's (Rev. J. G.) Petland Revisited. With 33 Illustrations. 3s. 6d.
  Wood's (Rev. J. G.) Strange Dwellings. With 60 Illustrations. 3s. 6d.
  Wood's (Rev. J. G.) Out of Doors. 11 Illustrations. 3s. 6d.

SMITH (R. Bosworth).
  CARTHAGE AND THE CARTHAGINIANS. With Maps, Plans, &c. Cr. 8vo. 6s.

SOPHOCLES. Translated into English Verse. By ROBERT WHITELAW, M.A., Assistant Master in Rugby School; late Fellow of Trinity College, Cambridge. Cr. 8vo. 8s. 6d.

STEPHEN (Sir James).
  ESSAYS IN ECCLESIASTICAL BIOGRAPHY. Cr. 8vo. 7s. 6d.

STEPHENS (H. Morse).
  A HISTORY OF THE FRENCH REVOLUTION. 3 vols. 8vo. Vols. I. and II. 18s. each.

STEVENSON (Robert Louis).
  A CHILD'S GARDEN OF VERSES. Small Fcp. 8vo. 5s.
  A CHILD'S GARLAND OF SONGS, Gathered from 'A Child's Garden of Verses'. Set to Music by C. VILLIERS STANFORD, Mus. Doc. 4to. 2s. sewed. 3s. 6d. cloth gilt.
  THE DYNAMITER. Fcp. 8vo. 1s. sewed. 1s. 6d. cloth.
  STRANGE CASE OF DR. JEKYLL AND MR. HYDE. Fcp. 8vo. 1s. sewed. 1s. 6d. cloth.

STEVENSON (Robert Louis) and OSBOURNE (Lloyd).
  THE WRONG BOX. Cr. 8vo. 3s. 6d.

STOCK (St. George).
  DEDUCTIVE LOGIC. Fcp. 8vo. 3s. 6d.

'STONEHENGE'.
  THE DOG IN HEALTH AND DISEASE. With 84 Wood Engravings. Square Cr. 8vo. 7s. 6d.

STRONG (Herbert A., M.A., LL.D.), LOGEMAN (Willem S.), and WHEELER (Benjamin Ide).
  INTRODUCTION TO THE STUDY OF THE HISTORY OF LANGUAGE. 8vo. 10s. 6d.

STURGIS (Julian, Author of 'My Friends and I,' 'Thraldom,' &c.).
  AFTER TWENTY YEARS, and other Stories. Cr. 8vo. 6s.

SULLY (James).
  THE HUMAN MIND: a Text-Book of Psychology. 2 vols. 8vo. 21s.
  OUTLINES OF PSYCHOLOGY. 8vo. 9s.
  THE TEACHER'S HANDBOOK OF PSYCHOLOGY. Cr. 8vo. 5s.

SUPERNATURAL RELIGION: an Inquiry into the Reality of Divine Revelation. 3 vols. 8vo. 36s.
  REPLY (A) TO DR. LIGHTFOOT'S ESSAYS. By the Author of 'Supernatural Religion'. 8vo. 7s. 6d.

SUTTNER (Bertha von).
  LAY DOWN YOUR ARMS (Die Waffen Nieder): The Autobiography of Martha Tilling. Translated by T. HOLMES. Cr. 8vo. 7s. 6d.

SWINBURNE (A. J., B.A.).
  PICTURE LOGIC: an Attempt to Popularise the Science of Reasoning. Post 8vo. 5s.

SYMES (J. E.).
  PRELUDE TO MODERN HISTORY: being a Brief Sketch of the World's History from the Third to the Ninth Century. With 5 Maps. Cr. 8vo. 2s. 6d.
  A COMPANION TO SCHOOL HISTORIES OF ENGLAND. Cr. 8vo. 2s. 6d.
  POLITICAL ECONOMY. With Problems for Solution, and Hints for Supplementary Reading. Cr. 8vo. 2s. 6d.

TAYLOR (Colonel Meadows, C.S.I., &c.).
  A STUDENT'S MANUAL OF THE HISTORY OF INDIA. Cr. 8vo. 7s. 6d.

THOMPSON (D. Greenleaf).
  THE PROBLEM OF EVIL: an Introduction to the Practical Sciences. 8vo. 10s. 6d.
  A SYSTEM OF PSYCHOLOGY. 2 vols. 8vo. 36s.
  THE RELIGIOUS SENTIMENTS OF THE HUMAN MIND. 8vo. 7s. 6d.
  SOCIAL PROGRESS: an Essay. 8vo. 7s. 6d.
  THE PHILOSOPHY OF FICTION IN LITERATURE: an Essay. Cr. 8vo. 6s.

THOMPSON (Annie).
  A MORAL DILEMMA: a Novel. Cr. 8vo. 6s.

THOMSON (Most Rev. William, D.D., late Archbishop of York).
OUTLINES OF THE NECESSARY LAWS OF THOUGHT: a Treatise on Pure and Applied Logic. Post 8vo. 6s.

THREE IN NORWAY. By Two of Them. With a Map and 59 Illustrations. Cr. 8vo. 2s. boards. 2s. 6d. cloth.

TOYNBEE (Arnold).
LECTURES ON THE INDUSTRIAL REVOLUTION OF THE 18TH CENTURY IN ENGLAND. 8vo. 10s. 6d.

TREVELYAN (Sir G. O., Bart.).
THE LIFE AND LETTERS OF LORD MACAULAY.
  Popular Edition. Cr. 8vo. 2s. 6d.
  Student's Edition. Cr. 8vo. 6s.
  Cabinet Edition. 2 vols. Cr. 8vo. 12s.
  Library Edition. 2 vols. 8vo. 36s.
THE EARLY HISTORY OF CHARLES JAMES FOX. Library Edition. 8vo. 18s. Cabinet Edition. Cr. 8vo. 6s.

TROLLOPE (Anthony).
THE WARDEN. Cr. 8vo. 1s. boards. 1s. 6d. cloth.
BARCHESTER TOWERS. Cr. 8vo. 1s. boards. 1s. 6d. cloth.

VERNEY (Frances Parthenope).
MEMOIRS OF THE VERNEY FAMILY DURING THE CIVIL WAR. Compiled from the Letters and Illustrated by the Portraits at Claydon House, Bucks. With a Preface by S. R. Gardiner, M.A., LL.D. With 38 Portraits, Woodcuts and Facsimile. 2 vols. Royal 8vo. 42s.

VILLE (George).
THE PERPLEXED FARMER: How is he to meet Alien Competition? Translated from the French by William Crookes, F.R.S., V.P.C.S., &c. Cr. 8vo. 5s.

VIRGIL.
PUBLI VERGILI MARONIS BUCOLICA, GEORGICA, ÆNEIS: The Works of Virgil, Latin Text, with English Commentary and Index. By B. H. Kennedy, D.D. Cr. 8vo. 10s. 6d.
THE ÆNEID OF VIRGIL. Translated into English Verse. By John Conington, M.A. Cr. 8vo. 6s.
THE POEMS OF VIRGIL. Translated into English Prose. By John Conington, M.A. Cr. 8vo. 6s.
THE ECLOGUES AND GEORGICS OF VIRGIL. Translated from the Latin by J. W. Mackail, M.A., Fellow of Balliol College, Oxford. Printed on Dutch Hand-made Paper. Royal 16mo. 5s.

WAKEMAN (Henry Offley, M.A.) and HASSALL (Arthur, M.A.).
ESSAYS INTRODUCTORY TO THE STUDY OF ENGLISH CONSTITUTIONAL HISTORY. By Resident Members of the University of Oxford. Cr. 8vo. 6s.

WALFORD (L. B., Author of 'Mr. Smith ').
THE MISCHIEF OF MONICA: a Novel. Cr. 8vo. 2s. 6d.
THE ONE GOOD GUEST: a Story. Cr. 8vo. 6s.
TWELVE ENGLISH AUTHORESSES. With Portrait of Hannah More. Cr. 8vo. 4s. 6d.

WALKER (Major A. Campbell-, F.R.G.S.).
THE CORRECT CARD: or, How to Play at Whist; a Whist Catechism. Fcp. 8vo. 2s. 6d.

WALPOLE (Spencer).
HISTORY OF ENGLAND FROM THE CONCLUSION OF THE GREAT WAR IN 1815 TO 1858. 6 vols. Cr. 8vo. 6s. each.
THE LAND OF HOME RULE: being an Account of the History and Institutions of the Isle of Man. Cr. 8vo. 6s.

WELLINGTON (Duke of).
LIFE OF THE DUKE OF WELLINGTON. By the Rev. G. R. Gleig, M.A. Cr. 8vo. 3s. 6d.

WEST (B. B.).
HALF-HOURS WITH THE MILLIONAIRES: Showing how much harder it is to spend a million than to make it. Cr. 8vo. 6s.

WEST (Charles, M.D., Founder of the Hospital for Sick Children).
THE MOTHER'S MANUAL OF CHILDREN'S DISEASES. Fcp. 8vo. 2s. 6d.

WEYMAN (Stanley J.).
THE HOUSE OF THE WOLF: a Romance. Cr. 8vo. 3s. 6d.

WHATELY (E. Jane).
ENGLISH SYNONYMS. Edited by R. Whately, D.D. Fcp. 8vo. 3s.
LIFE AND CORRESPONDENCE OF RICHARD WHATELY, D.D., late Archbishop of Dublin. With Portrait. Cr. 8vo. 10s. 6d.

WHATELY (Archbishop).
ELEMENTS OF LOGIC. Cr. 8vo. 4s. 6d.
ELEMENTS OF RHETORIC. Cr. 8vo. 4s. 6d.

[Continued on next page.

WHATELY (Archbishop)—*continued.*
LESSONS ON REASONING. Fcp. 8vo. 1s. 6d.
BACON'S ESSAYS, with Annotations. 8vo. 10s. 6d.

WHIST IN DIAGRAMS: a Supplement to American Whist, Illustrated; being a Series of Hands played through, Illustrating the American leads, the new play, the forms of Finesse, and celebrated coups of Masters. With Explanation and Analysis. By G. W. P. Fcp. 8vo. 6s. 6d.

WILCOCKS (J. C.).
THE SEA FISHERMAN, Comprising the Chief Methods of Hook and Line Fishing in the British and other Seas, and Remarks on Nets, Boats and Boating. Profusely Illustrated. Cr. 8vo. 6s.

WILLICH (Charles M.).
POPULAR TABLES for giving Information for ascertaining the value of Lifehold, Leasehold, and Church Property, the Public Funds, &c. Edited by H. BENCE JONES. Cr. 8vo. 10s. 6d.

WITT (Professor). Translated by FRANCES YOUNGHUSBAND.
THE TROJAN WAR. Cr. 8vo. 2s.
MYTHS OF HELLAS: or, Greek Tales. Cr. 8vo. 3s. 6d.
THE WANDERINGS OF ULYSSES. Cr. 8vo. 3s. 6d.
THE RETREAT OF THE TEN THOUSAND: being the Story of Xenophon's 'Anabasis'. With Illustrations. Cr. 8vo. 3s. 6d.

WOLFF (Henry W.).
RAMBLES IN THE BLACK FOREST. Cr. 8vo. 7s. 6d.
THE WATERING PLACES OF THE VOSGES. Cr. 8vo. 4s. 6d.
THE COUNTRY OF THE VOSGES. With a Map. 8vo. 12s.

WOOD (Rev. J. G.).
HOMES WITHOUT HANDS: a Description of the Habitation of Animals, classed according to the Principle of Construction. With 140 Illustrations. 8vo. 7s. net.
INSECTS AT HOME: a Popular Account of British Insects, their Structure, Habits and Transformations. With 700 Illustrations. 8vo. 7s. net.
INSECTS ABROAD: a Popular Account of Foreign Insects, their Structure, Habits and Transformations. With 600 Illustrations. 8vo. 7s. net.

WOOD (Rev. J. G.)—*continued.*
BIBLE ANIMALS: a Description of every Living Creature mentioned in the Scriptures. With 112 Illustrations. 8vo. 7s. net.
STRANGE DWELLINGS: a Description of the Habitations of Animals, abridged from 'Homes without Hands'. With 60 Illustrations. Cr. 8vo. 3s. 6d.
OUT OF DOORS; a Selection of Original Articles on Practical Natural History. With 11 Illustrations. Cr. 8vo. 3s. 6d.
PETLAND REVISITED. With 33 Illustrations. Cr. 8vo. 3s. 6d.
BIRD LIFE OF THE BIBLE. 32 Illustrations. Cr. 8vo. 3s. 6d.
WONDERFUL NESTS. 30 Illustrations. Cr. 8vo. 3s. 6d.
HOMES UNDER THE GROUND. 28 Illustrations. Cr. 8vo. 3s. 6d.
WILD ANIMALS OF THE BIBLE. 29 Illustrations. Cr. 8vo. 3s. 6d.
DOMESTIC ANIMALS OF THE BIBLE. 23 Illustrations. Cr. 8vo. 3s. 6d.
THE BRANCH BUILDERS. 28 Illustrations. Cr. 8vo. 2s. 6d.
SOCIAL HABITATIONS AND PARASITIC NESTS. 18 Illustrations. Cr. 8vo. 2s.

WORDSWORTH (Charles, D.C.L., Bishop of St. Andrews).
ANNALS OF MY EARLY LIFE, 1806-1846. 8vo. 15s.

WYLIE (James Hamilton).
HISTORY OF ENGLAND UNDER HENRY IV. 2 vols. Vol. I. 1399-1404. Cr. 8vo. 10s. 6d. Vol. II. [*In the Press.*

ZELLER (Dr. E.).
HISTORY OF ECLECTICISM IN GREEK PHILOSOPHY. Translated by SARAH F. ALLEYNE. Cr. 8vo. 10s. 6d.
THE STOICS, EPICUREANS AND SCEPTICS. Translated by the Rev. O. J. REICHEL, M.A. Cr. 8vo. 15s.
SOCRATES AND THE SOCRATIC SCHOOLS. Translated by the Rev. O. J. REICHEL, M.A. Cr. 8vo. 10s. 6d.
PLATO AND THE OLDER ACADEMY. Translated by SARAH F. ALLEYNE and ALFRED GOODWIN, B.A. Cr. 8vo. 18s.
THE PRE-SOCRATIC SCHOOLS: a History of Greek Philosophy from the Earliest Period to the time of Socrates. Translated by SARAH F. ALLEYNE. 2 vols. Cr. 8vo. 30s.
OUTLINES OF THE HISTORY OF GREEK PHILOSOPHY. Translated by SARAH F. ALLEYNE and EVELYN ABBOTT. Cr. 8vo. 10s. 6d.

www.ingramcontent.com/pod-product-compliance
Lightning Source LLC
Chambersburg PA
CBHW031937290426
44108CB00011B/594